advanced

Allvoca

빅데이터 기반 나에게 필요한 모든 영단어

위편삼절

공자가 주역을 자주 읽어 책을 묶은 가죽끈이 세 번이나 끊어졌다는 뜻으로
한 권의 책을 몇 십 번이나 되풀이해서 읽음을 의미한다

회독 시작일을 기록하세요

1회독	년	월	일
2회독	년	월	일
3회독	년	월	일
4회독	년	월	일
5회독	년	월	일

〈대한민국 영어 교육의 슬픈 현실〉

우리는,

수능 시험까지의 학창 시절 12년 동안 무수히 많은 영단어들과 씨름합니다.

성인이 되어 편입 시험을 위한 공부를 이어가기도 하며,

사회 진출을 위해 토익, 공무원 시험, 텝스 시험 등을 준비하고,

유학을 위해 TOEFL, IELTS, GRE, GMAT 등을 준비하기도 합니다.

또, 사회에 나와서는 회화가 부족하여 영어 회화 학원에 등록하기도 합니다.

여기에 슬픈 현실이 있습니다.

학습 자료를 통일하지 않고 매번 새로운 교재를 찾습니다.

그 결과, 학습이 누적되거나 반복되지 않고

우리의 영어 실력은 매번 초기화되다시피 합니다.

만약, 영단어 학습서를 통일하여 암기를 누적 & 반복해왔다면,

내 영어 실력이 지금보다 더 탄탄하지 않았을까요?

내 인생의 영단어는 『올보카 Basic & Advanced』 속 어휘 7,500개로 충분합니다.

매번 새로운 교재로 어휘력을 초기화하지 마시고, 이 교재만 반복학습하세요.

이것이 어휘 학습의 정석입니다.

저자 송승호

Allvoca
advanced

| 교재 소개

1. 우선순위 영단어장의 끝판왕

올보카는 빅데이터로 영단어의 우선순위를 정리한 단어장이다.

130억개 영단어 빅데이터를 정제하여 우선순위를 도출하고, 한국 영어학습환경 최적화 작업을 더해 교재를 완성하였다. 총 7,500개의 표제어로 구성된 『올보카 Basic & Advanced』는 주요 영문 텍스트에 99% 이상의 적용률(pg. 10 참조)을 자랑한다. 시험별 높은 적용률은 물론이고, 일반 영어에도 폭넓게 적용된다.

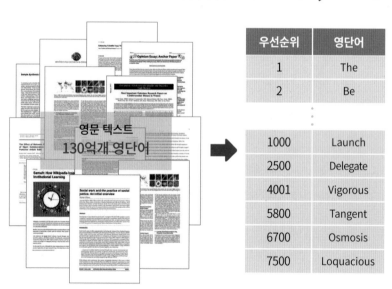

130억 개 영단어 >>>>> 우선순위 7,500개

우선순위	영단어
1	The
2	Be
⋮	
1000	Launch
2500	Delegate
4001	Vigorous
5800	Tangent
6700	Osmosis
7500	Loquacious

영문 텍스트
130억개 영단어

※ 영문 텍스트 130억 개 출처: 외국 서적, 신문기사, 웹문서 등 방대한 양의 영문 텍스트를 취합한 복수의 말뭉치 데이터베이스(corpus)

2. 올보카 제작 과정

첫째, 빅데이터를 활용하여 어휘의 우선순위를 계산했다.
130억 영문 텍스트 속 파생어 및 관련어휘를 표제어와 통합하는 작업을 거쳤고, 통합빈도수를 기준으로 표제어를 정렬했다. 또한, 주요 파생어들은 교재 속 표제어와 함께 표시하였다.

둘째, 특이 사례들은 순위를 조정하였다.
예를 들어, 초급 어휘인 'Giraffe(기린)'는 단순 빈도수 기준으로는 최고난도 어휘로 분류된다. 유아용 교재엔 자주 등장하지만 그 외의 텍스트엔 매우 드물게 등장하는 단어이기 때문이다. 올보카는 해당 어휘를 초급 어휘에 해당되도록 순위를 조정하는 등, 난이도 최적화 작업을 진행하였다.

셋째, 외래어는 별도 학습이 가능하도록 필터링하였다.
우리나라에서 유난히 많은 외래어가 사용되는 만큼, 상당수 어휘는 철자만 익히면 단번에 체득 가능하다. 예를 들어 Lingerie (란제리), Veranda (베란다), Bourgeois (부르주아) 등의 어휘는 얼핏 보면 생소하지만 발음과 스펠링만 익히면 손쉽게 외워진다. (p.291)

넷째, 일반 학습자 입장에서 불필요한 특수 용어들을 배제하였다.
일례로 'Paraffin' 이란 단어는 'C_nH_{2n+2}의 화학식으로 표현되는 알케인 탄화수소(등유)를 두루 일컫는 표현'인데, 빈도수로는 순위권에 들지만 일반적인 학습자에게 기대되는 어휘가 아니다. 또한, Google nGram 을 활용해 불필요한 고어들도 제거하였다.

다섯째, 교육부 지정 필수 영단어들은 우선순위 산정 시 가중치를 부여했다.
교육부가 공개한 필수 영단어 리스트는 영어 학습의 기초가 되는 어휘들을 담고 있다. 해당 어휘들에 가중치를 부여함과 동시에 교재 내에서 교육부 지정 단어임을 표시하였다. 이는 올보카를 우리나라 영어 학습환경에 최적화하기 위한 작업이었던 만큼 남녀노소 누구나 올보카로 평생 학습이 가능하다.

3. 모든 시험이 대비 가능한 All-in-One 영단어장

올보카 적용률

영어 시험들에 대한 『올보카 Basic & Advanced』의 적용률을 테스트해보았다. 아래 표에서 알수 있듯이, 사실상 모든 영어 시험은 올보카로 대비 가능하다. 게다가 CNN, TED 강연, 영화, 미드, 유명 연설 등 다양한 영어 콘텐츠에도 높은 적용률을 보이는 만큼 종합 영어 실력 향상에도 매우 효과적이다.

결국 '수능용 단어장', '토익용 단어장' 등 특정 시험 전용 단어장을 따로 살 필요가 없는 것이다. 따지고보면 매우 당연한 것인데, 대부분의 영어 시험은 문제은행식으로 출제되지 않기에 본인의 수준에 적합한 어휘들을 외우는 것이 가장 정직하고 효율적인 학습 방법인 것이다.

시험 영어	적용률		일반 영어	적용률
수능	99.8%		TED 강연	99.0%
공무원	99.4%		CNN	98.0%
TOEIC	99.3%		영화 (타이타닉)	98.9%
TOEFL	99.3%		미드 (프렌즈 시즌1)	99.3%
TEPS	99.2%		오바마 연설	99.8%
SAT	99.1%			

[커버리지 계산 기준] [수능 영어] - 20학년도 문제지 기준, [공무원영어] - '19 서울시 국가공무원 9급 공채 영어 필기시험 기준, [TOEIC] - ETS 공식 토익정기시험 기출문제집 최종회 문제지 기준, [TOEFL] - ETS 공개 공식 기출문제집 Set1 문제지 기준, [TEPS] - 텝스관리위원회 공식 뉴텝스 Sample Test 문제지 기준, [SAT] - College Board 제공 공식 SAT 최종회(8) 문제지 기준, [TED] - Top 4 영상 기준, [CNN] - 홈페이지 기사 제목 기준(5d), [영화] - 타이타닉 transcript 기준, [미드] - Friends Season 1 transcript 기준, [오바마] - 취임 연설 Yes We Can 기준/ 고유명사 제외 (인물명, 도시/국가명, 생소개념, 회사명 등), 의미 유추 가능 합성어 제외 『올보카 Basic & Advanced』 표제어 7,500개 및 파생어 기준 (미표시 확장어 포함) / 전체 확장 리스트는 ALLVOCA.com에서 제공 / 전체 적용률은 오차 ±2%

시험별 빈출 어휘

물론, 시험의 특성에 따라 출제 어휘가 특정 분야에 집중될 수는 있다. 예를 들어, 토익은 비즈니스 영어를 중점적으로 출제하여 "broker"이라는 단어의 빈도가 타 시험 대비 상대적으로 높다. 그래서 올보카는 각 시험별 최빈출 표현들을 도출하는 작업까지 진행했다. 시험별 역대 기출문제집, 공식문제집, 시험후기 등을 취합하여(아래 표 참조) 출제 빈도가 높거나 유의미한 단어들을 약 1,000~1,500개씩 추려냈고, 학습 시 참고할 수 있도록 표제어 옆에 해당 시험명을 표기해두었다. (p.12~15 참조)

시험	빈출 어휘 출처(산출 근거)
초중고	교육청 지정 필수 영단어
수능	19개년 기출 주요 어휘
공무원	15개년 기출 빈출 어휘
토익	10개년 기출 어휘
토플	iBT 12개년 기출 및 후기
텝스	10개년 기출 어휘
편입	10개년 전국 편입 기출
GRE, SAT	공식 기출 어휘, 후기 어휘

|시험별 학습 권장량

효과적인 학습을 위해선 명확한 목표 설정이 필수적이다. 아래 표는 학습자가 스스로 계획을 세울
수 있도록 돕는 학습가이드이다. 공식기출문제들의 어휘 및 lexile 지수 분석, 시험 간 점수 환산표,
실제 학생들의 통계 등을 바탕으로 시험 주요 구간 별 학습 권장량이 산정됐다.

올보카는 평생 치를 모든 영어 시험을 대비할 수 있도록 구성돼 있으니 본인의 목표 시험 성적대를
참고하여 학습 계획을 세우도록 하자. 그리고, 매년 어휘 학습을 초기화하지 말고 공부 흔적을 해
당 교재에 꾸준히 누적해나가길 추천한다.

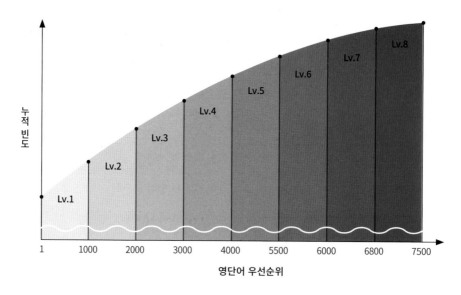

	Lv.1	Lv.2	Lv.3	Lv.4	Lv.5	Lv.6	Lv.7	Lv.8
수능	초등	중등	고등, 3~4등급	고3, 1~2등급	만점			
토익	토익 기초단어		650+	800+	940+	990		
텝스	텝스 기초단어		330+	400+	480+	520+	560+	600
토플	토플 기초단어		85+	95+	105+	110+	115+	120
공무원	공무원 기초단어			70	80	90	95~100	
편입	편입 기초단어				중위권	상위권		최상위
GRE	GRE 기초단어						GRE 빈출 단어	

＊올보카 Basic: Lv.1 ~ Lv.4 / 올보카 Advanced: Lv.5 ~ Lv.8

수능 영어

수능 영어에 출제되는 어휘는 철저히 "빈도수"로 결정된다.

평가원은 수능 출제 매뉴얼에서 다음과 같이 밝히고 있다. *"어휘수를 늘이되 사용 **빈도수가 높은 어휘**를 중심으로 … (중략) … 단, **빈도수가 낮은 어휘**를 사용해야하는 경우 주석을 달아주도록 한다."* 그러므로, 수능 어휘는 빈도수를 기준으로 학습해야 한다. 역대 수능 기출문제들을 분석한 결과, 수능 1~2 등급 목표 학생은 빈도수 #4000번(Lv.4)까지, 최상위권 학생은 #5500번(Lv.5)까지 학습하길 권장한다. Lv.6~8 은 일반 수능 수험생이 학습할 필요가 크지 않으며, 시험에 각주로 한글 뜻이 주어지는 단어들이 주로 해당 구간에 속해 있다.

	Lv.1	Lv.2	Lv.3	Lv.4	Lv.5	Lv.6	Lv.7	Lv.8
	~#1000	~#2000	~#3000	~#4000	~#5500	~#6000	~#6800	~#7500
수능	초등	중등	고등, 3~4등급	고3, 1~2등급	만점			

토익, 지텔프

ETS(토익 토플 공식 출제기관)의 Test User Guide엔 어휘의 빈도수(word frequency)가 시험 출제 시 활용된다고 명시되어 있다. 하여, 토익은 어휘 빈도수를 기준으로 학습하는 것이 효율적이다. Lv.4(~#4000)로 800점 이상의 안정적 상위권 달성이 가능하고 Lv.6 까지 학습 완료 시 어휘 때문에 문제를 틀리는 경우는 없을 것으로 보인다. 토익과 수능은 어휘의 난도 면에서 큰 차이를 보이지 않지만, 각 시험의 주요 어휘는 다소 상이하다. 각 표제어 우측 상단에 추가된 라벨을 참고하면서 학습하자.

	Lv.1	Lv.2	Lv.3	Lv.4	Lv.5	Lv.6	Lv.7	Lv.8
	~#1000	~#2000	~#3000	~#4000	~#5500	~#6000	~#6800	~#7500
토익	토익 기초단어		650+	800+	940+	990		
지텔프	지텔프 기초단어		32+	65+	95+	99+		

텝스

서울대 언어교육원이 주최한 텝스 20주년 학술대회에서 공개된 자료들에 '어휘 빈도수 (word frequency)'의 개념이 수차례 등장한다. 어휘의 빈도수가 TEPS 출제 시 활용되는 요소임은 틀림없어 보인다. 저자도 올보카 영단어 전체를 학습하고 시험에 응시하여 어휘 만점을 달성했다. 만점을 목표로 하는 학생은 Lv.8까지 학습해야겠지만, 아래 표를 참고해 각자의 학습 권장량을 확인하도록 하자. (최빈출 TEPS 어휘들은 토플과 상당 수 겹쳐 교재 내 라벨을 '토플'로 통합명시하였다.)

		Lv.1	Lv.2	Lv.3	Lv.4	Lv.5	Lv.6	Lv.7	Lv.8
		~#1000	~#2000	~#3000	~#4000	~#5500	~#6000	~#6800	~#7500
텝스	텝스 기초단어			330+	400+	480+	520+	560+	600

토플, 아이엘츠

토익 시험의 주관사인 ETS(Educational Testing Service)는 토플 시험도 관리 및 개발한다. 토익과 마찬가지로, TOEFL 공식 자료에는 "low frequency word"와 "high frequency word"등의 개념이 등장하고, 이를 성적대와 연결지어서 설명을 한다. 공식 기출문제들을 분석한 결과, 95+점이 목표인 학생은 #4000번까지, 115~120점이 목표인 학생은 #7500번까지 학습이 필요하다. 토플은 학생들의 실력 편차가 매우 큰 시험이기에, 본인 성적대에 적합한 어휘부터 암기하는 것이 가장 중요하다.

		Lv.1	Lv.2	Lv.3	Lv.4	Lv.5	Lv.6	Lv.7	Lv.8
		~#1000	~#2000	~#3000	~#4000	~#5500	~#6000	~#6800	~#7500
토플	토플 기초단어			85+	95+	105+	110+	115+	120
아이엘츠	아이엘츠 기초단어			6	6.5	7~7.5	8	8.5	9

공무원 영어

공무원 영어는 어휘 문제의 비중이 높은데다가 그 출제 범위가 매우 넓다. 따라서, 공무원 수험생은 자신의 목표 성적대까지 학습을 이어나가되 그 과정에서 '공무원' 빈출 라벨이 달린 어휘들은 빠짐없이 암기하도록 해야한다.

또한, '공무원 영단어' 암기 시작 전에 '수능 영단어'부터 끝내야 한다고 알려져있는데, 이는 사실상 올보카의 단계별 학습으로 해결 가능하다. 올보카는 Lv.3까지를 공무원 기초 단어(=수능 단어)로 분류하고 있으며 그 이후 Lv.4 이상부터 목표 성적별 학습량을 제시한다.

	Lv.1 ~#1000	Lv.2 ~#2000	Lv.3 ~#3000	Lv.4 ~#4000	Lv.5 ~#5500	Lv.6 ~#6000	Lv.7 ~#6800	Lv.8 ~#7500
공무원	공무원 기초단어			70	80	90	95~100	

편입, SAT, GRE

편입, SAT, GRE는 어휘 난이도가 가장 높은 시험들이다. 무턱대고 어려운 단어장을 사서 외우지 말고, 자신의 현 실력에 맞는 단어부터 차근차근 외우는 것이 가장 중요하다. 해당 시험들에선 Lv.1~4의 단어들이 '기초 단어'에 해당된다. 『올보카 Basic』은 말그대로 내 기본 실력을 다지고 빈틈이 없는지 체크하는 용도로 활용을 해야하며, 『올보카 Advanced』를 통해 시험용 어휘를 보충하도록 하자. 특히, SAT와 GRE에 빈출되는 최고난도 어휘도 Lv.7~8에 다수 포진되어 있으니 전 범위 학습을 권장한다. (최빈출 SAT 어휘들은 GRE와 상당 수 겹쳐 교재 내 라벨을 'GRE'로 통합명시하였다.)

	Lv.1 ~#1000	Lv.2 ~#2000	Lv.3 ~#3000	Lv.4 ~#4000	Lv.5 ~#5500	Lv.6 ~#6000	Lv.7 ~#6800	Lv.8 ~#7500
편입	편입 기초단어				중위권	상위권		최상위
SAT	SAT 기초단어				650+	720+		780+
GRE	GRE 기초단어					GRE 빈출 단어		

|구성과 특징

1
순번, 표제어, 발음 기호

130억 빅데이터에 기반한 진정한 우선순위 영단어! 빈도순으로 정렬되어 있다. 복잡한 발음 기호 대신 직관적인 발음 기호를 제공한다.

- Basic: #0001~#4000
- Advanced: #4001~#7500

2
주요 시험

시험별 최중요 어휘들은 표제어 우측 상단에 해당 시험명을 표기하였다. 각 시험마다 약 1,000~1,500개의 최중요 어휘가 표기되어 있다.

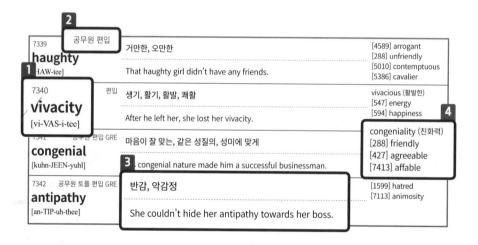

3
뜻, 예문

뜻과 예문이 위아래로 정리되어 있다. 교재 속 예문은 어휘 학습 구간에 적합한 난이도로 구성되어 있다.

(예문 해석 자료 ALLvoca.com 제공)

4
파생어, 관련어

우측열엔 (1) 주요 파생어 와 (2) 관련어가 실려 있다. 관련어들은 순번이 태깅되어 있어 연계 학습이 용이하다.

주요 접두사/접미사

접두사와 접미사는 단어의 형태를 확장시켜주고, 교재 속 파생어들을 이해하는데 큰 도움이 된다.
처음부터 모두 외워버리겠다는 생각보다는, 여러 번 훑어보면서 불참던 표현들만 가볍게 눈으로 익히자.

접두사	의미	예시	예시 뜻
pro, pre	앞에, 미리	predict	예측
re	다시, 뒤로	redo	재도전하다
in	안에; 아닌	interior	내부
un	아닌	uninterested	관심이 없는
dis	아닌	disadvantage	불리한
non	아닌	nonfiction	논픽션
anti	반대	antisocial	반사회적
counter, contra	반대	contradict	모순되다
mis	잘못	misunderstanding	오해
a	아닌; 진행 중인	atypical	비정상적
co, com	함께	co-worker	동료
inter	사이에	interaction	상호 작용
trans	가로질러	transaction	거래
sub	아래에	submarine	잠수함

접미사	예시	뜻
— 명사형 —		
tion, sion	celebration (celebrate)	축하 (축하하다)
ance, ence	existence (exist)	존재 (존재하다)
al	proposal (propose)	제안 (제안하다)
th	strength (strong)	힘 (힘 센)
ment, ness	movement (move)	움직임 (움직이다)
ity	equality (equal)	평등 (평등하다)
sis, ism	socialism (social)	사회주의 (사회의)
er, or	teacher (teach)	선생님 (가르치다)
age	marriage (marry)	결혼 (결혼하다)
hood	childhood (child)	어린 시절 (아이의)

5 접두사/접미사/어근 (p.18)

어휘 학습의 나비효과를 극대화할
수 있는 주요 접두사/접미사/어근
들이 정리되어 있다.

6 외래어 및 기타 (p.291)

우리나라에서 사용되는 주요 외래
어들은 별도 리스트로 제공된다. 발
음과 철자 위주로 가볍게 익히도록
하자.

외래어 및 기타 표현

무료 MP3 파일 제공 | Allvoca.com

외래어					
Accordion	아코디언	Blog	블로그	Chandelier	샹들리에
Adrenalin	아드레날린	Blouse	블라우스	Checkout	체크아웃
Album	앨범	Blu-Ray	블루레이	Cheetah	치타
Algorithm	알고리즘	Bonnet	자동차 본넷	Chef	셰프
Alibi	알리바이	Bouquet	부케	Cherry	체리
Almond	아몬드	Bourgeois	부르주아	Chess	체스
Alphabet	알파벳	Brassiere	브래지어	Chilli	칠리
Alps	알프스	Broccoli	브로콜리	Chimpanzee	침팬지
Aluminum	알루미늄	Brownie	브라우니	Chiropractic	카이로프랙틱
Amateur	아마추어	Brunch	브런치	Chocolate	초콜릿
Amen	아멘	Bulldog	불도그	Cholesterol	콜레스테롤
Ammonia	암모니아	Bulldozer	불도저	Christmas	크리스마스
Antenna	안테나	Burger	햄버거	Cigar	시가
Asparagus	아스파라거스	Burrito	브리토	Circus	서커스
Asphalt	아스팔트	Bus	버스	Clarinet	클라리넷
Aspirin	아스피린	Cafe	카페	Clover	클로버
		Caffeine	카페인	Cobalt	코발트색 (푸른)

INDEX

A							
		abrogate	7375	accomplice	6915	acronym	5327
		abrupt	4793	accomplish	1760	across	471
a	5	abruptly	4793	accomplishment	1760	act	82
A.M.	기타	abscess	6452	accord	479	action	82
abandon	2390	absence	2193	accordance	479	activate	3353
abash	7243	absent	2193	according	479	active	82
abate	5902	absolute	1124	accordingly	479	activist	3282
abatement	5902	absolutely	1124	accordion	외래어	activity	82
abbey	4620	absolution	6996	account	318	actor	82
abbreviate	4590	absolve	6996	accountable	318	actual	296
abbreviation	4590	absorb	1998	accountant	318	actually	296
abdicate	7198	absorption	1998	accounting	318	acuity	5998
abdication	7198	abstain	5316	accredit	2544	acuity	6946
abdomen	3420	abstention	5316	accredited	2544	acumen	6721
abdominal	3420	abstinence	5316	accrual	4331	acupuncture	5000
abduct	5187	abstract	2769	accrue	4331	acupuncturist	5000
abduction	5187	abstraction	2769	accumulate	2732	acute	3171
aberrant	6093	abstruse	7494	accuracy	1127	ad	704
aberration	6093	absurd	4103	accurate	1127	adage	6783
abet	7477	absurdity	4103	accusation	2120	adamant	6057

7 INDEX (p.297)

전체 단어를 abc 순으로 정리했
다. 모르는 영단어를 접하게 되면,
INDEX에서 찾아 학습을 할 수 있다.

| 주요 접두사/접미사

접두사와 접미사는 단어의 형태를 확장시켜주고, 교재 속 파생어들을 이해하는데 큰 도움이 된다.
처음부터 모두 외워버리겠다는 생각보단, 여러 번 훑어보면서 몰랐던 표현들만 가볍게 눈으로 익히자.

접두사	의미	예시	예시 뜻
pro, pre	앞에, 미리	predict	예측
re	다시; 뒤로	redo	재도전하다
in	안에; 아닌	interior	내부
un	아닌	uninterested	관심이 없는
dis	아닌	disadvantage	불리한
non	아닌	nonfiction	논픽션
anti	반대	antisocial	반사회적
counter, contra	반대	contradict	모순되다
mis	잘못	misunderstanding	오해
a	아닌; 진행 중인	atypical	비정상의
co, com	함께	co-worker	동료
inter	사이에	interaction	상호 작용
trans	가로질러	transaction	거래
sub	아래에	submarine	잠수함
de	아래로	decrease	감소하다
en	하게 만들다	enlarge	넓히다
be	완전히~하다	befriend	친구가 되다
per	완전히	perfect	완벽
fore	앞에, 미리	forecast	예측
ante	앞에, 이전	anterior	앞쪽의
post	뒤에, 이후	posterior	후방의
bene	좋은	beneficial	이로운
mal	나쁜	malfunction	오작동
auto	자동	automatic	자동
tele	원격	telephone	전화
ambi	두 개	ambiguous	모호한
uni, mono	1	unicorn	유니콘 (뿔 하나)
bi, tri, quad, oct	2, 3, 4, 8	triangle	삼각형
semi	1/2	semifinal	준결승
poly, multi	여러	multitasking	멀티태스킹
super	위, 우위	superior	우월한
bio	생물의	biology	생물학
eco	환경	ecology	생태학
geo	땅	geology	지질학
socio	사회	sociology	사회학

접미사	예시	뜻
– 명사형 –		
tion, sion	celebration (celebrate)	축하 (축하하다)
ance, ence	existence (exist)	존재 (존재하다)
al	proposal (propose)	제안 (제안하다)
th	strength (strong)	힘 (힘 쎈)
ment, ness	movement (move)	움직임 (움직이다)
ity	equality (equal)	평등 (평등하다)
sis, ism	socialism (social)	사회주의 (사회의)
er, or	teacher (teach)	선생님 (가르치다)
age	marriage (marry)	결혼 (결혼하다)
hood	childhood (child)	어린 시절 (아이)
– 형용사형 –		
ant, ent	pleasant (please)	기쁜 (기쁘게 하다)
ful	thankful (thank)	고마운 (고마워하다)
less (-)	hopeless (hope)	희망없는 (희망)
ous	humorous (humor)	유머러스한 (유머)
al, ly, y, ic	original (origin)	기원의 (기원)
ing, ive	excessive (excess)	과도한 (과잉)
able, ible	valuable (value)	가치있는 (가치)
ious	vicious (vice)	악랄한 (악)
– 동사형 –		
en	strengthen (strength)	강화하다 (힘)
ing	walking (walk)	걷는 중 (걷다)
ize, ise	familiarize (familiar)	익히다 (익숙한)
ify	simplify (simple)	단순화하다 (간단한)
– 부사형 –		
ly	simply (simple)	간단히 (간단한)
wise	otherwise (other)	그렇지 않으면 (다른)

| 주요 어근

한글에 한자(漢字)가 있다면 영어엔 어근(word root)이 있다.

최중요 어근들을 반복 학습함으로 어근에 대한 기본 감각을 기르자.

1순위 어근	어근 뜻	예시 1	예시 2
cogn	알다	recognize	cognitive
cred	믿다	credit	credible
dict	말하다	indicate	predict
duc	끌다	introduce	reduce
graph	그리다	calligraphy	autograph
grat	기쁨, 감사	gratitude	gracious
heri	상속	heritage	hereditary
ject	던지다	eject	reject
junct	연결하다	junction	join
just	올바른	justify	justice
leg	법	legal	legislation
medi	중간	medium	intermediate
mit	보내다	commit	emit
par	동등한	compare	parity
para	옆에, 초월	parasite	paranormal
path	느끼다	sympathy	psychopathy
pel	끌어내다	appeal	compel
plic	접다	complicated	replicate
port	운반하다	support	transport
pose	놓다	position	expose
rupt	깨다	corrupt	erupt
sect	자르다	section	segment
sequ	따르다	second	sequence
spec	보다	special	inspect
tain	잡다	contain	obtain
tract	끌다	attract	traction
val	힘 있는	value	prevail
vert	돌리다	advertise	convert
vis	보다	vision	invisible
voc	부르다	voice	vocal

2순위 어근	어근 뜻	예시
alter	다른	alternative
astr	별	astronaut
audi	듣다	audience
cede	가다	procedure
clin	기울이다	decline
fide	믿다	confidence
fort	힘	effort
frag	깨다	fraction
liber	자유	liberty
limin	경계	limit
log	말	dialogue
lumin	빛	illuminate
mand	명령	command
manu	손	manual
medic	의학	medical
mount	오르다	mountain
nom	이름	nomination
norm	규범	normal
ped	발	pedestrian
phon	소리	telephone
scrib	적다	describe
serv	지키다	conserve
spir	숨 쉬다	inspire
stat	서다	statue
terri	대지	territory
test	증언	testimony
vac	비어 있는	vacant
vict	이기다	victory
viv	살아있는	survive

Allvoca.com

수능	만점
공무원	80
토익	940+
지텔프	95+
텝스	480+
토플	105+
아이엘츠	7~7.5
편입	중위권
SAT	기초 단어
GRE	기초 단어

#4001~#5500

외국인으로서 중상급 수준의 어휘력이다.
구조화된 텍스트의 개요는 물론, 세부적인 내용까지도 이해할 수 있어 Google이나 Wikipedia 등을 이용한 영문 정보 탐색에도 무리가 없다. 레벨5 학습자들은 균형 잡힌 영어 실력을 위해 Input(어휘, 독해, 청해) 학습과 Output(말하기, 쓰기) 훈련을 병행하는 것이 좋다.

LEVEL **05**

4001	수능 토플 GRE	원기가 있는, 활기찬	vigor (힘, 원기)
vigorous			invigorating (활기차게 하는)
[VIG-er-uhs]		The vigorous hiker wanted to climb the highest mountain in the world.	[547] energetic

4002		전립선(의)	
prostate			
[PROS-teyt]		You should get a prostate check-up to make sure you are healthy.	

4003	공무원	~의 한 복판에, ~의 한창	[631] among
amid			[178] between
[uh-MID]		Amid the chaos, Romeo and Juliet fell in love.	

4004	고등 GRE	배반하다, 저버리다	betrayal (배신)
betray			[2399] abandon
[bih-TREY]		The spy betrayed his country.	

4005	공무원	1. 구멍, 틈새 2. 렌즈의 구경	
aperture			
[AP-er-cher]		There is a small aperture in the walls of the castle.	

4006	공무원 토플	괴기한, 기묘한	[1659] strange
bizarre			[1594] comical
[bih-ZAHR]		His bizarre behavior made everyone think he was crazy.	

4007	토익 토플	1. 위생 2. 위생학	[5424] sanitation
hygiene			[185] health
[HAHY-jeen]		To have good hygiene, you must wash your hands frequently.	

4008		신비의, 신비로운	mystic (신비주의의)
mystical			[1926] mysterious
			[923] spirituality
[MIS-ti-kuhl]		Unicorns are mystical animals.	[1375] magical

4009	고등	무례한, 버릇없는, 야만의	[3863] crude
rude			[1550] abusive
			[3824] impolite
[rood]		Eating food on public transportation is rude.	[4649] blunt

4010	수능	1. 미망인, 과부 2. 과부로 만들다	widowed (과부가 된)
widow			[5262] solitude
[WID-oh]		Wars increase the number of widows.	

4011	고등 토익	역겨운, 구역질나는	disgust (역겨움)
disgusting			[4403] repulsive
			[2830] horrible
[dis-GUHS-ting]		Rotten milk smells disgusting.	[3052] awful

4012		1. (식물의) 대, 줄기 2. (몰래) 따라다니다, 스토킹을 하다	stalker (스토커)
stalk			[1477] pursue
			[533] walk
[stawk]		The florist cut the stalk of the rose.	[3399] trunk

4013	수능	복수, 앙갚음, 보복	vengeance (복수)
revenge			[709] attack
[ri-VENJ]		I want to get revenge for my friend's death.	

4014	고등	놀라운, 굉장한	astonish (놀라게하다)
astonishing			[2336] overwhelming
			[887] amazing
[uh-STON-i-shing]		Traveling around the world is an astonishing accomplishment.	[959] surprising

4015	공무원 토플	편견, 고정 관념	stereotypical (진부한)
stereotype			[1122] categorize
[STER-ee-uh-tahyp]		Biased people have racial stereotypes.	[75] thought

4016	공무원 토플	미끄러지다, 부드럽게 나아가다	[1574] slide
glide			[2829] descend
[glahyd]		The figure skater glided on ice.	[3393] drift

4017		피스톤 (증기 기관 내에서 왕복 운동을 하는 기기)	[5405] reciprocating
piston			[603] generator
[PIS-tuhn]		The piston moves up and down in the car, keeping the machine functioning.	[2818] cylinder

4018	공무원 토플	1. 감소하다, 하락하다 2. 돌진하다, 뛰어들다	[2076] dive
plunge			[454] fall
[pluhnj]		The diver plunged into the pool.	[4063] descent

4019		1. (벌 등이) 쏘다 2. 찌르다 3. 따끔거리다	[2061] bite
sting			[1177] suffer
[sting]		A bee stung my arm yesterday.	[1745] hurt

4020		면도기	[2010] blade
razor			
[REY-zer]		Razors are used to shave beards.	

4021	공무원	의복, 의상, 의류	[1392] clothing
apparel			[889] equipment
[uh-PAR-uhl]		She was picky about choosing her apparel.	[1190] dress

4022	공무원	1. ~를 잘 견디다 2. ~에 저항하다	[1298] resist
withstand			[600] maintain
[with-STAND]		The house built with bricks could withstand the harsh winds.	[2087] combat
			[3113] cope

4023	토익	소방관	
firefighter			
[FAHYUHR-fahy-ter]		Firefighters are heroes.	

4024	공무원 토플	1. 참을 수 없음, 아량이 없음 2. 편협함, 옹졸함	tolerant (관대한)
intolerance			[3243] prejudice
[in-TOL-er-uhns]		Her intolerance of mistakes made her a bad teacher.	[5718] bigotry

4025	공무원	으깨다, 진압하다	[2692] crush
squash			[719] damage
[skwosh]		The cat squashed the bug with its paw.	[5134] extinguish

4026	공무원	위반하다, 침해하다	[1835] violate
infringe			[445] break
[in-FRINJ]		The police infringed on his privacy and read his emails.	[2628] breach
			[6623] contravene

4027	공무원 토플	1. 벙어리의, 무언의 2. 소리를 죽이다	[2044] silent
mute			[1813] speechless
[myoot]		A childhood accident caused her to become mute.	

4028	토플	1. (동물의) 무리 2. 목자, 양치기 3. 사람 짐승등을 모으다	[3947] flock
herd			[5445] brood
[hurd]		A herd of deer ran across the field.	

4029 **state-of-the-art** [steyt-ov-thee-ART]	최첨단의, 최신 기술의 Our science lab is equipped with state-of-the-art technology.	[60] brand-new [695] advanced [938] modern
4030　　　　토플 **dinosaur** [DAHY-nuh-sawr]	1. 공룡 2. 구시대적인 사람 The tyrannosaurus is the most famous dinosaur.	[3286] antiquated [6470] archaic
4031　　　　공무원 **assort** [uh-SAWRT]	분류하다, 체계화하다 Please assort the laundry into two piles.	assortment (분류, 모음) [1098] sort
4032 **snapshot** [SNAP-shot]	스냅 사진(을 찍다), 속사 He uploads snapshots of himself on social media.	[355] photograph [526] description
4033　　　고등 토플 **drown** [droun]	1. 물에 빠지다, 익사하다 2. 물에 빠트리다, 익사시키다 The child drowned in the lake.	[5278] submerge [363] die [6619] drench
4034　　토익 공무원 토플 **deteriorate** [dih-TEER-ee-uh-reyt]	악화되다, 수준이 떨어지다 The disease caused his memory to deteriorate.	[1792] decline [373] worsen [4389] crumble
4035　　　　공무원 **mankind** [MAN-kahynd]	인류, 인간 Mankind caused global warming	[463] humanity [907] animal
4036　　토익 공무원 토플 **soar** [sawr]	1. 치솟다, 높이 올라가다 2. 높이 (하늘을) 날다 The bird soared into the sky.	[836] rise [280] increase [4057] escalate [4092] ascend
4037　　　공무원 토플 **bail** [beyl]	보석금(을 내다) Rich criminals can pay bail.	bailout (긴급 원조) [1707] bond [2687] warrant
4038 **aerial** [AIR-ee-uhl]	공중의, 항공의 Helicopters and airplanes are aerial transportation vehicles.	[100] high
4039　　　공무원 토플 **frontier** [fruhn-TEER]	1. 국경, 경계 2. 개척의 영역 China wants to expand its frontier.	[1881] boundary [1823] border
4040 **homosexual** [hoh-muh-SEK-shoo-uhl]	동성애의 Some animals show homosexual behavior.	[2743] gay
4041 **flap** [flap]	1. 펄럭거리다, 퍼덕이다 2. 덮개 The bird flapped its wings.	[6239] flutter [2962] chaos
4042　　　　토익 **nap** [nap]	낮잠, 쪽잠 I am not sleepy because I took a nap.	[990] sleep

4043	공무원 토플	공감, 감정 이입(상대방의 감정에 대한 이해)	empathize (공감하다)
empathy			[3146] compassion
[EM-puh-thee]		He felt empathy for the main character.	[1251] appreciation
			[3321] sympathy

4044	토익 토플	1. 톤 (중량의 단위) 2. 다수의, 엄청난, 큰	[5265] hoard
ton			
[tuhn]		The packages each weigh 5 tons.	

4045	고등	휘파람(을 불다), 호각(을 불다)	[1396] warn
whistle			[6051] hiss
[HWIS-uhl]		She whistled to call her dog.	

4046		조작(하다), 전략적 행동(을 하다)	[82] action
maneuver			[3551] propel
[muh-NOO-ver]		The driver skillfully maneuvered through the crowded roads.	

4047	토플	1. 도랑 2. 버리다	[2718] gutter
ditch			
[dich]		The car fell in the ditch.	

4048		저장소, 창고	[2311] garage
depot			
[DEE-poh]		Farmers store grain and farming supplies in depots.	

4049	공무원 토플 GRE	중요하지 않은, 사소한, 보잘것없는	[1109] boring
trivial			[5696] commonplace
[TRIV-ee-uhl]		Don't worry. That's a trivial problem.	[6667] frivolous

4050	공무원 토플 GRE	1. 도랑, 참호 2. 도랑을 파다	[4047] ditch
trench			
[trench]		The soldiers stayed hidden in the trench.	

4051		중죄, 범죄	felon (중죄인)
felony			[967] crime
[FEL-uh-nee]		Stealing is a felony.	[2335] assault
			[6504] arson

4052	토익	~할 만한 가치가 있는	[30] useful
worthwhile			[428] beneficial
[WURTH-hwahyl]		Reading this book was worthwhile.	[991] advantageous

4053		1. 두피 2. 암표	scalper (암표상)
scalp			[3616] skull
[skalp]		He washed his hair and scalp.	

4054	공무원 토플 GRE	1. 만들다, 제작하다 2. 꾸미다, 위조하다	fabrication (지어낸 것)
fabricate			[842] construct
[FAB-ri-keyt]		The criminal fabricated a driver license.	[2435] assemble
			[5678] concoct

4055	수능 토플	주관적인	subjectivity (주관성)
subjective			subjectively (주관적으로)
[suhb-JEK-tiv]		Beauty is subjective.	[2753] biased

4056	공무원 토플 GRE	비유, 유사한 상황	analogous (유사한)
analogy			[582] similarity
[uh-NAL-uh-jee]		We are learning analogies in my literature class.	[572] comparison
			[2987] correlation

4057	공무원 토플	고조되다, 점증하다	escalation (점차 증가하는)
escalate			[239] grow
[ES-kuh-leyt]		The tension escalated.	[995] expand

4058	고등 토익	붙들어 매다, 단단히 고정하다 .	fastener (잠그는 것)
fasten			[361] secure
[FAS-uhn]		Please fasten your seatbelts.	[769] fix
			[2374] adhere

4059	공무원	얇은 조각, 박편	flaky (얇게 벗겨지는)
flake			[1853] chip
[fleyk]		Add coconut flakes to the cake to make it sweeter.	[409] bit
			[1533] leaf

4060	공무원 토플 GRE	1. 구분하다, 식별하다 2. 인식하다, 지각하다	discernment (구분 능력)
discern			discernible (식별할 수 있는)
[dih-SURN]		Can you discern a mouse and a rat?	[1885] perceive

4061	고등	1. 서로 다투다, 급히 움직이다 2. 기어오르다, 기다 3. 뒤볶다	[1333] struggle
scramble			[4662] melee
[SKRAM-buhl]		Passengers on the bus scrambled to find a seat.	

4062	토플	빛깔, 색채	[1900] shade
hue			[5614] tinge
[hyoo]		The sunset has an orange hue.	[5619] complexion

4063		1. 하강 2. 혈통, 내리받이	[454] fall
descent			[1574] slide
[dih-SENT]		The descent from the mountain took two hours.	[4018] plunge

4064	토익	주름	wrinkly (주름진)
wrinkle			[5326] crease
[RING-kuhl]		Getting wrinkles as you grow old is a natural process.	

4065		채플, 예배실	[867] church
chapel			[3959] sanctuary
[CHAP-uhl]		I went to pray at the chapel.	

4066		전쟁의, 호전적인	[1244] military
martial			
[MAHR-shuhl]		Martial laws give more power to military generals.	

4067	공무원 토플	교환하다, 교역하다	interchangeable (교환 가능한)
interchange			[1303] exchange
[in-ter-CHEYNJ]		The interchange of culture benefitted both countries.	

4068	공무원 GRE	정밀 검사, 조사	scrutinize (조사하다)
scrutiny			inscrutable (파악할 수 없는)
[SKROOT-n-ee]		The criminal's family received scrutiny.	[1302] examination
			[871] analysis

4069		기생충	parasitic (기생하는)
parasite			
[PAR-uh-sahyt]		Some parasites live inside their host.	

4070		쐐기 (물건의 사이를 벌리는 것)	[2967] squeeze
wedge			[3037] chunk
[wej]		Can you put a wedge under the door to keep it open?	

4071	토익	가뭄	[900] dryness
drought			[1091] lack
[drout]		The drought caused many plants to die.	[3915] scarcity

4072	공무원 토플	(하나의) 측면, 일면	multifaceted (다방면의)
facet			faceted (~면을 가진)
[FAS-it]		Judges try to understand every facet of the crime before reaching a verdict.	[1297] aspect [266] feature

4073	공무원	1. 종신 재직 자격 2. (재산, 지위) 보유 기간	[1066] administration
tenure			[1573] occupation
[TEN-yer]		All professors want to be guaranteed tenure.	

4074	토플	꽃가루	pollination (수분(受粉))
pollen			[2102] dust
[POL-uhn]		Bees collect pollen from flowers.	

4075	토플	1. 충치 2. 구멍, 움푹한 곳	[3993] hollow
cavity			[5398] crater
[KAV-i-tee]		You can prevent cavity by brushing your teeth.	

4076	공무원 토플	(비유 중) 은유	metaphorical (비유적인)
metaphor			metaphorically (비유적으로)
[MET-uh-fawr]		"My love is a rose" is a metaphor.	[397] image

4077	토플	끝이 뾰족해지다, 가늘어지다	[1756] decrease
taper			[5876] dwindle
[TEY-per]		Knives taper to a fine point.	[5902] abate

4078	공무원 토플 GRE	1. 돌발적인, 즉흥적인 2. 자발적인	spontaneously (돌발적으로)
spontaneous			spontaneity (돌발성)
[spon-TEY-nee-uhs]		She spontaneously proposed to him.	[1749] random

4079	토플	계급, 계층	[1274] rank
caste			[5110] stratum
[kast]		She is a member of the upper caste.	

4080	공무원 토플 GRE	성질, 성격	[2418] mood
temper			[1706] climate
[TEM-per]		The employees dislike his bad temper.	[2055] attitude

4081		1. (담배 등을) 피우다, 불다 2. 부풀어오른 형태	puffy (부풀어있는)
puff			[1568] blow
[puhf]		She puffed her cigarette.	[2018] breathe [6916] whiff

4082	토익 공무원 토플	밀집, (인구의) 과잉, 혼잡	congested (혼잡한)
congestion			[1635] overcrowding
[kuhn-JES-chuhn]		All drivers hate traffic congestion.	[228] full

4083		복숭아	peachy (복숭아빛의)
peach			
[peech]		Peaches are delicious.	

4084	고등 토플	멸종, 사멸	extinct (멸종한)
extinction			[363] death
[ik-STINGK-shuhn]		A meteor caused the extinction of dinosaurs.	[367] disappearance [1255] destruction

4085	공무원	판결, 평결	[540] answer
			[681] award
verdict			[1234] opinion
[VUR-dikt]		The judge reached a verdict.	

4086		세련된, 맵시 있는, 멋있는	[1486] smart
			[938] modern
chic			[1206] exclusive
[sheek]		Her outfit is chic.	[2425] elegant

4087	공무원 토플	1. 자양분을 주다, 거름을 주다 2. 기르다	nourishment (영양분)
			[3744] nurture
nourish			[1618] accommodate
[NUR-ish]		Please nourish the plants.	[3160] cultivate

4088		1. 라미네이팅하다, (종이를) 코팅하다 2. 층층이 쌓이게 하다	
laminate			
[LAM-uh-neyt]		You can laminate paper to make it more durable.	

4089		1. 거친 성격의, 야생의 2. 부랑자, 악당	[7337] scoundrel
			[4894] crook
rogue			
[rohg]		The war made him become rogue.	

4090		설사	
diarrhea			
[dahy-uh-REE-uh]		Diarrhea is the most common symptom of the disease.	

4091	토플	맛있는, 풍미 있는	savor (맛)
			unsavory (맛없는)
savory			[1065] tasty
[SEY-vuh-ree]		The pasta is savory.	[3557] appetizing

4092	토플	올라가다, 오르다	ascent (상승)
			[836] rise
ascend			[1493] lift
[uh-SEND]		The elevator ascended to the top of the building.	[1681] climb

4093	GRE	1. 독특한, 이상한 2. 변덕스러운	quirk (특이점)
			quirkiness (특이함)
quirky			[5202] eccentric
[KWUR-kee]		She loved his quirky personality.	[1659] strange

4094	공무원	메스꺼움, 속이 좋지 않은	nauseous (메스꺼운)
			nauseating (메스껍게하는)
nausea			nauseate (메스껍게 하다)
[NAW-zee-uh]		Her nausea was caused by the car ride.	[1906] sickness

4095	고등 토플	모방하다, 따라하다	imitation (모방)
			inimitable (모방 불가한)
imitate			imitator (모방자)
[IM-i-teyt]		Babies imitate their parents.	[3941] mimic

4096		사람의 대외적 성격, 꾸며진 성격	[466] character
			[134] personality
persona			
[per-SOH-nuh]		Her persona is much more pleasant than her true personality.	

4097	토익 토플	누적하는, 점증적으로	cumulus (응축된)
			cumulatively (누적되어)
cumulative			[280] increasing
[KYOO-myuh-luh-tiv]		The representative is elected by a cumulative vote.	

4098		유치원	
kindergarten			
[KIN-der-gahr-tn]		My son is in kindergarten.	

4099		대저택	[139] building
mansion			[3081] dwelling
[MAN-shuhn]		The rich celebrity lives in a mansion.	

4100	공무원 토플	포유동물	[109] creature
mammal			[2799] beast
[MAM-uhl]		Whales are mammals.	

4101	공무원 토플 편입	(아직 사실이 입증되지 못한 혐의 등을) 주장하다, 제기하다	allegation (혐의)
allege			allegedly (주장된 바에 따르면)
[uh-LEJ]		He alleged that he was the victim of a crime.	[2842] assert

4102		(곰, 사자, 이리 등의) 새끼	
cub			
[kuhb]		The bear looked after her cub.	

4103	수능	터무니없는, 불합리한	absurdity (불합리)
absurd			absurdly (불합리하게)
			[2708] ridiculous
[ab-SURD]		The student gave an absurd excuse that the dog ate his homework.	[306] unreasonable

4104		1. 손잡이 있는 컵, 머그잔 2. 도둑질 3. 얼굴	mugger (강도)
mug			[5487] jug
[muhg]		He poured the coffee into the mug.	[6422] dupe

4105	공무원 토플	최고조에 달하다, 극에 달하다	culmination (최고조)
culminate			[1868] peak
			[235] result
[KUHL-muh-neyt]		The athlete's efforts culminated in the gold medal.	[1592] cap

4106	공무원 토플	1. 던지다 2. 밀다, 밀치다 3. 요점, 취지	[1013] push
thrust			[1030] throw
			[1248] core
[thruhst]		She thrust the ball to her friend.	[6572] gist

4107	토플	그 이후로, 그 뒤로	[80] after
thereafter			
[thair-AF-ter]		The two friends had a big fight. Thereafter, they never talked to each other.	

4108	공무원 GRE	너무 이른, 때 아닌	prematurely (너무 이르게)
premature			[325] early
[pree-muh-CHOOR]		Premature births result in small babies.	[207] incomplete

4109	공무원 토플	1. 폭발하다 2. 분출하다	eruption (분출)
erupt			[2828] burst
			[367] appear
[ih-RUHPT]		The volcano erupted.	[1005] emerge

4110		(포도나무 등의) 덩굴 식물	
vine			
[vahyn]		The vines climbed up the castle walls.	

4111		1. 낟알, (곡식의) 알맹이 2. 요점, 핵심	[1248] core
kernel			[266] feature
			[1364] fruit
[KUR-nl]		A kernel got stuck in between his teeth.	[2206] grain

4112	토플	새기다	engraving (판화)
engrave			[670] draw
			[5458] embed
[en-GREYV]		They had their names engraved on the dining room table.	[5900] chisel

4113 공무원 토플 GRE **evoke** [ih-VOHK]	(기억, 감정 따위를) 불러일으키다, 환기하다	evocative (환기시키는) evocation (환기) [5433] elicit [1521] remind
	The letter from his dead mother evoked sorrow.	
4114 **miniature** [MIN-ee-uh-cher]	소형의, 모형의	[1869] tiny [219] small [외래어] mini
	The architect crafted a miniature golf course.	
4115 토익 **purse** [purs]	1. 돈주머니, 지갑 2. 핸드백, 소형 가방	[4180] pouch [1052] bag
	A thief stole her purse.	
4116 **confederate** [kuhn-FED-er-it]	1. 동맹한, 연합한 2. 남부파의, 남부 동맹의	confederation (연합) confederacy (연합) [1770] ally [2218] colleague
	Local farmers formed a confederate group to raise the price of crops.	
4117 **pier** [peer]	부두, 선창, 항구	[2992] dock
	The ship sailed towards the pier.	
4118 **stool** [stool]	(등, 팔걸이가 없는) 의자	[1014] seat
	Stools are uncomfortable to sit on.	
4119 공무원 **catastrophic** [kat-uh-STROF-ik]	대재앙의, 비극적인	catastrophe (재앙) [2257] disastrous [1223] dangerous [6222] calamitous
	He is suffering from a catastrophic illness.	
4120 공무원 **dementia** [dih-MEN-shuh]	치매	
	My grandmother is suffering from dementia.	
4121 고등 토익 **embassy** [EM-buh-see]	대사관	[4677] consulate
	If you get into an accident in a foreign country, go to the Korean embassy.	
4122 **runway** [RUHN-wey]	1. (모델 등의) 런웨이 2. (자동차 등의) 활주로, 주행로	[561] track [1210] path
	Models walked down the runway.	
4123 공무원 토플 GRE **arbitrary** [AHR-bi-trer-ee]	임의의, 멋대로의, 기분 내키는대로의	arbitrarily (임의대로) [1749] random [2747] discretionary [7268] capricious
	Nobody could challenge the arbitrary decisions of the dictator.	
4124 **psalm** [sahm]	찬송가, 성가	[4859] hymn [2468] verse
	The clergy sang psalms.	
4125 **slap** [slap]	(손바닥으로) 때리다, 치다	[5204] smack [578] hit [1568] blow
	She slapped his face.	
4126 공무원 **lottery** [LOT-uh-ree]	복권, 로또	[670] drawing [3370] gambling [5506] raffle
	He won the lottery.	

4127		구급차	
ambulance			
[AM-byuh-luhns]		Cars should move so that the ambulance can pass.	

4128		으깨다	[2692] crush
mash			[3328] chew
[mash]		Mash the potatoes and put in mayonnaise.	

4129	공무원 토플 GRE	1. 늘다, 증가하다 2. 늘리다	augmentation (증가)
augment			[280] increase
[awg-MENT]		Her anger towards her employee augmented.	[2915] amplify

4130	공무원	1. 난쟁이 2. 작은 3. 작게하다, 줄이다	[7093] midget
dwarf			[509] reduce
[dwawrf]		Snow White and the seven dwarves lived in the forest	

4131		별명, 약칭	[176] name
nickname			[7324] epithet
[NIK-neym]		My nickname for my boyfriend is honey.	

4132	공무원 편입 GRE	1. 배치하다 2. 보급하다 3. 투입하다	[186] open
deploy			[995] expand
[dih-PLOI]		The country was criticized for developing and deploying nuclear weapons.	

4133	공무원 토플 GRE	방해하다, 방해가 되다	hindrance (방해)
hinder			unhindered (방해받지 않는)
[HIN-der]		The tight dress hindered her breathing.	[4727] impede

4134	고등	시기하다, 부러워하다	enviable (부러운)
envy			envious (부러워하는)
[EN-vee]		I envy her good grades.	[3843] jealousy
			[1599] hatred

4135	토익	1. (머리) 빗 2. 빗질하다	
comb			
[kohm]		Please comb your hair before dinner	

4136	토익	목걸이	[4959] pendant
necklace			[2229] jewelry
[NEK-lis]		Can you help me take off my necklace?	[3992] choker

4137		1. 땋은 머리 2. 묶다, 땋다	[1218] wind
braid			
[breyd]		Her hair was separated into two braids.	

4138	고등 토익	1. 에스코트, 호위자 2. 호위하다, 호송하다	[2060] accompany
escort			[453] attendant
[ES-kawrt]		She asked her older brother to escort her to the ball.	

4139		1. 더미, 무더기 2. 쌓다	[2696] pile
heap			[2757] bundle
[heep]		There is a heap of hay in the barn.	[5317] clump

4140	공무원 토플 GRE	주로, 과반수의 경우에	predominately (주로)
predominantly			predominance (우위)
[pri-DOM-uh-nuhnt-lee]		People living in America are predominantly white.	[541] mainly
			[1291] chiefly

4141 **provision** [pruh-VIZH-uhn]	1. 규정, 조항 2. 공급, 지원 3. 식량 4. 대비 The agreement includes a provision prohibiting currency manipulation.	[671] supply [184] plan [1368] arrangement
4142 **crook** [krook]	사기꾼, 도둑 Lottery winners with little financial knowledge attract crooks.	[7269] swindler [1077] liar [2966] robber
4143 **troll** [trohl]	1. 트롤, 신화 속 괴물 2. 놀리다, 장난치다 Trolls in fairy tales live under bridges.	
4144 　　　　공무원 **infamous** [IN-fuh-muhs]	파렴치한, 악명높은 He is an infamous criminal.	infamy (악명) infamously (악명높게) [3902] notorious [1159] famous
4145 **pea** [PEE]	(완두) 콩 I don't like peas in my rice.	[외래어] olive
4146 **trivia** [TRIV-ee-uh]	1. 상식 퀴즈 2. 사소한 것 The highlight of the camp is the space trivia competition.	[6959] trifle [919] stuff [5782] memorabilia
4147 　　　　토플 **lush** [luhsh]	파릇파릇한, 싱싱한 The garden had many lush plants.	[1854] luxuriant [859] green [2258] dense [2566] abundant
4148 　　공무원 토플 **fragile** [FRAJ-uhl]	부서지기 쉬운, 약한 The dishes are very fragile.	fragility (부러지기 쉬움) [3126] delicate [1445] weak [3609] feeble
4149 　　　　공무원 **reckon** [REK-uhn]	~라고 생각하다, ~라고 가늠하다 I reckon Korea will win the World Cup next time.	reckoning (추산) [75] think [1282] calculate
4150 　　　　수능 **spit** [spit]	침(을 뱉다) Don't spit on the pavement.	[1675] rain
4151 　　　　공무원 **diaper** [DAHY-per]	기저귀 Babies use 6 diapers each day.	[4042] nappy [5458] embed [5900] chisel
4152 **warp** [wawrp]	1. 구부리다, 뒤틀다 2. 왜곡하다 The cardboard box had been warped by the rain.	[3159] distort [719] damage [2543] corrupt [5710] pervert
4153 **repercussion** [ree-per-KUHSH-uhn]	초래되는 결과, 영향 The president's remarks had serious repercussions for the global economy.	[1881] rebound [2167] backlash
4154 **sprout** [sprout]	싹이 트다, 자라다 The flowers sprouted.	[4181] germinate [1005] emerge

4155	공무원	1. 콩(과 관련된) 2. 간장	
soy [soi]		Soy is used to make various products such as tofu and milk.	

4156	토플	1. (보석) 호박 2. 호박색, 황색	[1779] yellow
amber [AM-ber]		Amber is used to make jewelry.	

4157	토익	모기	
mosquito [muh-SKEE-toh]		Mosquitos spread malaria.	

4158	공무원 토플	엉키다, 얽히다	entangle (얽히게하다) entanglement (말려듦)
tangle [TANG-guhl]		Her long hair got tangled in the fence.	[6954] jumble [1933] mess

4159	토플	질소	
nitrogen [NAHY-truh-juhn]		Plants absorb nitrogen from the soil.	

4160	공무원 토플	분산하다, 흩뜨리다	dispersion (분산된 상태) dispersal (확산)
disperse [dih-SPURS]		The crowds dispersed after the concert.	[3299] scatter [1241] circulate

4161	공무원 토플	유동, 변화	influx (유입) relux (역류, 썰물)
flux [fluhks]		Our company is in a state of flux.	[1178] flow [1463] transition

4162	공무원	1. 햇불, 토치, 손전등 3. 불로 태우다	[1224] burn [2851] lamp
torch [tawrch]		You should take a torch when going outside.	[4736] beacon

4163		최후의 막, 피날레	[592] finish [157] end
finale [fi-NAL-ee]		During the finale, all of the actors came out and bowed to the audience.	[1304] conclusion [5181] climax

4164		1. 항공로, (비행기의) 진입로 2. (숨을 들이쉬는) 기도	[2172] airline
airway [AIR-wey]		The plane landed on the airway.	

4165	공무원	납치하다	kidnapping (납치) kidnapper (납치범)
kidnap [KID-nap]		His daughter was kidnapped.	[5187] abduct [1344] capture

4166		1. 수탉 2. 위로 젖히다 3. 남성 성기	[204] man
cock [kok]		The cock wakes everyone up in the morning.	

4167		복실복실한, 솜털로 뒤덮인	fluff (솜털) [4580] fuzzy
fluffy [FLUHF-ee]		My puppy is white and fluffy.	[1245] soft [3415] feathery

4168	토플	1. ~라고 부르다, 별명을 붙이다 2. 음향 효과를 넣다	dubbing (영화 더빙) [176] name
dub [duhb]		My dog is dubbed 'Piggy' because it eats a lot of food.	[2034] designate [4131] nickname

4169	토플	다중의, 여럿의	[763] multiple
multi			
[MUHL-tee]		This machine serves multi purposes.	

4170	공무원 토플 GRE	완화하다	alleviation (완화)
alleviate			[1841] ease
			[1721] relieve
[uh-LEE-vee-eyt]		It is the government's role to alleviate poverty.	[7289] assuage

4171	공무원 토플	비평(하다), 비판(하다)	[898] criticism
critique			[1026] assessment
			[3582] thesis
[kri-TEEK]		I attended a lecture on how to write a movie critique.	[3802] appraisal

4172	토플	1. 균없는, 살균한 2. 불모의, 자식을 가지지 못하는	sterilization (살균)
sterile			sterilize (살균하다)
			sterility (불임)
[STER-il]		Surgical instruments must be sterile.	sterilizer (멸균장치)

4173		죽은, 돌아가신	[1186] dead
deceased			[2236] departed
[dih-SEEST]		I am sure your deceased grandfather is in heaven.	

4174		1. 화염 2. 활활 불타다	[1860] flame
blaze			[655] fire
[bleyz]		The blaze spread rapidly.	[6344] bonfire

4175	공무원 토플	1. (나무의) 수액 2. 활력, 기운 3. 활력을 짜내다, 약화시키다	[2028] drain
sap			
[sap]		Trees bleed sap when you cut them.	

4176	토플	여분의, 잉여의	[1738] excess
surplus			[98] addition
[SUR-pluhs]		Do you have any surplus clothes you would like to donate to charity?	[1148] leftover

4177	공무원 GRE	1. 비틀거리는, 넘어질 것 같은 2. 깜짝 놀랄 만한	stagger (비틀거리다)
staggering			[4014] astonishing
			[887] amazing
[STAG-uh-ring]		The drunk man was staggering in the streets.	[959] surprising

4178	공무원 토플	하급의, 열등한	inferiority (열등함)
inferior			[1173] poor
			[251] secondary
[in-FEER-ee-er]		The quality of crops produced this year is inferior to that of last year.	[327] lesser

4179		1. 별의 2. 최고의	interstellar (별들 간의)
stellar			[6617] astral
			[3543] astronomical
[STEL-er]		Stellar light reaches earth after many years.	[4661] cosmic

4180	토플	작은 주머니, 소형 보관함	[4115] purse
pouch			[1052] bag
[pouch]		She keeps money in her pouch.	[1824] pocket

4181		세균, 병원균	germinate (싹트다)
germ			germination (발생)
			[4771] microbe
[jurm]		Germs can cause many diseases.	[279] beginning

4182		엘프, 요정	[6797] pixie
elf			
[elf]		The elf promised to grant her wish.	

4183 **excursion** [ik-SKUR-zhuhn]	토익	1. 소풍, 견학 2. 탐험 The children were excited to go on an excursion.	[4309] outing [1811] cruise [3554] expedition
4184 **subtract** [suhb-TRAKT]	토익 공무원 토플	빼다, 감산하다 I will subtract the cost of the dishes from your salary.	subtraction (뺄셈) [2551] deduct [1282] calculate [3954] withhold
4185 **deaf** [def]		귀머거리의 He cannot hear you. He is deaf.	deafness (귀먹음) deafening (귀가 터질만 큼 시끄러운)
4186 **shrimp** [shrimp]		1. 새우 2. 난쟁이 Seagulls eat shrimp.	[6632] prawn [3609] feeble [6203] frail
4187 **panorama** [pan-uh-RAM-uh]		파노라마, 광경/영상, 전경 The skyscrapers make a beautiful panorama of Seoul.	panoramic (파노라마의) [116] view
4188 **cramp** [kramp]	공무원	1. 경련, (근육의 통증인) 쥐 2. 경련을 일으키다 You should stretch before swimming to prevent cramps.	[4366] ache [4819] constipation
4189 **curb** [kurb]	공무원	1. 자제하다, 억누르다 2. (자동차) 커브, 연석 I am curbing my desire for more food.	[2350] barrier [5126] ledge
4190 **steward** [STOO-erd]	토플	남자 승무원, 집사 The steward brought me a glass of water.	stewardess (여자 승무 원) [3176] custodian [1066] administrator
4191 **blink** [blingk]	고등	(눈을) 깜빡거리다 She blinked her eyes.	[외래어] wink [1670] flash [1962] shine [3841] flicker
4192 **greed** [greed]	고등	욕심 He had a lot of greed for money.	greedy (탐욕스러운) [7346] avarice [1738] excess
4193 **referendum** [ref-uh-REN-duhm]	공무원	국민투표 The government decides controversial issues through referendums.	[1027] election [2355] poll
4194 **tread** [tred]		밟다, 짓밟다 When you tread on autumn leaves they make a crunching sound.	[381] step [533] walk
4195 **hawk** [hawk]	토플	(새 중의) 매 Hawks are used by hunters.	hawkish (호전적인) [6670] peddle
4196 **masterpiece** [MAS-ter-pees]	공무원	걸작, 명작 This painting is a masterpiece.	[2963] gem

4197	수능	응시하다, 바라보다	[3184] stare
gaze			
[geyz]		The students gazed at the teacher with admiration.	

4198		벌거벗은, 나체의	nudity (노출)
nude			[3402] naked
[nood]		Ancient Greeks painted nude pictures.	[4593] bald

4199	토플	전체적인, 전체론의	[1546] comprehensive
holistic			[2769] abstract
[hoh-LIS-tik]		Try to have a holistic understanding of history.	[3203] integrated

4200	공무원	1. 따르다, 수긍하다 2. (상황을) 유지하다 3. 동의하는 판결을 내리다	[172] support
uphold			[1200] confirm
[uhp-HOHLD]		It is important to uphold the law.	[1934] advocate

4201		1. 쉽게 모양이 바뀌는 2. 플라스틱	plasticity (탄력성, 유연성)
plastic			[1309] flexible
[PLAS-tik]		Clay is a plastic material.	[3667] elastic

4202	공무원 토플 GRE	선전, 과장된 광고	propogate (번식하다, 널리 선전하다)
propaganda			[333] publicity
[prop-uh-GAN-duh]		During war, countries spread negative propaganda about each other.	[3989] hype

4203		기능 장애	dysfunctional (기능 장애가 있는)
dysfunction			[5054] malfunction
[dis-FUHNGK-shuhn]		She is suffering from liver dysfunction.	[2113] illness

4204		나무 상자, 나무틀	[569] box
crate			[783] cage
[kreyt]		There are apples in the crate.	

4205	공무원	1.어지럽히다, 난장판을 만들다 2. 어지럽게 흩어져 있는 것, 난장판	uncluttered (어수선하지 않은)
clutter			[1933] mess
[KLUHT-er]		The baby cluttered her toys around the room.	[6737] muddle

4206	고등	(축제, 행사 등의) 전날 밤	[388] night
eve			[5580] brink
[eev]		Santa Claus brings presents on Christmas Eve.	

4207		올빼미	[4498] burglar
owl			[5999] bandit
[oul]		Owls are active at night.	

4208	토플	살충제	
pesticide			
[PES-tuh-sahyd]		Try using pesticide if there are too many bugs in your house.	

4209	토플	열렬한, 적극적인	avidly (열렬하게)
avid			[3032] eager
[AV-id]		She is an avid learner.	[2131] enthusiastic
			[2427] devoted

4210	수능 토익 토플	1. 추론하다, 추측하다 2. 언급하다	inference (추론)
infer			inferential (추론의)
[in-FUR]		The detective inferred that she was the criminal.	[6353] deduce
			[614] measure

4211		1. 빤짝이다 2. 반짝이는 장식품/풀	glittering (반짝이는 상태)
glitter			glittery (반짝이는)
[GLIT-er]		Stars glitter in the night sky.	[1962] shine
			[3858] glamor

4212	공무원	수도사, 스님	
monk			
[muhngk]		Monks live in temples.	

4213	공무원	작업을 위탁하다, 외주하다	
outsource			
[OUT-sawrs]		Many US companies outsource work to Chinese companies.	

4214		유령, 환영	[2546] ghost
phantom			[4480] falsehood
[FAN-tuhm]		I saw a phantom of my dead grandmother.	[5801] hallucination

4215	토플	정화하다, 깨끗이 하다	purification (정화)
purify			[3028] cleanse
[PYOOR-uh-fahy]		You must purify water before drinking it.	

4216		뒷골목, 샛길	alleyway (=alley)
alley			[2112] lane
[AL-ee]		This alley reduces the time it takes to get to school.	

4217	토익 토플	안내서, 교본	[1433] manual
handbook			[195] directory
[HAND-book]		The camp gave all its students a handbook for surviving in the wild.	

4218		거인, 위인	titanic (거대한)
titan			[393] success
[TAHYT-n]		He is a titan in the technology industry.	[6709] behemoth

4219	공무원 토플	(한 곳으로) 모이다, 수렴하다	convergence (수렴)
converge			convergent (한 곳으로 모이는)
[kuhn-VURJ]		The roads all converge at the city hall.	[2435] assemble

4220	공무원	1. 배신자, 반역자 2. 매국노	[6467] renegade
traitor			[2456] deserter
[TREY-ter]		Since she told our secrets to the enemy she is a traitor.	[3483] conspirator

4221	공무원 토플	1. 기하급수적인 2. 지수의	exponentially (기하급수적으로)
exponential		The politician became exponentially more popular after the presidential debate.	
[ek-spoh-NEN-shuhl]			

4222		(달걀 따위를) 휘젓다, 휘두르다	[3133] whip
whisk			[3003] dash
[hwisk]		To make cookies, you must whisk two eggs.	[4463] dart
			[5531] fling

4223	토플	1. 윤곽 2. (화장으로) 윤곽을 잡다	contoured (윤곽이 있는)
contour			[2119] outline
[KON-toor]		His face has a sharp contour.	[1954] curve
			[4236] silhouette

4224		1. (특정 분야에) 영향력 있는 사람 2. 도사	[932] master
guru			[334] teacher
[GOOR-oo]		He is a fashion guru with more than 2 million followers.	

4225	수능	아는 사람, 지인	acquaint (알게되다)

acquaintance
[uh-KWEYN-tns]

He is not my friend. He's just an acquaintance.

[1560] familiarity
[288] friend
[500] associate

4226 토플
neurology
[noo-ROL-uh-jee]

신경학

Neurology studies the movement of neurons.

neurological (신경학의)
neurologist (신경과 전문의)

4227
funky
[FUHNG-kee]

1. 강력한 리듬의 2. (옷 등이) 트렌디한, 최신의

My teenage son likes funky music.

[3788] foul
[938] modern
[1064] earthy
[1417] fashionable

4228 수능 토플
vocational
[voh-KEY-shuh-nl]

직업상의, 직업의

You should consider attending a vocational school.

vocation (직업)
[321] professional

4229 공무원
funnel
[FUHN-l]

1. 깔때기 2. (깔때기로) 한 곳에 모으다

The campers used a funnel to collect rainwater.

[1919] pipe
[1185] channel
[1221] filter
[1652] tube

4230 공무원
orphan
[AWR-fuhn]

고아

Instead of giving birth, I want to adopt an orphan.

orphanage (고아원)
orphaned (고아가 된)

4231 공무원
evaporate
[ih-VAP-uh-reyt]

1. 증발하다 2. 증발시키다

Alcohol evaporates quicker than water.

evaporation (증발)
[367] disappear
[4160] disperse

4232 공무원 토플
loom
[loom]

어렴풋이 보이다, 근방에 (불길한 것이) 보이다, 희미하게 나타나다

Although the couple was happy, a serious problem was looming in the near future.

[1639] tower
[367] appear
[2234] brew

4233 토플
cannon
[KAN-uhn]

대포, 기관포

The soldiers used a cannon to attack the enemy ship.

[1330] gun
[578] hit
[4615] mortar

4234 토플
gravel
[GRAV-uhl]

자갈

Put gravel in the pot to help your plant grow.

[2895] irritate
[1777] sand

4235
jerk
[jurk]

1. 재수없는 사람 2. 홱 당기다

He is a jerk that swears all the time.

jerky (덜컥거리는)
[2644] fool
[5432] twitch

4236
silhouette
[sil-oo-ET]

실루엣, (어렴풋이 보이는) 윤곽, 그림자

The silhouette of the dancer was elegant.

[2119] outline
[53] likeness
[949] shape
[4223] contour

4237
duct
[duhkt]

(건물이나 기계 내부에 공기, 액체 등이 지날 수 있도록 만든) 관, 배관

The air travels through the ducts to the purifying machine.

[5704] conduit
[1652] tube

4238 토익
oval
[OH-vuhl]

1. 타원 2. 타원형의, 달걀 모양의

The building resembles an oval.

[5040] elliptical

4239	공무원	1. 확대하다 2. 과장하다	magnification (확대)
magnify			[2915] amplify
[MAG-nuh-fahy]		A loudspeaker magnifies sound.	[196] enlarge
			[4266] aggravate

4240	공무원 토플	좌우 대칭, 균형	symmetrical (대칭인)
symmetry			symmetric (대칭인)
[SIM-i-tree]		Faces with symmetry are considered beautiful.	[897] balance
			[582] similarity

4241	토플	1. 게 2. 매독 3. 심술쟁이	
crab			
[krab]		My favorite food is steamed crab.	

4242	고등 토플	과장하다, 허풍 떨다	exaggeration (과장)
exaggerate			[2915] amplify
[ig-ZAJ-uh-reyt]		He exaggerated his achievements on his resume.	[3159] distort

4243		르네상스, 문예부흥시대	[3215] revival
renaissance			[60] renewal
[ren-uh-SAHNS]		Michelangelo is a famous artist from the Renaissance.	[249] interest
			[5251] rejuvenation

4244	공무원	1. (시간의) 경과 2. 부주의, 실수	relapse (재발하다)
lapse			[621] fail
[laps]		Nobody noticed the time lapse.	[2628] breach
			[6615] blunder

4245	공무원	1. 느슨한, 느즈러진 2. 게으른	slacken (느슨해지다, 줄어들다)
slack			[1891] loose
[slak]		The slack knot became untied easily.	[3609] feeble

4246	토플	자수, 수놓기	embroidered (자수로 꾸며진)
embroidery			[5090] embellishment
[em-BROI-duh-ree]		Embroidery is a popular hobby for elderly women.	[1667] decoration

4247	토익	제빵류, 반죽과자	[외래어] cake
pastry			[2134] bread
[PEY-stree]		Pastry with fruit jam in the middle is called fruit tart.	

4248	공무원	1. 한바탕, 한참 2. (타격) 경기	[688] match
bout			[927] round
[bout]		Her occasional bouts of anger scared her children.	[1123] session
			[2113] illness

4249	공무원 GRE	1. 가차없는, 끈질긴 2. 냉혹한, 잔인한	relentlessly (끈질기게)
relentless			unrelenting (끊임없는)
[ri-LENT-lis]		She had relentless determination to finish the project.	relent (누그러지다)
			[7219] inexorable

4250	토익	여행스케줄, 여행기	[1288] route
itinerary			[1484] journey
[ahy-TIN-uh-rer-ee]		The travel agency provided an itinerary of the trip.	

4251	공무원 GRE	1. 민달팽이 2. 강타하다	sluggish (느린, 게으른)
slug			sluggishness (나태)
[sluhg]		Slugs eat cabbages.	[2594] punch
			[578] hit

4252	공무원	꾸물거리다, 어정거리다, 물러가지 않다	[537] remain
linger			[3393] drift
[LING-ger]		The boy lingered around the girl he liked.	

4253	토플	순례자, 방랑자	pilgrimage (순례) [472] traveler [1342] settler
pilgrim [PIL-grim]		Many pilgrims go to Jerusalem to see the holy city.	

4254	GRE	효력, 효능	efficacious (효력이 있는) [30] usefulness [2096] adequacy [2388] competence
efficacy [EF-i-kuh-see]		Has the efficacy of this medicine been proven?	

4255	토플	1. 털장식, 태슬장식 2. 앞머리	[1070] edge [5580] brink
fringe [frinj]		The dress was decorated with golden fringes.	

4256	토플	1. 대화 강조법, 수사학 (강조,변화,비유) 2. 미사	rhetorical (수사학의) rhetorically (수사적으로) [6692] oratory [6714] hyperbole
rhetoric [RET-er-ik]		His speech is convincing because of its great rhetoric.	

4257		1. 과격한 록 음악 2. 불량배, 양아치	[5640] thug [3097] bully
punk [puhngk]		The elderly do not like punk music.	

4258		1. 큰, 대 2. 뛰어난	[939] huge [893] extremely
mega [meg-uh]		Seoul is a mega city with a large population.	

4259	공무원 토플 GRE	애매한, 애매모호한	ambiguity (애매모호함) unambiguous (명확한) [3812] vague [5685] dubious
ambiguous [am-BIG-yoo-uhs]		He gave an ambiguous answer to the reporters.	

4260	공무원	1. 막히다 2. 막다, 막히게 하다	unclog (막힘을 제거하다) [849] block
clog [klog]		Hair clogged up the drain.	

4261	토익 공무원 토플	중요한, 꼭 해야 하는	[902] essential [898] critical [5093] compulsory
imperative [im-PER-uh-tiv]		It is imperative that you apologize to your friend.	

4262	토플	(깊은) 협곡	[5084] gorge
canyon [KAN-yuhn]		Many people travel to see canyons in the summer.	

4263	공무원 토플	힘을 쓰다, 영향을 끼치다	exertion (노력) [1044] exercise [140] apply
exert [ig-ZURT]		She exerted a positive influence on the children.	

4264	공무원 토플	1. (기금을) 기부하다 2. (능력을) 부여하다	endowment (기부) [1556] donate [5151] bestow
endow [en-DOU]		The corporation endowed the charity with 2 million dollars.	

4265		장애물, 어려움, 극복해야할 대상	[215] problem [665] difficulty [1817] complication
hurdle [HUR-dl]		Poverty is a hurdle to overcome.	

4266	공무원 토플	악화시키다	aggravation (악화) [373] worsen [2451] bother [2895] irritate
aggravate [AG-ruh-veyt]		The cold weather aggravated his fever.	

| 4267
sullen
[SUL-in] | 1. 시무룩한 2. 침울한, 맑지 못한 | [1632] severe |
| | Ted looked sullen after the test. | |

| 4268　　GRE
ostentatious
[os-ten-TEY-shuh s] | 허세가 있는 | [353] classy
[1677] grand
[5420] conspicuous |
| | I gave my wife a big, ostentatious engagement ring. | |

| 4269
chipmunk
[CHIP-muhngk] | 다람쥐 | [4656] squirrel |
| | A chipmunk dashed across our backyard. | |

| 4270　　공무원 토플
uplift
[uhp-LIFT] | 1. 향상시키다 2. 올리다 | [1493] lift
[619] hearten
[904] excite |
| | My mother tried to uplift our spirits. | |

| 4271
zinc
[ZINGk] | 아연 | [2016] silver
[847] gold
[1733] iron |
| | The chemical symbol of zinc is Zn. | |

| 4272
Easter
[EE-ster] | 부활절 | [5720] passover |
| | The family spent the Easter holiday at a beach. | |

| 4273　　공무원
miser
[MAHY-zer] | 구두쇠 | |
| | Louis, a self-proclaimed miser, amassed a great fortune. | |

| 4274　　GRE
bemoan
[bih-MOHN] | 슬퍼하다, 애도하다 | [5032] lament
[1782] complain
[6912] deplore |
| | He was bemoaning the fact that doctors charge so much. | |

| 4275　　공무원
gratitude
[GRAT-i-tood] | 감사(하는 마음) | [1251] appreciation
[1938] obligation
[2496] grateful |
| | Please have gratitude for the privileged life you are living. | |

| 4276
gown
[goun] | 1. (큰 행사에 입는 화려한) 드레스 2. (법관, 성직자 등의) 가운 | [1190] dress
[2729] costume |
| | I need to buy a gown for the wedding. | |

| 4277　　토플
fin
[fin] | (물고기) 지느러미 | [2432] flipper |
| | I could see the shark's fin from the boat. | |

| 4278
cane
[keyn] | 1. (나무) 지팡이, 막대기 2. 회초리 | [915] stick
[2001] pole
[2484] rod |
| | Gentlemen used to carry a black and white cane. | |

| 4279　　공무원 토플
repeal
[ri-PEEL] | 무효화하다, 폐지하다 | [1713] cancel
[4362] abolition |
| | The discriminatory law should be repealed. | |

| 4280
hull
[huhl] | 1. 선체, 배의 중심 부 2. 선체를 폭격하다 | [1120] frame |
| | The hull could accommodate up to 200 passengers. | |

4281	공무원 토플	역의, 반대의	inversion (도치, 전도)
inverted			invert (거꾸로하다)
[in-VUR-tid]		A quotation mark is sometimes called an inverted comma	[1845] reversed

4282		삼나무, 향나무	[859] evergreen
cedar			
[SEE-der]		Cedar is popularly used to build houses.	

4283	토플 GRE	힘든, 벅찬, 위압적인	daunt (겁먹게하다)
daunting			[1961] scary
			[896] serious
[dawn-ting]		Climbing a mountain is a daunting task.	[4839] baffle

4284		1. 멍, 타박상 2. 상처를 내다	[1745] hurt
bruise			[1043] injure
[brooz]		Athletes have many bruises on their legs.	[5579] blemish

4285	공무원	직물의, 옷감의	[1711] fabric
textile			[1993] fiber
[TEKS-tahyl]		The textile is too scratchy.	[2833] cloth

4286		연대, 대군	regimented (엄격히 관리 된)
regiment			
[REJ-uh-muh nt]		The marine regiments are deployed near the enemy nation.	[4666] battalion

4287		(송골)매	[4195] hawk
falcon			
[FAWL-kuh n]		Falcons have excellent eyesight.	

4288	수능	짐차, 사륜차	[553] carriage
wagon			[4442] caravan
[WAG-uhn]		Horses pulled the wagon.	

4289	공무원 토플	1. 거두다, 누리다 2. 베어들이다, 베다	reaper (농작물을 거두는 사람)
reap			[2515] harvest
[reep]		Please reap the success of your hard work.	[2177] derive

4290		1. 공명하다, 울려 퍼지다 2. 동의하다	resonance (공명, 공감)
resonate			[6534] resound
			[864] affect
[REZ-uh-neyt]		The sound of the bell resonated through the sky.	[2906] echo

4291		큰 걸음으로 걷다, 활보하다	[1975] pace
stride			[728] speed
			[4012] stalk
[strahyd]		The king strides through the castle.	[5525] stomp

4292	고등	꽃 피다, 번영하다	[3252] bloom
blossom			
[BLOS-uhm]		Flowers blossom in spring.	

4293		아첨하다, 알랑거리다	flattery (아첨)
flatter			flattered (으쓱해져 부끄 러운)
[FLAT-er]		The student flattered the professor to get better grades.	[2646] compliment

4294		향수	[3363] fragrance
perfume			[2944] scent
			[3604] aroma
[PUR-fyoom]		Are you wearing perfume?	[외래어] bouquet

4295		양치기, 목사	[609] guide
shepherd			[81] come
[SHEP-erd]		One shepherd looks after hundreds of sheep.	[4028] herder

4296	공무원	부수다, 깨트리다	[445] break
shatter			[2572] blast
[SHAT-er]		The glass was shattered because of the careless children.	[2828] burst

4297		명판, 틀	[1478] plate
plaque			[1667] decoration
[plak]		His award came with a plaque to hang on the wall.	[3421] badge

4298	공무원 토플	슬퍼하다, 애도하다	mourning (애도의)
mourn			mourner (문상객)
			mournful (애도하는)
[mawrn]		They mourned the death of their friends.	[3887] grieve

4299		동료, 친구	[3510] buddy
pal			[288] friend
[pal]		I don't have many pals because I'm new to town.	

4300	토익	팸플릿	[외래어] pamphlet
brochure			[240] booklet
[broh-SHOOR]		The brochure explained the dangers of smoking.	[704] advertisement

4301		학살하다, 죽이다	[682] kill
slay			[3541] assassinate
[sley]		The Nazis slew the Jews.	[4911] butcher

4302	토플	촉매, 촉진제	catalytic (촉매 작용의)
catalyst			catalysis (촉매)
			[2189] accelerator
[KAT-l-ist]		This fight was the catalyst for their divorce.	[323] cause

4303	공무원	뗏목	rafting (래프팅)
raft			[1414] boat
[raft]		The children sailed down the river on a raft.	[5839] barge

4304		박해하다, 괴롭히다	persecution (박해, 처형)
persecute			[3275] harass
[PUR-si-kyoot]		Why do people persecute others?	[4505] expel

4305		1. (씨) 뿌리다 2. 암돼지	sowing (씨를 뿌리는)
sow			[3299] scatter
			[239] grow
[soh]		Farmers sow their land in spring.	[4202] propagate

4306		1. 옛날을 회상하게 하는 2. 옛날을 회상하는 듯한	reminisce (추억을 회상하다)
reminiscent			reminiscence (회상)
[rem-uh-NIS-uhnt]		The movie was reminiscent of her childhood.	[591] suggestive

4307	고등	주먹(으로 치다)	fistful (한 움큼)
fist			[291] hand
[fist]		He punched his friend with his fist.	

4308		~하지 않는다면	[753] except
barring			
[BAHR-ing]		I will be there, barring unexpected hurricanes.	

4309	공무원	소풍, 여행	[4183] excursion [3554] expedition
outing [OU-ting]		I have a family outing this weekend.	

4310	토플	엿보다	[3315] glance [5682] peep
peek [PEEK]		She peeked in the room to check if it was empty.	

4311	토익 공무원 토플	구경꾼, 관찰자	[725] fan [3305] bystander
spectator [SPEK-tey-ter]		Many spectators came to watch the football match.	

4312		호두	
walnut [WAWL-nuht]		Walnuts are good for your health.	

4313	공무원 토플 GRE	존경, 숭배	revere (존경하다) [2568] worship [146] love [2728] admiration
reverence [REV-er-uhns]		He had reverence for his mentor.	

4314	토플	1. 십자군 전사 2. 투쟁가	crusade (투쟁) [1082] champion [172] supporter [1006] campaigner
crusader [kroo-SEY-der]		The Crusaders tried to recapture the Holy Lands.	

4315	공무원 토플	바다의, 해양의	[1950] marine [4510] aquatic [5983] nautical
maritime [MAR-i-tahym]		Maritime law states that this island belongs to Korea.	

4316		가져오다, 집어오다	[38] get [553] carry [890] earn
fetch [fech]		The dog fetched the ball.	

4317		새끼 고양이	
kitten [KIT-n]		My cat gave birth to kittens.	

4318	고등 토플	궁리하다	[1368] arrange
devise [dih-VAHYZ]		He devised a more efficient solution.	

4319	토플	알코올 음료, 주류	[5425] booze [1674] alcohol
liquor [LIK-er]		She is addicted to liquor.	

4320	수능	으르렁거리다	[6121] bellow [2572] blast [3172] shout [6145] barrage
roar [rawr]		The lion roared.	

4321	공무원	법정, 법관석	[626] court [515] board [530] committee
tribunal [trahy-BYOON-l]		After WWII, countries gathered to host an international war tribunal.	

4322	수능	사라지다, 소멸하다	[367] disappear [363] die
vanish [VAN-ish]		The magician vanished into thin air.	

4323	토익	1. 뷔페 2. 일격, 치다	[578] hit
			[5569] cafeteria
buffet			
[BUHF-it]		Don't eat too much. We are going to a buffet this evening.	

4324	토플	1. 두더지 2. (피부에 나는) 사마귀	[7147] freckle
mole			
[mohl]		Moles have bad eyesight.	

4325		우상, 숭배의 대상	idolize (우상화하다)
			[1704] hero
idol			[1772] legend
[AHYD-l]		She was the idol of all her students.	[4861] deity

4326		1. 발톱 2. 발톱으로 할퀴다	[2247] scratch
			[709] attack
claw			[4627] paw
[klaw]		Cats have sharp claws.	

4327		국수	
noodle			
[NOOD-l]		Many people eat noodles in Vietnam.	

4328	고등	여정, 항해	voyager (항해자)
			[1484] journey
voyage			
[VOI-ij]		Are you excited about the voyage next month?	

4329		자궁 경부의	cervix (자궁 경부)
cervical			
[SUR-vi-kuhl]		Cervical cancer is a serious health problem.	

4330		퓨마, 표범	[6191] cougar
panther			
[PAN-ther]		Panthers are endangered animals.	

4331	토플	1. 발생하다 2. 누적되다	accrual (발생)
			[2732] accumulate
accrue			[280] increase
[uh-KROO]		If you put your money in the bank, the interest accrues.	[5509] amass

4332		1. 굴러 넘어지다, 뒹굴다 2. 폭락하다, 하락하다	[454] fall
			[2596] dip
tumble			[2604] collapse
[TUHM-buhl]		The child tumbled on the bed.	[2829] descend

4333	토플	1. 퇴화, 퇴보 2. 역행, 되돌아감 3. 회귀	regress (되돌아가다)
			regressive (되돌아가는)
regression			[4244] relapse
[ri-GRESH-uhn]		Dementia causes mental regression.	

4334	공무원 토플 GRE	태만, 부주의, 무관심	negligent (무관심한)
			[453] inattentive
negligence			[621] failure
[NEG-li-juhns]		Police negligence caused the crime.	[654] disregard

4335	공무원	후회하다, 뉘우치다, 유감으로 생각하다	repentance (후회)
			repentant (후회하는)
repent			[2972] regret
[ri-PENT]		She repented for her sins.	[2637] apologize

4336		소리의, 음(파)의	supersonic (초음속의)
			[2020] auditory
sonic			
[SON-ik]		Radios receive sonic waves.	

4337			1. 약탈하다, 훔치다 2. 약탈품, 전리품		looting (약탈) [6512] plunder [2958] dough [5867] booty
loot [loot]			The thief looted the Mona Lisa.		

4338	토플	식물	[3265] flora [859] greenery
vegetation [vej-i-TEY-shuhn]		The drought killed all vegetation in the area.	

4339	수능	상속인, 후계자	heiress (상속녀) [1649] successor [2907] inheritor [3637] beneficiary
heir [air]		My daughter is the heir to my wealth.	

4340	1. 병소 2. 상해	[1218] wound [1043] injury [4284] bruise [4813] abrasion
lesion [LEE-zhuhn]	He has a brain lesion.	

4341	토플	(청중 앞에서) 읊다, 낭독하다	recital (발표회) recitation (낭독) [1201] repeat [698] communicate
recite [ri-SAHYT]		The student recited a poem.	

4342	학점, 성적 평점 (Grade Point Average)	
GPA [jee-pee-EY]	She has an excellent GPA.	

4343	(신체의) 골반	pelvic (골반의)
pelvis [PEL-vis]	He fractured his pelvis.	

4344	공무원 토플 GRE	영구적인, 지속적인, 끊임없는	perpetually (영구적으로) perpetuity (영속) [2557] persistent [340] often
perpetual [per-PECH-oo-uhl]		She felt perpetual sadness.	

4345	공무원	감귤류의 (식물)	[외래어] lemon
citrus [SI-truhs]		This region is famous for citrus production.	

4346	(기술자, 예술가 등의) 장인	[139] builder [5039] carpenter
artisan [AHR-tuh-zuhn]	He is a famous artisan.	

4347	벌집, 벌통	
hive [hahyv]	There are many bees in the hive.	

4348	카니발 축제, 유원지	[886] fair
carnival [KAHR-nuh-vuhl]	The children enjoyed the carnival.	

4349	1. 잘게 썰다 2. 잘게 썬 고기 요리	rehash (재탕(하다)) [4902] stew
hash [hash]	The cook hashed the meat.	

4350	공무원 토플 GRE	(부정적인 것의) 개시/시작	[279] beginning [3932] dawning
onset [ON-set]		Politicians predicted the onset of war.	

4351	공무원	1. 타악기 2. 충격, 진동	repercussion (영향) [3082] collision
percussion [per-KUHSH-uhn]		She plays a percussion instrument.	

4352	공무원 토플	숨어 있음, 잠복, 잠재	latent (잠복하는)
latency [LEYT-n-see]		The disease has a long phase of latency.	

4353		1. 육체화(한 것), 구체화(한 것) 2. ~의 전형, ~의 모범	reincarnation (환생) [3774] embodiment [627] example
incarnation [in-kahr-NEY-shuhn]		He is the incarnation of Christ.	

4354	토익 공무원	1. 준수하다, 따르다 2. 머무르다, 살다	[2516] endure [189] live [668] accept
abide [uh-BAHYD]		You should abide by the rules.	

4355	토플	(침을 바르고) 핥다	[966] touch
lick [lik]		The puppy licked the child.	

4356	토플	발굴하다, 파내다	excavation (발굴) excavator (굴착기) [2145] dig [3658] scrape
excavate [EKS-kuh-veyt]		Cultural artifacts were excavated.	

4357	공무원 토플	1. 재촉하다, 촉발시키다 2. 비 오다	precipitation (강수, 강우) [2189] accelerate [5296] expedite
precipitate [pri-SIP-i-teyt]		The events precipitated the company's filing for bankruptcy.	

4358		사과즙, 사이다	
cider [SAHY-der]		He is drinking cider.	

4359	공무원	향수(병), 회향(병)	nostalgic (향수를 일으키는) [103] longing [830] memory
nostalgia [no-STAL-juh]		Living abroad evokes nostalgia.	

4360		1. 아름다운, 우아한 2. 절묘한	exquisitely (아름답게) [542] beautiful [2312] charming [2728] admirable
exquisite [ik-SKWIZ-it]		She is exquisite.	

4361		도끼	axe (=ax)
ax [aks]		Use this ax to cut down the tree.	

4362	공무원 토플	폐지하다, 철폐하다	abolition (폐지) abolitionist (노예 제도 폐지론자) [7375] abrogate
abolish [uh-BOL-ish]		The law was abolished.	

4363		사상자, 조난자, 부상자, 사망자	[1518] victim [1568] blow [6222] calamity
casualty [KAZH-oo-uhl-tee]		The accident caused a large number of casualties.	

4364	토플	1. 후려치다, 쳐내다 2. (화면을) 넘기다	[1736] steal [4125] slap
swipe [swahyp]		She swiped the ball.	

4365 **flop** [flop]		1. 털썩 넘어지다, 털썩 떨어지다 2. 실패작	floppy (헐렁한) [621] failure [1331] hang [3329] bust
		The fish flopped onto the boat.	
4366 **ache** [eyk]	초등 토익	1. 아프다, 쑤시다 2. 아픔	headache (두통) [1745] hurt [1177] suffer [3497] misery
		My foot aches.	
4367 **primitive** [PRIM-i-tiv]	고등 토플	원시의, 원시적인	[7058] primordial [648] basic [6470] archaic
		Wheels are a primitive invention.	
4368 **bunny** [BUHN-ee]		토끼	[792] rabbit
		Bunnies eat grass.	
4369 **earl** [url]		(귀족의 호칭 중) 백작	
		The earl of Essex has a big castle.	
4370 **savior** [SEYV-yer]		구조자, 구세주	[429] protector [672] defender
		God is my savior.	
4371 **arcade** [ahr-KEYD]		1. 오락실 2. 아케이드, 유개도로, 상가	[2023] gallery [3106] mall
		The children went to the arcade.	
4372 **chalk** [chawk]		1. (칠판에 필기하기 위해 사용하는) 분필 2. 분필로 판서하다	[168] write
		The teacher took notes with the chalk.	
4373 **solicit** [suh-LIS-it]	공무원 편입	1. 간청하다, 요청하다, 부탁하다 2. 호객행위를 하다	solicitude (걱정) solicitation (요청) solicitous (걱정하는) [707] request
		It is illegal for public officials to solicit money or gifts in exchange for favors.	
4374 **onwards** [ON-werdz]	토플	~부터 계속, ~이후로 쭉	[713] forward
		From the 20th century onwards, technology has developed rapidly.	
4375 **thermostat** [THUR-muh-stat]		(자동) 온도 조절 장치	
		Our thermostat is broken.	
4376 **myriad** [MIR-ee-uhd]	공무원 토플	수많은, 무수한	[612] countless [157] endless [5265] hoard
		There is a myriad of options.	
4377 **halo** [HEY-loh]		(천사 등의) 후광	[257] light
		The angel had a halo.	
4378 **canopy** [KAN-uh-pee]	토플	덮개, 천막	
		There was a canopy above her bed.	

4379	토익	1. (특정 단체나 언론의) 방송, 소식, 뉴스 2. 게시(하다), 공지(하다)	[899] announcement
bulletin			[3475] dispatch
[BOOL-i-tn]		The audience watched the bulletin.	

4380	공무원	1. 범죄 과학 수사의 2. 법정의, 토론의	
forensic			
[fuh-REN-sik]		Forensic evidence revealed the criminal.	

4381	공무원	재정비하다, 재단장하다	refurbishment (재정비)
refurbish			[2956] renovate
			[777] paint
[ree-FUR-bish]		My parents refurbished my room.	[938] modernize

4382	공무원 토플	1. 동의어의 2. 유사한	synonym (유의어)
synonymous			antonym (반대어)
			[2013] equivalent
[si-NON-uh-muhs]		'Kind' and 'generous' are synonymous.	[326] connected

4383	토플	1. 경이적인, 굉장한 2. 자연 현상의	[2704] extraordinary
phenomenal			[959] surprising
			[1277] fantastic
[fi-NOM-uh-nl]		He has phenomenal strength.	

4384		1조(의)	[1390] billion
trillion			[5265] hoard
[TRIL-yuhn]		The company made a trillion dollars.	

4385		주의하다, 조심하다, 신중하다	[5308] heed
beware			
[bih-WAIR]		Beware of snakes.	

4386		1. 제대(하다) 2. 석방(하다), 면제(하다) 3. 해임(하다)	[438] release
discharge			[372] clearance
			[1785] pardon
[dis-CHAHRJ]		He has been looking forward to his military discharge.	

4387	수능 토플	도살(하다), 학살(하다)	[4789] massacre
slaughter			[682] kill
			[5975] annihilation
[SLAW-ter]		The butcher slaughtered the pig.	

4388		1. 짧은 막대 형태의 단추(로 고정하다)	[1032] switch
toggle		2. 버튼을 사용해 설정을 (빠르게) 변경하다	[2874] dial
			[3708] knob
[TOG-uhl]		The coat is fastened with toggles.	

4389	토플	1. 부서뜨리다, 가루로 만들다 2. 망하다	crumbly (부스러지기 쉬운)
crumble			[2604] collapse
			[445] break
[KRUHM-buhl]		The earthquake crumbled the buildings.	

4390	공무원 토플 GRE	1. (정치) 당파적인, 편향적인, 치우친 2. 지지자, 당원	bipartisan (양당 제휴의)
partisan			nonpartisan (무소속)
			partisanship (당파심)
[PAHR-tuh-zuhn]		Partisan politics is widespread these days.	[2753] biased

4391		1. (소규모의) 폭포 2. 떨어지다, 쏟아지다	[1470] stream
cascade			[5276] avalanche
			[6760] deluge
[kas-KEYD]		There is a cascade in the mountains.	

4392	공무원 토플 GRE	무경험자, 풋내기	[3753] rookie
novice			[193] learner
			[279] beginner
[NOV-is]		I'm not very good because I'm a novice.	

4393	공무원	비밀스럽게, 몰래	[1334] secrecy
stealth			
[stelth]		The robber moved in stealth mode.	

4394	공무원 토플	1. 전신 해골, 골격 2. 기계의 뼈대	[1120] frame
skeleton			[266] feature
[SKEL-i-tn]		There is a skeleton in the coffin.	[5743] scaffolding

4395	공무원	배아, 태아	[4181] germ
embryo			[279] beginning
[EM-bree-oh]		The embryo develops into a baby.	

4396	토플	소수의, 십진법의	
decimal			
[DES-uh-muhl]		Multiplying decimal numbers is hard.	

4397	토플	관료주의, 관료정치	bureaucratic (관료적인)
bureaucracy			bureaucrat (관료)
			[771] authority
[byoo-ROK-ruh-see]		The bureaucracy is inefficient.	[1066] administration

4398	고등	서두름, 성급함	hastily (성급하게)
haste			hasty (성급한)
			hasten (재촉하다)
[heyst]		Don't complete the task with haste.	[2136] rush

4399	토플	색조, 엷은 빛깔	[1590] tone
tint			[330] color
[tint]		The sky had an orange tint.	[5619] complexion

4400		(부글부글) 끓다, 끓이다	[2156] boil
simmer			[1224] burn
			[2535] bubble
[SIM-er]		The soup is simmering on the stove.	

4401	공무원 GRE	(음악, 연설 등을) 즉석으로 짓다, 즉흥적으로 마련하다	improvisation (즉흥)
improvise			[4951] brainstorm
[IM-pruh-vahyz]		She improvised a speech.	

4402		1. 매끄러운, 번지르르한 2. 교묘한, 교활한 3. 말솜씨가 번지르르한	[1410] smooth
slick			[165] easy
			[3256] greasy
[slik]		His hair looked slick.	

4403	토플	1. (공격자, 적 등을) 격퇴하다, 쫓아버리다 2. (제안, 구애 등을) 퇴짜 놓다	repellent (쫓아버리는)
repel			[6984] repulse
[ri-PEL]		The soldiers repelled the enemy.	[2869] confront

4404		발췌(하다), 인용(하다)	[1968] extract
excerpt			[876] mention
[EK-surpt]		The scientists quoted an excerpt from this book.	[3352] fragment

4405		1. (금속 중) 니켈 2. 5센트	[5130] dime
nickel			
[NIK-uhl]		Nickel is used to make batteries.	

4406	고등 토플	1. 달라붙다, 매달리다 2. 과도한 애착을 가지다, 집착하다	clingy (붙어서 떨어지지 않는)
cling			[915] stick
[kling]		Koalas cling to trees.	[2374] adhere

4407	공무원	조직적인, 체계적인	systemically (체계적으로)
systemic			[2042] fundamental
[si-STEM-ik]		This is a systemic problem.	

4408	공무원 토플 GRE	1. 흔들리다 2. 흔들다 3. 지배하다, 좌우하다	[1203] influence
sway			[2186] swing
[swey]		The trees swayed in the wind.	[7051] clout

4409	토익 공무원 토플	1. 결점, 단점 2. 약점	[991] disadvantage
drawback			[2657] defect
[DRAW-bak]		His drawback is that he is too emotional.	[3361] deficiency

4410		(자동차 등의) 헤드라이트, 전조등	
headlight			
[HED-lahyt]		Turn on the headlight when driving at night.	

4411		벼룩	[812] ant
flea			
[flee]		The dog has fleas.	

4412		때리다, 일격을 가하다	[1226] strike
bash			[578] hit
[bash]		The wrecking ball bashed the building.	[1134] celebration

4413	토플	왕조, 시대	[2461] empire
dynasty			[3017] regime
[DAHY-nuh-stee]		The Joseon dynasty ended in 1945.	

4414		(문장 구조를) 분석하다, (문법적 구성 요소로) 해부하다	[729] define
parse			[4210] infer
[pahrs]		The linguist parsed the sentence structure.	

4415	토플	이 책이나 문서 내에	
herein			
[heer-IN]		The author herein explains his opinions.	

4416	공무원 토플	1. 관개, (농업을 위해) 물을 끌어들이다 2. 상처부위를 소독하다, 세척하다	
irrigation			
[ir-i-GEY-shuhn]		Irrigation is important for farmers.	

4417	고등 토플	언어학상의, 언어의	linguistics (언어학)
linguistic			linguist (언어학자)
[ling-GWIS-tik]		There are many linguistic theories.	linguistically (언어학적으로)

4418		현기증나는, 어질어질한	dizziness (현기증)
dizzy			[2113] ill
[DIZ-ee]		The car ride made her dizzy.	[2672] distracted
			[6799] dazed

4419		1. 경사(도) 2. (온도, 기압 등의) 변화율	[3341] incline
gradient			[234] effect
[GREY-dee-uhnt]		The gradient is steep.	

4420		본래 상태로 되돌아가다	reversion (원상복귀)
revert			[364] return
[ri-VURT]		We reverted to the old rules.	[1666] reply
			[4651] degenerate

4421	공무원	(교회의) 제단, 제대	[4445] shrine
altar			
[AWL-ter]		I made a sacrifice at the altar.	

4422	토익	1. 부록 2. 부속물	[1242] attachment [1647] postscript [6920] addendum
appendix			
[uh-PEN-diks]		The appendix contains references.	

4423		1. 투자 수익률 (return on investment) 2. 왕의	
ROI			
[AHR-oh-ahy]		The business had a large ROI.	

4424	토플	해조류, 해초	
algae			
[AL-jee]		Algae reduce ocean pollution.	

4425	공무원	장수	[2108] durability [1751] permanence [2516] endurance
longevity			
[lon-JEV-i-tee]		Turtles are famous for longevity.	

4426		스나이퍼, 저격수	snipe (저격하다) [3541] assassin
sniper			
[snahy-per]		The sniper assassinated the king.	

4427	수능	가볍게 두드리다, 토닥거리다	[7056] caress [외래어] kiss
pat			
[pat]		I gave him a pat on the back.	

4428	토플	1. 석판, 두꺼운 판 2. 큰 조각	[3037] chunk [6777] hunk
slab			
[slab]		They used wooden slabs to build the house.	

4429	공무원	박애주의, 자선활동	philanthropic (박애주의의) philanthropist (자선가) [1840] charity [2507] generosity
philanthropy			
[fi-LAN-thruh-pee]		Philanthropy makes the world a better place.	

4430		1. 망명 2. 수용소, 도피처	[3959] sanctuary [13] haven [2423] immigration [2448] refuge
asylum			
[uh-SAHY-luhm]		Many refugees are seeking asylum.	

4431		1. 고정하다, 조이다, 잠그다 2. 버클, 잠금장치	[4152] warp
buckle			
[BUHK-uhl]		Buckle your pants.	

4432	토익	배구	
volleyball			
[VOL-ee-bawl]		She played volleyball with her friends.	

4433		1. (의성어) '핑' 소리를 내다 2. 연락하다, 문자하다	[2320] knock
ping			
[ping]		The microwave made a ping sound.	

4434	토플	조절하다, 변조하다	modulator (변조기) [1388] modify [123] change [7154] inflect
modulate			
[MOJ-uh-leyt]		The musician modulated the melody.	

4435	고등 토익	복도, 통로	[2289] avenue
aisle			[3869] corridor
[ahyl]		Students ran across the aisle.	

4436		명백한, 분명한	[1124] absolute
outright			[195] directly
[OUT-rahyt]		This is outright fraud.	[5392] downright

4437		석유	
petroleum			
[puh-TROH-lee-uhm]		The price of petroleum increased.	

4438		대나무	[4278] cane
bamboo			
[bam-BOO]		Pandas eat bamboo.	

4439	공무원 토플	덤불, 관목	shrubbery (=shrub)
shrub			[3546] bush
[shruhb]		They planted shrubs in the garden.	

4440		(창문이나 문짝) 한 판	
pane			
[peyn]		There was a scratch on the window pane.	

4441	공무원	다락방, 위층	lofty (높은, 숭고한, 거만한)
loft			aloft (높이, 위로)
[lawft]		Is there someone living in the loft?	[4772] attic [1759] apartment

4442	토플	여행자단, 서커스단	[1090] trailer
caravan			[6147] convoy
[KAR-uh-van]		The caravan travels across the country.	

4443	공무원 토플	먹을 수 있는, 식용의	inedible (먹을 수 없는)
edible			[1065] tasty
[ED-uh-buhl]		Is raw meat edible?	[5739] succulent

4444	공무원 토플	고갈하다, 소비하다	depletion (고갈)
deplete			[1756] decrease
[dih-PLEET]		Natural resources will be depleted soon.	[3326] bankrupt

4445		신전, 사당	enshrine (소중히 모시다)
shrine			[4065] chapel
[shrahyn]		The clergy prayed in the shrines.	[4421] altar

4446		1. (몸이나 마음을) 깨끗이하다 2. 정화하다	[3895] evacuation
purge			
[purj]		You should purge your mind of negative thoughts.	

4447		숯, 석탄	
charcoal			
[CHAHR-kohl]		Charcoal is used for heating.	

4448	토플	선서	[1300] promise
oath			[4976] deposition
[ohth]		The doctor took an oath of medicine.	

4449 **hone** [hohn]		1. (실력이나 능력을) 갈고닦다 2. (칼 등을) 날카롭게 하다	[193] learn
		Hone your artistic talents.	
4450 **infantry** [IN-fuhn-tree]		보병(대)	[1512] army
		The infantry invaded the other country.	
4451 **crest** [krest]	토플	1. (산, 물의) 정상 2. (가문의) 문장	crestfallen (낙심한, 풀죽은) [1868] peak [100] height
		The hikers finally reached the crest of the mountain.	
4452 **stray** [strey]	공무원	1. 길을 잃다, 헤매다 2. 길 잃은 사람/동물	astray (길을 잃어) [3039] wander [533] walk
		I found a stray dog.	
4453 **mercury** [MUR-kyuh-ree]	토플 GRE	1. (행성 중) 수성 2. 수은	
		Can you see Mercury?	
4454 **cuff** [kuhf]		1. (셔츠 등의) 소맷단 2. 손으로 때리기	[5204] smack [578] hit [2094] belt [3038] sock
		My cuffs got dirty.	
4455 **discourse** [DIS-kawrs]	수능 GRE	1. 담화, 담론 2. 강연(하다)	discursive (담론의, 두서없는) [698] communication [1411] conversation
		Engaging in discourse with people who disagree with you is important.	
4456 **exile** [EG-zahyl]	공무원 토플	1. 망명 2. 국외추방	[5349] banish [2423] immigration
		The prisoner was exiled.	
4457 **remit** [ri-MIT]	공무원	1. 면하다 2. 송금하다	remittance (송금) remission (사면) remiss (태만한) [396] send
		Her prison sentence was remitted to 5 years.	
4458 **disparity** [dih-SPAR-i-tee]	공무원 GRE	1. 격차, 다름 2. 불평등	disparate (다른) [4998] discrepancy [117] difference [1701] distinction
		There is a large income disparity between workers.	
4459 **tariff** [TAR-if]		관세	[1376] duty [160] payment [297] cost
		Imposing tariffs helps domestic producers.	
4460 **apt** [apt]	공무원	적합한, 적당한	aptly (적절히) aptitude (적성, 소질) [979] appropriate [988] suitable
		Is this an apt response?	
4461 **perimeter** [puh-RIM-i-ter]		1. 주위, 둘레 2. 방어선, 방어지대	[1823] border [1881] boundary [3443] confines
		Please don't cross the perimeters.	
4462 **azure** [AZH-er]		푸른색, 하늘색	[934] blue
		The azure shirt suited him well.	

4463	공무원 토플	1. (던지는) 창, 침 2. 쏜살같이 뛰어가다	[3003] dash
dart			[986] fly
[dahrt]		She threw a dart to the target.	[1507] bound

4464	공무원	횡단하다, 가로 건너다	traversal (횡단하는)
traverse			[1161] cross
[TRAV-ers]		They traversed across the country.	

4465		오줌 누다	
pee			
[pee]		If you need to pee, go to the bathroom.	

4466		1. 시골풍의, 전원의 2. 소박한, 꾸밈없는	[5590] austere
rustic			
[RUHS-tik]		I want a rustic garden.	

4467	공무원 토플 GRE	1. 세속적인 2. 현세의	secularism (세속주의)
secular			[511] materialistic
[SEK-yuh-ler]		Making money is a secular desire.	[1284] civil
			[4313] irreverent

4468		1. (구호를) 외치다 2. 구호 3. 노래하다	[3172] shout
chant			[4859] hymn
[chant]		The clergy chanted a prayer.	[5255] mantra

4469	고등 토플	턱	
chin			
[chin]		His chin is pointy.	

4470		한 겹, 한 가닥	pliers (집게)
ply			pliable (휘기 쉬운)
[plahy]		A ply of thread in her shirt became undone.	

4471		1. 매춘부 2. 매춘 행위	prostitution (매춘)
prostitute			[4899] hustler
[PROS-ti-toot]		Prostitutes are often abused.	

4472	공무원	(수리를 목적으로) 분해하다	[123] change
overhaul			[401] improve
[oh-ver-HAWL]		The engineer overhauled the car.	[769] fix

4473	고등	연민, 동정, 유감	pitiful (불쌍한)
pity			[3146] compassion
[PIT-ee]		Please have pity for those who are less fortunate than you.	[3321] sympathy
			[5920] condolence

4474	공무원 토플	(동물이나 사람의) 측면, 옆구리	[642] join
flank			
[flangk]		You have a bruise on your flank.	

4475		1. 극찬(하다) 2. 열변을 토하다	[7124] babble
rave			
[reyv]		The old women raved about her son.	

4476		1. 미식가 2. 미식가에게 적합한 수준의	[6581] connoisseur
gourmet			
[goor-MEY]		This restaurant satisfied the picky gourmet.	

4477 **pellet** [PEL-it]	토플	알갱이	[409] bit [2677] bullet [2924] pill
		The pellet from the gun injured the bird.	
4478 **terminology** [tur-muh-NOL-uh-jee]		(전문가들이 사용하는) 용어, 술어	[880] language [6101] jargon
		Doctors use medical terminology.	
4479 **decree** [dih-KREE]	토플	1. 법령, 판결 2. (법령 등을) 포고하다, 선포하다	[82] act [290] order [899] announcement
		The judge declared a new decree.	
4480 **false** [fawls]	고등	거짓의, 부정의	falsely (허위로) falsehood (거짓) [2552] fake
		The candidate's claims were mostly false.	
4481 **entail** [en-TEYL]	공무원	~을 수반하다, ~을 필요로 하다	[527] involve [235] result
		Love entails sacrifice.	
4482 **denote** [dih-NOHT]		암시하다, 의미하다	[872] indicate [221] signify
		Her smile denoted that she agreed.	
4483 **dilemma** [dih-LEM-uh]		딜레마, 난관	[6625] predicament [665] difficulty [2063] crisis [3088] embarrassment
		This is a moral dilemma.	
4484 **rag** [rag]	공무원 토플	누더기	ragged (누더기의)
		The poor child was wearing rags.	
4485 **whereby** [hwair-BAHY]		~에 의하여, ~으로	[1121] thus
		She signed an agreement whereby her company would decrease prices.	
4486 **spear** [speer]		1. 창 2. (창으로) 찌르다	[4504] lance [915] stick [6927] bayonet
		Spears are pointy.	
4487 **spinach** [SPIN-ich]	공무원	시금치	[859] green
		Many children dislike spinach.	
4488 **fuss** [fuhs]		야단법석, 난리	fussy (까탈스러운) [7127] commotion [1581] confusion [2665] disturbance
		Stop making a fuss.	
4489 **meadow** [MED-oh]		목초지, 풀밭	[4717] pasture
		Cows are grazing in the meadow.	
4490 **hoop** [hoop]	토플	1. 후프, 고리(형의 물건) 2. 굴렁쇠	[1271] ring
		The gymnast jumped through the hoop.	

4491	공무원	(북미의) 대초원	[4489] meadow [4717] pasture
prairie [PRAIR-ee]		There is a little house in the prairie.	

4492		1. (대학교 등의) 총장 2. 수상	[2199] premier [626] court [771] authority
chancellor [CHAN-suh-ler]		The chancellor gave a speech.	

4493	토플	1. 도래 2. 출현, 강림	[81] coming [279] beginning [950] arrival
advent [AD-vent]		The advent of the computer changed society.	

4494		소용돌이(치다)	[6111] whirl [1960] spin [5089] churn
swirl [swurl]		The water swirled down the drain.	

4495	공무원	유혹하다, 꾀다	enticement (유혹하다, 꾀다) [3966] lure [1069] attract
entice [en-TAHYS]		Sellers entice customers with sales techniques.	

4496	공무원 토플	늪	swampy (질퍽퍽한) [6442] inundate [5092] bog
swamp [swomp]		Alligators live in swamps.	

4497	고등	(남자) 조카	[980] father [1189] brother
nephew [NEF-yoo]		My nephew is 5 years old.	

4498	공무원	도둑질, 절도	burglar (도둑) burglarize (도둑질하다) [2966] robbery [967] crime
burglary [BUR-gluh-ree]		Burglary is a serious crime.	

4499	토플	~에 능통한, ~에 상식이 많은	[7128] shrewd [1588] intelligence
savvy [SAV-ee]		Savvy engineers can fix the problem.	

4500		1. 작품을 선별하다, 전시를 총괄하다 2. 부목사	curator (큐레이터) [2973] pastor
curate [KYOOR-it]		The priest was sick so the curate lead the ceremony instead.	

4501		1. (구타, 상처 등을) 가하다, 입히다 2. (벌 등을) 주다, 가하다	infliction (가함) [2405] impose
inflict [in-FLIKT]		Don't inflict pain on people you love.	

4502		1. 집단, 무리 2. (고대 로마) 군대	[2713] companion [172] supporter [5514] comrade
cohort [KOH-hawrt]		The teenager cohort likes pop music.	

4503	토익 토플	환불, 리베이트	[1624] discount [200] allowance [5902] abatement
rebate [REE-beyt]		The customer asked for a rebate.	

4504		1. 창(으로 찌르다) 2. (상처 부위를) 절개하다	[4486] spear
lance [lans]		Soldiers used to use a lance.	

4505		쫓아내다, 추방하다	expulsion (추방)
expel			[4980] eject
[ik-SPEL]		The student was expelled.	[2577] dislodge

4506		(총계를) 계산하다	[508] total
tally			[688] match
[TAL-ee]		Tally the profits for today.	[2355] poll

4507	토익 공무원	~에 유창한, ~에 뛰어난	fluency (유창함)
fluent			fluently (유창하게)
[FLOO-uhnt]		She is fluent in English.	[1410] smooth
			[169] read

4508	공무원	슬픔, 불행	sorrowful (슬퍼하는)
sorrow			[3887] grief
[SOR-oh]		The mourners expressed sorrow.	[1692] sadness
			[4829] agony

4509	토플	꾸미다, 장식하다	adornment (장식품)
adorn			unadorned (간소한)
[uh-DAWRN]		She adorned her bag with beads and buttons.	[1667] decorate
			[542] beautify

4510	토플	수중의, 물의	[1950] marine
aquatic			[2143] floating
[uh-KWAT-ik]		Jellyfish are aquatic animals.	[5758] amphibious

4511	GRE	독특한, 특유한	peculiarity (특이함)
peculiar			peculiarly (특이하게)
[pi-KYOOL-yer]		He has a peculiar hobby.	[1659] strange
			[1701] distinct

4512		1. 가사 2. 허드렛일, 자질구레한 일	[1039] task
chore			[1259] assignment
[chawr]		It's your turn to do the chores.	[2760] burden

4513		1. 인도적인 2. 친절한, 자상한	inhumane (비인간적인)
humane			humanely (자비롭게)
[hyoo-MEYN]		Prisoners should be treated in a humane manner.	[410] kind
			[696] approachable

4514		1. 잘라내다, 쳐내다 2. 건자두	pruning (잔가지를 잘라내다)
prune			[2263] trim
[proon]		The gardener pruned the branches of the tree.	[673] replace

4515		박자, 속도, 템포	[외래어] rhythm
tempo			[728] speed
[TEM-poh]		The tempo of the music was slow.	[3213] momentum
			[6070] cadence

4516	공무원	1. (특정분야를) 탐구하다 2. (무언가를 찾기 위해) 샅샅이 들추다	[4356] excavate
delve			[1004] investigate
[delv]		The student delved into the field of science.	[2390] inquire
			[5942] burrow

4517		주석, 주해	annotate (주석을 달다)
annotation			[525] comment
[an-uh-TEY-shuhn]		The book has helpful annotations.	[3816] glossary

4518		(군대의) 중위	[2759] deputy
lieutenant			
[loo-TEN-uhnt]		The lieutenant commanded her soldiers.	

4519	공무원	송어	[983] fish
trout		There are many trouts in the river.	
[trout]			

4520		적, 앙숙	[1548] enemy
foe			[2835] adversary
[foh]		He is my foe, not a friend.	[5020] antagonist

4521		토네이도, 큰 회오리 바람	[2202] twister
tornado			[1878] storm
[tawr-NEY-doh]		The tornado caused massive damages on the country.	[5374] cyclone

4522		1. 메시아, 구세주 2. 예수	[1393] god
messiah			[2986] saint
[mi-SAHY-uh]		When is the messiah coming?	

4523	공무원	1. (구운 빵) 한 덩어리 2. 게으름 피우다	[2856] lounge
loaf			[4541] bun
[lohf]		I would like a loaf of bread.	[외래어] cake

4524	고등 공무원 토플	절망	[3497] misery
despair			[2653] desperation
[dih-SPAIR]		The moaned in despair.	[5443] gloom
			[6156] anguish

4525	고등 토익	정돈하다, 깔끔히 하다	untidy (깔끔하지 못한)
tidy			[2920] neat
[TAHY-dee]		Please tidy your room.	[290] orderly
			[3740] sleek

4526		연소, 산화	combustible (불이 쉽게 붙는)
combustion			[1224] burning
[kuhm-BUHS-chuhn]		Combustion of fossil fuels produces energy.	[3367] ignition

4527	공무원 토플 GRE	1. 불투명한 2. 이해하기 어려운, 복잡한	opacity (불투명함)
opaque			[3751] obscure
[oh-PEYK]		The river water is opaque.	[1363] cloudy

4528	공무원 GRE	경계하는, 주의하는	vigil (불침번)
vigilant			vigilance (경계)
[VIJ-uh-luhnt]		Please be vigilant at night.	[2038] alert
			[453] attentive

4529		1. 완벽한 보기, 전형 2. 학문관	[431] model
paradigm			[627] example
[PAR-uh-dahym]		She is the paradigm for all students.	

4530	공무원	주인공	[1704] hero
protagonist			
[proh-TAG-uh-nist]		The protagonist won the war.	

4531	공무원 GRE	시대에 뒤쳐진, 구식의	[4927] obsolete
outdated			[988] unsuitable
[out-DEY-tid]		Your discriminatory beliefs are outdated.	[3286] antiquated
			[6470] archaic

4532		그로셰 뜨개질, 코바늘 뜨개질	[2003] hook
crochet			[3167] mesh
[kroh-SHEY]		She learned how to crochet.	[3871] ornament

4533	공무원 토플 GRE	유해한, 해가 되는	detriment (손상)
detrimental			[1708] harmful
[de-truh-MEN-tl]		Smoking is detrimental for your health.	[1223] dangerous [1255] destructive

4534	토익 공무원 토플	적응하다, 익숙해지다	unaccustomed (익숙하지 않은)
accustom			[1706] acclimate
[uh-KUHS-tuhm]		I became accustomed to American culture.	[1415] adapt

4535	공무원 토플	취임(식)의, 개회(식)의	inauguration (취임식)
inaugural			[510] original
[in-AW-gyer-uhl]		The CEO gave an inaugural speech.	

4536	공무원	충실도, (약속의) 엄수	infidelity (바람피는 행위)
fidelity			[1380] faithfulness
[fi-DEL-i-tee]		Fidelity is an important trait in a partner.	[2267] loyalty [2427] devotion

4537	공무원 GRE	1. 소중히 여기다, 아끼다 2. 고이 간직하다	[2040] treasure
cherish			[622] remember
[CHER-ish]		Please cherish my present.	[2728] admire [2940] adore

4538	공무원 토플	1. 전염병 2. 유해성의	[3766] plague
epidemic			[2113] illness
[ep-i-DEM-ik]		The epidemic killed many birds.	[5417] contagious [6385] endemic

4539		초조하다, 애타다	[1133] worry
fret			[2451] bother
[fret]		Don't fret about the problem.	[4829] agonize

4540		1. 확 당기다, 비틀다 2. (공구 중) 렌치 3. 마음 아픔	[2202] twist
wrench			[315] dislocate
[rench]		She wrenched the door handle.	[1218] wind [2140] bend

4541		1. (빵 중) 번 2. 묶은 머리	[981] roll
bun			[999] bottom
[buhn]		I would like jam on my bun.	[2134] bread [외래어] doughnut

4542		신화(집)	mythological (신화의)
mythology			[309] belief
[mi-THOL-uh-jee]		The mythology was about Zeus.	[1219] theory [1772] legend

4543		(금속원소 중) 티탄, 티타늄	[4218] titan
titanium			
[tahy-TEY-nee-uhm]		Titanium is a sturdy metal.	

4544		1. 매달아 올리다 2. (투석기로) 던지다	[5531] fling
sling			[1030] throw
[sling]		The workers had to sling the cargo onto the ship.	[5774] dangle

4545	GRE	고집이 강한, 완고한, 완강한	stubbornly (완강하게)
stubborn			stubbornness (완강함)
[STUHB-ern]		Not many people like him because he is stubborn.	[7326] obstinate [652] determined

4546	공무원	인류학	anthropologist (인류학자)
anthropology			anthropological (인류학의)
[an-thruh-POL-uh-jee]		Anthropology is the study of society and culture.	[405] sociology

4547 공무원 GRE	조용한, 평온한	tranquility (고요함)
tranquil		tranquilizer (진정제)
[TRANG-kwil]	The riverside was tranquil.	[2260] calm [1384] peaceful

4548 GRE	앞의, 앞서	forego (앞서다)
foregoing		[477] above
[fawr-GOH-ing]	The foregoing discussion has ended.	

4549	(아이스하키 원반인) 퍽	
puck		
[puhk]	The puck slid into the goal.	

4550	1. 소년 2. 젊은이	[1093] boy
lad		[1545] male
[lad]	Lad, can you help me?	[1580] fellow

4551 공무원	(가을의) 낙엽	[1533] leaf
foliage		[4338] vegetation
[FOH-lee-ij]	Autumn foliage is beautiful.	

4552 토플	(화폐, 책, 표석 등에) 새겨진 글	inscribe (새기다)
inscription		[4112] engraving
[in-SKRIP-shuhn]	There is an inscription on the stone.	[3848] caption

4553 공무원	잇따르다, 이어지다	ensuing (잇따르는)
ensue		[155] follow
[en-SOO]	Punishment ensued the crime.	[2035] arise [6948] befall

4554 공무원 토플	빙하	[5581] iceberg
glacier		
[GLEY-sher]	Glaciers are melting.	

4555 고등 토플	1. 장애 2. 강자에게 불리한 추가 조건	handicapped (장애가 있는)
handicap		[4133] hindrance
[HAN-dee-kap]	She has a handicap.	[991] disadvantage

4556	운, 라임	[2468] verse
rhyme		[2871] poem
[rahym]	Good poems should rhyme.	[6070] cadence

4557 수능	1. 흘겨보다, 째려보다 2. 쨍한 빛	glaring (눈부신)
glare		glaringly (눈부시게)
[glair]	He glared at me.	[1860] flame [2945] glow

4558 토플	(국외) 추방	deport (추방하다)
deportation		[4505] expulsion
[dee-pawr-TEY-shuhn]	There are different opinions surrounding the deportation of refugees.	[128] displacement [4926] eviction

4559 공무원 GRE	초월하다, 넘어서다	transcendental (초월적인)
transcend		[1983] exceed
[tran-SEND]	Love transcends borders.	[3844] eclipse

4560	지도책, 도감	[162] design
atlas		[670] drawing
[AT-luhs]	The atlas has a map of the world.	

4561		행복, 흡족	blissful (행복이 넘치는)
bliss			[594] happiness
[blis]		Good food and good company brings bliss in our lives.	[6761] euphoria

4562		1. 정당하게, 정식으로 2. 제시간에	unduly (과도하게)
duly			[879] properly
[DOO-lee]		He was a duly elected president.	[662] correctly
			[979] appropriately

4563	공무원 토플	1. 길들이다 2. 길들여진, 순한	untamed (길들여지지 않은)
tame			[496] subdue
[teym]		Humans have tamed many animals.	[2065] gentle

4564	공무원	부산스러운, 붐비는	bustle (분주히 돌아다니다)
bustling			
[BUHS-uhl-ing]		The market is bustling with people.	

4565	공무원	이름의, 명목상의, 허울만의	nominally (명목상)
nominal			[6232] ostensible
[NOM-uh-nl]		That is just a nominal apology.	

4566	공무원	(사건의) 여파, 결과	[1746] consequence
aftermath			[831] impact
[AF-ter-math]		The aftermath of the war was devastating.	

4567		경험적인, 실증적인	empirically (경험적으로)
empirical			[492] practical
[em-PIR-i-kuhl]		Empirical evidence proves that global warming is true.	[1285] true
			[1461] experimental

4568		(군대의) 대	[500] association
brigade			
[bri-GEYD]		The brigade waited for the orders of the commander.	

4569	토익 공무원	1. 청사진(을 마련하다) 2. 자세한 계획(을 세우다)	[573] preparation
blueprint			[1720] draft
[BLOO-print]		Blueprints provide detailed information about the building.	

4570	공무원 GRE	분개, 분노	resent (분노하다)
resentment			resentful (분하게 여기는)
[ri-ZENT-muhnt]		She felt resentment towards the criminal.	[3130] bitterness
			[7113] animosity

4571		독점	monopolize (독점하다)
monopoly			[131] leadership
[muh-NOP-uh-lee]		There is a monopoly in the oil market.	[265] holding
			[5596] cartel

4572	공무원 토플 GRE	흩뿌리다, 파급하다	dissemination (확산)
disseminate			[1373] spread
[dih-SEM-uh-neyt]		The media disseminated fake news.	[704] advertise
			[899] announce

4573		꼭두각시, 인형	puppeteer (인형을 조종하는 자)
puppet			[801] doll
[PUHP-it]		She controlled the puppet.	

4574	토플	1. 얕은 언덕 2. 언덕을 쌓다	[4139] heap
mound			[2696] pile
[mound]		The children hid behind the small mound.	

4575	히스패닉의, 라틴 아메리카의	
hispanic		
[hi-SPAN-ik]	Hispanic food contains a lot of spices.	

4576	양을 재다	quantifiable (수치화할 수 있는)
quantify		quantification (수치화)
[KWON-tuh-fahy]	It is difficult to quantify how many people were at the protest.	[614] measure

4577 수능	1. 유모 2. (아이를) 애지중지하다	[1217] nurse
nanny		
[NAN-ee]	We are looking for a nanny.	

4578	물집(이 생기다), 수포(가 생기다)	blistering (매우 더운)
blister		[2535] bubble
[BLIS-ter]	I have blisters from walking too long.	[719] damage [6452] abscess

4579	시초, 발단	[279] beginning
inception		[1378] initiation
[in-SEP-shuhn]	The inception of organisation was two years ago.	[5404] outset

4580 토플	보풀이 일어난, 보송보송한	fuzz (솜털)
fuzzy		[372] unclear
[FUHZ-ee]	My sweater is fuzzy.	[891] hairy [2574] faint

4581	살인	[1741] murder
homicide		[967] crime
[HOM-uh-sahyd]	There was a homicide yesterday.	[3541] assassination

4582	(맥주의 일종인) 에일	[1765] beer
ale		[2234] brew
[eyl]	He drinks ale.	

4583	복고풍의, 재유행하는	[2623] vintage
retro		[1417] old-fashioned
[RE-troh]	This shop specializes in retro clothing.	

4584	(질병의 치료를 위해) 처방되거나 권장된 식습관	[776] procedure
regimen		[외래어] menu
[REJ-uh-muhn]	Please follow the regimen recommended by the doctor.	

4585	(육군, 공군, 해병대의) 대령, 연대장	[1012] commander
colonel		
[KUR-nl]	The colonel ordered his soldiers to march.	

4586	1. 영적 교감, 교섭 2. 종교적 성찬식	commune (교감하다)
communion		[1580] fellowship
[kuh-MYOON-yuhn]	I encountered my dead grandmother's spirit during the communion.	[698] communication [2783] intimacy

4587	1. 부업 2. (경기장의) 측선 3. 출전이나 참가를 제한하다	
sideline		
[SAHYD-lahyn]	She is a teacher who uploads videos on youtube on the sideline.	

4588	(어패류 중) 굴	[5840] clam
oyster		
[OI-ster]	Oysters have hard shells.	

4589 공무원 토플 **arrogant** [AR-uh-guhnt]	자만한, 거만한 He is too arrogant.	arrogance (자만) arrogantly (거만하게) [7339] haughty [1636] proud
4590 **abbreviation** [uh-bree-vee-EY-shuhn]	약자, 약어 UN is an abbreviation for United Nations.	abbreviate (약자로 줄여 쓰다) [738] contraction
4591 **tendon** [TEN-duhn]	(근육을 구성하는 줄) 건, 힘줄 His tore his tendons during exercise.	[4888] ligament [5450] hamstring
4592 **infrared** [IN-fruh-red]	적외선의 We cannot see infrared rays with our bare eyes.	
4593 **bald** [bawld]	대머리의 He is almost bald.	[2117] bare [5989] barren
4594 **cucumber** [KYOO-kuhm-ber]	오이 There are cucumbers in this sandwich.	
4595 **aforementioned** [uh-FAWR-men-shuhnd]	앞서 말한 The aforementioned argument is convincing.	[477] above [674] previous [761] introductory
4596 토플 **hemisphere** [HEM-i-sfeer]	(지구의) 반구 I live on the Northern hemisphere.	[661] half [2936] fraction
4597 공무원 **turf** [turf]	1. (한 나라의) 영역 2. 잔디 3. 경마 The ball landed in their turf.	[2351] grass [2999] lawn [외래어] carpet
4598 **wand** [wond]	1. (마술사의) 지팡이 2. 지휘봉 I have a magic wand.	[6377] baton
4599 공무원 **synergy** [SIN-er-jee]	시너지 효과, 공동 상승 작용 Their cooperation resulted in synergy.	[2147] cooperation [30] usefulness
4600 토익 **beforehand** [bih-FAWR-hand]	이전에, 사전에 I should have warned you beforehand.	[119] before [325] earlier [726] sooner
4601 **levy** [LEV-ee]	1. 과세하다, 징세하다 2. 추가적인 부담을 주다 The government levied a large tax.	[415] charge [1376] duty [2760] burden
4602 GRE **perennial** [puh-REN-ee-uhl]	1. 영원한, 끝이 없는 2. 다년생의 He is destined to be a perrenial all-star.	perennially (영속적으로) [225] always [260] continual [2463] chronic

4603	토플	1. (천 등으로) 덮다, 걸치다 2. 긴 커튼	drapery (긴 커튼)
drape			[231] cover
[dreyp]		She draped her shoulders with a shawl.	[1392] clothe
			[5101] cloak

4604		거위	[기타] turkey
goose			
[goos]		The goose lives in this lake.	

4605	토익 공무원 토플	여기다, 간주하다, 생각하다	[75] think
deem			[200] allow
[deem]		I deem it an honor to be invited.	[1041] assume

4606		1. 감각을 잃은, 무딘 2. 감각을 잃게 하다	numbness (저림)
numb			[383] insensible
[nuhm]		The cold made her finders numb.	[117] indifferent
			[863] painless

4607		1. 예고하다, 알리다 2. 전령관, 보도자	heraldic (문장에 대한)
herald			unheralded (미리 알려지
[HER-uhld]		The weather forecaster heralded rain.	지 않은)
			[221] sign

4608		(화폐 등의) 가치의 하락	depreciate (가치가 하락
depreciation			하다)
[dih-pree-shee-EY-shuhn]		There has been a massive depreciation of the dollar.	[509] reduction
			[5628] deflation

4609	토플	1. 분비물, 분비액 2. 분비 작용	secrete (분비하다)
secretion			[415] discharge
[si-KREE-shuhn]		The secretion of snails is transparent and slimy.	

4610	공무원 토플 GRE	조심성 있는, 신중한	prudence (조심성)
prudent			prudential (신중한)
[PROOD-nt]		She is prudent.	prudently (신중하게)
			[256] careful

4611		고난이도 묘기, 스턴트	[1595] trick
stunt			[3951] feat
[stuhnt]		The athlete performed an amazing stunt.	

4612		명랑한, 흥겨운	merrily (명랑하게)
merry			[594] happy
[MER-ee]		He has a merry personality.	[862] drunk
			[2488] cheerful

4613		1. (곡식 중) 귀리 2. 귀리가 포함된	[2206] grain
oat			
[oht]		Horses eat oat.	

4614	토플	안마당, 안뜰	[2999] lawn
courtyard			[3581] patio
[KAWRT-yahrd]		Children are playing in the courtyard.	

4615	토플	시멘트와 모래의 혼합물	brick-and-mortar (소매
mortar			오프라인 가게의)
[MAWR-ter]		Bricks need to be stacked with mortar.	[2374] adhesive
			[3782] cement

4616		1. 하사관 2. 중사 3. 경사	[2048] captain
sergeant			[2759] deputy
[SAHR-juhnt]		The sergeant was in charge of many soldiers.	

4617 **clot** [klot]		1. 응고된 덩어리 2. 응고되다	[5317] clump
		There was a small clot in her blood.	
4618 **detergent** [dih-TUR-juhnt]	공무원	세제	[559] cleaner [1313] solvent
		He used detergent to remove the stain.	
4619 **dorm** [dawrm]		기숙사	dormitory (=dorm) [1759] apartment [4659] hostel
		I live in the dorm.	
4620 **abbey** [AB-ee]	토플	수도원, 수녀원	[4676] monastery [5390] nunnery
		There is an abbey on the mountain.	
4621 **forthcoming** [FAWRTH-kuhm-ing]	공무원	곧 닥쳐올, 곧 일어날	[696] approaching [726] soon [2207] anticipated
		There is a forthcoming disaster.	
4622 **hut** [huht]	고등	오두막, 임시 숙소	[5457] shack [569] box
		Up to four people can sleep in this hut.	
4623 **ashamed** [uh-SHEYMD]		부끄러워하는, 창피해하는	unashamedly (부끄러움 없이) [3088] embarrassed [2637] apologetic
		Don't be ashamed of your mistakes.	
4624 **outage** [OU-tij]	토익	(정전, 단수 등의) 서비스나 공익 사업의 끊김	[621] failure
		There was an electricity outage.	
4625 **concise** [kuhn-SAHYS]		간결한, 짧은	concisely (간결하게) [1671] brief [6327] succinct
		The speech was concise and touching.	
4626 **pantry** [PAN-tree]		식료품실	[3169] closet [5053] cellar
		There are snacks in the pantry.	
4627 **paw** [paw]	공무원	1. 동물의 발 2. 동물의 발로 차거나 긁다	
		Puppies have four paws.	
4628 **peg** [peg]		1. 고정 핀 2. 고정하다	[1753] pin [769] fix [2884] rope
		Use this peg to hang the pictures.	
4629 **intrinsic** [in-TRIN-sik]	공무원 GRE	근본적인, 고유한	intrinsically (근본적으로) [3211] inherent [648] basic [838] elemental
		You should identify the intrinsic cause of the problem.	
4630 **jog** [jog]	고등 토익	조깅하다, (운동을 위해) 달리다	[152] run
		Jogging is a good exercise.	

4631	지하철	[766] underground
metro		[2075] railway
[ME-troh]	The metro is a cheap and convenient way of traveling.	

4632	1. 덜컹거리다 2. 흔들다 3. 신경질나게 하다	rattlesnake (방울뱀)
rattle		[1969] shake
[RAT-l]	The car rattled because of the bumpy road.	[2612] jar [2689] bounce

4633	공무원 GRE	피하다, (교묘히) 모면하다	evasion (모면)
evade			evasive (회피하는)
[ih-VEYD]		The company tried to evade paying taxes.	[848] avoid [3567] bypass

4634	공무원 토플 GRE	왔다갔다 양극으로 진동하다	oscillation (진동)
oscillate			[3888] fluctuate
[OS-uh-leyt]		The Korean stock market is known to oscillate frequently.	[2186] swing [7153] lurch

4635	(공원이나 정원에 있는 별장 등의) 장식용 건물	[5880] marquee
pavilion		[854] structure
[puh-VIL-yuhn]	There is a pavilion in the park.	

4636	공무원 토플	앙금	sedimentary (앙금의)
sediment			[1827] deposit
[SED-uh-muhnt]		There are sediments in the water.	

4637	1. 설교 2. 잔소리	[2385] lecture
sermon		[1035] advice
[SUR-muhn]	The priest gave a sermon.	[1813] speech [6402] exhortation

4638	공무원 토플	만장일치의, 이구동성의	unanimously (만장일치로)
unanimous			unanimity (만장일치)
[yoo-NAN-uh-muhs]		There was unanimous agreement.	[1409] united

4639	굴, 소굴	[6864] lair
den		[2886] cave
[den]	Rabbits live in a den.	

4640	GRE	이례적인 현상, 불규칙한 현상, 변칙	anomalous (이례적인)
anomaly			[649] abnormality
[uh-NOM-uh-lee]		This is just an anomaly.	[117] difference [6093] aberration

4641	1. 용광로 2. 화덕	[3387] stove
furnace		[710] heater
[FUR-nis]	The furnace is used to make pots.	[2156] boiler

4642	고등 토플	1. 기뻐 날뛰다, 열광하다 2. 벌레 윙윙 소리 3. 소문, 루머	[6428] murmur
buzz			[4320] roar
[buhz]		Fans buzzed around the singer.	[5031] hum

4643	주의 깊은, 경계하는	unwary (부주의한)
wary		[2149] cautious
[WAIR-ee]	You should be wary when walking around at night.	[453] attentive [1133] worried

4644	1. (성과에 대한) 보수 2. 관대함 3. 풍부함	bountiful (풍부한)
bounty		[1360] reward
[BOUN-tee]	If you find the criminal, I will give you a large bounty.	[984] gift [991] advantage

4645		고생, 고뇌	woefully (비참하게, 고뇌에 차서)
woe			[3497] misery
[woh]		The tales of woe made me have empathy for him.	[1692] sadness

4646		1. (카드 등을) 뒤섞다 2. (발을) 질질 끌다	shuffling (발을 끌며)
shuffle			reshuffle (조직 개편)
[SHUHF-uhl]		You should shuffle the cards again.	[533] walk [2074] drag

4647	공무원	차별대우, 분리 정책	segregate (차별하다)
segregation			[892] separation [2625] discrimination
[seg-ri-GEY-shuhn]		Segregation is illegal.	[6568] apartheid

4648		회상, 상기, 기억	[830] memory
recollection			[4306] reminiscence
[rek-uh-LEK-shuhn]		I have no recollection of hitting him.	

4649	공무원	1. (날이) 무딘, 뾰족하지 않은 2. 솔직한, 꾸밈없는	bluntly (직설적으로)
blunt			[3731] dull
[bluhnt]		The knife is blunt.	[1404] honest

4650		대각선의, 비스듬한	diagonally (대각선으로)
diagonal			[6258] oblique [2946] slope
[dahy-AG-uh-nl]		Draw a diagonal line across the page.	[5730] slanted

4651	공무원	퇴보, 악화	degenerative (퇴행성의)
degeneration			degenerate (퇴보하다) [4034] deterioration
[dih-jen-uh-REY-shuhn]		The disease causes degeneration of mental capabilities.	[373] worsening

4652	토익 공무원 GRE	그럴듯한, 믿을 만한	implausible (믿기 힘든)
plausible			plausibility (그럴듯함) [963] conceivable
[PLAW-zuh-buhl]		Her argument is plausible.	[1209] credible

4653	공무원	(죽음을 초래할 수준으로) 치사적인, 유독한	[1186] deadly
lethal			[1223] dangerous
[LEE-thuhl]		This is a lethal poison.	[1255] destructive

4654	토플	(걸터)앉다	[1573] occupy
perch			
[purch]		The bird perched on the branch.	

4655	토플	1. 자식, 자손 2. 성과	[235] result
offspring			[970] baby
[AWF-spring]		He has three offspring.	[5445] brood

4656		다람쥐	
squirrel			
[SKWUR-uhl]		Squirrels eat acorns.	

4657		(묽은) 수프	[2738] soup
broth			
[brawth]		If you are sick, you should drink broth.	

4658		1. 내륙의, 내지의 2. 내국의, 국내의	[1864] interior
inland			[1327] coastal
[IN-luhnd]		Inland Australia has many deserts.	

4659 **hostel** [HOS-tl]	호스텔, 숙박소	[외래어] hotel [3425] inn
	They stayed at a hostel.	

4660 공무원 GRE **bolster** [BOHL-ster]	1. 지지하다 2. 지지대	[1007] strengthen [1338] aid [1566] boost
	The pillars bolstered the building.	

4661 **cosmic** [KOZ-mik]	1. 우주의 2. 광활하다	cosmos (우주) [1462] universal [196] large [721] global
	Scientists are trying to resolve cosmic mysteries.	

4662 **melee** [MEY-ley]	1. 소동, 소란 2. 혼란스러운 군중	[5620] fray [2665] disturbance [5960] brawl
	There is a melee outside.	

4663 공무원 토플 **manifold** [MAN-uh-fohld]	1. 다양한 2. 다방면의	[1535] diverse [1717] conflicting
	There are manifold applications of this technology.	

4664 **prenatal** [pree-NEYT-l]	출생 전의	postnatal (출생 후의)
	Prenatal check-ups are essential.	

4665 공무원 **indictment** [in-DAHYT-muhnt]	기소, 고발	indict (기소하다) [415] charge [898] criticism [4101] allegation
	He filed an indictment of the perpetrator.	

4666 토플 **battalion** [buh-TAL-yuhn]	대부대, 대군	[500] association [1512] army [3976] contingent
	There are three battalions that are undefeated.	

4667 토플 **plaster** [PLAS-ter]	1. 석고 2. 석고를 바르다	[2374] adhesive [3782] cement
	Plaster is used to make statues.	

4668 **cove** [kohv]	1. 비바람이 없는 작은 만 2. 녀석, 자식	[4751] inlet
	Many animals stayed at the cove for shelter.	

4669 **prefix** [PREE-fiks]	접두사	[5953] preface
	Un- is a common prefix.	

4670 **ailment** [EYL-muhnt]	질병, 질환	ailing (병을 앓고있는) [2113] illness [446] condition [4366] ache
	She is suffering from an ailment.	

4671 **redeem** [ri-DEEM]	1. (실수를) 만회하다, 상환하다 2. (죄로부터) 구원하다	redemption (만회, 상환, 구원) [401] improve [588] reclaim
	There seems to be no way to redeem it.	

4672 **bloat** [bloht]	1. 부풀다, 붓다 2. 부풀게하다	[2740] swell [239] grow [2579] inflate
	If you eat too much, your stomach will bloat.	

4673	공무원	1. 암시적인, 함축적인 2. 절대적인, 의심없는	implicitly (암시하는, 절대적으로)
implicit			[2494] implied
[im-PLIS-it]		There was an implicit agreement among the members.	[503] contained

4674	공무원	1. 담보(로 내 놓은) 2. 부수적인	[361] security
collateral			[251] secondary
[kuh-LAT-er-uhl]		I used my house as collateral to get a loan.	[6068] ancillary

4675	토플	요새, 안전지대	[5857] stronghold
fortress			[2350] barrier
[FAWR-tris]		The king ran away to the fortress.	[5901] citadel

4676		수도원	[4620] abbey
monastery			
[MON-uh-ster-ee]		The monastery gave shelter to people who lost their homes due to the fire.	

4677		영사관	consul (영사)
consulate			[4121] embassy
[KON-suh-lit]		If you get in an accident, go to the Korean consulate.	[1558] ministry

4678	공무원 토플	1. 말다툼, 언쟁(하다) 2. 불평(하다)	quarrelsome (호전적인)
quarrel			[2329] dispute
[KWAWR-uhl]		He quarrels with his sister all the time.	[962] argument
			[6808] altercation

4679	토플	영웅담, 무용담	[1772] legend
saga			
[SAH-guh]		The saga is about Hercules.	

4680	공무원 토플 GRE	1. 포착하기 어려운, 용케 빠져나가는 2. 기억하기 어려운	elude (피하다)
elusive			[4633] evasive
[ih-LOO-siv]		The answer is elusive.	[665] difficult
			[2554] fleeting

4681		전등, 랜턴	[2851] lamp
lantern			[4736] beacon
[LAN-tern]		You should use a lantern to navigate in the dark.	[4780] flashlight

4682		점성술 (별의 위치로 길흉을 파악하는 것)	[6035] horoscope
astrology			
[uh-STROL-uh-jee]		Astrology suggests there is a connection between the stars and individual destiny.	

4683	토플	조랑말	[1689] horse
pony			
[POH-nee]		The little girl rode a pony.	

4684	공무원 GRE	회고적인, 지난 일을 돌이켜 생각하다	retrospect (회상)
retrospective			[6511] retroactive
[re-truh-SPEK-tiv]		This is a retrospective apology for my past actions.	[341] historical
			[1108] reflective

4685	고등	바지	[2666] pants
trousers			
[TROU-zerz]		Should I wear trousers or a skirt?	

4686		1. (회사들의) 협회, 조합 2. 배우자권	[500] association
consortium			[148] company
[kuhn-SAWR-shee-uhm]		The pharmaceutical companies created a consortium.	[765] club

4687 **ingest** [in-JEST]	1. (음식물을) 섭취하다 2. (지식을) 받아들이다 Infants can't ingest food properly yet.	ingestion (섭취) [677] consume [601] eat [1998] absorb
4688 **soluble** [SOL-yuh-buhl]	용해될 수 있는, 가용성의 This medicine is soluble.	insoluble (용해되지 않는) [3086] dissolved
4689 고등 토플 **censorship** [SEN-ser-ship]	검열 제도 Internet censorship in China is very strict.	[7141] censured [1472] restriction
4690 **blizzard** [BLIZ-erd]	눈보라 The blizzard caused many car accidents.	[4357] precipitation [6903] gale
4691 공무원 **hefty** [HEF-tee]	1. 크고 강한, 억센 2. (숫자가) 상당한, 큰 He is a hefty young man.	[1716] massive [196] large [1328] fat [6260] colossal
4692 토익 공무원 **skim** [skim]	1. 훑어 읽다 2. (기름이나 거품을) 떠내다 She skimmed through the book.	[2559] foam [470] remove [3315] glance [4843] graze
4693 공무원 **corpse** [kawrps]	시체, 송장 Corpses become cold.	[335] body
4694 공무원 **recess** [ri-SES]	1. 휴식, 휴가 2. (의회 등의) 휴회 3. 우묵 들어간 곳 The students play games during recess.	[445] break [3165] pause
4695 **paradox** [PAR-uh-doks]	역설, 모순 Paradoxes are hard to understand.	paradoxical (역설의) paradoxically (역설적으로) [4103] absurdity
4696 공무원 **stark** [stahrk]	1. 명백한 2. 완전한 The teacher's stark anger scared the students.	[2939] harsh [229] simple [785] ugly [4649] blunt
4697 **aide** [eyd]	부관, 보좌관 The principal has an aide.	[636] assistant [2759] deputy
4698 **latch** [lach]	고리쇠 Don't forget to fasten the latch.	[1104] lock
4699 **paranoid** [PAR-uh-noid]	망상성의 Don't be so paranoid.	paranoia (망상증) [2693] insane [1133] worried
4700 **charismatic** [kar-iz-MAT-ik]	카리스마 있는 She is a charismatic leader.	charisma (카리스마) [2312] charming [1069] attractive [1365] appealing

4701	공무원	부끄러움, 굴욕	humiliate (부끄럽게 하다)
humiliation			[2621] shame
[hyoo-mil-ee-EY-shuhn]		Her face turned red because of humiliation.	[1581] confusion

4702		울다, 눈물 흘리다	[3887] grieve
weep			[1782] complain
[weep]		The child is weeping.	[2068] cry

4703	공무원	가해자, 범인	perpetrate (죄를 범하다)
perpetrator			[2661] offender
			[967] criminal
[PUR-pi-trey-ter]		He is the perpetrator of this crime.	[3541] assassin

4704		비행, 경범죄	demeanor (품행, 행실)
misdemeanor			[1584] offense
			[1930] evil
[mis-di-MEE-ner]		He was punished for his misdemeanor.	[5939] transgression

4705	토익 공무원	지연하다, 미루다	postponement (연기)
postpone			[1697] delay
			[769] fix
[pohst-POHN]		The deadline for the assignment was postponed.	[3651] defer

4706	토익	사기, 의욕, 의기	[923] spirit
morale			[270] pleasure
			[2055] attitude
[muh-RAL]		The soldiers had high morale.	[2418] mood

4707		1. 표기법, 기수법 2. 표기, 표시, 기록	notate (기록하다)
notation			[606] documentation
[noh-TEY-shuhn]		Artists understand musical notation.	

4708	공무원	~을 삼가다, 억제하다	[5316] abstain
refrain			
[ri-FREYN]		Refrain from biting your nails.	

4709		초음파	
ultrasound			
[UHL-truh-sound]		The doctor used an ultrasound to see the baby.	

4710		1. 음력의 2. 달의	[2021] moon
lunar			
[LOO-ner]		Lunar New Year is in late January.	

4711	토플	(동물, 기생충 등의) 감염	infest (감염하다)
infestation			[3766] plague
			[3358] curse
[in-fe-STEY-shuhn]		The farm is suffering from mice infestation.	[5417] contagion

4712		너비, 폭	[2153] scope
breadth			[103] length
[bredth]		The breadth of this room is wide.	

4713		1. 급류 2. 폭포처럼 쏟아짐	torrential (폭포같은)
torrent			[2126] flood
			[4391] cascade
[TAWR-uhnt]		The canoe sailed through the torrent.	[5265] hoard

4714	공무원 토플 GRE	1. 확산 2. 증식, 급증	proliferate (확산하다)
proliferation			[1373] spread
[pruh-lif-uh-REY-shuhn]		The proliferation of nuclear weapons is dangerous.	

4715		양배추	[외래어] kale
cabbage [KAB-ij]		Rabbits eat cabbage.	

4716	공무원	무신론자, 신이나 종교를 믿지 않는 사람	atheism (무신론) [4467] secular
atheist [EY-thee-ist]		Atheists do not go to church.	[7369] agnostic

4717		목초지, 목장	[4489] meadow [2351] grass
pasture [PAS-cher]		There are many sheep gazing in the pasture.	[4843] grazing

4718	공무원	남성적인, 남자다운	masculinity (남성성) [1545] male
masculine [MAS-kyuh-lin]		You don't have to be masculine.	[204] manly [7305] macho

4719		1. (술 중) 럼주 2. 기이한	[2115] curious [1659] strange
rum [ruhm]		He drank too much rum.	

4720	공무원 GRE	1. 본래의, 원래의 2. 청정한	[5515] immaculate [559] clean
pristine [PRIS-teen]		The book is in its pristine condition.	[3872] intact

4721	GRE	1. 억압적으로 홍보하다, 강매하다 2. 과하게 칭찬하거나 자랑하다	[2650] boast [2458] praise
tout [tout]		The insurance company touted their product.	[6019] laud

4722	GRE	망상, 착각	delusional (망상의) deluded (망상의)
delusion [dih-LOO-zhuhn]		Don't fool yourself with delusions.	[1073] dream [75] thought

4723		일화	anecdotal (일화의) [377] story
anecdote [AN-ik-doht]		The lecturer told an anecdote about herself.	[1455] episode

4724	공무원	그런데도 불구하고, ~할지라도	[3048] nevertheless [1184] despite
notwithstanding [not-with-STAN-ding]		I was upset. Notwithstanding, I remained calm.	

4725	토플	친근성, 친밀감	[247] closeness [3321] sympathy
affinity [uh-FIN-i-tee]		Some people have a natural affinity with children.	[3570] affection

4726	토플	1. 목재 2. 느리고 어설프게 이동하다	lumbering (느리게 움직 이는)
lumber [LUHM-ber]		We need more wood to make lumber.	[3688] timber

4727	공무원 토플 GRE	방해하다, 저해하다	impediment (방해물) unimpeded (방해받지 않은)
impede [im-PEED]		She impeded the progress of the plan.	[4133] hinder

4728	공무원	열망 받는, (많은 이들이) 갈망하는	covet (갈망하다) covetous (탐욕스러운)
coveted [KUHV-iti d]		A diplomat is a coveted profession.	[1100] desired [3388] crave

4729 **latitude** [LAT-i-tood]	토플	위도	
		Different countries have different latitudes.	
4730 **plank** [plangk]		(두꺼운 나무) 판자	[515] board [1071] platform [4726] lumber
		She used a wooden plank to build the shed.	
4731 **plural** [PLOO R-uhl]		복수(형)	[422] several
		The plural of apple is apples.	
4732 **siege** [seej]	토플	1. 포위하다 2. 포위 작전	[6321] blockade [247] closure [2294] invade [외래어] barricade
		The criminals were sieged by the police forces.	
4733 **starch** [stahrch]	공무원	1. 전분, 녹말 2. (의류에) 풀을 먹이다	
		Starch is used to bake bread.	
4734 **pallet** [PAL-it]		1. 운송되어야하는 화물을 쌓아두는 깔판 2. 주걱 3. 화가의 팔레트	
		Cargo is stacked on the pallet	
4735 **clown** [kloun]		1. 광대 2. 익살꾼	[2293] joker [1594] comedian [3837] wit
		Clowns can juggle balls.	
4736 **beacon** [BEE-kuhn]		1. 횃불, 봉화 2. 신호	[2979] lighthouse [3884] flare [4196] masterpiece [4681] lantern
		The villagers lit a beacon.	
4737 **muse** [myooz]		1. (예술적) 영감의 대상 2. 고뇌하다, 고민하다	[2805] meditate [282] consider
		My girlfriend is my muse.	
4738 **trumpet** [TRUHM-pit]		1. 트럼펫(을 연주하다) 2. 자기 자랑을 하다	[3045] horn [899] announce
		I can play the trumpet.	
4739 **tedious** [TEE-dee-uhs]	공무원 토플 GRE	지루한, 따분한	tedium (지루함) [1109] boring [2465] annoying [7418] banal
		This task is tedious.	
4740 **annuity** [uh-NOO-i-tee]		연금	
		The insurance company gives her an annuity of $2,000.	
4741 **darn** [dahrn]		1. 젠장 2. (옷의 구멍을) 짜깁다	[2360] sew
		Darn, I made a mistake.	
4742 **noun** [noun]		명사	
		Nouns can be the subject of a sentence.	

4743		투쟁적인, 호전적인	militancy (교전 상태)
militant			[7260] belligerent
[MIL-i-tuhnt]		The soldiers were militant.	[2842] assertive
			[7358] bellicose

4744		밀다, 밀치다	[1013] push
shove			[2145] dig
[shuhv]		He shoved me.	[5267] cram

4745		1. 유황의 2. 황녹색의	sulphur (=sulfur)
sulfur			
[SUHL-fer]		This pill contains only a little sulfur.	

4746	공무원	1. 굉장히 2. 최대의, 극치의	[1046] maximum
utmost			[229] simply
[UHT-mohst]		This issue is of the utmost importance.	[1124] absolute

4747		췌장	
pancreas			
[PAN-kree-uh s]		The pancreas regulates blood sugar levels.	

4748		노즐, 주둥이	[2309] nose
nozzle			[5299] faucet
[NOZ-uh l]		Water is leaking from the nozzle.	

4749	토익	이로 말미암아, 이로 인해	[1121] thus
hereby			
[heer-BAHY]		I hereby declare you man and wife.	

4750	공무원	항공 우주 사업(의)	
aerospace			
[AIR-oh-speys]		The aerospace industry is rapidly developing.	

4751		1. 작은 물줄기 2. 후미, 구멍	[365] entry
inlet			[3832] basin
[IN-let]		Langstone river is an inlet of the English Channel.	

4752		한 단체를 상징하는 노래, 성가	[4859] hymn
anthem			[3980] chorus
[AN-thuh m]		We sing the national anthem at school.	[4468] chant

4753		1. 육욕, 색욕 2. 열망	lusty (열정적인, 건장한)
lust			[1100] desire
[luhst]		Lust and love are different feelings.	[3388] craving

4754		암탉	[1640] chicken
hen			[4604] goose
[hen]		The hen lays eggs.	

4755		따로 감춰두다, 숨겨두다	[1262] hide
stash			[2227] inventory
[stash]		The squirrel stashed its acorns in a hole in the tree.	[3431] cache

4756		1. 돼지 2. 욕심쟁이 3. 전부 차지하다	[2872] pig
hog			[6250] boar
[hawg]		Hogs eat a lot of food.	

4757	공무원	1. 능력, 재능 2. 독창성	[1372] talent
flair			[111] ability
[FLAIR]		Her flair differentiated her from everyone else.	[171] experience
			[4460] aptitude

4758		아니, 절대	[6234] nay
nope			[67] no
[nohp]		Is he kind? Nope. He is very selfish.	

4759		1. 아바타, 분신 2. (신의) 화신	[5868] epitome
avatar			[5537] archetype
[AV-uh-tahr]		Using a virtual avatar, you can chat with people all over the world.	

4760	토플	(역사적 의미를 가진) 유물, 고적	[3286] antique
relic			[956] evidence
[REL-ik]		The museum collects historical relics.	

4761	토플	1. (예술 작품의) 영감 2. 화려한 무늬, 패턴	[1279] theme
motif			[963] concept
[moh-TEEF]		What was her motif for the novel?	[외래어] logo

4762	토플	야만적인, 사나운	[1547] wild
savage			[3041] brutal
[SAV-ij]		Soldiers during war can be savage.	[3470] cruel

4763		격노, 분격	[3161] rage
wrath			
[rath]		She feared her father's wrath.	

4764		1. 뉘앙스 2. (감지하기 어려운) 변화	[1900] shade
nuance			[266] feature
[NOO-ahns]		His facial expressions convey many nuances.	[1701] distinction
			[외래어] gradation

4765		1. 만지작거리다 2. (전통 음악 연주에 사용되는) 바이올린	fiddler (바이올린 연주자)
fiddle			[966] touch
[FID-l]		She fiddled with her hair.	[2644] fool
			[6831] fidget

4766		(단체, 조직 간의) 연락, 상통	[460] contact
liaison			[698] communication
[lee-ey-ZAWN]		Frequent liaison is essential for cooperation to succeed.	

4767	공무원 토플	정확히 가리키다, 정확히 짚다	[539] identify
pinpoint			[630] explain
[PIN-point]		Can you pinpoint the cause of the accident?	[1439] diagnose

4768		(사람의) 미묘한 분위기	[3914] ambience
aura			[266] feature
[AWR-uh]		He had a gloomy aura.	[1297] aspect

4769	공무원 토플	기관차	locomotion (이동할 수 있는 힘)
locomotive			[외래어] engine
[loh-kuh-MOH-tiv]		Locomotives significantly reduced travel time.	

4770		성실한, 진지한	earnestly (진지하게)
earnest			earnestness (진지함)
[UR-nist]		She is an earnest worker.	[896] serious
			[652] determined

4771	공무원	1. 미생물 2. 세균	microbial (미생물의)
microbe			[외래어] virus
[MAHY-krohb]		Microbes cause diseases.	

4772		다락방	[4441] loft
attic			
[AT-ik]		They keep old toys in the attic.	

4773	공무원	1. 황혼, 여명 2. 쇠퇴기	[5415] dusk
twilight			[445] break
[TWAHY-lahyt]		She woke up at twilight.	[955] sunset

4774	공무원	파충류	
reptile			
[REP-til]		Lizards are reptiles.	

4775	공무원	1. 균형을 잡다 2. 우아함 3. ~할 준비가 되어있는	[897] balance
poise			[1110] confidence
[Poiz]		The penguin poised for a few seconds before jumping into the sea.	[2260] calmness

4776		1. 아주 반짝이는, 눈부신 2. 대단한	dazzle (감탄시키다)
dazzling			[2513] gorgeous
			[1397] bright
[DAZ-uhl-ing]		The lights are dazzling.	[2178] brilliant

4777	토플	방사능의	radioactivity (방사능)
radioactive			[2089] radiation
			[1223] dangerous
[rey-dee-oh-AK-tiv]		Radioactive matter is toxic.	[3220] contaminated

4778	공무원 토플 GRE	놀라게 하다, 당황하게 하다	startling (놀라게 하는)
startle			[1728] shock
			[2408] alarm
[STAHR-tl]		The dog startled her.	[3594] frighten

4779	공무원	억압, 탄압	repress (억압하다)
repression			repressive (억압적인)
			[3210] suppression
[ri-PRESH-uh n]		Constant repression of his anger caused him to suffer.	[2294] invade

4780		1. 손전등, 플래시 2. 섬광	[4162] torch
flashlight			[257] light
[FLASH-lahyt]		Stop pointing your flashlight at my face.	

4781	공무원 토플 GRE	1. 기발한, 독창적인 2. 교묘한	ingenuity (창의력)
ingenious			[3031] clever
			[109] creative
[in-JEEN-yuhs]		I have an ingenious idea to get us through this problem.	[1119] imaginative

4782	공무원 토플	죽다, 썩다, 소멸되다	perishable (썩기 쉬운)
perish			[2438] expire
			[363] die
[PER-ish]		That cabbage has perished.	[3025] cease

4783		1. 사소한, 하찮은 2. 옹졸한 3. 소규모의	[237] unimportant
petty			[327] lesser
			[6667] frivolous
[PET-ee]		I can't be bothered with such petty inquiry.	

4784		반~, 반대하는	[1169] opposed
anti			[2835] adverse
			[5443] gloomy
[AN-tahy]		He supports the anti-smoking law.	

4785 **fluorescent** [floo-RES-uhnt]		형광(의) LEDs are much more energy efficient than fluorescent lights.	fluorescence (형광) [5565] luminous [1397] bright
4786 **cockpit** [KOK-pit]		조종석 The captain is going to give us a tour of the cockpit.	[2642] cabin [3752] compartment
4787 **flirt** [flurt]		1. (남녀가 서로)즐기다, 추파를 던지다 2. 바람둥이 My dog was flirting with my neighbor's dog.	flirty (추파를 던지는) flirtatious (=flirty)
4788 **ponder** [PON-der]	공무원 토플	숙고하다 She continued to ponder the problem.	ponderous (너무 신숙한, 크고 무거운) [282] consider [3697] contemplate
4789 **massacre** [MAS-uh-ker]	공무원	대량 학살(하다) He could barely survive the massacre.	[4387] slaughter [2014] defeat [3541] assassination
4790 **stint** [stint]		1. 일정 동안의 복무, 근무 2. 아끼다, 절약하다 3. 제한 I worked at a burger shop as a short stint.	[1259] assignment [1376] duty
4791 **glossary** [GLOS-uh-ree]		용어 해설 사전 Please refer to the glossary.	[3702] dictionary
4792 **maid** [meyd]		가정부 I am closer to my maid than I am to my own family.	
4793 **abruptly** [uh-BRUHPT-lee]	공무원	1. 갑자기, 불쑥 2. 퉁명스럽게, 무뚝뚝하게 The meeting was ended abruptly when the fire alarm went off.	abrupt (갑작스러운) [1730] suddenly
4794 **tack** [tak]		1. 방향 2. 방침 3. 고정하다 4. 압정 The new project will take a different tack.	[2204] nail
4795 **afflict** [uh-FLIKT]	토플	1. 괴롭히다, 피해를 끼치다 2. (병에)시달리다 I don't want to afflict you with my issues.	affliction (고통) [1446] trouble [1177] suffer [2465] annoy
4796 **serene** [suh-REEN]	GRE	1. 평온한, 고요한, 온화한 2. 맑은 She has a serene face.	serenity (평온함) [2260] calm [694] comfortable [775] composed
4797 **evangelist** [ih-VAN-juh-list]		1. 전도사 2. 신약 복음서의 저자 He is a very faithful evangelist.	evangelize (전도하다) [1213] missionary [2131] enthusiast [2973] pastor
4798 **layman** [LEY-muhn]		1. 전문 교육을 받지 않은 자 2. 평신도 To the layman, the paper was unreadable.	[4467] secular

4799		배설물의	defecate (배변하다)
fecal			[2543] corrupt
[FEE-kuh l]		The well contained fecal matter from humans or cows.	[4011] disgusting

4800		변화가 힘들 정도로 확고해지다	[6407] encroach
entrench			[729] define
[en-TRENCH]		Racism is deeply entrenched in the American society.	[5458] embed

4801		1. 잔디가 나는 흙 2. (영국 은어) 놈	[4597] turf
sod			
[sod]		Sod is grass and the layer of soil just below it.	

4802	GRE	거친, 투박한, 굵은	coarsely (거칠게)
coarse			[4009] rude
[kawrs]		The coarse sand was rough under my feet.	[1719] rough

4803		압류	foreclose (압류하다, 방해하다)
foreclosure			[1206] exclusion
[fawr-KLOH-zher]		His entire property went into foreclosure.	

4804	토익	1. (밭을)갈다, 경작하다 2. 쟁기 3. 제설하다 4. (역경을 딛고)나아가다	[3160] cultivate
plow			
[plou]		You need to plow the land before planting seeds.	

4805	토플	1. 예복 2. 가운	[1190] dress
robe			[2729] costume
[rohb]		She put on her robe.	

4806		1. (남학생의)대학교 동아리, 사모임 2. 우애, 형제애, 박애 3. 협회, 조합	fraternal (형제의)
fraternity			[1189] brotherhood
[fruh-TUR-ni-tee]		He joined a fraternity when he was a freshman.	[288] friendship
			[3692] guild

4807		말린 풀	[6540] fodder
hay			[2351] grass
[hey]		We stacked the hay over at the barn.	

4808	토플	벽화	[355] photograph
mural			[777] painting
[MYOO R-uh l]		She painted a huge mural on the side of the building.	

4809		딱정벌레	[1331] overhang
beetle			[417] oversize
[BEET-l]		Beetles are insects.	[986] fly

4810	토플	간헐적인	intermittently (간헐적으로)
intermittent			intermission (휴식 시간)
[in-ter-MIT-nt]		Intermittent rain cooled down the temperature.	[5966] sporadic

4811	토익	참치, (참)다랑어	
tuna			
[TOO-nuh]		Do you want some tuna?	

4812	토플	1. 몫, 할당량/액 2. 최소 득표수	[2487] allocation
quota			[4933] allotment
[KWOH-tuh]		She was given a quota of tickets to sell.	

4813 abrasive [uh-BREY-siv]	토플	1. 연마재(의) 2. 마찰이 있는(인간관계), 거슬리는	abrasion (마찰에 의한 마모/긁힘) [1719] rough [2465] annoying
		He scratched his arm against an abrasive paper.	
4814 incubator [IN-kyuh-bey-ter]	토플	인큐베이터, 부화기, 배양기	incubation (부화) incubate (배양하다)
		Her baby spent two weeks in an incubator.	
4815 dune [doon]	토플	사구, 모래언덕	[3199] ridge
		We saw many sane dunes in the desert.	
4816 poultry [POHL-tree]		가금(류의 고기)	[1640] chicken [2974] duck
		I don't eat meat or poultry.	
4817 arsenal [AHR-suh-nl]	토플	무기(고), 병기고	
		The country is willing to give up its nuclear arsenal.	
4818 retarded [ri-TAHR-did]	공무원 토플	1. 지체되는, 저지되는 2. 정신 지체의, 발달이 늦은	retardation (지연) [1697] delayed
		Our economic development has been retarded by the lack of domestic demand.	
4819 constipation [kon-stuh-PEY-shuhn]		변비	[717] irregularity [738] contraction [4366] ache
		She is suffering from constipation.	
4820 genital [JEN-i-tl]		생식기의	genitalia (성기) [773] sexual
		The genital area needs to be kept clean.	
4821 memoir [MEM-wahr]		회고록, 회상록, 전기	[2850] autobiography [318] account [4723] anecdote
		He wrote a memoir of his long trip to Barcelona.	
4822 lettuce [LET-is]		양상추	[4715] cabbage
		Bacon goes well with lettuce.	
4823 stationary [STEY-shuh-ner-ee]	토플	1. 정지된, 고정된 2. 변하지 않는	[2557] persistent [142] still [948] immobile [1688] motionless
		The car crashed into a stationary bus.	
4824 underlying [UHN-der-lahy-ing]		기저의, 기저에 놓여있는, 기초의	underlie (~의 기초가 되다) [648] basic [838] elemental
		What was the underlying cause of the fire?	
4825 trajectory [truh-JEK-tuh-ree]		1. 궤적, 궤도, 탄도 2. (질병의)양상	[1040] progress [1954] curve [3219] orbit
		The missile is following its trajectory.	
4826 emblem [EM-bluhm]	공무원 GRE	상징	emblematic (상징적인) [1700] symbol [221] signified [3421] badge
		The national emblem of Canada is a maple leaf.	

4827	공무원 토플	1. 철회하다, 취소하다 2. 움츠리다, 집어넣다	retractable (넣었다 뺄 수 있는)
retract			[2082] withdraw
[ri-TRAKT]		The president retracted his statement.	

4828	공무원	1. 나머지, 잔존물, 유물, 남아있는 2. 그루터기	[3635] remainder [125] part
remnant			[409] bit
[REM-nuhnt]		Hostility between the two countries is a remnant from colonial days.	[3352] fragment

4829	공무원	고통, 고뇌	agonizing (괴로운) agonize (괴로워하다)
agony			[863] pain
[AG-uh-nee]		He screamed in agony.	[1692] sadness

4830		1. 깎다, 자르다 2. 부러지다	shears (큰 가위) [2263] trim
shear			[445] break
[sheer]		Don't shear the sheep.	[3982] mow

4831		삼각대	
tripod			
[TRAHY-pod]		Bring a camera and a tripod.	

4832		연단, 지휘대, 시상대	[1071] platform [852] stage
podium			
[POH-dee-uhm]		She stepped up to the podium.	

4833		1. 종말, 파멸 2. 대재앙 3. 묵시, 천계	apocalyptic (종말론의) [157] end
apocalypse			[5975] annihilation
[uh-POK-uh-lips]		We might one day die of nuclear apocalypse.	[7435] cataclysm

4834	수능 토플	전신, 전보(를 보내다)	[1028] wire [2494] imply
telegraph			[3515] summons
[TEL-i-graf]		She received telegraphy from her mother.	

4835	토익 공무원 토플 GRE	1. 체포하다, 검거하다 2. 이해하다, 터득하다	apprehension (걱정, 불안, 체포)
apprehend			apprehensive (걱정하는, 이해하는)
[ap-ri-HEND]		The criminal was apprehended.	

4836	토플	끔찍한, 소름끼치는, 무시무시한	horrifically (끔찍하게) [3052] awful
horrific			[1728] shocking
[haw-RIF-ik]		The bomb attack was just horrific.	[5666] appalling

4837		(스포츠)대표팀	[2632] squad
varsity			
[VAHR-si-tee]		He joined the varsity team.	

4838		쌍안경	
binoculars			
[buh-NOK-yuh-lerz]		These binoculars are out of focus.	

4839	토플 GRE	1. 당황하게 만들다, 어안이 벙벙하게 만들다 2. 좌절시키다, 방해하다	baffling (이해하지 못해 당황한)
baffle			[1581] confuse
[BAF-uhl]		The bad news totally baffled her.	[887] amaze

4840	공무원	1. 평형, 균형 2. 안정, 평정	[897] balance [582] similarity
equilibrium			[775] composure
[ee-kwuh-LIB-ree-uhm]		The country's economy must be in equilibrium.	[2260] calmness

4841			
rejoice [ri-JOIS]	기뻐하다, 흐뭇해하다		[1134] celebrate [5334] revel
	I rejoice to see you again.		

4842	토플		
choreography [kawr-ee-OG-ruh-fee]	안무		choreographer (안무가) [1316] dance
	His choreography is favored by many people.		

4843	토플		
graze [greyz]	1. 풀을 뜯다/먹이다 2. 방목하다 3. 긁히다, 까지다		[3658] scrape
	I saw a couple of cows grazing peacefully.		

4844	공무원		
forfeit [FAWR-fit]	1. (권리 등을) 잃다, 포기하다 2. 몰수하다, 박탈하다		forfeiture (몰수) [435] lose
	He forfeited his right to the throne.		

4845	공무원 GRE		
meticulously [muh-TIK-yuh-luh-slee]	꼼꼼하게, 세심하게, 면밀하게		meticulous (꼼꼼한) [256] carefully
	This project has been meticulously planned.		

4846	공무원		
proverb [PROV-erb]	속담, 격언		[6783] adage
	I like referring to proverbs.		

4847	토플 GRE		
canon [KAN-uhn]	규범, 표준		[516] rule [6090] tenet [6520] precept
	Against newspaper canon, the reporter refused to exaggerate the story.		

4848	토플 GRE		
deflect [dih-FLEKT]	1. 방향을 돌리다 2. 빗나가다 3. 회피하다, 모면하다		deflection (굴절) [3904] divert [2140] bend [6169] avert
	He tried to deflect the attention of the people from the issue.		

4849			
niece [nees]	(여자) 조카		[790] cousin [809] aunt
	My niece is three years old.		

4850			
grin [grin]	싱긋 웃다, 씩 웃음		[1931] smile [7043] smirk
	She grinned.		

4851			
dean [deen]	대학의 학장		[2005] principal [1066] administrator [1637] legislator
	The dean wants to see you.		

4852	토익 공무원		
courier [KUR-ee-er]	1. 배달원, 택배원 2. 특사		[3839] messenger
	The courier will be arriving soon.		

4853	공무원		
annex [uh-NEKS]	1. (영토 등을) 무력으로 합병(하다) 2. 부속 건물, 신관		annexation (합병) [5016] append [2294] invade [4422] appendix
	Hawaii was annexed to the United States in 1898.		

4854	공무원 GRE		
divergence [dih-VUR-juhns]	1. (의견 등의)차이 2. 분기		divergent (분기하는) diverge (분기하다) [117] difference [4458] disparity
	The party needs to overcome a great divergence of opinions among members.		

4855		유충, 유생, 애벌레	
larva			
[LAHR-vuh]		A caterpillar is a larva.	

4856	공무원	1. 움푹 팬 곳, 함몰 2. 우그러뜨리다 3. 훼손	[4918] incision
dent			[5019] imprint
[dent]		There is a dent in the back of the car.	[5182] indentation

4857	공무원 토플	위험(성), 위기	perilous (위험한)
peril			[2553] hazard
[PER-uhl]		My life is in peril right now.	[361] insecurity
			[531] risk

4858		1. (신체의)앞의, 앞부분의 2. ~전의, ~보다 이전의 3. (뇌 구조상의)전측	[712] prior
anterior			
[an-TEER-ee-er]		The term anterior refers to the front of a body.	

4859		찬송가, 찬가, 찬미가	[4752] anthem
hymn			[4468] chant
[him]		The service began with a hymn.	

4860		용암	
lava			
[LAH-vuh]		A volcano emits lava.	

4861		1. 신 2. 신전	[1393] goddess
deity			[2519] divinity
[DEE-i-tee]		A religious group of people knelt before the deity.	[4325] idol

4862		눈의 망막	[3316] pupil
retina			
[RET-n-uh]		His retina has been damaged.	

4863		1. 신조, 신념 2. 사도 신경	[3022] doctrine
creed			[5572] dogma
[kreed]		Human rights are universal regardless of race or creed.	

4864	공무원 GRE	무모한, 부주의의, 제멋대로인	recklessly (무모하게)
reckless			recklessness (무모함)
[REK-lis]		He is a reckless teenager.	[3986] rash
			[3452] shallow

4865		1. 쓰레기(같은 것) 2. 헛소리	[3490] garbage
rubbish			[3461] junk
[RUHB-ish]		Your essay is rubbish.	[3571] debris
			[3748] litter

4866		(잘)들리는	inaudible (들리지 않는)
audible			[1371] detectable
[AW-duh-buhl]		Her voice was not audible at all.	[4185] deafening

4867	토플	1. 코의 2. 비음의	[2309] nose
nasal			
[NEY-zuhl]		He suffered from nasal congestion.	

4868	공무원 GRE	1. 취하지 않은, 맑은 정신의 2. 냉정한 3. 수수한	sobering (정신이 깨게 하는)
sober			[2260] calm
[SOH-ber]		I'm trying to stay sober.	[3449] restrained

4869 **skillet** [SKIL-it]	냄비, 팬	[2959] bucket
	She boiled an egg in a small skillet.	

4870 토플 **apex** [EY-peks]	꼭대기, 절정, 정상	apical (정점의) [1868] peak [4105] culmination
	He finally reached the apex of the mountain.	

4871 토플 **mania** [MEY-nee-uh]	(열)광, 매니아	maniac (미치광이) [1475] passion [1776] craze [2131] enthusiasm
	She is a mania for sports cars.	

4872 공무원 **subordinate** [suh-BAWR-dn-it]	1. 하위의, 하급자 2. 종속의 3. 부차적인	subordination (종속) [4178] inferior [251] secondary
	Senior officers spend some time to train their subordinates.	

4873 공무원 **blush** [bluhsh]	1. 얼굴이 붉어지다 2. 부끄러워하다 3. 홍조	[3115] flush [7263] wince
	You always blush in front of him.	

4874 **haze** [heyz]	1. 안개 2. (정신이)몽롱한 상태 3. 안개로 뒤덮다 4. 괴롭히다	hazy (안개가 낀) [1363] cloud [2672] distraction
	I can barely see what's in front of me in such a thick haze.	

4875 공무원 **honeymoon** [HUHN-ee-moon]	신혼여행(을 가다)	[279] beginning
	We're going on a month long honeymoon.	

4876 토플 **conquest** [KON-kwest]	1. 정복 2. 점령(지)	[1795] victory [2294] invasion [4853] annexation
	The country continued to expand its territory by conquest.	

4877 공무원 토플 **agitation** [aj-i-TEY-shuhn]	1. 불안, 동요 2. 흥분 3. 시위, 소요	agitate (동요시키다) agitator (선동자) [5480] turmoil [1133] worry
	The earthquake caused a high level of agitation among people.	

4878 공무원 GRE **perseverance** [pur-suh-VEER-uhns]	인내(심), 끈기	persevere (인내하다) [2557] persistence [652] determination [1348] dedication
	Her years of perseverance finally paid off.	

4879 **petal** [PET-l]	꽃잎	[2809] needle
	Rose petals tend to be very soft.	

4880 수능 토플 **peasant** [PEZ-uh nt]	1. 소작농 2. 농부, 농민	[1050] farmer [1332] laborer
	Our family comes from a long line of peasants.	

4881 토익 토플 **reflex** [REE-fleks]	반사 신경, 반사 작용	[1158] automatic [1228] reaction
	The boy has good reflexes.	

4882 토플 **longitude** [LON-ji-tood]	경도	longitudinal (경도의) [2656] diameter [4712] breadth
	Can you give me the longitude of your current location?	

4883 **auxiliary** [awg-ZIL-yuh-ree]	1. 보조의 2. 추가의 3. 조동사 4. 보조원	[2033] accessory [6068] ancillary
	The factory keeps an auxiliary power system.	

4884 공무원 **usher** [UHSH-er]	1. 안내원 2. 안내하다	[4138] escort [81] come
	Opera had already started, so the usher didn't let us in.	

4885 공무원 **smuggle** [SMUHG-uhl]	밀반입하다, 밀수하다, 밀매하다, 빼돌리다	smuggler (밀수범) [2894] sneak [1262] hide [1872] export
	I tried to smuggle some candy out of the cafeteria.	

4886 **mar** [mahr]	손상시키다, 망쳐놓다	[2896] spoil [719] damage [4284] bruise [6125] blight
	His reputation will be forever marred by this single mistake.	

4887 공무원 GRE **eradicate** [ih-RAD-i-keyt]	1. 뿌리뽑다, 근절하다 2. 전멸시키다	eradication (근절) [1626] eliminate [673] replace [4362] abolish
	You need to eradicate sugar from your diet if you want to live.	

4888 **ligament** [LIG-uh-muhnt]	인대	[3344] knot [1942] screw [4158] tangle
	He suffered ligament damage in his knee from a car accident.	

4889 **artillery** [ahr-TIL-uh-ree]	1. 대포 2. 포병(대)	[1170] battery [4233] cannon
	Our opponent is armed with heavy artillery.	

4890 **gymnastics** [jim-NAS-tiks]	체조	gymnast (체조선수) gymnastic (체조) [1044] exercise
	She shows great talent in gymnastics.	

4891 수능 GRE **cynical** [SIN-i-kuhl]	1. 냉소적인 2. 빈정대는, 비꼬는 3. 부정적인	[882] distrustful [1607] selfish
	He might have tried to be funny, but he was too cynical.	

4892 **brow** [brou]	1. 이마 2. 눈썹 3. (벼랑) 꼭대기	[1868] peak [1921] eyebrow
	He wrinkled his brow.	

4893 **snug** [snuhg]	1. 포근한, 아늑한 2. 딱 맞는 3. 작은 방	[694] comfortable
	I feel so snug when I hug my golden retriever.	

4894 공무원 **crooked** [KROOK-id]	1. 비뚤어진, 구부러진, 굴곡있는 2. 부정직한	[2140] bent [95] uneven [1954] curved
	She gave him a crooked smile.	

4895 **tang** [TANG]	톡 쏘는 맛, 냄새	[5379] zest [1065] taste
	This Thai curry has a nice tang.	

4896 공무원 **mediocre** [mee-dee-OH-ker]	1. 평범한, 보통의 2. 썩 좋지 않은	mediocrity (평범함) [727] average [1173] poor [2073] decent
	Their new song is mediocre compared to the last album.	

4897	공무원 토플	1. 떼 2. 군중 3. 떼지어 다니다, 무리지어 다니다	[1635] crowd
swarm			[81] come
[swawrm]		We were swarmed by bees after touching the hive by mistake.	[3947] flock

4898	유성, 별똥별	meteorite (운석)
meteor		
[MEE-tee-er]	A meteor big enough can kill all humanity.	

4899	1. 열정적으로 일하다 2. 밀어내다 3. 재촉하다, 서두르다 4. 번잡, 혼잡	hustler (사기꾼)
hustle		[2136] rush
[HUHS-uhl]	She finally became successful after years of hustling.	[807] hurry [4630] jog

4900	석영	[2371] crystal
quartz		
[kwawrts]	This cup is made from quartz.	

4901	1. 모범생, 괴짜 2. 얼간이	nerdy (괴짜스러운)
nerd		[4937] geek
[NURD]	He is the biggest nerd in our school.	[2644] fool [4235] jerk

4902	1. 스튜 2. 끓이다	[2156] boil
stew		[2234] brew
[stoo]	Her mom has the best stew recipe.	[외래어] pie

4903	1. 뇌물 2. 뇌물을 주다, 뇌물로 매수하다	bribery (뇌물 수수)
bribe		[2543] corrupt
[brahyb]	I tried to bribe a police officer but was arrested for it.	[1991] compensation [2593] manipulation

4904	1. 이유, 근거 2. 이성	[630] explanation
rationale		[1219] theory
[rash-uh-NAL]	You shouldn't make a big decision like this without any rationale.	[2592] excuse

4905	그 안에, 그 점에서	[477] above
therein		
[thair-IN]	She works hard and therein lies the key to her success.	

4906	1. 개과의 동물, 개(의) 2. 송곳니	[734] dog
canine		
[KEY-nahyn]	The fox is a canine animal.	

4907	1. 연합체 2. 기업 조합	[1403] union
syndicate		[500] association
[SIN-di-kit]	He is the leader of the crime syndicate of this city.	[5596] cartel

4908	1. 덮개, 커버 2. 장식품	upholster (가구를 덮다)
upholstery		[3238] cushioning
[uhp-HOHL-stuh-ree]	She wrapped herself around the upholstery.	

4909	토플	1. 그루터기 2. 남은 부분 3. 선거 유세 4. 난처하게 하다	[2475] puzzle
stump			[3291] ignorant
[stuhmp]		They used the stump as a table.	

4910	토익	1. 크레인 2. 학, 두루미 3. (목을) 길게 빼다	[5695] hoist
crane			
[kreyn]		The crane operator suffered a heart attack while on duty.	

4911 고등 butcher [BOOCH-er]	1. 정육점(주인) 2. 도살하다 3. 학살하다	butchery (도살) [4387] slaughter [682] killer
	My butcher saves the best cuts for me.	
4912 공무원 GRE lucrative [LOO-kruh-tiv]	수익성이 있는, 이익이 있는	[1087] profitable [991] advantageous
	This business opportunity will be lucrative for both of us.	
4913 strait [streyt]	1. 해협 2. 궁핍, 곤경	[6625] predicament
	The ship will be arriving at the strait soon.	
4914 snag [snag]	1. (뜻밖의)문제 2. 걸리다, 찢다 3. 날카로운 부분	[4934] hitch [215] problem [1642] bug [2350] barrier
	She likes me - the only snag is that I am married.	
4915 공무원 토플 GRE culprit [KUHL-prit]	1. 범인, 주범 2. 장본인	[967] criminal [4051] felon
	Diesel cars are the main culprit of air pollution.	
4916 wield [weeld]	1. 행사하다, 지배하다 2. 휘두르다	unwieldy (다루기 힘든) [2186] swing [140] apply [273] control
	As soon as he got promoted, he started wielding his authority.	
4917 hem [hem]	1. (옷의)단 2. 단을 올리다	[3166] rim [2360] sew
	The hem on his pants needs sewing.	
4918 incise [in-SAHYZ]	칼로 베다, 새기다, 절개하다	incision (절개) incisive (날카로운) incisor (앞니) [742] score
	My name was incised in the wooden slate.	
4919 potion [POH-shuhn]	1. 물약 2. 묘약 3. 1회의 분량	[6455] elixir [862] drink
	My mother got me a potion that should cure my stomach ache.	
4920 gala [GEY-luh]	1. 축제 2. 경축 행사	[462] party [378] joyful [3674] festive
	I made this dress by myself for the gala tomorrow.	
4921 bylaw [BAHY-law]	1. 규칙 2. 조례	[921] regulation [82] act [218] case [516] rule
	One of the bylaws prohibits smoking in the workplace.	
4922 sabbath [SAB-uhth]	안식일	
	He won't answer your call, he's on a Sabbath.	
4923 tad [tad]	조금, 약간, 소량	[409] bit
	My score is a tad bit higher than his.	
4924 turret [TUR-it]	1. 작은 탑, 포탑 2. (전투기의)조종석	[1639] tower
	We need to keep this turret at all times to fight back the enemy.	

4925 **posterior** [po-STEER-ee-er]	1. 뒤의, 후면의 2. 후두개 3. 엉덩이	[1664] rear [999] bottom
	The soccer player tore the posterior ligament behind his knee.	
4926 **eviction** [ih-VIK-shuh n]	쫓아냄, 퇴거, 축출	evict (쫓아내다) [4505] expulsion
	We received the eviction notice from the bank after not paying the mortgage.	[1610] dispossession [4980] ejection
4927 공무원 GRE **obsolete** [ob-suh-LEET]	1. 구식의, 시대에 뒤쳐진 2. 쓸모없는	[4531] outdated [1417] old-fashioned [3286] antiquated [6470] archaic
	Your phone is so obsolete.	
4928 **genesis** [JEN-uh-sis]	1. 기원, 발생 2. 창세기	[1729] origin [279] beginning [6972] provenance
	This project had its genesis three years earlier.	
4929 토플 **reverberate** [ri-VUR-buh-reyt]	울리다, 반향하다	reverb (에코) [2906] echo [2915] amplify [6534] resound
	Her voice reverberates so amazingly on the stage.	
4930 토플 **chronological** [kron-l-OJ-i-kuh l]	시간 순의, 연대기의	chronology (연대기) [1861] sequential [341] historical
	Can you name all the president in chronological order?	
4931 공무원 GRE **superficial** [soo-per-FISH-uh l]	1. 깊이 없는, 가벼운, 천박한 2. 피상적인, 표면적인 3. 겉으로 드러나는, 표면의	superficially (표면적으로 는) [3452] shallow [6667] frivolous
	She seemed like a very superficial person.	
4932 **superhero** [SOO-per-heer-oh]	슈퍼히어로, 영웅	[1704] hero
	Batman is my son's favorite superhero.	
4933 공무원 **allotment** [uh-LOT-muhnt]	1. 분배, 배당 2. 할당량	allot (할당하다) [2487] allocation [200] allowance [671] supply
	The budget allotment for each city has been poorly assigned.	
4934 **hitch** [hich]	1. 얻어타다 2. 매다, 묶다 3. 문제 4. 매듭	[4914] snag [55] go [4409] drawback [4992] glitch
	Can I hitch a ride to the train station?	
4935 **dominion** [duh-MIN-yuh n]	1. 지배(권), 통치(권) 2. 영토 3. 주권 4. 영연방 자치령	[516] rule [131] leadership
	The country holds dominion over a vast area.	
4936 **parole** [puh-ROHL]	1. 가석방, 집행유예 2. 가석방시키다	[3643] probation [2181] liberate
	She was released on parole.	
4937 **geek** [geek]	1. 괴짜, 별난 사람 2. 광	geeky (괴짜스러운) [4901] nerd [3350] freak
	What a geek you are.	
4938 **ape** [eyp]	1. 유인원 2. 영장류 3. 흉내내다	[3941] mimic [3647] emulate [4095] imitate
	Some argue that humans evolved from apes.	

4939 **bombard** [bom-BAHRD]	1. 퍼붓다 2. 공격하다 3. 폭격하다	[2059] bomb [264] ask [2104] batter [6145] barrage
	I was bombarded with questions after giving my presentation.	
4940 　　　　공무원 토플 GRE **imminent** [IM-uh-nuhnt]	1. 임박한, 일촉즉발의, 곧 닥친 2. 절박한	[5339] impending [385] certain [918] immediate [4621] forthcoming
	I can feel the imminent danger of climate change.	
4941 **nipple** [NIP-uhl]	젖꼭지, 유두	[2173] chest
	Moments after a puppy was born, it looked for the mother's nipple.	
4942 　　　　　공무원 **hypnosis** [hip-NOH-sis]	최면(상태)	hypnotize (최면을 걸다) [5675] coma [6767] slumber
	She put me on hypnosis as an interrogation method.	
4943 　　　　　토플 **chimney** [CHIM-nee]	굴뚝	[2130] stack
	Santa was too fat that he got stuck in the middle of a chimney.	
4944 　　　　　토플 **marital** [MAR-i-tl]	1. 결혼생활의 2. 부부의	premarital (혼전의) [1018] marriage [1336] wedded [7229] matrimonial
	The couple has marital problems.	
4945 **dummy** [DUHM-ee]	1. 인체 모형, 마네킹 2. 모조품 3. 바보, 멍청이	[2644] fool
	He confused a dummy laying down on the street with a real person.	
4946 **salute** [suh-LOOT]	1. 경례하다 2. 경의를 표하다 3. 거수 경례, 인사	[1111] welcome [2025] acknowledge [2458] praise [2702] bow
	The president saluted the public.	
4947 **graft** [graft]	1. 이식(하다) 2. 뇌물	[3385] implant [1404] dishonesty
	He had to get a skin graft to treat his wounds.	
4948 　　　　공무원 **freeway** [FREE-wey]	고속도로	[2201] highway [3504] artery
	Traffic is unbearable on the freeway today.	
4949 　　공무원 토플 **sprawling** [sprawl-ing]	1. 제멋대로 뻗어나가는 2. 불규칙하게 넓어지는	sprawl (손발을 쭉 뻗어 눕다) [4365] flop
	So many spiders are sprawling out of that little hole.	
4950 **revamp** [ree-VAMP]	개조하다, 수리하다	[2071] alter [559] clean [1667] decorate [4472] overhaul
	I've revamped my old bike.	
4951 　　　　　토익 **brainstorm** [BREYN-stawrm]	1. 브레인스토밍(하다), 아이디어를 구상하다 2. 갑자기 사고가 정지되는 현상	[3023] deliberate [6134] antics
	Let's have a brainstorm session to come up with the solution.	
4952 **rant** [rant]	소리치다, 큰소리로 불평하다	ranting (소리치기) [4475] rave [1782] complain
	He started ranting when he got drunk.	

4953	GRE	1. 과다, 과잉 2. 다혈증	[98] addition [6760] deluge
plethora [PLETH-er-uh]		Her paper contained a plethora of detail.	

4954		1. 동족의, 혈족의 2. 유사한, 비슷한	[572] comparable [582] similar [4056] analogous
akin [uh-KIN]		Although not related, she felt very akin to her friend.	

4955	공무원	1. 자르다, 절단하다 2. 끊다, 분리하다	severance (분리) [892] separate [326] disconnect [3508] detach
sever [SEV-er]		I had to sever my arm because the injury was too severe.	

4956	공무원	위험	jeopardize (위험에 처하게 하다) [2553] hazard [4857] peril
jeopardy [JEP-er-dee]		I can't put my family's life in jeopardy just because I need some money.	

4957	GRE	1. 증명하다, 입증하다 2. 증언하다 3. 맹세시키다	attestation (입증) [2291] testify [121] show [1986] authenticate
attest [uh-TEST]		Can you attest to your innocence in the court of law?	

4958	공무원 토플	1. 체력, 스태미나 2. 지구력, 인내력 3. 정력	[2516] endurance [547] energy [652] determination
stamina [STAM-uh-nuh]		I can't go on with such low stamina.	

4959		펜던트, (목걸이)장식	[4136] necklace
pendant [PEN-duhnt]		Her grandmother gave her a diamond pendant.	

4960		1. 불구로 만들다, 제기능을 못하게 만들다 2. 장애, 불구자 3. 손상	crippled (불구의, 절름발이의) [4964] lame [1255] destroy
cripple [KRIP-uhl]		The car accident left him crippled for life.	

4961	고등	찬장, 식기장	[2372] cabinet [1104] locker [3169] closet
cupboard [KUHB-erd]		Can you please put the dishes in the cupboard?	

4962	공무원	1. 광신도 2. ~에 열광하는 사람	fanatical (광적인) [5469] zealot [82] activist [2129] addict
fanatic [fuh-NAT-ik]		He became a religious fanatic.	

4963		과수원	[3877] grove [640] plantation [1068] garden
orchard [AWR-cherd]		Try these peaches from my family's orchard.	

4964		1. 불충분한, 앞뒤가 맞지 않는 2. 다리를 저는, 절뚝거리는	[1445] weak [1043] injured [3116] sore
lame [leym]		What a lame excuse for being late to work.	

4965	토플	1. (in lieu of 의 형태로 쓰이는 경우) ~의 대신으로, ~대신에 2. 장소	[574] instead
lieu [loo]		He takes dividends in lieu of salary.	

4966	토플	침, 타액	[4150] spit
saliva [suh-LAHY-vuh]		I was so dehydrated that I didn't have any saliva in my mouth.	

4967 **eclectic** [ih-KLEK-tik]	GRE	다양한 구성의, 독특한	[604] varied [1535] diverse [1630] broad
		She has such an eclectic group of friends.	

4968 **duel** [DOO-uhl]		1. 결투 2. 다툼, 싸움, 투쟁	[697] fight [4248] bout
		I challenged him to a fencing duel.	

4969 **cadet** [kuh-DET]		사관 후보생	[92] student [399] youth
		Her son is a cadet at the school.	

4970 **anarchy** [AN-er-kee]		1. 무정부 상태 2. (사회의)무질서 3. 난장판	anarchism (무정부주의) [1581] confusion [2962] chaos
		The country is in a state of anarchy.	

4971 **alas** [uh-LAS]		1. 아아(슬픔, 안타까움의 소리) 2. 유감스럽게도	[992] unfortunately
		She is so in love with him, but alas he is not.	

4972 **trilogy** [TRIL-uh-jee]		3부작	
		She finally completed the last novel of the trilogy.	

4973 **comet** [KOM-it]		혜성	
		I have never witnessed a comet before.	

4974 **lubrication** [LOO-bri-key-shuh n]	토플	윤활, 매끄럽게 함	lubricate (윤활유를 바르 다)
		We need some lubrication for the car's front axle.	

4975 **wherein** [hwair-IN]	토플	1. 어디에서, 어떤 점에서 2. 그 점에서 3. 거기서	
		I would like to live in a country wherein human rights are respected.	

4976 **deposition** [dep-uh-ZISH-uhn]		1. 증언, 녹취 2. 퇴적(물) 3. 퇴위	depose (권력자를 퇴위시 키다) [470] removal [6185] impeachment
		We need your deposition for this trial.	

4977 **dire** [dahyuh r]	토플	1. 매우 심각한, 엄청난, 끔찍한 2. 긴급한	[896] serious [898] critical [3171] acute
		Expect dire consequences when you enter the hostile territory.	

4978 **wreath** [reeth]		1. 화환 2. 화관 3. 고리 모양	[6575] garland [외래어] bouquet
		The president laid a wreath at the war memorial.	

4979 **rake** [reyk]		1. 긁어모으다 2. 갈퀴(질하다) 3. 훑다	[966] touch [4135] comb [5498] scour
		I raked up so many points playing video games.	

4980 **eject** [ih-JEKT]		1. 내쫓다 2. 튀어나오다 3. 배설하다	ejection (방출, 분출) [4505] expel [2689] bounce [5349] banish
		I was ejected out of a theater for being too loud.	

4981	공무원	이기다, 능가하다	[724] excel
trump			
[truhmp]		Love trumps superficial differences.	

4982		1. 삼위 일체 2. 3인조	[기타] three
trinity			
[TRIN-i-tee]		Supply, demand and price form a great trinity.	

4983		가발	
wig			
[wig]		I wore a wig to disguise myself.	

4984	공무원	1. 숨어있다, 잠복하다 2. 도사리다 3. 속임수	[3096] creep
lurk			[5971] crouch
[lurk]		He could feel the tiger lurking behind the bushes.	

4985		1. 별자리, 성좌 2. 집합체	[669] star
constellation			[410] kind
[kon-stuh-LEY-shuhn]		What is your favorite constellation?	

4986	공무원 GRE	1. 악성의 2. 악의 가득한	malign (해로운, 악성의)
malignant			[3963] malicious
[muh-LIG-nuhnt]		His tumor turned out to be malignant.	[1074] cancerous
			[1186] deadly

4987		1. 과육 2. 걸쭉한 것	[2655] paste
pulp			[5369] slime
[puhlp]		I like orange juice with some pulp.	

4988		1. 온도계 2. 체온계	[1541] instrument
thermometer			[4375] thermostat
[ther-MOM-i-ter]		It became so hot that the thermometer exploded.	

4989	토플	1. 정체기, 안정기 2. 안정, 정체 상태가 지속되다 3. 고원	[690] highland
plateau			[2053] elevation
[pla-TOH]		The company's sales have finally reached a plateau.	[3165] pause

4990		빈혈(증)	anaemia (빈혈)
anemia			
[uh-NEE-mee-uh]		She is suffering from anemia.	

4991	공무원	1. 격동의, 격변의 2. 난기류의 3. 사나운	turbulence (난기류)
turbulent			[1547] wild
[TUR-byuh-luhnt]		After years of a turbulent relationship, they finally got a divorce.	[604] variable
			[2332] bumpy

4992		작은 문제, 작은 기술상의 결함	[2643] flaw
glitch			[1642] bug
[glich]		Can you fix the glitch in the monitor?	[2657] defect
			[4934] hitch

4993		1. 탈출 2. 이동, 이주	[2236] departure
exodus			[3895] evacuation
[EK-suh-duhs]		The old town is facing an exodus of its young people.	

4994		황도대, 12궁, 12가지 별자리	[2429] forecast
zodiac			
[ZOH-dee-ak]		Virgo is the sixth sign of the zodiac.	

4995	공무원 GRE	1. 노끈 2. 꼬다	intertwine (뒤엉키게 하다)
twine			[1459] string
[twahyn]		My cat loves to play with a ball of twine.	[1218] wind
			[3596] yarn

4996	공무원 토플 GRE	1. 다작하는 2. 다산하는, 열매를 많이 맺는 3. 많은	[109] creative
prolific			[284] decisive
[pruh-LIF-ik]		He was a prolific writer, publishing over 60 books in his lifetime.	[1199] rich

4997		1. 뇌진탕 2. 충격	[831] impact
concussion			[1043] injury
[kuhn-KUHSH-uhn]		She seems to have suffered a concussion after a car accident.	[2332] bump

4998	토익 공무원 GRE	별개의, 개별적인, 분리된	discrepancy (불일치, 모순)
discrete			[892] separate
[dih-SKREET]		Each student had his own discrete identity.	[1701] distinct

4999	공무원	1. 불쌍한, 애처로운 2. 한심한 3. 슬픈	pathos (연민을 부르는 힘)
pathetic			[3497] miserable
[puh-THET-ik]		I felt so pathetic after being dumped.	[2465] annoying

5000		침술, 침 치료	acupuncturist (침술사)
acupuncture			[5232] sedative
[AK-yoo-puhngk-cher]		Have you thought about acupuncture therapy for your back pain?	

5001		골키퍼	
goalie			
[GOH-lee]		Our amazing goalie stopped all 10 attempts.	

5002	공무원 GRE	1. 암시하다, 시사하다, 넌지시 비추다 2. 언급하다, ~에 관해 말하다	allusion (암시)
allude			[504] refer
[uh-LOOD]		The president alluded to the issue in his speech.	[876] mention

5003	공무원	1. (계약서에)규정하다, 명시하다 2. 보장하다, 약속하다	stipulation (계약, 약정)
stipulate			[434] specify
[STIP-yuh-leyt]		The regulations stipulate that all procedures must comply with safety standards.	[1447] guarantee
			[2034] designate

5004	공무원	1. 특징 2. 품질 증명, 보증 딱지(를 붙이다)	[266] feature
hallmark			[872] indication
[HAWL-mahrk]		One hallmark of a good student is his ability to focus.	[외래어] trademark

5005	공무원	구두법, 구두점	punctuate (강조하다)
punctuation			
[puhngk-choo-EY-shuhn]		You need to use the correct and proper punctuation in your essay.	

5006		1. 의미의, 의미론적인 2. 어의의	semantically (의미론적으로)
semantic			[4417] linguistic
[si-MAN-tik]		He has difficulty performing semantic processing when reading.	

5007	공무원 토플	보복, 복수, 앙갚음	retaliate (보복하다)
retaliation			retaliatory (보복적인)
[ri-tal-ee-EY-shuhn]		They killed the terrorists in retaliation.	[4013] revenge
			[2344] punishment

5008	공무원	자랑(하다), 떠벌리다, 허풍(떨다)	[2650] boast
brag			[5242] crow
[brag]		Stop bragging about yourself.	

5009 토익 토플 **gossip** [GOS-uhp]	1. 소문, 험담(하다) 2. 수다, 잡담 I don't like to be involved in gossips about my friends.	[392] talk [1411] conversation [2045] chatter [4642] buzz
5010 공무원 GRE **contempt** [kuhn-TEMPT]	1. 경멸, 멸시, 업신여김 2. 모욕, 치욕 3. 무시 She showed strong contempt for incompetent coworkers.	contemptuous (경멸하는) [6409] scorn [1599] hatred
5011 **snare** [snair]	1. 덫, 함정 2. 유혹 3. 덫에 걸리게 하다 A rabbit was caught in a snare.	ensnare (유혹하다) [2067] trap [6921] ploy
5012 **dissertation** [dis-er-TEY-shuhn]	(학위)논문 My dissertation was met with so many questions.	[2563] essay [3582] thesis
5013 공무원 **stigma** [STIG-muh]	오명, 오점, 낙인 I cannot live the rest of my life with the stigma of a murderer when I am innocent.	stigmatize (낙인찍다) [2097] disgrace [1896] stain [2621] shame
5014 **chime** [chahym]	1. (종, 시계가)울리다, 시각을 알리다 2. 소리 The chime of the clock woke me up from the nap.	[1271] ring
5015 **liquidation** [lik-wi-DEY-shuhn]	1. 청산, 정리, 파산 2. 현금화 A liquidation specialist came to evaluate our assets.	liquidate (청산하다) [1342] settlement [247] close [372] clearance
5016 **append** [uh-PEND]	1. 덧붙이다, 첨가하다, 첨부하다 2. 부가하다 Can you append this message at the end of the letter?	appendage (첨가물) [1242] attach [6054] affix
5017 **apparatus** [ap-uh-RAT-uhs]	1. 기구, 장치 2. 조직체, 기관 I don't need any apparatus to fix this.	[562] device [2766] appliance
5018 **wee** [wee]	1. 매우 작은, 적은, 조금 2. 오줌 He needs a wee drop of milk in his coffee.	[1869] tiny [219] small [3790] microscopic
5019 공무원 **imprint** [IM-print]	1. 각인(시키다), 강한 인상을 주다 2. 찍다, 새기다, 인쇄하다 3. 자국 Our short meeting left a strong imprint on each other.	[837] mark [221] signature [624] print
5020 GRE **antagonist** [an-TAG-uh-nist]	1. (주인공의)대립자, 상대역 2. 적대자, 저항자 The main antagonist of this novel dies at the end.	antagonistic (대립하는) antagonism (적대감) antagonize (적으로 돌리다)
5021 **reinstate** [ree-in-STEYT]	1. 복귀시키다 2. 원상태로 회복시키다 I've been reinstated after years of false accusation.	reinstatement (복귀, 복직) [1563] restore [303] employ
5022 **ripple** [RIP-uhl]	1. 영향 2. 잔물결(을 일으키다), 파문(을 일으키다) Her small action caused a ripple effect that impacted the whole town.	[1354] wave

| 5023 **undulate** [UHN-juh-leyt] | 1. 물결 모양의, 물결치다 2. 기복이 있다 | undulating (물결 모양의) [1354] wave [2186] swing [5545] wobble |
| | The photographer took several shots of the undulating slopes. | |

| 5024 토플 **paleontology** [pey-lee-uhn-TOL-uh-jee] | 고생물학 | [3535] archaeology [4356] excavation |
| | Paleontology focuses on using fossils to look into ancient times. | |

| 5025 **chopsticks** [CHOP-stiks] | 젓가락 | |
| | David started using chopsticks when he was 2 years old. | |

| 5026 GRE **deprecate** [DEP-ri-keyt] | 1. 강한 반대 의견을 내다 2. 업신여기다 | [7021] disparage [709] attack |
| | Such conduct should be strongly deprecated. | |

| 5027 **molar** [MOH-ler] | 어금니 | [1805] tooth |
| | Many of his teeth, even his molar, were missing. | |

| 5028 **strut** [struht] | 1. 뽐내며 걷다, 활보하다 2. 지주, 버팀목 | [7083] swagger [533] walk |
| | My daughter strutting always makes me laugh. | |

| 5029 공무원 **laden** [LEYD-n] | 잔뜩 실은, 가득한 | lading (화물) [844] loaded |
| | This container is laden with fresh oranges from California. | |

| 5030 공무원 **incumbent** [in-KUHM-buhnt] | 1. 현직자, 재직자 2. 재임 중인 | [658] necessary |
| | The incumbent mayor resigned immediately after being accused. | |

| 5031 **hum** [huhm] | 1. 콧노래를 부르다, 흥얼거리다 2. 윙윙 거리다 3. 활기차다 | [4642] buzz [4320] roar [5385] moan |
| | We started humming out our favorite song together. | |

| 5032 공무원 GRE **lament** [luh-MENT] | 1. 애통해하다, 통탄하다 2. 애도 | lamentation (애도) lamentable (애통한) [4298] mourn [4274] bemoan |
| | They all lamented her death at the funeral. | |

| 5033 **shovel** [SHUHV-uhl] | 삽(질하다), 삽으로 옮기다 | [3595] scoop |
| | Can you shovel out the rock in the yard? | |

| 5034 공무원 토플 **grim** [grim] | 1. 암울한, 우울한 2. 엄숙한 3. 음침한, 스산한 | grimly (암울하게) grimace (찡그린 얼굴(을 하다)) [5443] gloomy |
| | Their future seems grim after they suffered a death in the family. | |

| 5035 공무원 토플 GRE **ubiquitous** [yoo-BIK-wi-tuhs] | 어디에나 존재하는, 아주 흔한 | ubiquity (어디에나 존재함) [313] omnipresent [2443] widespread |
| | Telephone booths used to be ubiquitous, but not anymore. | |

| 5036 공무원 **coup** [koo] | 1. 쿠데타 2. 큰 성공 | [82] action [1030] overthrow [3951] feat |
| | The coup was failed once people started rebelling. | |

5037			
rift	균열, (찢어진)틈		[1800] split
[rift]			[962] argument
	My foot got stuck in the rift.		[2628] breach

5038			
solidarity	연대(감), 결속, 단결		[1409] unity
[sol-i-DAR-i-tee]			[172] support
	You can feel the solidarity of the people at the strike.		[427] agreement
			[3538] consensus

5039	토익 공무원		
carpenter	목수		carpentry (목수업)
[KAHR-puhn-ter]			[139] builder
	The carpenter did a fine job making the bookcase.		[4346] artisan

5040	토플		
elliptical	1. 타원형의 2. 생략된, 함축된 3. 타원형 운동기구		ellipse (타원)
[ih-LIP-ti-kuhl]			
	The elliptical orbits of the planets were first discovered by Kepler.		

5041			
secluded	1. 한적한, 외딴 2. 격리된, 남들과 접촉이 거의 없는		seclusion (격리)
[si-KLOO-did]			[2243] isolated
	His hometown is a secluded island with a small population.		[1208] distant
			[2456] deserted

5042			
temporal	1. 시간의, 시간 제약의 2, 현세의, 속세의		[4467] secular
[TEM-per-uhl]			[511] materialistic
	Our time with our parents is limited and temporal.		[1017] frequency
			[1064] earthly

5043			
snippet	1. 한 토막, 단편, 작은 조각 2. 자투리		[3352] fragment
[SNIP-it]			[409] bit
	I can't believe you found such valuable information from a small snippet.		

5044	공무원		
underpin	1. 뒷받침하다, 근거를 대다 2. 지지하다, 밑에서 떠받치다 3. 보강하다		underpinning (기반, 토대)
[uhn-der-PIN]			[643] matter
	She presented data to underpin her argument.		

5045			
sublime	1. 숭고한, 멋진, 장엄한 2. 황당한		sublimation ((화학) 승화)
[suh-BLAHYM]			sublimate (긍정적으로 승화시키다)
	There is something sublime about a perfectly executed figure skating routine.		[1677] grand

5046	공무원		
decipher	판독, 해독하다, 암호를 풀다		cipher (암호)
[dih-SAHY-fer]			[490] decode
	Can you decipher this code?		[317] understand
			[871] analyze

5047			
proponent	지지자		[105] backer
[pruh-POH-nuhnt]			[172] supporter
	His opinion is gaining a lot of proponents.		[1934] advocate

5048			
camel	낙타		
[KAM-uhl]			
	I haven't tried camel meat yet.		

5049	토익		
vase	꽃병		[503] container
[veys]			[2612] jar
	This vase was made in the 18th century.		

5050			
algebra	대수학		[1282] calculation
[AL-juh-bruh]			[5451] calculus
	Matrix algebra was such a challenging course.		

5051 **rover** [ROH-ver]	토플	1. 탐사선 2. 방랑자, 유랑자	[3039] wanderer [734] dog
		They are sending a rover to the moon for the expedition.	

5052 **purport** [per-PAWRT]		1. 주장하다, ~이라 칭하다 2. 취지, 요지	purportedly (알려진 바 에 의하면) [3162] pretend
		The theory purports to explain a correlation between the two phenomena.	

5053 **cellar** [SEL-er]		지하 저장고	[3178] basement [1759] apartment
		Can you grab a bottle of wine from the cellar?	

5054 **malfunction** [mal-FUHNGK-shuhn]	토익	오작동(하다), 고장, 기능 불량	[621] failure [1642] bug [2657] defect
		Production has come to a stop due to a malfunction in the assembly line.	

5055 **char** [chahr]	토플	숯으로 만들다, 숯이 되다, 까맣게 타다	[5899] scorch [1224] burn
		This BBQ is charred perfectly for my taste.	

5056 **permeate** [PUR-mee-eyt]	공무원	1. 스며들다, 배어들다 2. 침투하다 3. 퍼지다	impermeable (액체를 통 과시키지 않는) [5171] pervade [6656] imbue
		Water will permeate through the concrete wall.	

5057 **ivory** [AHY-vuh-ree]		1. 상아(색) 2. 상아로 만든 물건	[617] white
		She looks good in her ivory dress.	

5058 **kite** [kahyt]		연	
		They are flying kites to celebrate the holiday.	

5059 **intoxicate** [in-TOK-si-keyt]		1. 취하게 하다 2. 흥분(도취)시키다, 열중시키다 3. 중독시키다	intoxication (취한 상태) [4877] agitate [5094] arouse
		I can't believe she was intoxicated with just one sip of beer.	

5060 **sacrament** [SAK-ruh-muhnt]		1. 성례 2. 성찬	sacramental (신성한) [4586] communion
		He received the sacrament on bended knee.	

5061 **prom** [prom]		(미국 고등학교)졸업 무도회	[1316] dance [4920] gala
		She couldn't find the right dress for the prom.	

5062 **exacerbate** [ig-ZAS-er-beyt]	공무원 토플 GRE	악화시키다	exacerbation (악화) [4266] aggravate [373] worsen [2465] annoy
		I don't want to exacerbate the situation.	

5063 **alchemy** [AL-kuh-mee]		1. 연금술 2. 마력	alchemist (연금술사) [3054] wizardry
		People once believed that with alchemy, it was feasible to make gold from lead.	

5064 **snatch** [snach]	공무원 토플	1. 빼앗다, 강탈하다 2. 움켜쥐다, 붙잡다	[1757] grab [2897] rip [5043] snippet
		A thief snatched my purse.	

5065 **jade** [jeyd]	1. 옥, 비취(색) 2. 지치게 하다 3. 야윈 말 Her grandmother gave her a jade necklace.	jaded (싫증난)
5066　　토익 공무원 토플 편입 **fiscal** [FIS-kuh l]	재정상의, 회계의 The nation is going through fiscal problems.	[433] financial [597] economic [1192] budgetary
5067 **infiltrate** [in-FIL-treyt]	침투하다, 스며들다 We shouldn't let vile ideology infiltrate our children's minds.	infiltration (침투) [3056] penetrate [266] feature [5056] permeate
5068　　　　공무원 **replenish** [ri-PLEN-ish]	보충하다, 채우다 I feel the need to replenish my energy levels.	replenishment (보충) [685] refill [2330] refresh
5069 **hypertension** [hahy-per-TEN-shuh n]	고혈압 Obesity is closely linked to hypertension.	
5070 **handset** [HAND-set]	1. 핸드세트 2. 송수화기, 휴대폰 He always carries his radio handset to the gym.	
5071　　　토플 GRE **equitable** [EK-wi-tuh-buhl]	1. 공평한, 공정한 2. 동등한, 균등한 Any country should pursue a more equitable distribution of wealth.	inequitable (불공정한) [886] fair [2073] decent
5072 **incarceration** [in-kahr-suh-REY-shuh n]	감금, 투옥, 징역 A large amount of government budget is spent on incarceration each year.	incarcerate (감금하다) [1561] imprisonment [3366] captivity [3443] confinement
5073　　　　공무원 **applaud** [uh-PLAWD]	1. 박수갈채하다 2. 칭찬하다 The audience applauded when he finished singing.	applause (박수) [2458] praise [1072] approve [2488] cheer
5074 **cuddle** [KUHD-l]	껴안다, 포옹(하다) He loves cuddling his little dog.	[5775] clasp [7056] caress [외래어] kiss
5075　　　　공무원 **verge** [vurj]	1. 경계, 한계, 가장자리 2. 도로변, 변두리 I was on the verge of tears.	[557] almost [1070] edge [5580] brink
5076 **migraine** [MAHY-greyn]	편두통 She gets migraines right before it rains.	[4366] headache
5077　　　　GRE **novelty** [NOV-uh l-tee]	새로움, 참신함, 신형의 The internet is no longer a novelty.	[1103] freshness [1165] innovation [2115] curiosity
5078 **rectify** [REK-tuh-fahy]	바로잡다, 교정하다, 수정하다 We need to rectify the situation right away.	rectifier (바로잡는 사람) [769] fix [1947] amend [3113] cope

5079 **comma** [KOM-uh]	쉼표	
	You forgot to put a comma between these two words.	

5080 **surreal** [suh-REE-uhl]	초현실적인, 꿈같은	surrealism (초현실주의) [1659] strange
	The movie was a surreal mix of reality and imagination.	

5081　　수능 토플 GRE **naive** [nah-EEV]	순진무구한, 속기 쉬운	naively (순진하게) [2898] innocent [882] trusting [3291] ignorant
	It's naive of you to believe that.	

5082 **snail** [sneyl]	달팽이	
	She accidentally stepped on a snail.	

5083 **kettle** [KET-l]	주전자	
	He put the kettle on the stove.	

5084 **gorge** [gawrj]	1. 협곡, 골짜기 2. 실컷 먹다	[4262] canyon [7080] chasm
	The wind was blowing down the gorge.	

5085　　토플 **cortex** [KAWR-teks]	피질	[3608] crust
	His visual cortex has been damaged.	

5086　　공무원 GRE **hamper** [HAM-per]	1. 방해하다, 저해하다 2. (손)바구니	[4133] hinder
	The factory's old facility can hamper the production line.	

5087 **homage** [HOM-ij]	경의, 존경, 충성	[1059] respect [2458] praise [3651] deference [5397] allegiance
	That poem was written to pay homage to T.S. Eliot.	

5088　　수능 **sniff** [snif]	1. 킁킁 냄새맡다 2. 코를 훌쩍이다 3. 생각, 낌새 4. 콧방귀 뀌다	[1836] smell [1371] detect [2018] breathe [3990] inhale
	My dog sniffed my mom's luggage.	

5089 **churn** [churn]	1. 거세게 휘젓다, (속이)뒤틀리다 2. 고객 이탈 3. 동요하다	[4877] agitate [2156] boil
	It was very painful to feel my stomach churn with bad memories.	

5090　　공무원 GRE **embellish** [em-BEL-ish]	1. 장식하다, 꾸미다 2. 미화하다	embellishment (장식, 꾸밈) [1667] decorate [4509] adorn
	I am going to embellish my room with new drawings.	

5091 **continuum** [kuhn-TIN-yoo-uhm]	~의 연속, 연속체	discontinuity (단절) [1751] permanence [260] continuity
	She was mesmerized by the color continuum of the rainbow.	

5092 **bog** [bog]	1. 늪지, 수렁, 소택지 2. 화장실	boggy (늪의) [5713] marsh [2658] toilet
	She sank deep into the bog.	

5093	수능 GRE	의무적인, 필수의, 강제의	[2365] mandatory
compulsory			[395] forced
[kuhm-PUHL-suh-ree]		Attendance is compulsory for all students.	[658] necessary

5094	공무원	1. 자극하다, 불러일으키다 2. 각성시키다, 깨우다, 자극하다	arousal (자극, 흥분)
arouse			rouse (잠에서 깨우다, 신 나게 하다)
[uh-ROUZ]		His constant teasing aroused my anger.	[2819] awaken

5095	공무원	1. 가장 중요한, 주요한 2. 최고의	[1291] chief
paramount			[541] main
[PAR-uh-mount]		Safety is considered paramount in our company.	[1140] outstanding
			[4140] predominant

5096	공무원	1. 집행관, 보안관 2. 육공군 원수	
marshal			
[MAHR-shuhl]		He saw a marshal on the finish line with a yellow flag.	

5097		1. 모터사이클 경주(장) 2. 고속도로	
speedway			
[SPEED-wey]		This track is not suitable for competitive speedway.	

5098		외치다, 함성을 지르다	exclamation (감탄)
exclaim			[3172] shout
[ik-SKLEYM]		She could not help exclaiming at how much her niece had grown.	[2842] assert

5099	공무원	근처, 주변, 근접	[3588] proximity
vicinity			[128] place
[vi-SIN-i-tee]		It's not even in the vicinity of what we agreed on.	[1246] neighborhood

5100		향유, 연고	balmy (부드러운)
balm			[6110] ointment
[bahm]		Apply some balm on your face.	[외래어] lotion

5101	GRE	1. 망토 2. 가리다, 숨기다	[997] surface
cloak			[5309] mantle
[klohk]		She wore a red cloak.	[5449] camouflage

5102		1. 요람 2. 발상지 3. 안다, 흔들어 어르다	[5544] crib
cradle			[1120] frame
[KREYD-l]		Her son was sleeping in the cradle.	

5103		1. 늘어지다, 처지다 2. 약화되다, 하락하다	saggy (축 처진)
sag			[6638] droop
[sag]		Our skin starts to sag as we get older.	[5398] crater

5104	공무원 토플	고통(을 안겨주다), 괴롭히다	tormentor (고통을 안겨 주는 사람)
torment			[3530] torture
[tawr-MENT]		She decided not to torment her mom anymore.	[4795] affliction

5105		버드나무	[958] tree
willow			[외래어] olive
[WIL-oh]		He drew a golden willow and a maple tree.	

5106	공무원	1. 불법화하다, 금지하다 2. (사회에서)매장하다, 추방하다 3. 무법자, 추방자	[2343] prohibit
outlaw			[967] criminal
[OUT-law]		The president agreed to outlaw abortion.	[4894] crook
			[5999] bandit

5107 **hound** [hound]	1. 사냥개 2. 맹렬히 쫓다, 추적하다 Hounds are known to chase after foxes.	[734] dog [155] follow
5108　　　토익 **attire** [uh-TAHYUHR]	의복, 복장, 옷차림새 Are jeans appropriate attire for a wedding?	[1392] clothing [4021] apparel
5109 **sloppy** [SLOP-ee]	1. 엉성한, 대충하는 2. 단정치 못한 3. 감상적인 He was fired for his sloppy work.	[256] careless [3424] awkward
5110　　　토플 **stratum** [STREY-tuhm]	1. (사회)계층 2. 지층, 단층 They are good friends even though they come from different strata of society.	
5111 **upstream** [UHP-streem]	1. 상류로(향하는), 흐름을 거슬러 올라가는 2. 원재료의 Salmons are known to swim upstream to spawn.	
5112 **impart** [im-PAHRT]	1. 전하다, 알리다, 나눠 주다 2. 덧붙이다, 첨가하다 The professor tried hard to impart her knowledge and skill.	[191] tell [698] communicate [2902] convey
5113 **admiral** [AD-mer-uhl]	해군 대장, 제독, 해군 장성 사령관 The president mentioned the brave admiral in his speech.	
5114　　　공무원 **drizzle** [DRIZ-uhl]	1. 조금 붓다, 뿌리다 2. 이슬비(가 내리다) I drizzled some chocolate syrup over my brownie.	[2024] shower [1675] rain [1997] spray [5714] dribble
5115 **orb** [awrb]	1. 구, 구체 2. 천체 3. 안구 She could see the vast orb of the sun.	[3317] sphere
5116　　공무원 GRE **transient** [TRAN-shuhnt]	1. 일시적인, 순간적인 2. 덧없는 3. 단기 체류의 The doctor said my fever was transient.	transitory (=transient) [1648] temporary [604] variable [2554] fleeting
5117 **whopping** [HWOP-ing]	터무니없는, 엄청난, 몹시 She told a whopping lie.	[939] huge [196] large [1716] massive [6260] colossal
5118 **avenger** [uh-VEN-jer]	복수자, 원수 갚는 사람 The avenger sought retaliation.	avenge (복수하다)
5119 **motto** [MOT-oh]	1. 모토, 좌우명 2. 표어 The motto of the company is to be innovative at all times.	[외래어] slogan [6783] adage
5120 **tinker** [TING-ker]	1. 땜질하다, 서투르게 고치다, 손보다 2. 땜장이 My dad likes doing some tinkering in the basement.	[4765] fiddle [1933] mess [6293] dabble

5121 **stink** [stingk]	1. 악취(를 풍기다) 2. 평판이 나쁘다 --- Your shoes stink.	[1836] smell [2944] scent [7126] stench
5122 **whine** [hwahyn]	1. 징징대다, 우는 소리(를 하다), 낑낑대다 2. 불평 --- Stop whining like a baby.	whiner (징징대는 사람) [5385] moan [1782] complain [6393] gripe
5123 공무원 **relegate** [REL-i-geyt]	1. 좌천시키다, 강등시키다 2. 이관하다, 위임하다 --- She has been relegated to the position of secretary.	relegation (좌천) [5409] consign [882] entrust
5124 **lore** [lawr]	1. 지식, 학문 2. 전승, 전통 --- European lore depicts the serpent as the evil animal.	folklore (민속 이야기) [461] science [309] belief [772] knowledge
5125 공무원 GRE **ecstasy** [EK-stuh-see]	황홀(경), 무아의 경지 --- She was in ecstasy when he kissed her.	ecstatic (황홀한) [6069] rapture [270] pleasure [6761] euphoria
5126 **ledge** [lej]	1. 좁은 선반 2. (해안부근의)암초 --- He decorated the window ledge with beautiful flowers.	[1070] edge [3199] ridge
5127 토플 **torso** [TAWR-soh]	몸통, 상체, 토르소(몸통 조각상) --- She couldn't take her eyes off of his naked torso.	[3399] trunk [3314] bronze [3329] bust
5128 GRE **construe** [kuhn-STROO]	1. 이해하다, 해석하다 2. 구문 분석 --- How would you construe his behavior?	misconstrue (오해하다) [1651] interpret [729] define [4210] infer
5129 **plum** [pluhm]	1. 자두 2. 알짜배기의 --- I ate three plums for lunch.	[101] great
5130 **dime** [dahym]	다임(10센트 동전) --- Can I borrow a dime?	[1443] cent
5131 **mite** [mahyt]	1. 진드기 2. 조금, 약간 --- The mite is barely visible to the naked eyes.	[1642] bug [3036] insect [6297] wretch
5132 공무원 토플 **lavish** [LAV-ish]	1. 호화로운, 사치스러운 2. 후한, 아낌없이 주는 --- The family has such a lavish lifestyle.	lavishly (호화롭게) [1854] luxurious [1432] substantial [4644] bountiful
5133 **horde** [hawrd]	(큰)무리, 군중 --- A horde of children chased after an ice cream truck.	[1635] crowd [2692] crush
5134 토익 **extinguish** [ik-STING-gwish]	1. (불을)끄다, 진화하다 2. (희망을)잃게 하다, 전멸시키다 --- Carbon dioxide is often used to extinguish the fire.	extinguisher (소화기) [6199] quench

5135		적갈색(의)	[1858] brown
auburn [AW-bern]		He has beautiful auburn hair.	

5136		1. 저글링하다 2. 두가지 일을 동시에 하다 3. 속이다, 사기치다	[2593] manipulate [1030] throw
juggle [JUHG-uhl]		She knows how to juggle with four balls.	[2071] alter [4646] shuffle

5137		1. 관심을 끌다, 주목시키다 2. 고정시키다 3. 대갈못	riveting (확 주목시키는) [447] focus
rivet [RIV-it]		The complex plot of the novel was riveting.	[4058] fasten [4698] latch

5138		1. 경고 2. 발명 특허권 보고 신청 3. 소송 절차 정지 통고	[2149] caution [6418] admonition
caveat [KAV-ee-aht]		Before concluding the deal, you should thoroughly consider the caveat.	

5139		심문, 질문(함)	interrogate (심문하다) [263] question
interrogation [in-ter-uh-GEY-shuhn]		He finally confessed after three days under interrogation.	[1302] examination

5140		기념품	[6874] memento [984] gift
souvenir [soo-vuh-NEER]		Did you bring any souvenirs back from the trip?	

5141		1. 코뿔소(의) 2. 우울, 의기소침, 침울 3. 파산된	rhinoceros (=rhino)
rhino [RAHY-noh]		White rhinos are rarer than the black ones.	

5142		수류탄, 소화탄	[2059] bomb
grenade [gri-NEYD]		The grenade blew up right in front of him.	

5143	공무원	1. 스며들게 하다, 서서히 불어넣다 2. 주입하다, 고취시키다	[3539] infuse [864] affect
instill [in-STIL]		I tried hard to instill trust in my boyfriend.	[3874] diffuse [4572] disseminate

5144		1. 민중 지도자 2. 단, 연단	
tribune [TRIB-yoon]		A tribune's veto didn't prevent the Senate from passing a bill.	

5145		1. 분석, 검사 2. 시금(하다), 시험(하다)	
assay [a-SEY]		The researcher conducted an assay to study the composition.	

5146	공무원	1. ~하지 않도록 2. ~을 두려워하여	
lest [LEST]		You shouldn't be mean to your friends, lest you turn them into enemies.	

5147	공무원 토플 GRE	1. 사망, 서거, 죽음 2. 폐지, 소멸 3. 양도(하다)	[157] end [2236] departure
demise [dih-MAHYZ]		Everyone was shocked by his sudden demise.	[2604] collapse

5148	공무원	1. 저명한, 유명한 2. 탁월한	eminently (현저히) preeminence (탁월함)
eminent [EM-uh-nuhnt]		My professor is one of the world's most eminent biologists.	[1159] famous [1059] respected

| 5149
dismantle
[dis-MAN-tl] | GRE | 1. 철거하다, 분해하다 2. 폐지하다 | [2435] disassemble
[3962] demolish |
| | | The furniture needs to be dismantled so that it can be transported. | |

| 5150
patriarch
[PEY-tree-ahrk] | | 가장, 족장, 창설자 | patriarchy (가부장제)
matriarch (여성 가장, 여성 족장)
[2493] elder |
| | | My father is the patriarch of our family. | |

| 5151
bestow
[bih-STOH] | 공무원 | 수여하다, 주다, 부여하다 | [91] give
[1129] confer
[3030] bequeath |
| | | She needs to bestow more time to work. | |

| 5152
astronaut
[AS-truh-nawt] | | 우주비행사 | [1976] pilot |
| | | The little boy dreams of becoming an astronaut. | |

| 5153
blockbuster
[BLOK-buhs-ter] | | 블록버스터(유명한 책이나 영화) | |
| | | This new film will be a real blockbuster. | |

| 5154
exemplary
[ig-ZEM-pluh-ree] | 공무원 GRE | 모범적인, 전형적인, 본보기인 | exemplar (모범)
[431] model
[478] commendable
[724] excellent |
| | | The couple has an exemplary marriage. | |

| 5155
banquet
[BANG-kwit] | 토익 토플 | 1. 연회, 향연 2. 성찬 | [3578] feast
[3674] festivity |
| | | Do you know how many people will be attending the banquet? | |

| 5156
smear
[smeer] | 토플 | 1. 얼룩 2. (기름 따위로)더럽히다, 비방하다 3. 문질러 지우다 | [1896] stain
[1914] dirty
[3428] blur |
| | | There's a smear on your pants. | |

| 5157
schema
[SKEE-muh] | | 1. 개요, 설계 2. 도표, 도식 | [1724] scheme
[573] preparation |
| | | Mental schemas that establish the ground for interpretation are different among individuals. | |

| 5158
aerobic
[ai-ROH-bik] | 공무원 토플 | 1. 유산소의, 에어로빅 2. 호기성의, 호균성의 | [555] airy |
| | | Running is an example of aerobic exercise. | |

| 5159
ratify
[RAT-uh-fahy] | 공무원 | 비준하다, 승인하다 | ratification (승인)
[1072] approve
[221] sign
[1200] confirm |
| | | Five countries have ratified the treaty. | |

| 5160
ark
[ahrk] | | 1. (노아의)방주 2. 계약의 궤 | [1414] boat |
| | | The movie depicted the story of Noah's ark. | |

| 5161
pun
[puhn] | | 말장난, 농담 | [2293] joke |
| | | He made a pun that nobody understood. | |

| 5162
kinetic
[ki-NET-ik] | 공무원 | 1. 운동의(에 의한) 2. 속도 | kinetics (운동학)
[1634] dynamic
[2031] animated
[3873] lively |
| | | Potential energy can be converted to kinetic energy. | |

5163 공무원 토플 **dissipate** [DIS-uh-peyt]	1. 흩뜨리다, 소멸시키다 2. 낭비하다 She opened the window to dissipate the heat.	dissipation (흐트림) [4160] disperse [4444] deplete
5164 토플 **rooster** [ROO-ster]	수탉 I woke up to the sound of a rooster crowing.	[1640] chicken [4604] goose
5165 **raven** [REY-vuhn]	1. 까마귀 2. 새까만 The raven is often misidentified as a crow.	
5166 **astound** [uh-STOUND]	놀라게하다, 경악시키다 He always astounds us with his sense of humor.	astounding (놀라운) [4014] astonish [959] surprise
5167 **bronco** [BRONG-koh]	(북미 서부의)야생마 He has experience of riding a bronco.	[1689] horse
5168 토플 **grapple** [GRAP-uhl]	1. 고심하다 2. 맞붙어 싸우다 The government is grappling with the problem of air pollution.	[1333] struggle [697] fight [2787] contend [2869] confront
5169 토플 **uterus** [YOO-ter-uhs]	자궁 Women's uterus tends to swallow during menstruation.	uterine (자궁의) [5396] womb
5170 공무원 GRE **benign** [bih-NAHYN]	1. 양성의(악성의 반대) 2. 상냥한, 온화한 A benign tumor doesn't need to be removed.	[410] kind [1571] favorable [2065] gentle [6008] benevolent
5171 공무원 GRE **pervasive** [per-VEY-siv]	1. 만연하는, 구석구석 깃든, 퍼지는 2. 스며드는 Drug abuse is still a pervasive problem in our society.	pervade (만연하다) [2443] widespread [485] common [1079] obvious
5172 토플 **dissent** [dih-SENT]	1. 반대(의견) 2. 의견을 달리하다 There is no time for dissent.	[427] disagree [6006] discord
5173 공무원 토플 **pebble** [PEB-uhl]	자갈, 조약돌 She found a beautiful pebble on the beach.	[1010] rock [1064] earth [4234] gravel
5174 **dermatologist** [dur-muh-TOL-uh-jist]	피부과 전문의 You should see a dermatologist for skin issues.	dermal (피부에 관한) dermatology (피부학)
5175 고등 **darling** [DAHR-ling]	1. 자기야(사랑하는 사람을 부를 때 쓰는 애칭) 2. 사랑하는 My darling, I love you so much.	[146] love
5176 **psychotic** [sahy-KOT-ik]	정신병의, 정신병 환자 He is suffering from a psychotic disorder.	psycho (정신병 환자) [2693] insane

5177		1. 고글, 수경, 보안경 2. 눈을 부릅뜨고 보다	
goggle			
[GOG-uhl]		You forgot to put your goggles on.	

5178	공무원 토플	유목민(족), 방랑자	nomadic (유목의)
nomad			[3039] wanderer
[NOH-mad]		I hope to become a nomad one day.	[2423] migrant [4253] pilgrim

5179		도르래	
pulley			
[POOL-ee]		She lifted that stone with a rope and a pulley.	

5180		(회의를)주재하다, 사회를 보다, 의장이 되다	[273] control
preside			[1066] administer
[pri-ZAHYD]		The chairman will preside at the meeting.	[1544] chair

5181		1. 클라이맥스, 절정, 최고점 2. 절정에 이르다	climactic (절정의)
climax			[1868] peak
[KLAHY-maks]		I stopped watching the movie right before the climax.	

5182		1. (줄의 첫 머리를, 행을)들여쓰다 2. 주문(하다)	indentation (들여쓰기)
indent			[1766] tear
[in-DENT]		You are recommended to indent the first line of a paragraph.	

5183	공무원	1. 무심코, 우연히 2. 부주의로	inadvertent (의도치 않은)
inadvertently			[1527] unintentionally
[in-uhd-VUR-tn-tlee]		The couple inadvertently left the restaurant without paying the tip.	[4334] negligently

5184	공무원	거대한, 거인 같은	[939] huge
gigantic			[196] large
[jahy-GAN-tik]		He owns a gigantic house.	[2777] enormous [6260] colossal

5185		1. 블레이저 2. 선전하는 사람, 퍼뜨리는 사람	[외래어] jacket
blazer			[1587] coat
[BLEY-zer]		I need a blouse to go with this blazer.	

5186		1. 기질, 성향 2. 배치	[3341] inclination
disposition			[5619] complexion
[dis-puh-ZISH-uhn]		My brother has a cheerful disposition.	

5187		유괴, 납치	abduct (유괴하다)
abduction			[4165] kidnapping
[ab-DUHK-shuhn]		She was abducted by aliens in her dream.	[2860] rape

5188		1. 초승달 모양 2. 이슬람교	
crescent			
[KRES-uhnt]		There is a crescent moon up in the sky.	

5189	공무원 GRE	만족(감), 충족, 희열	gratifying (만족감을 주는)
gratification			gratify (만족시키다)
[grat-uh-fi-KEY-shuhn]		This boring job gives no gratification.	[1267] satisfaction

5190	공무원	위협(하다), 협박(하다)	menacing (위협적인)
menace			[1205] threat
[MEN-is]		Dogs without a leash are a public menace.	[531] risk [2553] hazard

5191 **fume** [fyoom]	공무원	1. 연기, 매연 2. 화를 내다	[3161] rage [5558] bristle
		Car exhaust fumes are the main cause of air pollution.	
5192 **cod** [kod]		1. 대구(생선) 2. 가짜의, 속이기	
		She doesn't like seafood except for cod.	
5193 **militia** [mi-LISH-uh]		민병대, 의용군, 시민군	[1244] military
		The militia was called to put down the riot.	
5194 **buoy** [BOO-ee]	공무원 GRE	1. 부표 2. 뜨다, (물에)띄우다 3. 기분이 들뜨다	buoyancy (물에뜨는 부력) buoyant (부양성 있는) [4736] beacon
		Buoys in the ocean mark the boundary of the safety zone.	
5195 **tamper** [TAM-per]	공무원 토플	1. 조작하다, 변경하다 2. 간섭하다 3. 만지작 거리다	[719] damage [5120] tinker [6655] meddle
		It is impossible to tamper data stored in a blockchain.	
5196 **nuisance** [NOO-suhns]		1. 골칫거리, 성가신 물건/행위/사람 2. 방해	[215] problem
		Weeds are a nuisance in the springtime.	
5197 **garner** [GAHR-ner]		1. 얻다, 모으다 2. 저장하다, 축적하다	[5509] amass
		The company's new product garnered much attention from the audience.	
5198 **martyr** [MAHR-ter]		1. 순교자 2. ~으로 괴로워하는 사람	[7087] scapegoat
		Jesus is a martyr who sacrificed his life for everyone else.	
5199 **splendid** [SPLEN-did]	공무원	1. 근사한, 훌륭한, 멋진 2. 인상적인	splendidly (근사하게) [101] great [542] beautiful [7017] baroque
		She has done a splendid job.	
5200 **farewell** [fair-WEL]	토익	작별(인사)	[817] goodbye
		I said a long-overdue farewell to my friend.	
5201 **hijack** [HAHY-jak]		1. (배, 비행기 등을)납치하다, 약탈하다 2. 이용하다, 장악하다	
		The terrorist group tried to hijack a plane.	
5202 **eccentric** [ik-SEN-trik]	공무원 GRE	괴짜(의), 별난, 괴상한	eccentricity (괴상함) [4006] bizarre [1776] crazy [2115] curious
		People didn't like him for his eccentric behavior.	
5203 **spindle** [SPIN-dl]		1. 물레가락 2. 축, 굴대 3. 방추	
		She accidentally pricked her finger on the sharp end of the spindle.	
5204 **smack** [smak]		1. 때리다, 부딪치다 2. 맛, 풍미, 향기	[4125] slap [578] hit [2991] bang
		She never smacks her children.	

5205 **vanguard** [VAN-gahrd]	1. 선봉, 선두 2. 선구자, 선발대	[552] forefront [외래어] engineer
	The company is in the vanguard of technological advances.	
5206 **grievance** [GREE-vuhns]	불만, 불평거리	[1782] complaint [308] hardship [3887] grief
	An employee can file a formal grievance if he receives a lower salary than other colleagues.	
5207 토익 토플 **auditorium** [aw-di-TAWR-ee-uhm]	강당, 객석, 청중석, 관중석	
	The school's auditorium has been renovated.	
5208 **skew** [skyoo]	1. 왜곡하다 2. 비스듬한, 비대칭의, 비뚤어지게	[2202] twist [719] damage [2071] alter [2753] bias
	Inaccurate data can skew the results of the survey.	
5209 **hardcore** [HAHRD-kawr]	1. 절대적인, 단호한, 철저한 2. 강경파	[1979] habitual [2129] addicted
	Thanks to his hardcore dedication to his schoolwork, he got all A's for the semester.	
5210 **asteroid** [AS-tuh-roid]	소행성	[721] globe [1064] earth
	Fourteen known asteroids lie between Mars and Jupiter.	
5211 **autograph** [AW-tuh-graf]	사인(을 하다), 서명(을 하다)	[221] sign [2864] endorsement
	Can I get your autograph?	
5212 토플 **allure** [uh-LOOR]	1. 매력 2. 매혹하다, 꾀다	alluring (매혹적인) [1069] attract [1365] appeal [4700] charisma
	The allure of the stage drew her back to performing.	
5213 공무원 GRE **refractive** [ri-FRAK-tiv]	굴절하는, 굴절에 의한	refraction (굴절) refract (굴절시키다)
	Rays with different refractive properties form light.	
5214 **kiosk** [KEE-osk]	1. 키오스크(간이 매점) 2. 공중전화 박스	[3373] booth [1340] pop-up
	He bought cigarettes at the kiosk.	
5215 토플 **pneumonia** [noo-MOHN-yuh]	폐렴	
	She suffered from pneumonia.	
5216 **pigeon** [PIJ-uhn]	비둘기	[2076] dove
	I hate pigeons on the street.	
5217 공무원 GRE **humility** [hyoo-MIL-i-tee]	겸손	[796] shyness [3179] humble
	Humility is the foundation of all virtue.	
5218 **mast** [mast]	돛대, 깃발	[2001] pole
	The mast is used to guide the boat.	

5219 **ballistic** [buh-LIS-tik]		1. 탄도(학)의 2. 격노하다, 격분하다	[3161] enraged
		North Korea developed ballistic missiles.	
5220 **havoc** [HAV-uhk]	공무원 토플	1. 파괴, 혼란 2. 침해	[2962] chaos [1223] danger [6222] calamity [7435] cataclysm
		The government's regulations would wreak havoc on the economy.	
5221 **surcharge** [SUR-chahrj]		추가요금, 할증금, 추징금	[415] overcharge [160] payment [305] price [1537] expense
		There is a surcharge for extra luggage.	
5222 **lotus** [LOH-tuhs]		연(꽃)	[718] situated
		She loves the smell of lotus leaves.	
5223 **genocide** [JEN-uh-sahyd]	공무원	대량 학살, 집단/민족 학살	[6524] carnage
		The dictator was accused of genocide.	
5224 **maze** [meyz]	공무원	미로, 미궁	[6020] labyrinth [1926] mystery
		She couldn't get out of the maze.	
5225 **intercourse** [IN-ter-kawrs]		1. 육체적 관계 2. 교류, 교제, 소통	[698] communication [2783] intimacy
		Certain diseases can be transmitted through sexual intercourse.	
5226 **mariner** [MAR-uh-ner]		선원, 뱃사람, 수부	[2088] sailor
		The old mariner became sick of waters.	
5227 **manor** [MAN-er]		1. 영지, 장원 2. (경찰의)관할 지역	[4099] mansion
		He became rich after inheriting the manor from his father.	
5228 **formidable** [FAWR-mi-duh-buhl]	공무원	1. 엄청난, 어마어마한 2. 강력한, 위협적인, 무서운	[201] powerful [1223] dangerous [4283] daunting
		The challenge they were facing was a formidable one.	
5229 **almighty** [awl-MAHY-tee]	공무원	1. 전능한 2. 대단한, 대단히 3. 신	
		I swear by Almighty God to tell the truth.	
5230 **recline** [ri-KLAHYN]		기대게하다, 눕히다, 뒤로 젖히다	recliner (뒤로 기댈 수 있 는 의자) [6776] repose [2856] lounge
		She reclined her seat to take a quick nap.	
5231 **hostage** [HOS-tij]	수능	인질, 볼모	[1561] prisoner [3366] captive
		The criminals released the hostages.	
5232 **sedative** [SED-uh-tiv]	공무원	1. 진정제 2. 가라앉히는	sedate (진정시키다) [4547] tranquilizer
		The doctor prescribed the patient a sedative to help him sleep.	

5233	공무원 토플 GRE	무자비한, 가차없는, 냉혹한	ruthlessly (무자비하게)
ruthless			[2947] merciless
[ROOTH-lis]		The dictator was notorious for his ruthless behavior.	[3041] brutal
			[3470] cruel

5234	공무원 토플	1. 파열(하다), 찢다 2. 결렬, 단절, 불화	[445] break
rupture			[719] damage
[RUHP-cher]		The old pipe has been ruptured.	[2628] breach

5235		1. 어치(새 종류) 2. 얼간이, 시골뜨기	
jay			
[jey]		Jays are her favorite birds.	

5236	토플	보리	[6540] fodder
barley			[2699] corn
[BAHR-lee]		This beer is made from barley.	

5237		1. 부랑자, 게으름뱅이 2. 엉덩이 3. ~을 얻다	[7001] tramp
bum			[999] bottom
[buhm]		He looks like a bum with that nasty hair.	[7443] derelict

5238		으스스한, 무시무시한	[1961] scary
spooky			[2763] chilling
[SPOO-kee]		We sat down to tell spooky tales.	[3096] creepy
			[3594] frightening

5239		1. 개자식, 놈 2. 사생아, 서자 3. 가짜의, 잡종의	
bastard			
[BAS-terd]		He was a bastard to his girlfriend.	

5240		1. 휙 돌다, 미끄러지다 2. 많음, 다량	[4139] heap
slew			[2566] abundance
[sloo]		The car slewed violently on the icy road.	[3100] aggregation

5241	공무원	잔혹 행위, 포악	atrocious (잔혹한)
atrocity			[3681] outrage
[uh-TROS-i-tee]		The terrorist group committed atrocities against innocent people.	[2585] horror
			[3470] cruelty

5242	토플	1. 까마귀 2. 수탉의 울음소리, 환성 3. 자랑하다	[5008] brag
crow			[2611] tweet
[kroh]		Crows are black.	[2650] boast

5243	공무원	2개국어를 구사하는	lingual (언어의)
bilingual			
[bahy-LING-gwuh l]		He is virtually bilingual in English and French.	

5244		(in tandem 으로 쓰일 경우) ~와 함께, 동시에, 나란히	[148] company
tandem			[765] club
[TAN-duh m]		She is working in tandem with her counterpart at the company.	

5245		1. 희미하게 빛나다, 어렴풋이 비치다 2. 미광	shimmering (희미하게 빛나는)
shimmer			[1962] shine
[SHIM-er]		Her reflection was shimmering on the water.	[6675] glimmer

5246	공무원	1. 노골적인, 뻔한 2. 소란스러운, 시끄러운 3. 야한	blatantly (노골적으로)
blatant			[1079] obvious
[BLEYT-nt]		He was angry at her blatant remark.	[4623] unashamed
			[5420] conspicuous

5247 공무원	불면증	[990] sleeplessness
		[714] restlessness
insomnia		[2819] awake
[in-SOM-nee-uh]	She suffered from insomnia.	

5248	1. 지친, 피곤한 2. 싫증나는 3. 지루하게 하다, 싫증나다, 지치게하다	weariness (피로)
		[1399] tired
weary		[1109] bored
[WEER-ee]	I've grown weary of all your complaints.	[4011] disgusted

5249	더러운, 추잡한	filth (쓰레기)
		[1914] dirty
filthy		
[FIL-thee]	What a filthy lie you told.	

5250 공무원 GRE	실용적인, 실제적인	pragmatism (실용주의)
		[492] practical
pragmatic		[135] businesslike
[prag-MAT-ik]	We need to implement more pragmatic measures.	

5251 공무원	다시 젊어지게 하다, 활력을 회복하다, 회춘하다	rejuvenation (활력충전)
		rejuvenated (활력이 충
rejuvenate		전된)
[ri-JOO-vuh-neyt]	A cup of lemon water makes me feel rejuvenated.	[1563] restore

5252 공무원 GRE	산문(체), 일반문	prosaic (평범한)
		[775] composition
prose		[2563] essay
[prohz]	I prefer reading prose to poetry.	

5253	1. 지붕널 2. 간판 3. 조약돌	
shingle		
[SHING-guhl]	They are repairing their house's shingle roof.	

5254	1. 칭찬, 포상 2. 수상 3. 명예	[2458] praise
		[681] award
accolade	The professor's approval was the highest accolade she could have	[1701] distinction
[AK-uh-leyd]	ever asked for.	[5741] kudos

5255	만트라, 기도 또는 명상 때 외는 주문	[4859] hymn
		[외래어] melody
mantra		
[MAN-truh]	He recites his mantra before going to bed.	

5256	1. 부패성의 2. 패혈증의	antiseptic (소독제)
		[1374] infected
septic		
[SEP-tik]	If you don't treat that cut, it may go septic.	

5257	~보다 우수하다, ~를 능가하다	[3970] surpass
		[152] outrun
outperform		[1983] exceed
[out-per-FAWRM]	His company always outperforms its competitors.	

5258	직접으로, 바로	
firsthand		
[FURST-hand]	I've experienced the earthquake firsthand.	

5259	점성, 끈적함	viscous (점성이 있는)
		[915] stickiness
viscosity		
[vi-SKOS-i-tee]	Honey has a higher viscosity than water.	

5260	1. 불황 2. 폭락(하다), 급감(하다)	[1792] decline
		[1788] crash
slump		[2604] collapse
[sluhmp]	The stock market is in a slump.	[5398] crater

5261 **syringe** [suh-RINJ]	1. 주사기 2. (귀 따위를)씻어 내다	[2809] needle
	You should never reuse syringes.	
5262　　　　공무원 토플 GRE **solitary** [SOL-i-ter-ee]	혼자의, 고독한, 외딴	solitude (고독) [2843] lone [1440] retiring
	She spent the holiday in solitary.	
5263　　　　　　토플 **schizophrenia** [skit-suh-FREE-nee-uh]	조현병, 정신 분열증	schizophrenic (정신 분 열증 환자) [4699] paranoia [2693] insanity
	He was diagnosed with schizophrenia.	
5264 **moose** [moos]	큰 사슴	[5884] elk
	I haven't tasted moose meat yet.	
5265 **hoard** [hawrd]	비축(하다), 저장(하다)	hoarder (비축하는 사람) [2732] accumulation [5689] backlog
	They started to hoard food to prepare for the huge storm.	
5266　　　　　공무원 GRE **innate** [ih-NEYT]	타고난, 선천적인	innately (선천적으로) [838] elemental
	She has an innate talent for music.	
5267 **cram** [kram]	1. 벼락치기 하다 2. 밀어 넣다	[919] stuff [685] fill [844] load [1635] crowd
	They are cramming for the exam tomorrow.	
5268 **shrug** [shruhg]	(양손바닥을 위로 하여)어깨를 으쓱하다	[5692] nudge
	He gave a little shrug and walked away.	
5269　　　　　　토플 **serpent** [SUR-puhnt]	뱀	[3001] snake [6634] viper
	The wire was coiled like a serpent.	
5270 **amidst** [uh-MIDST]	~가운데	[631] among [178] between
	I enjoy working amidst clutter.	
5271　　　　　　공무원 **venom** [VEN-uhm]	1. 독 2. 앙심, 악의	venomous (독성있는) [2686] poison [1599] hatred [3130] bitterness
	That snake's venom is very lethal.	
5272　　공무원 토플 GRE **lucid** [LOO-sid]	1. 명백한, 명료한 2. 투명한, 맑은 3. 의식이 또렷한	elucidate (상세히 설명하 다) lucidity (명료함) elucidation (설명)
	Her explanation was lucid and concise.	
5273 **tug** [tuhg]	힘껏 잡아당기다, 끌다	[912] pull [2074] drag
	The baby tugged on his mom's arm.	
5274 **marrow** [MAR-oh]	1. 골수 2. 동행, 동료	[1248] core
	She received a bone marrow transplant.	

5275	토플	활판술, 인쇄술	[775] composition
typography			
[tahy-POG-ruh-fee]		Normally, the typography and the book design go hand in hand.	

5276		눈사태, 산사태	[6145] barrage
avalanche			[6760] deluge
[AV-uh-lanch]		They were killed in an avalanche while skiing.	

5277		나방	[799] butterfly
moth			[812] ant
[mawth]		Is that a butterfly or a moth?	

5278	공무원 토플	1. 잠수하다, 물속에 가라앉다 2. 감추다	[3523] immerse
submerge			[2733] soak
[suhb-MURJ]		He submerged into a deep sleep.	[6760] deluge

5279		확인하다, 알아내다, 규명하다	[652] determine
ascertain			[1200] confirm
[as-er-TEYN]		The probe team will ascertain the truth.	

5280	공무원	1. 약물, 마약 2. 멍청이 3. 정보	doping (약물 복용, 도핑)
dope			[2995] weed
[dohp]		They were arrested for selling dope.	[2644] fool
			[3666] idiot

5281		기사, 기병대, 기갑부대	
cavalry			
[KAV-uh l-ree]		The cavalry was carrying a shield.	

5282		역의, 반대의, 거꾸로 된	inversely (반대로)
inverse			[1845] reverse
[in-VURS]		He and she have inverse personalities.	[1717] conflicting

5283	공무원	경멸하다	[1599] hate
despise			[6745] abhor
[dih-SPAHYZ]		She despises people who smoke.	[6925] deride

5284	GRE	전복시키다, 뒤엎다	subversive (전복시키는)
subvert			[3943] undermine
[suhb-VURT]		The rebels attempted to subvert the government.	[1203] influence
			[2543] corrupt

5285		1. 우르르 소리를 내다 2. 알아내다 3. 패싸움(을 하다)	rumbling (우르르 소리를 내는)
rumble			[3694] thunder
[RUHM-buhl]		The rumble of the thunder eventually diminished.	[4320] roar

5286		1. 졸, 앞잡이 2. 노리개	[3242] pledge
pawn			[1518] victim
[pawn]		He was used as a political pawn by the president.	

5287		1. 부풀다, 볼록하다, 툭 튀어나오다 2. 돌출부	[2740] swelling
bulge			[3684] lump
[buhlj]		Her cheeks bulged with a bite of an apple.	

5288	공무원	광란, 열광, 광분	frenzied (광적인)
frenzy			[3576] fury
[FREN-zee]		They screamed in a frenzy of excitement.	[1776] craze
			[2665] disturbance

5289		1. 횡설수설하는, 두서없는 2. 사방으로 뻗은	ramble (정처없이 거닐다)
rambling			[3039] wandering
[RAM-bling]		The chairman gave a rambling speech.	[533] walker
			[1488] disjointed

5290	공무원 토플	1. 먹이를 찾다 2. 사료	[6540] fodder
forage			[4135] comb
[FAWR-ij]		At night, wild boars came down to the town to forage for food.	

5291		수수께끼, 난제	[5599] enigma
riddle			[263] question
[RID-l]		Let's solve this riddle.	[1088] complexity
			[6823] conundrum

5292	공무원 GRE	망각, 의식하지 못하는	oblivious (망각한)
oblivion			[589] nothingness
[uh-BLIV-ee-uhn]		She often drinks herself into oblivion.	[1095] forgetful

5293	공무원	유혹하다, 꾀어내다	seduction (성적 유혹)
seduce			seductive (유혹하는)
[si-DOOS]		He was trying to seduce his coworker.	[3966] lure
			[4004] betray

5294	공무원	엄숙한, 근엄한, 진지한	solemnly (근엄하게)
solemn			solemnity (근엄함)
[SOL-uhm]		She looked very solemn as she spoke to him.	[896] serious
			[3897] dignified

5295		4중주(단), 4인조	[기타] four
quartet			
[kwawr-TET]		The quartet will be performing tomorrow.	

5296	토익	1. 재빨리 해치우다, 신속히 처리하다 2. 촉진시키다	expedited (촉진된)
expedite			[2189] accelerate
[EK-spi-dahyt]		I'm here to help you expedite your plans.	[636] assist

5297	토플	1. 던지다 2. (욕을)퍼붓다 3. 토하다	[1030] throw
hurl			[655] fire
[hurl]		She desperately wanted to hurl herself into his arms.	[5531] fling

5298		1. 함정, 유혹 2. 위험	[2067] trap
pitfall			[215] problem
[PIT-fawl]		I failed to avoid that pitfall.	[665] difficulty
			[1223] danger

5299		수도꼭지	[2223] valve
faucet			[4748] nozzle
[FAW-sit]		He forgot to turn off the faucet.	

5300	공무원 GRE	불길한	omen (징조)
ominous			[1205] threatening
[OM-uh-nuhs]		Those dark clouds looked very ominous.	[896] serious
			[1223] dangerous

5301	공무원	강제, 강요	coerce (강요하다)
coercion			coercive (강압적인)
[koh-UR-shuhn]		He told the truth under coercion.	[1494] violence
			[3630] intimidation

5302		1. 모낭 2. 난포	[891] hair
follicle			
[FOL-i-kuhl]		Hair sprays may block hair follicles.	

| 5303 | 공무원 | 위조(하다), 모조(하다), 흉내(내다) | counterfeiter (위조범) [2552] fake |
| **counterfeit** [KOUN-ter-fit] | | She bought a counterfeit watch. | [732] illegal [931] copied |

| 5304 | 토플 | 석호, 늪, 못 | [3196] pond |
| **lagoon** [luh-GOON] | | They found a beautiful, blue lagoon. | |

| 5305 | | 1. 변하다, 바뀌다 2. 형태 | [1453] transform [1388] modify |
| **morph** [mawrf] | | Stem cells can morph into many different cells. | [2071] alter |

| 5306 | | 1. 더미, 뭉치, 짐짝 2. 뭉치다, 짐짝을 만들다 | [2757] bundle [4058] fasten |
| **bale** [beyl] | | She slept on a bale of straw last night. | |

| 5307 | | 1. 부스러기 2. 소량 | [3269] scrap [409] bit |
| **crumb** [kruhm] | | She brushed the bread crumbs off the table. | |

| 5308 | 공무원 | 주의를 기울이다, 조심하다 | [481] notice |
| **heed** [heed] | | He paid no heed to her warning. | |

| 5309 | | 1. 역할, 책임 2. 덮개, 외투 3. 덮다 | [5101] cloak [131] leadership |
| **mantle** [MAN-tl] | | He inherited his father's mantle. | [2990] veil |

| 5310 | | 1. 토할 것 같다 2. 재갈(을 물리다) 3. 언론탄압, 보도 금지령 4. 개그 | [2293] joke [6153] hoax |
| **gag** [gag] | | That awful smell made her gag. | |

| 5311 | | 섞이다, 어울리다, 돌아다니다 | [1620] blend [656] mix |
| **mingle** [MING-guhl] | | He didn't know how to mingle with the crowd. | |

| 5312 | | 1. 낱알 모양의 2. 오돌토돌한 | [2206] grainy [1719] rough |
| **granular** [GRAN-yuh-ler] | | A granular salt takes a long time to melt. | |

| 5313 | | 1. (가볍게)두드리다 2. 바르다, 칠하다 3. 소량 | [1838] tap [2768] rub |
| **dab** [dab] | | She dabbed a little bit of foundation onto her face. | [5744] blob |

| 5314 | | 콜라주, 모음(집) | |
| **collage** [kuh-LAHZH] | | He made a collage of stamps. | |

| 5315 | | 1. 전조 2. 선구자, 선배 | [5953] preface |
| **precursor** [pri-KUR-ser] | | The stock market crash was just a precursor to greater economic depression. | |

| 5316 | 공무원 토플 | 1. 끊다, 자제하다, 삼가다 2. 기권하다 | abstinence (절제) abstention (기권) |
| **abstain** [ab-STEYN] | | I am going to abstain from drinking alcohol. | [4708] refrain [848] avoid |

117

5317 **clump** [kluhmp]	1. 응집하다 2. 무거운 발걸음 소리 3. (나무, 덤불 등의)무리, 무더기	[2070] bunch
		[2757] bundle
	Brown rice doesn't clump together very well.	[5265] hoard
		[5744] blob

| 5318 **savannah** [suh-VAN-uh] | 사바나, 열대초원 | |
| | He hoped to walk across the savannah with his wife. | |

5319 토플 **orchid** [AWR-kid]	1. 난초 2. 연자주빛의	[외래어] lavender
		[330] color
	She grows a rare orchid.	

5320 **platter** [PLAT-er]	1. 타원형의 큰 접시 2. 레코드, 음반	[1478] plate
		[332] food
	He served the meat on a beautiful platter.	[1633] disc
		[1758] dish

5321 공무원 **clergy** [KLUR-jee]	성직자들	cleric (성직자)
		[2472] priesthood
	Many of the clergies attended the ceremony.	

5322 공무원 **temperament** [TEM-per-uh-muhnt]	1. 기질, 성미 2. 괴팍함	temperamental (변덕스러운)
		[2103] disposition
	She has the right temperament for the job.	[2055] attitude

5323 **coffin** [KAW-fin]	관	[6796] casket
		[4204] crate
	They watched as the coffin was lowered into the grave.	

| 5324 **detox** [DEE-toks] | 해독(하다) | [2473] detoxification |
| | She is on a detox diet. | |

5325 **thrift** [thrift]	절약, 검약	thrifty (검소한)
		[5592] frugality
	He became a man of fortune thanks to his virtues of thrift and hard work.	[5590] austerity

5326 **crease** [krees]	1. 주름 2. 구기다, 구겨지다	[4064] wrinkle
		[7047] crumple
	There were creases in his uniform.	

| 5327 공무원 **acronym** [AK-ruh-nim] | 두문자어, 약어 | [4590] abbreviation |
| | Do you know what this acronym stands for? | |

| 5328 **peppermint** [PEP-er-mint] | 페퍼민트, 박하 | [3128] mint |
| | I would like a peppermint candy. | |

5329 **rodent** [ROHD-nt]	설치류(쥐, 다람쥐 등)	[2098] mouse
		[4368] bunny
	Rodents have large teeth.	[6133] hare

| 5330 **kneel** [neel] | 무릎 꿇다 | [2702] bow |
| | He knelt to pray. | |

5331 **wade** [weyd]	(물, 진흙 속을)헤치며 건너다, 간신히 나아가다	[3700] paddle [2367] bathe
	They had to wade through the river to the opposite side.	

5332 **symposium** [sim-POH-zee-uhm]	심포지엄, (학술)토론회	[외래어] seminar [647] discussion [1578] convention
	The symposium will last for two days.	

5333 **surname** [SUR-neym]	성	
	How do you spell your surname?	

5334 **revel** [REV-uhl]	1. (술 마시고)흥청거리다 2. 왁자지껄한 잔치	
	The team went to a bar to revel in their victory.	

5335 **scavenger** [SKAV-in-jer] 토플	1. 쓰레기를 뒤지는 사람 2. 도로 청소부	scavenge (쓰레기를 뒤지다) [420] collector
	Her dog is a scavenger, always looking through the trash can.	

5336 **brim** [brim]	1. 가장자리 2. (모자의)챙 3. 가득 채우다, 넘치려 하다	[1070] edge
	The waitress filled our glasses to the brim.	

5337 **apron** [EY-pruhn]	1. 앞치마 2. 격납고	
	She looks good in that yellow apron.	

5338 **bluff** [bluhf]	1. 허세(부리다) 2. 엄포(를 놓다) 3. 절벽	[1595] trick
	He has a bluff way of speaking.	

5339 **impending** [im-PEN-ding]	1. 임박한, 금세 일어날 것 같은 2. 절박한	[4940] imminent [696] approaching [726] soon [2234] brewing
	The actor announced his impending retirement.	

5340 **miscellaneous** [mis-uh-LEY-nee-uhs]	잡다한, 여러 종류의	misc (=miscellaneous) [1535] diverse [7404] sundry
	The junk shop is selling miscellaneous items.	

5341 **fleece** [flees]	양털, 플리스(직물)	[3378] wool [2439] defraud [2774] cheat
	She bought a jacket lined with fleece.	

5342 **nook** [nook]	구석(진 곳), 후미진 곳	[1324] corner [6580] crevice
	I couldn't find my earrings even though I searched every nook and cranny.	

5343 **spade** [speyd]	1. 삽, 가래 2. 스페이드(카드)	[5033] shovel
	He brought back a garden spade and a spray nozzle.	

5344 **badger** [BAJ-er]	1. 오소리 2. 조르다, 괴롭히다	[3275] harass [2465] annoy [3097] bully [5597] nag
	Badgers can dig deep holes.	

5345	토플	1. 마법을 쓰다 2. 탄원하다, 간청하다 3. ~을 상기시키다	[4113] evoke
conjure [KON-jer]		He can conjure a dove out of a hat.	[3388] crave

5346	토익	1. 각서, 비공식 서한 2. 제안서 3. 메모	[외래어] memo
memorandum [mem-uh-RAN-duhm]		The two countries signed a memorandum.	[810] diary [899] announcement

5347	말벌	[5986] hornet
wasp [wosp]	She was stung by a wasp.	

5348	1. 뒤덮다 2. 감추다, 가리다 3. 수의 4. 장막	[997] surface
shroud [shroud]	Air pollution shrouds our cities in clouds of hazardous smog.	[5101] cloak

5349	1. 몰아내다, 떨쳐버리다 2. 추방하다	banishment (추방) [4505] expel
banish [BAN-ish]	I am trying to banish that evil thought from my mind.	[2703] dismiss [5938] dispel

5350	1. 졸이다 2. 밀렵하다 3. 가로채다, 도용하다, 침범하다	poacher (밀렵꾼) [1736] steal
poach [pohch]	They poached pears in red wine.	[4646] reshuffle [4885] smuggle

5351	1. (털을)뽑다 2. 구해내다, 빼내다 3. 꺾다 4. 용기	[929] courage [2865] bravery
pluck [pluhk]	She doesn't know how to pluck her eyebrows.	[3886] grit [5064] snatch

5352	주머니, 낭	[4180] pouch
sac [sak]	Our lungs have millions of tiny air sacs.	

5353	1. 노새 2. 슬리퍼	[5611] donkey
mule [myool]	He has never ridden a mule before.	

5354	1. 병동 2. (ward off로 쓰일 경우) 피하다	[1661] guard
ward [wawrd]	After surgery, I had to remain in my ward for 7 days.	[635] department

5355	하수구	[2028] drain
sewer [SOO-er]	My wedding ring fell into the sewer.	[2718] gutter

5356	지급 불능, 파산	solvent (지급 가능한, 용매)
insolvency [in-SOL-vuhn-see]	The rise in personal insolvencies hints at a national recession.	[3326] bankruptcy [445] breakdown

5357	부드러운, 매우 연한	[2065] gentle [3126] delicate
tender [TEN-der]	He gave the baby a tender kiss.	[6165] supple

5358	끝내다, 해지하다, 해고하다	terminator (근절시키는 자, 몰살자)
terminate [TUR-muh-neyt]	The company terminated my contract.	[3158] abort [4362] abolish

| 5359 **tower** [TOU-er] | 1. 탑, 타워 2. 우뚝 솟다 | [1604] column [3970] surpass |
| | The Eiffel tower is a major tourist attraction. | |

| 5360 **bleachers** [BLEE-cherz] | 경기장 외야 관람석 | [외래어] benches |
| | The ball flew into the bleachers. | |

| 5361 **alumni** [uh-LUHM-nahy] | 졸업생, 동문 | alumnus (동창) |
| | I ran into a Harvard alumni at the conference. | |

| 5362 **stern** [sturn] | 엄하다, 엄격하다 | sternly (엄격히) [1632] severe [2287] strict [5034] grim |
| | He is a stern dad. | |

| 5363 **twitter** [TWIT-er] | 1. 새가 지저귀다 2. (SNS) 트위터 | [6934] chirp [5009] gossip |
| | Birds were twittering all around us. | |

| 5364 **menstruate** [MEN-stroo-eyt] | 월경하다 | [1178] flow |
| | She started menstruating at the age of 14. | |

| 5365 공무원 **lice** [lahys] | (머리의) 이 | louse (lice의 단수형) |
| | The old man had lice in his hair. | |

| 5366 토플 **reed** [reed] | 갈대 | |
| | The birds build their nests with reed. | |

| 5367 **analog** [AN-l-awg] | 아날로그인 | |
| | Analog computers are a thing of the past. | |

| 5368 **exposition** [ek-spuh-ZISH-uhn] | 1. 설명, 해설 2. 전시회, 전람회 | expository (설명하는) expo (=exposition) [1526] exhibition [630] explanation |
| | His exposition contains many meaningful details. | |

| 5369 **slime** [slahym] | 1. 점액 2. 물때 | slimy (끈적한) [6363] muck [5715] goo [5957] ooze |
| | Slimes form in a wet condition. | |

| 5370 **moss** [maws] | 이끼 | mossy (이끼로 덮인) |
| | The rocks were covered with moss. | |

| 5371 GRE **maverick** [MAV-er-ik] | 1. 독단적인 사람, 독불장군 2. 이단아 3. 개성인 | [3398] nonconformist |
| | She was recognized as a bit of a maverick. | |

| 5372 공무원 **gasp** [gasp] | 1. (놀라서) 숨이 막히다 2. 헐떡거리며 말하다 | [2666] pant [2018] breathe [5098] exclamation [6010] whoop |
| | He gasped in pain. | |

5373		긴 여정	[1484] journey
odyssey			[1040] progress
[OD-uh-see]		The film portrays the main character's odyssey to find his true love.	[1490] adventure
			[4183] excursion

5374	토플	사이클론, (인도양 등의)열대성 저기압	[1878] storm
cyclone			[2202] twister
[SAHY-klohn]		The cyclone struck our town last night.	

5375	공무원	1. 게걸스럽게 먹다 2. 집어삼키다 3. 탐독하다	[677] consume
devour			[1255] destroy
[dih-VOU-uhr]		She devoured the entire chocolate cake.	[1998] absorb

5376		1. 술 취한 2. 주정뱅이	drunken (술 취한)
drunk			drunkenness (취한 상태)
[druhngk]		He was too drunk to remember anything.	[1434] stoned

5377		권총 케이스	
holster			
[HOHL-ster]		She put her gun back in its holster.	

5378		도마뱀	[6923] gecko
lizard			[1052] bag
[LIZ-erd]		Lizards can regenerate their tails.	

5379		1. 열정 2. 풍미, 묘미	zesty (열정적인, 풍미의)
zest			[2131] enthusiasm
[zest]		He has a great zest for life.	[1471] flavoring

5380		1. 현장 2. 무대 3. 로컬(컴퓨터 용어)	[128] place
locale			[315] location
[loh-KAL]		The director has found the perfect locale for his new film.	[347] locality

5381	토플	1. 유료 도로 2. (무기) 창 3. 민물고기	turnpike (유료 도로)
pike			[4948] freeway
[pahyk]		I have to drive down the pike to get to work.	[848] avoid

5382	공무원	1. 반박하다, 논박하다, 공박하다 2. 부인하다	refutation (반박)
refute			irrefutable (반박 불가능한)
[ri-FYOOT]		I wish I could refute your argument.	[1037] disprove
			[612] counter

5383		풍자, 비꼼	satirical (풍자적인)
satire			[5462] sarcasm
[SAT-ahyuhr]		The movie was a clever satire on American politics.	[898] criticism
			[6569] banter

5384		결점, 단점, 흠	[2643] flaw
shortcoming			[215] problem
[SHAWRT-kuhm-ing]		The employee only has a minor shortcoming.	[2657] defect
			[3361] deficiency

5385	공무원	1. 신음(하다), 끙끙거리다 2. 불평(하다), 한탄(하다)	[5915] groan
moan			[1782] complain
[mohn]		He was moaning in pain.	[1936] sigh
			[6393] gripe

5386	GRE	1. 무신경한, 무관심한 2. 거만한, 오만한 3. 기사, 호위무사	[3719] knight
cavalier			[6691] condescending
[kav-uh-LEER]		She lives a cavalier life, not thinking about the future.	

5387 **adjective** [AJ-ik-tiv]	형용사	
	How many adjectives are in that paragraph?	

5388 **cartilage** [KAHR-tl-ij]	연골(조직)	[1646] bone
	Joints are typically surrounded by cartilages.	

5389 **dissect** [dih-SEKT]	1. 해부하다 2. 분석하다 3. 나누다	dissection (해부) [871] analyze [92] study
	He dissected a frog in his biology class.	

5390　　수능 **nun** [nuhn]	수녀, 여승	[1622] sister
	The orphanage is run by a nun.	

5391　　공무원 **delinquent** [dih-LING-kwuhnt]	1. 체납되어 있는, 연체된 2. 비행의, 불량의	delinquency (청소년의 비행) [496] overdue [967] criminal
	He has been delinquent in paying his taxes.	

5392 **downright** [DOUN-rahyt]	완전히, 아주, 철저히	[3013] utter [207] completely [4436] outright
	The man was downright rude to her.	

5393　　공무원 **kin** [kin]	친족, 친척	kinship (혈족관계) kindred (=kin)
	His kin is planning on visiting him.	

5394 **frantic** [FRAN-tik]	1. 제정신이 아닌, 심히 흥분한, 미친 2. 정신없이 서두는	frantically (미친듯이) [1133] worried [1987] angry [4877] agitated
	She became frantic when she thought she lost her child.	

5395 **wiggle** [WIG-uhl]	(짧고 빠르게) 꼼지락거리다, 씰룩대다, 뒤흔들다	[2186] swing
	He wiggled his toes out of boredom.	

5396 **womb** [woom]	자궁, 뱃속	[5169] uterus [1864] interior
	She has a baby in her womb.	

5397　　토플 **allegiance** [uh-LEE-juhns]	충성	[2267] loyalty [1348] dedication [2374] adherence
	I give my full allegiance to the company.	

5398 **crater** [KREY-ter]	분화구, 큰 구멍	[1320] hole [1756] decrease [1773] mouth
	Lava was oozing out of the crater.	

5399 **cheesy** [CHEE-zee]	1. 저급한, 유치한 2. 치즈 맛이 나는	[1230] cheap [1776] crazy
	That teen movie was so cheesy.	

5400　　GRE **venerable** [VEN-er-uh-buhl]	공경/존경할 만한	venerate (존경하다) veneration (존경, 공경) [4313] revered [1677] grand
	He works at a venerable institution.	

5401		고명(을 얹다), 장식을 달다	
garnish			
[GAHR-nish]		The chef garnished the dish with mint sprigs.	

5402	공무원 토플	히스테리, 병적 흥분, 열광	[5288] frenzy
hysteria			[1198] fear
			[4877] agitation
[hi-STER-ee-uh]		She was on the verge of hysteria.	[7009] delirium

5403		자기(제품)	[1796] pottery
porcelain			[3540] ceramic
[PAWR-suh-lin]		These cups are porcelain.	

5404	토플	착수, 발단, 최초	[279] beginning
outset			
[OUT-set]		We knew we were going to fail from the outset.	

5405	공무원	상호간의, 호혜적인	reciprocity (서로 도움이
reciprocal			되는 관계) reciprocate
			(보답하다, 답례하다)
[ri-SIP-ruh-kuhl]		Our relationship is based on reciprocal trust and respect.	[2730] mutual

5406	공무원	1. 엄중한, 엄격한 2. 긴박한, 절박한	[2287] strict
stringent			[1022] demanding
			[1507] binding
[STRIN-juhnt]		The government introduced a new set of stringent regulations.	

5407		태아	
fetus			
[FEE-tuhs]		All major body organs are already present in a fetus.	

5408		1. 체로 거르다 2. 면밀히 조사하다 3. 분리하다, 가려내다	[6535] sieve
sift			[871] analyze
			[1004] investigate
[sift]		Sift the flour, baking powder, and salt into a large bowl.	[4135] comb

5409	토익	탁송(물), 배송(물)	consign (위탁하다)
consignment			[499] delivery
			[1062] distribution
[kuhn-SAHYN-muhnt]		We will ship this consignment of clothes pretty soon.	

5410		1. 고삐 2. 통솔권 3. 억제하다, 통제하다	[4189] curb
rein			[131] leadership
[reyn]		The donkey responded to even the slightest pull on the rein.	

5411		1. 부속, 부가 2. 부가사(문법)	[5016] appendage
adjunct			[919] stuff
[AJ-uhngkt]		He was an adjunct professor.	

5412	토익	출납원, 계산원	[318] accountant
cashier			[3472] clerk
[ka-SHEER]		Don't forget to pay the cashier.	

5413	공무원	1. 프리즘, 분광기 2. 각기둥	
prism			
[PRIZ-uhm]		A prism refracts sunlight into various colors.	

5414	공무원	겁쟁이, 비겁한(사람)	cowardly (검쟁이다운)
coward			[1640] chicken
			[970] baby
[KOU-erd]		Stop being a coward and speak up for yourself.	[6974] wimp

5415 **dusk** [duhsk]	땅거미, 황혼, 해질녘	dusky (어둑어둑한) [4773] twilight
	He works from dawn to dusk.	

5416 **cactus** [KAK-tuhs]	선인장	
	You don't need to water your cactus.	

5417 공무원 **contagious** [kuhn-TEY-juhs]	(접촉)전염성의	[1374] infectious [1186] deadly [2113] ill [6385] endemic
	This infection is highly contagious.	

5418 공무원 GRE **scribe** [skrahyb]	서기, 필기자	circumscribe (경계에 선 을 긋다, 제한하다) [2213] journalist
	In the old days, illiterate people would often hire scribes.	

5419 공무원 GRE **impeccable** [im-PEK-uh-buhl]	결점없는, 완벽한	impeccably (결점없이) [414] perfect [4360] exquisite [5515] immaculate
	He has an impeccable work ethic.	

5420 공무원 **conspicuous** [kuhn-SPIK-yoo-uhs]	두드러진, 눈에 잘 띄는, 뚜렷한	inconspicuous (두드러 지지 않은) [1079] obvious [1582] apparent
	The shy girl hates being conspicuous among her colleagues.	

5421 **roundabout** [round-uh-BOUT]	1. 우회적인, 둘러가는, 완곡한 2. 로터리	[1908] circuitous [195] indirect
	He took a roundabout route to avoid the traffic.	

5422 **anal** [EYN-l]	1. 항문의 2. 꼼꼼한	[4488] fussy
	He had an injury to the anal sphincter.	

5423 고등 **cape** [keyp]	1. 망토 2. 곶, 갑	[5101] cloak
	Was she wearing a cape?	

5424 토플 **sanitation** [san-i-TEY-shuhn]	1. 위생(시설) 2. 하수구 설비	[4007] hygiene [559] cleanliness
	Many people in the world still don't have access to the sanitation system.	

5425 **booze** [booz]	술(을 들이키다)	boozy (술취한) [862] drink [1674] alcohol
	She bought some booze for the party.	

5426 공무원 토플 GRE **sparse** [spahrs]	부족한, 희박한, 드문	sparsely (드물게) [6382] scanty [197] little [1017] infrequent
	He only has a sparse amount of hair.	

5427 **quaint** [kweynt]	예스러운, 색다른, 기발한	[1843] odd [1417] old-fashioned [2115] curious [4006] bizarre
	We visited the quaint town over the weekend.	

5428 **aerodynamic** [air-oh-dahy-NAM-ik]	공기역학의	[3740] sleek
	The aerodynamic design of the car makes it steady even in the harsh wind.	

5429 **giggle** [GIG-uhl]		낄낄거리다 He just couldn't stop giggling.	[1863] laugh [5601] chuckle
5430 **prognosis** [prog-NOH-sis]		1. 진찰 2. 경과 예측, 예상 Surveys prove that doctors are overly optimistic when making a prognosis.	[2429] forecast [1439] diagnosis [1452] prediction
5431 **berth** [burth]		1. (선박, 기차의)침상, 숙소 2. 품다, 정착하다 The passenger slept on the berth.	[2992] dock [1389] port
5432 **twitch** [twich]		1. 경련(이 오다), 씰룩거리다 2. 홱 잡아당기다 I had a twitch in my left eye.	[4235] jerk [4191] blink [6239] flutter
5433 **elicit** [ih-LIS-it]	GRE	이끌어 내다, 유도해 내다, 도출하다 The comedian failed to elicit laughter from the audience.	[4113] evoke
5434 **boycott** [BOI-kot]		보이콧(하다), 불매(하다) People decided to boycott the company's products.	[2030] reject [848] avoid
5435 **pamper** [PAM-per]		소중히 하다, 애지중지하다 Mothers often pamper their children.	[3592] indulge [5189] gratify
5436 **slit** [slit]		구멍, 틈(을 만들다) She slit open the envelope.	[1800] split [4005] aperture [5562] cleavage
5437 **vandalism** [VAN-dl-iz-uhm]		기물 파손, 만행 He was charged with vandalism after spraying some paint on the sculpture.	vandalize (기물을 파손하다) [2821] mischief
5438 **jihad** [JI-hahd]		1. 종교적 투쟁, 지하드 2. 성전 This region is becoming a hotbed of global jihad.	jihadist (종교 투쟁자) [4314] crusade
5439 **vertex** [VUR-teks]		꼭짓점, 정점, 최고점 He likes eating pizzas from the vertex to the crust.	[1868] peak [1488] joint
5440 **assimilate** [uh-SIM-uh-leyt]	토플	1. 동화되다, 흡수하다, 비슷해지다 2. 이해하다 She was required to assimilate into the new environment.	assimilation (흡수) [1998] absorb [614] measure [1546] comprehend
5441 **karma** [KAHR-muh]	공무원	인과응보, 업보 She strongly believes in karma.	[3007] fate
5442 **relish** [REL-ish]	GRE	1. 즐기다 2. 맛, 풍미, 향기 I relish a long hot bath after a hectic day at work.	[53] like [5379] zest

5443	공무원 토플 GRE	우울한, 어두운, 비관적인	[6493] dismal
gloomy			[1363] cloudy
[GLOO-mee]		Their future looks very gloomy.	[5795] bleak

5444	공무원 GRE	일상적인, 현세의, 속세의	[2503] ordinary
mundane			[70] day-to-day
[muhn-DEYN]		She loves enjoying a mundane evening at home.	[7418] banal

5445	1. 곰곰히 고민하다 2. (알을)품다 3. 종족	[1133] worry
brood		[4655] offspring
[brood]	There's no need to brood over this issue.	

5446	1. 주둥이, 입부분 2. 총구 3. 재갈을 물리다, 입마개를 씌우다	[2044] silence
muzzle		[439] stop
[MUHZ-uhl]	My dog has a flat muzzle.	

5447	공무원 GRE	잠자는, 휴면기의, 활동휴지중인	dormancy (휴면 상태)
dormant			[105] backward
[DAWR-muhnt]		Many animals are dormant in winter.	[990] asleep

5448	1. 회색의 2. 으스스한	grizzled (머리 색이 회색인)
grizzly		
[GRIZ-lee]	I have never seen a grizzly bear before.	[2154] gray

5449	공무원 GRE	카모플라주(하다), 위장(하다), 속이다	[3948] disguise
camouflage			[2144] mask
[KAM-uh-flahzh]		He attempted to camouflage his real personality.	[5101] cloak

5450	1. 오금의 힘줄, 뒷다리 관절의 힘줄 2. 방해하다	[4960] cripple
hamstring		[5797] debilitate
[HAM-string]	The runner accidentally pulled his hamstring.	

5451	미적분(학)	[1420] mathematics
calculus		[1282] calculation
[KAL-kyuh-luhs]	She didn't pass the calculus exam.	[5050] algebra

5452	1. 정부, 애인 2. 여주인 3. 여교사	[1662] lady
mistress		
[MIS-tris]	The politician had many mistresses.	

5453	(스케이트, 아이스)링크	[482] field
rink		[2292] gym
[ringk]	They skated around the rink.	

5454	1. 실질적인, 본질적인 2. 명사의	[1432] substantial
substantive		[541] main
[SUHB-stuhn-tiv]	The company needs to make substantive changes to survive.	

5455	1. 돌리다, 회전하다 2. 회전대, 회전 고리	[3522] pivot
swivel		[278] turn
[SWIV-uhl]	Can you swivel your head?	[3577] revolve

5456	1. 마취약의, 마취성의 2. 마약 3. 진정제, 수면제	[953] drug
narcotic		[2260] calming
[nahr-KOT-ik]	Morphine is a narcotic.	

5457 **shack** [shak]	오두막, 판잣집, 가건물	[4622] hut [189] live [2642] cabin [3357] cottage
	The poor family lived in a shack.	
5458 토익 토플 편입 **embed** [em-BED]	깊이 박다, 끼워 넣다	imbedded (내장된) [3385] implant [86] include [247] enclose
	There were many jewels embedded in the crown.	
5459 **howl** [houl]	1. (울부)짖다, 아우성치다 2. 윙윙거림(바람 소리)	[4320] roar [2068] cry [5746] growl [5915] groan
	The dogs were howling last night.	
5460 편입 **synopsis** [si-NOP-sis]	개요, 요약, 적요	[1764] summary [1592] recap
	This is a five-page synopsis of the 200-page book.	
5461 편입 **stout** [stout]	1. 짜리몽땅한, 통통한 2. 용감한, 굳센	[498] strong [1328] fat
	She didn't like her stout body.	
5462 토플 편입 **sarcastic** [sahr-KAS-tik]	비꼬는, 빈정거리는	sarcasm (비꼼, 풍자) [3248] ironic [1565] acid
	Stop being sarcastic.	
5463 **bravo** [BRAH-voh]	브라보(감탄사)	[3724] acclaim
	I gave my daughter a bravo after she demonstrated her piano skills.	
5464 **parrot** [PAR-uht]	1. 앵무새 2. 앵무새처럼 말을 되풀이하다 (혹은 그런 사람)	[2906] echo [1201] repeat [4341] recite
	He keeps a parrot as a pet.	
5465 **limp** [limp]	1. (다리를)절뚝거리다 2. 기운이 없는, 축 처진	[7271] hobble [259] listless [3494] stumble
	She was limping slightly.	
5466 편입 **celestial** [suh-LES-chuhl]	하늘의, 천체의, 천국의	[2519] divine [542] beautiful [2221] angelic
	I don't believe in celestial creatures.	
5467 **trolley** [TROL-ee]	1. 손수레, 카트 2. 노면 전차	[2717] cart [1633] disk [외래어] drum
	She rolled the trolley across the floor.	
5468 **spool** [spool]	실을 감는 패(에 감다)	[3713] reel [1218] wind [2818] cylinder
	Can you pass me that spool of black thread?	
5469 편입 GRE **zeal** [zeel]	열의, 열중	zealous (열성적인) zealot (열광자) [2131] enthusiasm [652] determination
	Nothing could suppress his zeal for politics.	
5470 **physics** [FIZ-iks]	물리학	
	Chemistry and physics are two important fields of study.	

5471			
muffle	1. 소리를 죽이다 2. 덮다, 감싸다		muffler (머플러, 소음기)
			[5984] stifle
[MUHF-uhl]	They put a carpet over the floor to muffle some of the noise.		[1186] deaden
			[3136] dampen

5472	공무원 토플 편입		
famine	기근, 식량부족		[2470] hunger
			[3497] misery
[FAM-in]	The famine killed so many people.		[4071] drought

5473			
dove	1. 비둘기 2. dive의 과거형		[367] disappear
			[2596] dip
[duhv]	The dove is a symbol of peace.		

5474	토플 편입 GRE		
exalt	1. 칭찬하다, 칭송하다 2. 승격/격상시키다		exaltation (칭송)
			[2133] glorify
[ig-ZAWLT]	The professor exalted him for his outstanding research.		[2458] praise
			[7455] extol

5475			
clinch	1. 매듭짓다, 결론을 내리다 2. 성사시키다 3. 끌어안음		[1342] settle
			[319] win
[klinch]	The company hopes to clinch the deal.		[1592] cap
			[1808] assure

5476			
bingo	1. 빙고(게임) 2. 옳지, 맞았어		
[BING-goh]	Do you want to play bingo?		

5477			
beep	경적(소리를 내다) 삐/삑(소리를 내다)		
[beep]	She beeped the horn.		

5478			
adjoining	인접하는, 부근의		adjoin (인접해있다)
			[3239] adjacent
[uh-JOI-ning]	The two families booked adjoining rooms at the hotel.		[347] local
			[6356] contiguous

5479	토플 편입		
subside	가라앉다, 침전하다, 잠잠해지다		subsidence (가라앉음, 감퇴)
			[3435] diminish
[suhb-SAHYD]	Her leg pain subsided after she took the medicine.		[2829] descend

5480	공무원 편입		
turmoil	혼란, 소동, 파란		[1581] confusion
			[2288] anxiety
[TUR-moil]	The teacher could not handle the turmoil in her classroom.		[2665] disturbance

5481			
sheath	칼집, 케이스		[231] covering
[sheeth]	You should always carry the blade in its sheath.		

5482			
notary	공증인		notarized (공증받은)
[NOH-tuh-ree]	We need this document verified by a notary.		

5483			
zucchini	주키니(서양호박)		
[zoo-KEE-nee]	She cooked zucchini pasta for dinner.		

5484	공무원 토플 편입 GRE		
aristocracy	귀족 사회, 귀족주의		aristocrat (귀족)
			[2392] elite
[ar-uh-STOK-ruh-see]	Most countries are no longer ruled by the aristocracy.		

5485 **boulder** [BOHL-der]	큰 바위	[1010] rock [1064] earth [4234] gravel
	A boulder has a smooth surface.	

5486 **tummy** [TUHM-ee]	배	[3325] belly [3420] abdomen
	The baby was up all night with a tummy ache.	

5487 **jug** [juhg]	주전자, 항아리	[1451] bottle
	He filled the jug with cold milk.	

5488 **dagger** [DAG-er]	단도, 단검, 비수	[2080] knife [2010] blade [6927] bayonet
	Put the dagger back in its sheath.	

5489 **temperance** [TEM-per-uhns]	절제, 금주	[2196] moderation [4868] sober
	Temperance enhances many physical features.	

5490 공무원 **uptake** [UHP-teyk]	1. 섭취, 흡수 2. 이해	[2531] intake
	Drinking too much alcohol can reduce the uptake of some important nutrients.	

5491 토플 **quarry** [KWAWR-ee]	1. 채석장 2. 캐내다, 찾아내다 3. 사냥감	[3868] prey
	He works at the rock quarry.	

5492 **nugget** [NUHG-it]	1. (귀금속) 덩어리 2. 가치있는 것	[3684] lump
	She was digging the ground to find a gold nugget.	

5493 공무원 편입 **tyranny** [TIR-uh-nee]	압제, 독재	tyrant (폭군) [3005] dictatorship [771] authoritarianism [3470] cruelty
	After the fall of the dictator, the country finally became free from tyranny.	

5494 **swan** [swon]	백조	
	The swans are white.	

5495 **casserole** [KAS-uh-rohl]	캐서롤 (냄비째 내놓는 찜류의 요리)	[4902] stew
	She cooks the best casserole in the world.	

5496 **grille** [gril]	(쇠)창살, 그릴	[2508] grill
	They were separated by a grille.	

5497 편입 **detract** [dih-TRAKT]	1. 손상시키다, 떨어뜨리다 2. (주의를)딴 데로 돌리다	[3435] diminish
	These minor faults do not detract from the overall quality of the film.	

5498 공무원 **scour** [SKOUuhr]	1. 문질러 닦다, 청소하다 2. 뒤지다, 찾아 헤매다	[3537] scrub
	She scoured the sink all day.	

5499		
puncture	1. (타이어)펑크(가 나다), 구멍(을 뚫다) 2. (자존심 등이)없어지게 하다	[3818] pierce
[PUHNGK-cher]		[1766] tear
	The tire was punctured by a nail.	

5500		
buffalo	버팔로(아메리카 들소), 물소	[5913] bison
[BUHF-uh-loh]	Buffalos and cows look the same to me.	

Allvoca.com

#5501~#6000

외국인으로서 상급 수준이며 토익 만점 또는 토플 110점 이상의 어휘력이다. 불편함 없이 영문 소설을 읽는 것이 가능한데, 종종 섬세한 뉘앙스를 이해하지 못하는 일이 발생한다. 그러므로 레벨6 학습자에게는 해외 베스트셀러를 활용한 보충 학습을 추천한다. NYT Best Seller, Amazon Best Seller 등을 참고하라.

LEVEL **06**

5501		
caterpillar	애벌레, 모충	[4855] larva
[KAT-uh-pil-er]	This caterpillar will turn into a butterfly.	

5502 공무원 편입		
livelihood	생계, 살길, 민생	[303] employment [1063] income
[LAHYV-lee-hood]	She is earning her livelihood as a translator.	

5503		
bandage	붕대(를 감다)	
[BAN-dij]	He put a bandage on her arm.	

5504 편입		
watershed	분수령, 중대한 분기점	[1147] milestone
[WAW-ter-shed]	Getting into a prestigious college was a watershed moment in her life.	

5505		
lily	백합	
[LIL-ee]	She likes the smell of lilies.	

5506		
raffle	1. 추첨식 판매법 2. 복권 판매 3. 폐물, 쓰레기	[4126] lottery [2212] betting [3370] gamble
[RAF-uhl]	Many people purchased tickets for a raffle at the fair.	

5507		
cremation	화장, 소각	cremate (시체를 화장하다) [6879] incinerating
[KREE-mey-shuh n]	Her grandmother's cremation was a sad affair.	

5508		
canister	깡통, 금속 용기	[503] container [1557] bowl [3832] basin
[KAN-uh-ster]	She was carrying around a cookie canister.	

5509 공무원 토플		
amass	모으다, 축적하다, 쌓다	[2732] accumulate [420] collect [2435] assemble
[uh-MAS]	He has amassed a huge fortune from his film.	

5510		
treble	1. 3배의, 3개 파트의 2. 높은 음역대	[2912] triple
[TREB-uhl]	She earns treble my salary.	

5511		
crimson	1. 진홍색 2. 새빨개지다	[5987] scarlet [6025] maroon
[KRIM-zuhn]	Crimson is my favorite color.	

5512 편입 GRE		
succumb	굴복하다, 지다	[2116] yield [2702] bow
[suh-KUHM]	She thought he would succumb to her charm.	

5513 편입		
unravel	풀다, 해결하다, 해명하다	[1313] solve [317] understand [1172] resolve
[uhn-RAV-uhl]	He unraveled the long rope.	

5514 편입		
comrade	동지, 동무(공산국에서 쓰는 호칭)	[3510] buddy [51] co-worker [288] friend
[KOM-rad]	They visited their injured comrade.	

5515 공무원 편입	오점없는, 흠없는, 깨끗한	immaculately (흠 잡을 것 없이)
immaculate [ih-MAK-yuh-lit]	After hours of cleaning, the house looks immaculate.	[940] spotless [559] clean

5516 공무원 편입 GRE	사악한, 불길한, 험악한	[5300] ominous
sinister [SIN-uh-ster]	The town looked sinister just in time for Halloween.	[1930] evil [4977] dire

5517 공무원 편입 GRE	1. 잠정적인 2. 망설이는, 머뭇거리는	tentatively (망설이며)
tentative [TEN-tuh-tiv]	Due to the bad weather, the plane's arrival time is tentative.	[3227] hesitant [385] uncertain [1342] unsettled

5518 공무원 편입 GRE	1. 단조로운, 개성없는 2. 순한, 상냥한	[3731] dull
bland [bland]	He has a bland personality.	[1109] boring [5779] stale [7418] banal

5519	1. 발사체, 발사 무기 2. 추진하는	[외래어] missile
projectile [pruh-JEK-til]	The projectile exploded after hitting a building.	[2888] rocket

5520 토플	1. 터키석 2. 청록색	
turquoise [TUR-koiz]	She likes wearing her turquoise necklace.	

5521	불가사리	
starfish [STAHR-fish]	John discovered a starfish in the ocean.	

5522	녹다, 해동하다, 누그러지다	[2362] melt
thaw [thaw]	The snow finally began to thaw.	[3086] dissolve [3249] defrost

5523 토플	몰수하다, 압수하다	confiscation (몰수)
confiscate [KON-fuh-skeyt]	The teacher confiscated her phone.	[2664] seize [979] appropriate

5524 편입	은밀한, 비밀의, 숨은	covertly (은밀히)
covert [KOH-vert]	The police finally discovered the criminal's covert plan.	[1334] secret [1262] hidden [7474] surreptitious

5525	발을 구르다, 쿵쿵	[2609] stamp
stomp [stomp]	He stomped his foot out of frustration.	[533] walk

5526 공무원	상품, 제품, 도자기류	tableware (식탁용 식기류)
ware [wair]	The shop owner reduced the price of the ware he was selling.	[1711] fabric [3320] commodity

5527 공무원 편입	열거하다, 나열하다, 세다	enumeration (열거)
enumerate [ih-NOO-muh-reyt]	It is hard to enumerate all the people who have helped me over the years.	[507] itemize [675] register [1282] calculate

5528	대걸레(로 닦다)	[6214] swab
mop [mop]	The students volunteered to mop the classroom floor.	[1357] wash [2791] towel [외래어] sponge

5529 **violet** [VAHY-uh-lit]	1. 보라색 2. 제비꽃	[2745] purple
	I'm wearing a violet dress today.	

5530 **knuckle** [NUHK-uhl]	손가락 마디, 주먹	[1488] joint
	She cracked her knuckles.	

5531 **fling** [fling]	1. 내던지다 2. 퍼붓다 3. 즐기다	[2890] toss [1030] throw
	He flung his arms around her.	

5532 **deacon** [DEE-kuhn]	부제, (교회)집사	[1558] minister
	He was the deacon of a local church.	

5533 토플 **vertebrate** [VUR-tuh-brit]	척추 동물	vertebra (척추) invertebrate (무척추동물) [4100] mammal [109] creature
	The body of a vertebrate is symmetrical on both sides.	

5534 **facade** [fuh-SAHD]	1. (건물의) 외관, 정면 2. (실제와는 다른) 겉모습, 허울	[552] front [330] color [1404] dishonesty [3006] exterior
	The facade of the church is beautifully decorated.	

5535 편입 **protrude** [proh-TROOD]	튀어나오다, 내밀다, 돌출되다	protrusion (돌출) [5287] bulge
	My neighbor's car always protrudes into my driveway.	

5536 토익 **concierge** [kon-see-AIRZH]	(아파트나 건물의) 관리인, 수위	[453] attendant
	The concierge opened the door for me.	

5537 **archetype** [AHR-ki-tahyp]	(사물의 기준이 되는 형) 전형	archetypal (전형적인) [4529] paradigm [627] example
	Germany is the archetype of a post-reunification country.	

5538 공무원 편입 **erroneous** [uh-ROH-nee-uhs]	오류가 있는, 잘못된	[906] wrong [662] incorrect [2138] faulty [4480] false
	She made an erroneous assumption about me.	

5539 **homestead** [HOHM-sted]	(집과 부속지를 포함하는) 농가	[1428] estate [4963] orchard
	The couple moved to the countryside and set up a homestead.	

5540 **whey** [hwey]	(우유에서 지방을 제거한 액체인) 유장	
	Whey is used to produce cheese and butter.	

5541 **precinct** [PREE-singkt]	(경찰 행정 목적으로 나뉜 도시 등의) 구역	[1155] district [1246] neighborhood
	The crime rate in this precinct is very high.	

5542 **stepfather** [STEP-fah-ther]	새아빠, 양아버지	stepmother (새엄마) stepson (의붓아들) stepdaughter (의붓딸)
	He is not my biological father. He is my stepfather.	

5543 theorem [THEE-er-uhm]	GRE	(수학이나 과학 등의) 정리, 명제	[1115] proposition [6355] axiom
		The scientific theorem confused the students.	

5544 crib [krib]		(빗장으로 보호된) 유아용 침대	[5102] cradle [2774] cheat [3971] bunk [5948] cot
		The baby fell out of her crib.	

5545 wobble [WOB-uhl]		흔들리다, 불안정하다	wobbly (흔들리는) [4408] sway [2186] swing [6501] falter
		The shelf will wobble if you put anything heavy on it.	

5546 lineage [LIN-ee-ij]		가문, 혈통	[3776] clan [4063] descent
		Noble families in England have a royal lineage.	

5547 partake [pahr-TEYK]	공무원	1. (제공된 음식이나 음료를) 섭취하다 2. 참여하다, 같이하다	partaker (참여자) [601] eat
		Would you like to partake some cheese?	

5548 gravy [GREY-vee]		(육즙으로 만든 소스인) 그레이비, 고기 소스	[1190] dressing
		Try dipping the bread in gravy.	

5549 conservatory [kuhn-SUR-vuh-tawr-ee]		1. 온실 2. 음악이나 인문학 중심 대학	
		Plants are growing in the conservatory.	

5550 obscene [uhb-SEEN]		외설한, 추잡한	obscenity (외설함) [1914] dirty [4802] coarse
		Children should not watch obscene movies.	

5551 warden [WAWR-dn]		감시인, 교도관	[2617] guardian [1066] administrator
		The warden is monitoring the prisoners.	

5552 vogue [vohg]	토플	인기, 유행	[1417] fashion [735] popularity
		Short skirts became the vogue.	

5553 shin [shin]		1. 정강이 2. (팔과 다리를 사용해 나무 등을) 타고 올라가다	[1493] lift
		The football player bruised her shin.	

5554 madam [MAD-uhm]		(격식있는 상황에서 여성을 칭하는 호칭인) 마담, 부인	[307] woman
		Madam, could you please help me?	

5555 hotline [HOT-lahyn]	토익	(상담이나 특정 문제 해결을 위한) 직통 전화	
		There is a national hotline for people suffering from depression.	

5556 saline [SEY-leen]		1. 염분을 포함한, 소금의 2. 짠	salinity (염분) [5732] briny
		The students used saline solution for the science experiment.	

5557	편입	1. 소음, 소란 2. (테니스나 배드민턴 등에 사용되는) 라켓	
racket			
[RAK-it]		Where is this terrible racket coming from?	

5558	공무원	1. 짧은 털(을 곤두세우다) 2. ~이 가득하다, ~으로 뒤덮이다	
bristle			
[BRIS-uh l]		The old man had a few white bristles on his chin.	

5559	공무원 토플 편입	딱딱하지만 부서지기 쉬운, 부러지기 쉬운	[1445] weak
brittle			
[BRIT-l]		When you become old, your bones become brittle.	

5560		수직의, 직각을 이루는	[2302] vertical [1233] straight
perpendicular			
[pur-puhn-DIK-yuh-ler]		The cliff was nearly perpendicular.	

5561		(빨리 멈추거나 방향을 전환하는 도중) 미끄러지다	[2086] slip [1574] slide [3393] drift [4016] glide
skid			
[skid]		The bus skidded to a halt.	

5562		1. 균열, 분열 2. 가슴골	cleave (나누다, 고수하다) [920] division [117] difference [5037] rift
cleavage			
[KLEE-vij]		There is a cleavage between the rich and the poor.	

5563	편입	동굴, 땅굴	[2886] cave
cavern			
[KAV-ern]		The cavern remained unexplored for centuries.	

5564		1. 보초, 파수병 2. 파수병을 두다, 보초를 세우다	[1661] guard
sentinel			
[SEN-tn-l]		A soldier stood sentinel at the gates of the castle.	

5565	공무원 편입	빛나는, 밝은	luminary (발광체, 전문가) [1397] bright [2178] brilliant [6193] incandescent
luminous			
[LOO-muh-nuhs]		The luminous glow of the moon lit up the night sky.	

5566		백혈병	
leukemia			
[loo-KEE-mee-uh]		She is suffering from leukemia.	

5567	토플	너비에 비해 길이가 긴, 길쭉한	elongation (늘어남) elongate (잡아 늘이다) [1605] stretched
elongated			
[ih-LAWNG-gey-tid]		Giraffes have elongated necks.	

5568	토플	석공직, 석공업	mason (석공)
masonry			
[MEY-suh n-ree]		Her hands became rough from masonry.	

5569	토익	구내 식당, 급식실	[외래어] cafe
cafeteria			
[kaf-i-TEER-ee-uh]		The students went to the cafeteria to have lunch.	

5570	편입	1. 국외 거주자, 본인의 국적과 다른 나라에서 사는 사람 2. 국외 거주자의	expat (=expatriate) [4456] exile [2423] immigration
expatriate			
[eks-PEY-tree-eyt]		She is a Korean expatriate living in America.	

5571	자만심이 강한	[4589] arrogant
		[7067] brash
cocky		
[KOK-ee]	The host of the party was cocky to all guests.	

5572 토플 편입 GRE	(부정할 수 없는 진리로 여겨지는) 교리, 교의	dogmatic (고집이 강한)
		[3022] doctrine
dogma		[1219] theory
[DAWG-muh]	Copernicus rejected the scientific dogma of the 16th century.	[4863] creed

5573	1. 낙하산 2. (긴급 상황에서) 기존의 절차 외의 방식으로 고용되다	[396] send
parachute		
[PAR-uh-shoot]	She was severely injured because her parachute failed to open.	

5574 공무원 GRE	과소비하는, 사치스러운	extravagance (사치)
		extravaganza (화려한 쇼)
extravagant		[1738] excessive
[ik-STRAV-uh-guhnt]	Taking taxis is extravagant.	[1130] expensive

5575	개집	[2642] cabin
		[247] enclosure
kennel		
[KEN-l]	The dog sleeps in the kennel.	

5576	1. 둥글고 납작한 것 2. 귓불	
lobe		
[lohb]	The lobes of the leaf were even.	

5577	악어	
crocodile		
[KROK-uh-dahyl]	Crocodiles eat small animals and fish.	

5578	속임수, 술책, 트릭	gimmicky (속임수의)
		[562] device
gimmick		
[GIM-ik]	The politician's policies were only gimmicks.	

5579 편입	1. 흠, 결점 2. 손상시키다, 흠을 내다	unblemished (흠집 없는)
		[2643] flaw
blemish		[1043] injury
[BLEM-ish]	She has a few blemishes on her skin.	[6036] blot

5580 공무원	1. 가장자리, 끝 2. (어떤 일이 일어나기) 직전, 찰나	[1070] edge
		[3957] periphery
brink		[4255] fringe
[bringk]	The car stopped at the brink of the cliff.	

5581	빙산	[4554] glacier
iceberg		
[AHYS-burg]	Icebergs are melting due to global warming.	

5582	1. (기업이나 단체의 회계 정보를 기록한) 원장, 회계책 2. (무덤의) 대석	
ledger		
[LEJ-er]	The spending of our company is recorded in the ledger.	

5583	1. 여물통 2. (액체가 통과할 수 있게 만든) 배수로	[4050] trench
trough		
[trawf]	The horse is drinking out of the water trough.	

5584	1.거대한 2. (동물) 매머드	[5184] gigantic
		[196] large
mammoth		[2777] enormous
[MAM-uh th]	The Great Depresion was a financial crisis of mammoth proportions.	[6260] colossal

5585		
thorn [thawrn]	(식물의) 가시	thorny (가시가 많은) [3057] spike
	Roses have thorns.	

5586 공무원 편입 GRE		
denounce [dih-NOUNS]	(공공연히) 비난하다, 고발하다	denunciation (비난) [3417] condemn [2120] accuse [2316] blame
	The public denounced the corrupt politician.	

5587		
fumble [FUHM-buhl]	1. 더듬거리다, 어설프게 다루다 2. 실수, 과오, 과실	[7164] grope [6866] botch
	The player fumbled and missed the ball.	

5588 편입 GRE		
paternity [puh-TUR-ni-tee]	아버지임, 부계	paternal (아버지의) [980] fatherhood [1619] birth [3455] ancestry
	The police tracked down the paternity of the child.	

5589		
ovulation [OV-yuh-ley-shuh n]	배란	ovulate (배란하다)
	Ovulation occurs every 28 days.	

5590 공무원 편입 GRE		
austerity [aw-STER-i-tee]	1. 궁핍을 참고 견디는 것 2. 엄숙, 엄격	austere (엄격한) [1632] severity [2788] poverty [3400] rigor
	The war caused citizens to suffer from austerity.	

5591		
utensil [yoo-TEN-suh l]	도구, 기구	[1541] instrument [889] equipment [2766] appliance
	You need writing utensils to take the exam.	

5592 공무원 편입		
frugal [FROO-guh l]	검소한, 절약하는, 알뜰한	frugality (근검절약) [5325] thrifty [256] careful [5917] canny
	He has frugal spending habits.	

5593		
prank [prangk]	장난(치다)	prankster (장난을 치는 사람) [2293] joke [5310] gag
	The children played a prank on their friend.	

5594		
freebie [FREE-bee]	공짜로 얻는 것, 경품, 사은품	[313] present
	Children can get a freebie toy with this meal.	

5595		
reverend [REV-er-uh nd]	1. 목사 2. 성직자	[2472] priest
	The reverend gave a touching sermon.	

5596		
cartel [kahr-TEL]	카르텔, (기업이나 국가들의) 연합	[882] trust [4686] consortium [6371] conglomerate
	OPEC is a cartel of oil producing countries.	

5597		
nag [nag]	1. 잔소리, 괴롭힘 2. 바가지 긁다, 잔소리하다	nagging (잔소리하는) [829] scold [395] force [2465] annoy
	My mom keeps nagging me.	

5598 공무원 편입 GRE		
adept [uh-DEPT]	1. 숙련된, 능숙한 2. 고수	[908] expert [111] able [1760] accomplished
	He is adept at lying.	

5599 공무원 편입 GRE	수수께끼, 불가사의	enigmatic (불가사의한) [5291] riddle [1926] mystery [2475] puzzle
enigma [uh-NIG-muh]	The disappearance of the plane was an enigma.	

5600	툴툴거리다, 불평하다	[5915] groan
grunt [gruhnt]	She grunted that the work was too tiring.	

5601	킬킬 웃다, 싱글싱글 웃다	[5429] giggle [1863] laugh
chuckle [CHUHK-uhl]	He chuckled as he watched TV.	

5602	장난꾸러기의, 못된	[3791] wicked [1930] evil
naughty [NAW-tee]	The naughty children threw their toys on the floor.	

5603	야만인, 미개한 사람, 교양없는 사람	[4762] savage [2084] monster
barbarian [bahr-BAIR-ee-uhn]	Europeans in the 17th century thought all Africans were barbarians.	

5604	전갈	
scorpion [SKAWR-pee-uhn]	Some scorpions are poisonous.	

5605	(폭식, 폭음 등 무언가를) 과도하게 함, 흥청망청함	
binge [binj]	He went on a spending binge and bought five shirts.	

5606 GRE	1. 심사 2. 판결	adjudicate (판결하다) adjudicator (재판관)
adjudication [uh-joo-di-KEY-shuhn]	The professors were in charge of adjudication of the competition.	

5607	우화, 비유담	[2547] fable [2450] tale
parable [PAR-uh-buhl]	The parable of the rabbit and the turtle teaches children the importance of diligence.	

5608 편입 GRE	(어떤 일이) 일어나지 않게 하다, 방해하다	[740] prevent [3025] cease [6169] avert
preclude [pri-KLOOD]	Her disease precluded her from living a normal life.	

5609	계피	
cinnamon [SIN-uh-muhn]	I love cinnamon rolls.	

5610	어뢰(를 사용하여 공격하다)	[3732] wreck [1255] destroy [2015] soldier [5985] guerrilla
torpedo [tawr-PEE-doh]	The ship was hit with a torpedo.	

5611	1. 당나귀 2. 고집이 센 사람, 바보	[1689] horse [2644] fool
donkey [DONG-kee]	The donkey ate a carrot.	

5612 공무원 토플	1. 날씬한 2. 가느다란 3. 마른, 빈약한	[3259] slim [3126] delicate [4148] fragile
slender [SLEN-der]	She is slender.	

5613 **flask** [flask]	1. (과학 실험 용도의) 플라스크 2. (음료를 담는) 작은 병 There are flasks in the laboratory.	[1451] bottle [7008] canteen
5614 편입 **tinged** [TINJ d]	엷게 칠해진 The leaves were tinged red in fall.	tincture (~의 흔적) [4399] tinted [6656] imbue
5615 **pry** [prahy]	1. 꼬치꼬치 캐묻다 2. 지레(로 들춰내다) Please don't pry into about my personal life.	[1004] investigate [3392] poke
5616 공무원 편입 GRE **eloquent** [EL-uh-kwuhnt]	유창한, 화술이 뛰어난 She is an eloquent speaker.	eloquently (유창하게) [3560] articulate [864] affecting [6411] ardent
5617 편입 **paralyze** [PAR-uh-lahyz]	1. 마비시키다 2. 능력을 퇴화하다 He cannot walk because he is paralyzed.	[4960] cripple [1255] destroy [3962] demolish
5618 편입 GRE **whimsical** [HWIM-zi-kuhl]	1. 변덕스러운 2. 특이한, 별난 He is a whimsical person who keeps changing his mind.	whim (갑작스러운 기분) whimsy (특이한) [7268] capricious [514] funny
5619 GRE **complexion** [kuhm-PLEK-shuhn]	1. 피부색 2. 안색, 얼굴빛, 표정 She had a dark and healthy complexion.	[266] feature [330] coloring [4062] hue
5620 **fray** [frey]	1. 닳다, 해지다 2. 마모되다 3. 소동, 싸움 Clothes fray quickly if you wear them often.	[5960] brawl [445] break [4662] melee
5621 편입 **injunction** [in-JUHNGK-shuhn]	(법원에서 내리는) 행동 중지 명령 The judge issued an injunction to stop companies from increasing oil prices.	[2062] ban [6418] admonition
5622 GRE **overt** [oh-VURT]	명백한, 분명한 His hostility was overt.	overtly (명백히) [1079] obvious [65] known [933] definite
5623 공무원 편입 **pinnacle** [PIN-uh-kuhl]	1. 정점 2. (높은) 산봉우리 This invention is the pinnacle of the scientist's career.	[1868] peak [4105] culmination [4870] apex
5624 **triathlon** [trahy-ATH-luhn]	트라이애슬론, (철인) 3종 경기 A triathlon is composed of running, cycling, and swimming.	
5625 **barb** [bahrb]	(미늘이나 가시 등) 뾰족한 것 The fish is hooked on the barb.	barbed (가시가 있는) [3057] spike [898] criticism [2534] arrow
5626 GRE **syllable** [SIL-uh-buhl]	(단어의 한) 음절 The word window has two syllables.	

5627	GRE	(한 민족이나 단체의) 기풍, 정신	[923] spirit
ethos			[1219] theory
[EE-thos]		Our national ethos respects the elderly.	[1355] mentality
			[3642] ideology

5628		~에서 공기를 빼다, 수축하다	deflation (물가 하락)
deflate			deflationary (물가 하락의)
[dih-FLEYT]		The balloon was deflated.	[3179] humble

5629		1. (고기 등을) 잘게 다지다 2. 종종 걷다	[533] walk
mince			[2560] grind
[mins]		Mince the meat and add it to the stew.	[4389] crumble

5630	편입	불법의, 무허가의	[732] illegal
illicit			[3590] forbidden
[ih-LIS-it]		Cocaine is an illicit drug.	[5717] adulterous
			[7029] bootleg

5631		1. (소리, 맛, 색 등이) 부드럽고 감미로운 2. 잘 익은	[1245] soft
mellow		3. (성격이) 느긋하고 태평한	[2260] calm
[MEL-oh]			[3126] delicate
		She has a soft, mellow voice.	[4091] savory

5632	공무원	1. 정신없는, 난장판의 2. 흥분한, 열광적인	[2962] chaotic
hectic			[7255] boisterous
[HEK-tik]		Her schedule is full and hectic.	

5633		1. 사마귀 2. (나무) 옹이 3. 흠집, 결점	[4324] mole
wart			[5579] blemish
[wawrt]		He has a wart on his foot.	

5634		1. 문어 2. 낙지	
octopus			
[OK-tuh-puhs]		An octopus has eight limbs.	

5635		자몽	
grapefruit			
[GREYP-froot]		Grapefruit is bittersweet.	

5636		곡예사	acrobatics (곡예)
acrobat			[4332] tumbler
[AK-ruh-bat]		The acrobat performed an amazing trick.	[1316] dancer
			[4735] clown

5637	편입	1. 밧줄로 매다, 연결시키다 2. (핸드폰을 활용해) 인터넷에 연결하다	untethered (연결이 안된)
tether			[1507] bind
[TETH-er]		The cow was tethered to the tree.	[2605] cord
			[3212] harness

5638	편입	1. (원의 둘레인) 원주 2. ~의 둘레	[4461] perimeter
circumference			[7212] girth
[ser-KUHM-fer-uhns]		The circumference of the circle is 10cm.	

5639	편입	내성적인 사람	introverted (내성적인)
introvert			[1225] reserved
[IN-truh-vurt]		He is introverted and shy.	[2843] loner

5640		불량배, 폭력배	[3541] assassin
thug			[5999] bandit
[thuhg]		He was attacked by thugs at night.	

5641	자위 행위를 하다	masturbation (자위)
masturbate [MAS-ter-beyt]	Many people feel uncomfortable talking about masturbation.	

5642 공무원 편입	솔직한, 숨김없는	candidly (솔직하게) [2168] frank
candid [KAN-did]	The couple had a candid talk about their relationship.	[1404] honest [2107] forthright

5643	(잡힌 포로에 대한) 몸값, 배상금	[4605] redeem [305] price
ransom [RAN-suhm]	The terrorists demanded a large ransom.	

5644 GRE	1. 매개자, 중재자 2. 중간 단계의, 중간 수준의	[2586] intermediate [993] judge
intermediary [in-ter-MEE-dee-er-ee]	The detective communicated with the suspect through an intermediary.	[2654] broker

5645	1. 자갈 2. (도로나 거리에) 자갈을 깔다 3. (구두를) 만들거나 수선하다	cobbled (자갈이 많은) [207] complete
cobble [KOB-uhl]	The car drove over the cobbles.	[2435] assemble

5646 토플	(액체다) 조금씩 떨어지다, 똑똑 흐르다	[241] leave [3096] creep
trickle [TRIK-uhl]	Water trickled from a hole in the machine.	[3406] crawl

5647 GRE	1. 마음아픈 슬픔의, 신랄한 2. (맛이나 향이) 톡 쏘는	poignancy (날카로움) [1692] sad
poignant [POIN-yuhnt]	It is poignant that the soldier died on her birthday.	[2665] disturbing [3130] bitter

5648 공무원 토플 편입	1. 간절히 ~하고 싶어하다, 염원하다 2. 동경하다, 그리워하다	yearning (갈망하다) [1100] desire
yearn [yurn]	The prisoner yearned for freedom.	[83] want [4366] ache

5649	1. 바보같은 2. 장난끼 넘치는	goof (바보같은 짓을 하다) [3103] silly
goofy [GOO-fee]	He is not smart. He is goofy.	[1776] crazy

5650 공무원 편입	신나는, 즐거운, 유쾌하게 만드는	exhilaration (활기) [904] exciting
exhilarating [ig-ZIL-uh-rey-ting]	Riding a rollercoaster is exhilarating.	

5651	지진의	[6841] tectonic
seismic [SAHYZ-mik]	The scientists predicted seismic activity will occur next week.	

5652	1. (과음 이후의) 숙취 2. 후유증 3. 잔여물	[341] historical [4366] headache
hangover [HANG-oh-ver]	I have a bad hangover from the party yesterday.	

5653	1. 선술집 2. 여관, 여인숙	[3425] inn [851] bar
tavern [TAV-ern]	We went to get a drink from the local tavern.	[외래어] hotel

5654	1. 토막, 동강 2. (발가락을) 찧다	stubby (뭉툭한) [4865] rubbish
stub [stuhb]	Did you throw away your ticket stubs?	

5655	공무원	새어나오다, 스며 나오다	[2028] drain
seep			[2707] bleed
[seep]		Blood seeped out the wound.	

5656	GRE	1. 마법, 신비한 것, 불가사의한 것 2. 신비하다, 초자연적이다	
occult			
[uh-KUHLT]		The old man claims to have occult powers.	

5657	공무원 토플 편입	미신	superstitious (미신을 믿
superstition			는)
[soo-per-STISH-uhn]		He believes in superstitions like Bigfoot.	

5658	토플 편입	1. 돌풍 2. (감정 등이) 돌발스러운 것	[452] fit
gust			[2572] blast
[guhst]		A gust of wind blew in through the window.	[3447] breeze

5659	편입	1. 지출금, 지불금 2. 영업비	disburse (지불하다)
disbursement			[160] payment
[dis-BURS-muhnt]		The finance department monitors the company disbursements.	[1130] expenditure
			[6884] outlay

5660		다각형	[949] shape
polygon			
[POL-ee-gon]		A triangle is a polygon with three sides.	

5661	편입	1. (~가 잘보이는) 위치, 장소 2. 우월함, 유리한 상황	[991] advantage
vantage			
[VAN-tij]		From her vantage point, she could see the beach.	

5662		가계, 가문, 족보	[5546] lineage
pedigree			
[PED-i-gree]		I don't care about the pedigree of my pet.	

5663		산수, 계산, 연산	[1420] mathematics
arithmetic			[575] computation
[uh-RITH-muh-tik]		The student failed the arithmetic test.	[1282] calculation

5664	토플 편입	불화, 다툼	[4678] quarrel
feud			[962] argument
[fyood]		It is time to resolve the long feud between the two nations.	[6808] altercation

5665		1. (음식을 액체에) 담그다, 적시다 2. 빠트리다, 빠지게 하다	[3523] immerse
dunk			[2733] soak
[duhngk]		Dunk your donut in coffee.	

5666	편입	섬뜩한, 끔찍한	appalled (섬뜩해하는)
appalling			[3561] dreadful
[uh-PAW-ling]		Murder is an appalling crime.	[2408] alarming
			[2830] horrible

5667		퇴폐적인 (사람), 전락한 (사람)	decadence (타락)
decadent			[4651] degenerate
[DEK-uh-duhnt]		Many people criticize the decadent behavior of the youth.	[1930] evil
			[1980] immoral

5668	공무원 토플	배설하다, 분비하다	excretion (배설)
excrete			[1626] eliminate
[ik-SKREET]		Our body excretes toxins from the body through sweat.	[4609] secrete

5669　　　공무원 GRE **galvanize** [GAL-vuh-nahyz]	1. 의욕을 증진시키다, 동기를 부여하다 2. 아연으로 도금하다 Her parent's support galvanized her to audition.	galvanized (도금된) [2297] stimulate [959] surprise [4014] astonish
5670　　　　　　GRE **meridian** [muh-RID-ee-uhn]	1. (지구의 양 극을 지나는 원) 자오선 2. 자오선의 The meridian is an imaginary line that crosses the North Pole and the South Pole.	
5671　　　공무원 GRE **upbeat** [UHP-beet]	1. (성격이) 긍정적인, 경쾌한 2. (음악에서의) 상승되는 기조 Her upbeat personality made everyone happy.	[2488] cheerful [594] happy [5194] buoyant
5672 **ballast** [BAL-uhst]	1. (배 등이 안정감있게 항해할 수 있도록 두는 무게감 있는 물건인) 밸러스트, 바닥짐, 모래주머니 2. 바닥짐을 두다 Hot air balloons should always travel with a ballast on windy days.	[737] weight [4840] equilibrium
5673 **clockwise** [KLOK-wahyz]	시계방향으로 도는, 오른쪽으로 도는 Turn the lid clockwise to open the bottle.	
5674　　공무원 토플 편입 GRE **affluent** [AF-loo-uhnt]	부유한, 풍족한 She grew up in an affluent family.	affluence (부) [1855] wealthy [3323] prosperous
5675 **coma** [KOH-muh]	혼수상태, 코마 She woke up from the coma after 10 days.	[6183] trance [2574] faint [5292] oblivion [6767] slumber
5676　　　　공무원 **encyclopedia** [en-sahy-kluh-PEE-dee-uh]	백과사전 The encyclopedia contains diverse information.	
5677 **sanitary** [SAN-i-ter-ee]	위생적인, 청결한 The hospital is a sanitary environment.	sanitize (위생적으로 청소하다) [4007] hygienic
5678　　공무원 편입 GRE **concoction** [kon-KOK-shuhn]	혼합물, 혼합 조제물 If you are ill, you should drink this herbal concoction.	concoct (만들다) [656] mixture [332] food [2234] brew
5679　　　　　토플 **eerie** [EER-ee]	음산한, 으스한 The haunted house was eerie.	eerily (음산하게) [5917] uncanny [3594] frightening
5680 **autopsy** [AW-top-see]	(사망 원인을 밝히기 위해 시체를) 부검하다 The police sent the body to the hospital for an autopsy.	
5681　　공무원 토플 편입 GRE **hereditary** [huh-RED-i-ter-ee]	유전의, 세습의 Allergies may be hereditary.	heredity (유전) [2907] inherited [1524] genetic [3079] inborn
5682 **peep** [peep]	1. 훔쳐보다 2. (병아리 등이) 삐약거리다 3. 투정, 불만 She peeped into the empty room.	[4310] peek [3315] glance [6699] hoot

5683 **mermaid** [MUR-meyd]	(신화 등에 등장하는) 인어	
	Mermaids have long, shiny tails.	

5684 토익 **carton** [KAHR-tn]	(판지) 상자, (음식이나 액체를 담는) 곽, 통	[503] container [4204] crate
	Please recycle the milk carton.	

5685 편입 GRE **dubious** [DOO-bee-uhs]	미심쩍은, 수상한	[962] arguable [1849] debatable
	Your argument seems dubious but I will believe you.	

5686 공무원 **uprising** [UHP-rahy-zing]	반란, 폭동	[2690] rebellion [7194] insurrection [7210] mutiny
	There was an uprising against the corrupt ruler.	

5687 **typeface** [TAHYP-feys]	서체, 글씨체	[외래어] font
	Adults prefer a large typeface.	

5688 토플 GRE **amplitude** [AM-pli-tood]	1. 진폭 2. 넓이, 폭	[3934] magnitude
	The scientists tried to detect the amplitude of the waves.	

5689 **backlog** [BAK-lawg]	(특히 밀린 업무의) 축적된 것, 축적량	[1697] delay [2227] inventory [5947] stockpile
	She has a huge backlog of assignments to finish.	

5690 GRE **syllabus** [SIL-uh-buhs]	강의 소개, 교수 요목	[2091] curriculum [5460] synopsis
	Read the syllabus before signing up for the class.	

5691 편입 **perforated** [PUR-fuh-rey-tid]	구멍이 있는, 뚫린	perforation (구멍) perforate (구멍을 뚫다) [3818] pierced [445] broken
	The paper is perforated.	

5692 **nudge** [nuhj]	슬쩍 찌르다	[1013] push
	I nudged my friend to get her attention.	

5693 **gastric** [GAS-trik]	(장기 중) 위의, 위와 관련된	[3420] abdominal
	He has a gastric ulcer.	

5694 공무원 편입 **cumbersome** [KUHM-ber-suhm]	성가신, 방해가 되는	[4916] unwieldy [30] useless [2490] bulky [2760] burdensome
	Some people think bicycle helmets are cumbersome.	

5695 토플 **hoist** [hoist]	들어올리다, 끌어올리다	[1493] lift [3621] erect [6613] heave
	Can you help me hoist my bag?	

5696 공무원 토플 GRE **commonplace** [KOM-uhn-pleys]	1. 흔해빠진, 평범한 2. 상투적인	[2503] ordinary [947] customary [5444] mundane
	Environmentally friendly products are increasingly commonplace.	

| 5697
screenplay
[SKREEN-pley] | 시나리오, 대본 | [1647] script
[266] feature
[2848] cinema |
| | The author wrote a brilliant screenplay. | |

| 5698
showdown
[SHOH-doun] | 최후의 대결, 막판, 결전 | [2869] confrontation
[962] argument
[2063] crisis
[3437] clash |
| | The two presidential candidates had a showdown. | |

| 5699
pact
[pakt] | 협정, 계약 | [738] contract
[427] agreement
[1368] arrangement
[2421] compact |
| | The two companies signed a pact. | |

| 5700   공무원 편입
tremble
[TREM-buhl] | 1. 떨다, 진동하다 2. 떨게하다, 진동시키다 | [1969] shake
[3172] shout
[6239] flutter
[6740] quiver |
| | He trembled with fear. | |

| 5701
excise
[EK-sahyz] | 1. 국내 소비세(를 부과하다), 물품세(를 부과하다) 2. 삭제하다 | excision (삭제)
[1376] duty
[4459] tariff
[5221] surcharge |
| | The government increased the excise on cigarettes. | |

| 5702
veto
[VEE-toh] | 거부권(을 행사하다), 금지권(을 행사하다) | [2030] reject
[1655] denial
[2062] ban
[3590] forbid |
| | China will veto this proposal. | |

| 5703
testicle
[TES-ti-kuhl] | 고환 | [1054] ball
[4820] genitalia |
| | Males have two testicles. | |

| 5704   GRE
conduit
[KON-dwit] | 1. 도관, 수도 2. 연결로 | [1185] channel
[1116] modality
[1919] pipe
[4237] duct |
| | Water passed through the city conduits. | |

| 5705   토플 편입
meteorology
[mee-tee-uh-ROL-uh-jee] | (대기의 현상들을 연구하는 학문인) 기상학 | meteorologist (기상학
자)
[1294] weather |
| | Meteorology is the study of weather and changes in the atmosphere. | |

| 5706
pimple
[PIM-puhl] | 여드름, 뾰루지 | [3785] acne
[5579] blemish |
| | It is natural for teenagers to have pimples. | |

| 5707   공무원 편입
prowess
[PROU-is] | 1. 뛰어난 솜씨, 숙련됨 2. 용기 | [929] courage
[171] experience
[4460] aptitude |
| | Everyone marveled at her athletic prowess. | |

| 5708   토플
translucent
[trans-LOO-suhnt] | (빛만 통과하는) 반투명한 | [2413] transparent
[5565] luminous |
| | The china bowl is translucent. | |

| 5709
marina
[muh-REE-nuh] | (모터보트, 요트 등의) 정박소, 항구 | [2595] harbor |
| | The boats dock at the marina at night. | |

| 5710
pervert
[per-VURT] | 1. 변질된, 도착된 2. 변태 | perversion (틀린 해석)
[2543] corrupt
[373] worsen
[2265] weirdo |
| | The judges perverted the court of justice by punishing the wrong person. | |

5711 **fiance** [fee-AHN-sey]	약혼자	
	My fiance is beautiful and kind.	

5712 **fiduciary** [fi-DOO-shee-er-ee]	1. 신용의, 신탁의 2. 수탁자, 수탁인	[882] trustee [429] protective
	He breached his fiduciary duty to watch over her money.	

5713 **marsh** [mahrsh]	습지, 늪	marshy (습지의) [4496] swamp
	Alligators are living in the marsh.	

5714 **dribble** [DRIB-uhl]	1. (공 등을) 드리블하다, 튕기다 2. (군침을) 흘리다 3. 가랑비(가 내리다)	[5646] trickle [5114] drizzle [5957] ooze
	Dribble the ball to the right.	

5715 **gooey** [GOO-ee]	끈적거리는, 달라붙는	goo (끈적한 것) [915] sticky [1245] soft [5259] viscous
	Glue is gooey.	

5716 편입 GRE **quintessential** [kwin-tuh-SEN-shuhl]	대표적인, 전형적인	quintessentially (본질적 으로) [2262] supreme [972] typical
	Fish and chips is the quintessential British food.	

5717 **adultery** [uh-DUHL-tuh-ree]	간통	adulterer (간통자) [4536] infidelity
	He was enraged to find out that his wife had committed adultery.	

5718 공무원 편입 **bigotry** [BIG-uh-tree]	1. 편견, 편협 2. 고집, 완고함	bigot (편협한 사람) [494] mindset [2625] discrimination [2753] bias
	Racial bigotry must be eradicated.	

5719 **ventricle** [VEN-tri-kuhl]	(심장이나 뇌의) 실	
	The heart has two ventricles.	

5720 **passover** [PAS-oh-ver]	(이집트 탈출을 기념하는 이스라엘 민족의 축제인) 유월절	[4272] Easter
	Passover is celebrated in March or April.	

5721 공무원 편입 GRE **dialect** [DAHY-uh-lekt]	방언, 지방어, 사투리	[1813] speech [2880] accent
	She speaks in a southern dialect.	

5722 **tenor** [TEN-er]	1. 의의, 취지 2. (알토와 바리톤 사이의 음역인) 테너	[1590] tone [2418] mood [6572] gist
	The general tenor of the conference was to find ways to mitigate climate change.	

5723 공무원 **plummet** [PLUHM-it]	(수직으로) 떨어지다, 급격히 저하하다	[4018] plunge [454] fall [1788] crash [2604] collapse
	The value of oil plummeted.	

5724 **blitz** [blits]	1. (군대가) 급습하다 2. 분투하다	[2335] assault [4939] bombardment
	Many people died during the blitz.	

5725 편입 GRE	~에 대한 혐오, 증오	averse (싫어하는)
aversion		[1599] hatred
	I have an aversion to spiders.	[2467] allergy
[uh-VUR-zhuhn]		[7113] animosity

5726 공무원 토플 편입 GRE	(논리적) 오류, 착오	fallacious (틀린)
fallacy		[75] thought
	The notion that the poor are not hardworking is a fallacy.	[3383] deception
[FAL-uh-see]		[4480] falsehood

5727 편입	1. (특정한 감정을) 모으다, 용기를 내다 2. (군인들을) 소집하다	
muster		
	She mustered the courage to ask him out.	
[MUHS-ter]		

5728 공무원	1. 구혼하다, 구애하다 2. ~의 지지를 얻기 위해 노력하다	[1477] pursue
woo		[1603] pitch
	She tried to woo him with a love song.	[3160] cultivate
[woo]		

5729	습진	
eczema		
	Children often suffer from eczema.	
[EK-suh-muh]		

5730	1. 기울다 2. 기울어지게 하다 3. 특정한 (정치적, 사상적) 견해가 있다	[1572] angle
slant		[2304] leaning
	The Leaning Tower of Pisa is slanted.	[2946] slope
[slant]		

5731 토익	호화로운, 호화판의	[1854] luxurious
deluxe		[1130] expensive
	They stayed at a deluxe hotel room.	[2425] elegant
[duh-LUHKS]		

5732	1. 소금물 2. 바닷물	[3245] vinegar
brine		
	Brine is used to preserve fish and vegetables.	
[brahyn]		

5733	변두리, (중심가의) 주변	[3044] suburbs
outskirts		[3957] periphery
	They lived on the outskirts of town.	
[OUT-skurts]		

5734	폭발하다, 터뜨리다	detonation (폭파)
detonate		detonator (기폭 장치)
	The terrorists threatened to detonate the bomb.	[2058] explode
[DET-n-eyt]		[2572] blast

5735	거름(을 주다), 비료(를 주다)	[676] droppings
manure		[3953] compost
	Manure helps plants grow.	
[muh-NOOR]		

5736 편입	1. 긴장감 2. 걱정, 불안	suspenseful (긴장이 넘 치는)
suspense		[2305] tension
	The movie built up suspense.	[2288] anxiety
[suh-SPENS]		

5737 편입 GRE	바꾸다, 대체하다	[673] replace
supersede		[516] overrule
	Smartphones have superseded flip phones.	
[soo-per-SEED]		

5738	(식물의 생식 세포인) 포자, 홀씨	[1449] seed
spore		
	Mushrooms reproduce through spores.	
[spawr]		

5739 공무원 편입		
succulent	1. (과일 등이) 즙이 많은 2. (이야기 등이) 흥미로운	[1937] delicious [1065] tasty [2064] moist [6660] luscious
[SUHK-yuh-luhnt]	She bit into a succulent peach.	

5740		
fixation	(병적인 수준의) 집착	fixate (꽂혀 있는) [2876] obsession [249] interest [2469] fascination
[fik-SEY-shuhn]	The child has a fixation on this doll.	

5741		
kudos	1. 명예, 영예 2. 칭찬, 축하	[2458] praise [5073] applause
[KOO-dohz]	Being a politician has some kudos attached to it.	

5742 공무원		
trespass	1. (타인의 영역을) 침입하다, 침범하다 2. 방해하다	trespasser (무단침입자) [5939] transgress [530] commit [4704] misdemeanor
[TRES-puhs]	Don't trespass my territory.	

5743		
scaffolding	1. (공사 중 임시로 세운 가설물인) 비계 2. 비계 재료	[1120] frame
[SKAF-uhl-ding]	We will tear down the scaffolding after construction.	

5744		
blob	방울, 액체 덩어리	[940] spot [1168] river [3297] bead
[blob]	There is a blob of paint on the wall.	

5745		
contraceptive	피임기구, 피임약	contraception (피임) [외래어] condom
[kon-truh-SEP-tiv]	Contraceptives prevent unwanted pregnancies.	

5746		
growl	1. (맹수가) 으르렁거리다 2. (낮은 목소리로) 화내다	[7081] snarl [5459] howl [5600] grunt
[groul]	The dog growled at me.	

5747		
mercenary	1. 용병 2. 돈을 받고 일하는	[1607] selfish
[MUR-suh-ner-ee]	The country doesn't have enough soldiers so they recruited mercenaries.	

5748 편입		
derail	탈선하다, 이탈하다	derailment (탈선) [5878] thwart [1788] crash [4133] hinder
[dee-REYL]	The car was derailed.	

5749		
indemnify	(법률적으로) 배상하다, 보상하다, 보호하다	indemnity (배상, 보호) [1991] compensate
[in-DEM-nuh-fahy]	The company promised to indemnify the consumers.	

5750		
anoint	1. (종교 의례로) 머리에 기름을 바르다 2. ~를 후계자로 선정하다	[5829] consecrate [1918] bless
[uh-NOINT]	The bishop will be anointed at the ceremony today.	

5751		
alligator	악어	
[AL-i-gey-ter]	Alligators are used to make purses.	

5752 공무원 토플 편입 GRE		
wane	1. 줄어들다, 기울다 2. 종말에 가까워지다, 약해지다	[1792] decline [327] lessen [5902] abate [6835] atrophy
[weyn]	The waning moon seemed ominous.	

5753		(다른 나라로) 이주하다	emigration (이주)
emigrate			[2387] migrate
[EM-i-greyt]		The family planned to emigrate to America.	[2236] depart

5754	편입 GRE	1. 향(을 피우다) 2. 화나게 하다	[6719] infuriate
incense			[2465] annoy
			[3604] aroma
[IN-sens]		Please light up the incense.	[3640] odor

5755	공무원 편입	가명, 일명	
alias			
[EY-lee-uhs]		The author used an alias to publish her books.	

5756	공무원 편입	1. 기념일 2. 축제	jubilation (환희)
jubilee			jubilant (좋아하는)
[JOO-buh-lee]		The town held a jubilee to celebrate the king's long reign.	[1134] celebration

5757	공무원	1. 신장, 키 2. 위상, 명성	[524] standing
stature			[111] ability
[STACH-er]		She is a woman of tall stature.	

5758	토플 편입	1. 양서류의 2. 수륙 양용의	amphibious (양서류)
amphibian			[811] frog
[am-FIB-ee-uhn]		Frogs are amphibians.	[7140] salamander

5759		1. (식물 등이) 시들다 2. 시들게 하다	[6638] droop
wilt			[3435] diminish
[wilt]		The flower wilted.	[3767] glaze

5760	토플	노른자위	
yolk			
[yohk]		Separate the egg yolk and the egg white.	

5761		1. 전망, 풍경 2. 예상, 기대, 희망	[116] view
vista			
[VIS-tuh]		She was amazed by the vista of the mountains.	

5762	공무원 편입 GRE	쓸데없는, 무의미한, 무용한	futility (무의미함)
futile			[30] useless
			[1364] fruitless
[FYOOT-l]		He is very stubborn so trying to convince him is futile.	[3993] hollow

5763		순경, 경관	[1371] detective
constable			
[KON-stuh-buh l]		The constable patrolled the streets.	

5764		1. 시집, 선집, 문집 2. 앨범	
anthology			
[an-THOL-uh-jee]		I would like a Shakespeare anthology for my birthday.	

5765	토플	1. (매, 독수리 등) 육식조 2. (작은) 공룡	
raptor			
[RAP-ter]		Raptors eat mice.	

5766	공무원	잠복(하다), 매복(하다)	[2067] trap
ambush			
[AM-boo sh]		The thieves ambushed the woman on the streets.	

5767	편입	고양이과의	[1361] catlike
feline			[2097] graceful
[FEE-lahyn]		Tigers are part of the feline family.	

5768	편입	1. 구슬리다, 설득하다 2. 형태를 갖추게 하다, 다듬다	[3205] persuade
coax			[4495] entice
[kohks]		He coaxed her into listening to him.	

5769		1. (최후의 만찬 때 쓴) 잔, 성배 2. 열망의 대상	
grail			
[greyl]		The grail can turn water into wine.	

5770		(램프나 양초의) 심지	
wick			
[wik]		Light fire on the candle wick.	

5771	편입 GRE	위선자	hypocritical (위선의)
hypocrite			[3162] pretender
[HIP-uh-krit]		She is a hypocrite who supports animal rights but also eats meat.	[1077] liar
			[5718] bigot

5772		1. 정강이 2. 손잡이, 자루	[2110] stem
shank			
[shangk]		The short pants revealed his shanks.	

5773	편입	1. 고의로 파괴(하다) 2. 방해(하다) 3. 반항(하다)	[3943] undermine
sabotage			[719] damage
[SAB-uh-tahzh]		She sabotaged my plan.	[1255] destruction
			[2573] disruption

5774	토플	1. 달랑거리다 2. 매달다 3. 매달리다	[1331] hang
dangle			[4041] flap
[DANG-guhl]		Earrings are dangling from her hears.	[6638] droop

5775	공무원 토플	1. 꼭 쥐다 2. 걸쇠(를 채우다), 버클(을 채우다)	[3233] clutch
clasp			[553] carry
[klasp]		The child clasped her mother's hand.	

5776	공무원	역경, 시련, 고난	[2063] crisis
ordeal			[4829] agony
[awr-DEEL]		He was sick and tired after his ordeal.	[6156] anguish

5777		샤먼, 무당	
shaman			
[SHAH-muhn]		They called a shaman to drive out evil spirits.	

5778	편입 GRE	1. 참고 문헌 목록 2. 작가의 저서 목록	
bibliography			
[bib-lee-OG-ruh-fee]		Please refer to the bibliography to find the source of this information.	

5779	공무원	1. 굳어진, 신선치 않은 2. 창의성이 없는	[194] musty
stale			[1836] smelly
[steyl]		This bread is stale.	[3457] nasty

5780		1. (어떤 감정을) 자극하다, 유발하다 2. 격려하다	[3638] provoke
incite			[929] encourage
[in-SAHYT]		The proposal incited feelings of love.	[4877] agitate
			[7477] abet

5781 공무원 토플 **playwright** [PLEY-rahyt]	극작가	[1024] author
	There were five playwrights involved in writing this script.	
5782 **memorabilia** [mem-er-uh-BIL-ee-uh]	(중요한 사건이나 사람과 관련된) 기념품	[622] remembrances
	The museum displayed WWII memorabilia.	
5783 **grub** [gruhb]	1. 유충 2. 음식 3. (땅을) 파다	[332] food [3464] worm
	After six months, the grub will become a beetle.	
5784 **annum** [AN-uhm]	(금융 목적으로 사용되는) 해, 년	
	The interest rate is 2% per annum.	
5785 공무원 토플 편입 **plight** [plahyt]	1. 고난, 역경, 어려움 2. 서약, 맹세	[6625] predicament [446] condition [2063] crisis
	We should empathize with the plight of the poor.	
5786 **tingle** [TING-guhl]	1. 따끔거리다 2. 따끔거리게 하다 3. 조마조마하다	[2338] thrill [1177] suffer
	My nose is tingling with the cold.	
5787 **queer** [kweer]	1. 기묘한 2. 동성애의	[4511] peculiar [2140] bent
	The movie that we watched was queer.	
5788 **stoke** [stohk]	1. (난로 등의) 불을 때다 2. (어떤 감정을) 선동하다	[1292] fuel [1033] feed [1224] burn [2491] stir
	He stoked up the fire to light the room.	
5789 **puddle** [PUHD-l]	웅덩이	[1349] pool [3196] pond
	Don't step in the puddle.	
5790 **turntable** [TURN-tey-buhl]	턴테이블, 회전반	
	A record is playing on the turntable.	
5791 토플 **ultraviolet** [uhl-truh-VAHY-uh-lit]	자외선(의)	
	Humans cannot see ultraviolet rays.	
5792 **nip** [nip]	1. 꼬집거나 살짝 깨물다 2. 홀짝 마시다 3. 훔치다	[3709] pinch [986] fly
	The cat nipped its owner's hand.	
5793 토플 **spruce** [sproos]	1. 가문비나무 2. (패션) 최신 유행의, 이쁘게 하다	[2920] neat [1667] decorate
	The spruce tree is evergreen.	
5794 토플 **dorsal** [DAWR-suhl]	(물고기의) 등의	
	Fish have dorsal fins.	

5795	공무원 편입	1. 황량한 2. 쌀쌀하고 우울한	[5443] gloomy
bleak			[2763] chilly
[bleek]		There are no plants on the bleak field.	[5590] austere

5796	편입	재난, 사고, 불운	hapless (불운한)
mishap			[1597] accident
[MIS-hap]		The successful event passed without mishap.	[621] fail
			[6222] calamity

5797	편입	쇠약하게 하는, 약화하는	[2198] exhausting
debilitating			[373] bad
[dih-BIL-i-tey-ting]		The disease is debilitating.	[4960] cripple
			[6001] attenuate

5798		오타, 오자	[624] misprint
typo			[621] fail
[TAHY-poh]		I found a typo in this book.	[3383] deception
			[6615] blunder

5799	편입	1. 수비대(를 파견하다) 2. 요새, 부대	[5857] stronghold
garrison			[1275] encampment
[GAR-uh-suhn]		The garrison defended the town.	

5800	GRE	1. 주제에서 벗어나는 2. 접선(의)	[6356] contiguous
tangent			
[TAN-juhnt]		We were discussing a serious issue when Tom got off on a tangent.	

5801	공무원	1. 환각 2. 환청	hallucinate (환각을 느끼다)
hallucination			[3462] illusion
[huh-loo-suh-NEY-shuhn]		Drinking too much alcohol can cause hallucinations.	[4214] phantom

5802	GRE	(두 가닥을) 엮다, 잇다, 꼬다	[1018] marry
splice			[4947] graft
[splahys]		Splice the rope to make it durable.	

5803		고양이의 수염	[891] hair
whisker			
[HWIS-ker]		The cat had white whiskers.	

5804		1. 간부회의 2. (정치적) 논의, 토의	[1578] convention
caucus			[276] meet
[KAW-kuhs]		Many stockholders participated in the caucus.	[1502] gathering

5805		포기하다, 없이하다	[6063] renounce
forgo			[2399] abandon
[fawr-GOH]		My colleague decided to forgo her career for motherhood.	[7198] abdicate

5806		두부	
tofu			
[TOH-foo]		Tofu is made from soybeans.	

5807		빠짐없고 포괄적인, 총망라한	[2139] thorough
exhaustive			[1546] comprehensive
[ig-ZAWS-tiv]		An exhaustive approach is needed in legal investigations.	[5676] encyclopedic

5808	토플 GRE	(빛, 열, 소리 등을) 발산하다, 내보내다	emanation (발산)
emanate			
[EM-uh-neyt]		The lamp emanated light and heat.	

5809 공무원 GRE **amalgamation** [uh-mal-guh-MEY-shuhn]	연합하다, 혼합하다, 섞다	amalgam (아말감, 혼합물)
	The organization was formed by the amalgamation of several smaller groups.	[613] combination [2582] fusion

5810 **deli** [DEL-ee]	(치즈, 샐러드 등을 판매하는) 간편식품 판매점	
	I went to the local deli to buy cheese.	

5811 편입 **insurgent** [in-SUR-juhnt]	폭도, 반란자	insurgency (반란) [2690] rebel
	The government imprisoned the insurgents.	

5812 **outpost** [OUT-pohst]	1. (본거지로부터 떨어져서 배치된) 군대의 전초 2. (제국이나 국가의 중심으로부터) 떨어진, 외곽의	[1342] settlement [4039] frontier
	The outpost prevented any surprise attacks.	

5813 **hazelnut** [HEY-zuhl-nuht]	개암, 헤이즐넛	hazel (개암나무)
	Hazelnuts have a hard shell.	

5814 편입 **taint** [teynt]	오염(하다), 더럽히다	[1896] stain [719] damage [5013] stigma [5579] blemish
	His reputation became tainted.	

5815 공무원 편입 GRE **tenacity** [tuh-NAS-i-tee]	끈기, 완강함	tenacious (집요한) [4878] perseverance [652] determination [929] courage
	Tenacity is an admirable trait.	

5816 공무원 **gestation** [je-STEY-shuhn]	1. 임신/잉태 기간 2. (아이디어 등의) 발달 기간	gestational (임신의) [1638] pregnancy [75] thought
	The gestation for a human baby is 10 months.	

5817 **barber** [BAHR-ber]	1. 이발사 2. 이발하다	
	I went to the barber to get a haircut.	

5818 토플 **tertiary** [TUR-shee-er-ee]	1. 제 3의, 3차의 2. 3번째로 중요한	[기타] third [251] secondary
	The tertiary industry in Korea has developed rapidly.	

5819 토익 **photocopy** [FOH-tuh-kop-ee]	(사진) 복사(하다)	photocopier (복사기) [931] copy
	Please photocopy these essays for me.	

5820 **indigo** [IN-di-goh]	인디고, 남색	[4462] azure
	Indigo is a mix of blue and purple.	

5821 **pedagogy** [PED-uh-goh-jee]	교육(학)	pedagogical (교육의) [334] teaching
	The most important aspect of pedagogy is love and respect.	

5822 **cornea** [KAWR-nee-uh]	(눈의 투명한 막인) 각막	corneal (각막의)
	He had a scratch on his cornea.	

5823		
acclimate [AK-luh-meyt]	1. 익히다, 순응시키다 2. (장소, 기후 등에) 익숙해지다	[4534] accustom
	The zoo animals had become acclimated to the crowd noise.	

5824		
squeak [skweek]	찍찍 울다, 끽끽 울다	squeaky (삐걱삐걱 소리가 나는) [6960] creak [6807] screech
	The mouse squeaked.	

5825 공무원 편입		
procrastination [proh-kras-tuh-NEY-shuh n]	농땡이 피우다, 미루다, 지연시키다	procrastinate (미루다) procrastinator (미루는 사람) [1697] delay
	Procrastination delays progress.	

5826 공무원 편입 GRE		
morbid [MAWR-bid]	1. 죽음에 관한 관심이 넘치는 2. 병적인, 우울한	mobidity (병적 상태) [5443] gloomy [363] death
	Having a morbid fascination with blood, he liked vampires.	

5827 편입 GRE		
erratic [ih-RAT-ik]	1. 변덕스러운, 일정치 않은 2. 기괴한	erratically (변덕스럽게) [717] irregular [604] variable [649] abnormal
	She is an erratic person who cannot make a decision.	

5828 토플		
leopard [LEP-erd]	표범	[외래어] cheetah [4330] panther
	Leopards are endangered animals.	

5829 편입		
consecrate [KON-si-kreyt]	1. 신성하게 하다, 정화하다 2. 바치다, 희생하다	consecration (신성화) [1348] dedicate [1918] bless
	The church has not been consecrated yet.	

5830		
physique [fi-ZEEK]	체격, 신체	[949] shape
	He has a powerful physique.	

5831		
petite [puh-TEET]	몸집이 작은, 조금한	[1869] tiny [3259] slim [7073] diminutive [7139] dainty
	She is beautiful and petite.	

5832		
spout [spout]	1. 뿜어내다 2. 주둥이, 분출구	[6323] gush [1168] river
	The factory spouted out carbon emissions.	

5833		
superannuated [soo-per-AN-yoo-ey-tid]	1. 오래되어 쓸모없는 2. 시대에 맞지 않는	superannuation (연금) [4927] obsolete [1803] ancient
	The general was superannuated after being injured.	

5834 편입		
subpoena [suh-PEE-nuh]	1. 소환장 2. (소환장으로) 소환하다	
	The court sent a subpoena to the suspect.	

5835		
foray [FAWR-ey]	1. 침략하다, 약탈하다 2. 새로운 분야를 시도하다	[2580] raid [982] attempt [2294] invasion
	The army made a foray against the enemy nation.	

5836		
exfoliate [eks-FOH-lee-eyt]	박피하다, 벗기다	[3014] peel
	Exfoliate your face with a facial scrub.	

5837 **pep** [pep]	원기, 기운, 활력 He was full of pep and decided to exercise.	[4733] starch
5838 **prospectus** [pruh-SPEK-tuhs]	(학교, 회사, 단체 등의) 취지서, 안내서 The company handed out its prospectus to university students.	[2119] outline [2610] catalog [5690] syllabus
5839　　　　토플 **barge** [bahrj]	1. 주제넘게 나서다, 끼어들다　2. 거룻배, 짐배 Please don't barge into my room.	[1414] boat [986] fly [4303] raft
5840 **clam** [klam]	(대합)조개 Clams can be found in the sea and mud.	[3307] shellfish
5841　　　　편입 **quarantine** [KWAWR-uhn-teen]	검역(하다), 격리(하다) Health experts quarantined infected patients.	[2243] isolate [3390] detention
5842 **orthopedic** [awr-thuh-PEE-dik]	1. 정형외과의　2. 정형외과의사 You should go see an orthopedic surgeon about your injury.	
5843　　공무원 편입 GRE **homogeneous** [hoh-muh-JEE-nee-uhs]	동종의, 동일한 Korea is a homogeneous society.	homogeneity (동질성) [2887] alike [582] similar
5844 **jockey** [JOK-ee]	1. 경마의 기수　2. 경쟁하다 She is a famous jokey.	[757] rider [51] work
5845 **squid** [skwid]	오징어 A squid has ten limbs.	
5846　　공무원 편입 **ferocious** [fuh-ROH-shuhs]	흉악한, 사나운 Tigers are ferocious.	ferocity (사나움) ferociously (사납게) [4762] savage [1223] dangerous
5847　　　　편입 **peruse** [puh-ROOZ]	1. 숙독하다, 꼼꼼히 읽다　2. 점검하다 The student is perusing her textbook.	[4068] scrutinize [169] read [871] analyze [1413] browse
5848 **fudge** [fuhj]	1. (설탕과 버터 등으로 만든 사탕의 일종인) 퍼지　2. 허위, 날조 Fudge is very sticky.	[외래어] chocolate [577] solution [4242] exaggerate [4633] evade
5849　　공무원 편입 **dilate** [dahy-LEYT]	1. 확장하다, 팽창하다　2. 확장시키다 Her pupils dilated.	dilation (팽창) [995] expand [239] grow [7032] expound
5850 **raisin** [REY-zin]	건포도 There are raisins in the cereal.	[803] grape

5851	토플 편입	지구의, 육지의, 지상의	extraterrestrial (지구 밖, 외계의)
terrestrial [tuh-RES-tree-uhl]		Terrestrial animals are suffering from global warming.	[1064] earthly

5852		접미사	[6054] affix
suffix [SUHF-iks]		Anti- is a common suffix.	

5853		1. (장식으로 사용하는) 깃털 (뭉치) 2. 깃털로 장식하다 3. (깃털 모양으로) 퍼지다	plumage (깃털) [2436] pride [227] line
plume [ploom]		Her hat is decorated with ostrich plumes.	

5854		1. 젖을 떼다 2. (의존하던 것으로부터) 떼어 놓다, 단념시키다	[3662] discourage
wean [ween]		The mother weaned her baby off milk.	

5855		1. (골프에서 티와 그린 사이의 잔디인) 페어웨이 2. 항로	
fairway [FAIR-wey]		The ball landed on the fairway.	

5856	공무원	1. 측정기준, 평가기준 2. 미터법	[1318] metrical
metric [ME-trik]		The metric for judging swimming is speed.	

5857		근거지, 본거지, 요새	[5901] citadel [128] place [4675] fortress [6860] bastion
stronghold [STRAWNG-hohld]		The army captured the last stronghold of the enemy.	

5858	편입 GRE	서투른, 어설픈	clumsily (서투르게) clumsiness (서투름) [3424] awkward [2490] bulky
clumsy [KLUHM-zee]		He is a clumsy worker who makes many mistakes.	

5859	공무원 편입	1. 광택, 광휘 2. 코팅	lackluster (윤기 없는) [2178] brilliance [270] pleasure [1397] brightness
luster [LUHS-ter]		The luster of the stars is beautiful.	

5860		1. 뜨거운, 타는 듯한 2. 비판적인	[1224] burning [896] serious [1589] baking [4174] blazing
searing [SEER-ing]		The summer weather is searing.	

5861		방귀(뀌다)	
fart [fahrt]		He farted quietly.	

5862	GRE	재채기하다	
sneeze [sneez]		When someone sneezes, you should say "bless you".	

5863		1. 뛰어난, 멋진 2. 맵시 있는	[2920] neat [30] useful [724] excellent
nifty [NIF-tee]		This is a nifty tool that has many functions.	

5864	편입 GRE	사분면, 사분원, 사분의	[1351] quarter [기타] fourth
quadrant [KWOD-ruhnt]		Please focus on the first quadrant.	

5865		
floss	치실(을 사용하다), 플로스(를 사용하다)	[2605] cord
[flaws]	Doctors recommend using floss twice a week.	

5866	GRE	
denominator	분수의 분모	numerator (분수의 분자) [618] figure [1712] statistic
[dih-NOM-uh-ney-ter]	The denominator of 1/3 is 3.	

5867		
booty	1. 전리품, 포획물 2. 엉덩이	[4337] loot [2896] spoils [6512] plunder
[BOO-tee]	The army gained booty from attacking the citizens.	

5868	공무원 편입	
epitome	전형, 대표적인 것	epitomize (전형을 보여 주다) [262] ideal [3774] embodiment
[ih-PIT-uh-mee]	She is the epitome of a kind grandmother.	

5869	공무원 GRE	
predicate	1. 단언하다, 주장하다 2. 근간으로 삼다 3. (문장의 구조 중) 술부	predicated (~에 입각한) [3611] proclaim [614] measure
[PRED-i-keyt]	Don't predicate that she is the criminal before further investigations.	

5870	공무원 편입	
detour	1. 우회(하다) 2. 우회로	[3910] deviation [1094] direction [3904] diversion
[DEE-toor]	The car made a rapid detour.	

5871	공무원 편입	
taunt	조소(하다), 조롱(하다)	[3772] tease [1550] abuse [6925] derision
[tawnt]	Her friends taunted her for being fat.	

5872	GRE	
pessimistic	비관적인	pessimism (비관주의) pessimist (비관주의자) [1315] negative [1780] depressed
[pes-uh-MIS-tik]	He is not hopeful and is always pessimistic.	

5873		
populism	(시민의 뜻을 따른다는 명목의 정치인) 포퓰리즘, 인민주의	[2503] ordinary
[POP-yuh-liz-uhm]	Lower taxes and increased welfare is based on populism.	

5874		
glee	환희, 유쾌	gleefully (유쾌하게) [594] happiness [2069] delight [6846] elation
[glee]	He danced with glee.	

5875		
otter	수달	
[OT-er]	Otters eat fish.	

5876	공무원 편입	
dwindling	(수가) 줄어드는	dwindle (수가 줄어들다) [3808] decay [5902] abate
[DWIN-dling]	The eagle population is dwindling.	

5877	공무원	
parlor	1. 거실 2. 객실 3. 가게	
[PAHR-ler]	They watched TV in the parlor.	

5878	공무원 편입 GRE	
thwart	1. 방해하다, 훼방하다 2. 좌절시키다	[439] stop [612] counter [6059] circumvent
[thwawrt]	The politician thwarted her opponent.	

5879	편입	1. 견실한, 부동의 2. 의리있는	steadfastly (확고하게)
steadfast			[2267] loyal
[STED-fast]		Their relationship is steadfast.	[4354] abiding
			[6057] adamant

5880		1. 큰 천막 2. (행사의) 가장 중요한	[외래어] tent
marquee			[541] main
[mahr-KEE]		The birthday party will be held in a marquee.	

5881	공무원	콧수염	
mustache			
[MUHS-tash]		He is growing a mustache.	

5882		1. 덤벨, 아령 2. 얼간이, 바보	[4945] dummy
dumbbell			[2644] fool
[DUHM-bel]		Exercising with dumbells can make your muscles stronger.	

5883		1. 달려들다, 뛰어들다 2. 찌르다	[4106] thrust
lunge			
[luhnj]		The player lunged to catch the ball.	

5884		큰 사슴, 엘크	[5264] moose
elk			
[elk]		Many elks live in Canada.	

5885	공무원 편입	어리석은 행동, 실수	[2644] foolishness
folly			[1776] craziness
[FOL-ee]		The plan is folly.	[2459] stupidity
			[4103] absurdity

5886	공무원 편입	1. 촉각의 2. 촉각으로 구분할 수 있는	[6030] palpable
tactile			
[TAK-til]		Your tactile senses intensify at night.	

5887		1. (군인들을 수용하는) 막사 2. (노동자들의) 숙소	[1351] quarters
barracks			
[BAR-uhks]		The soldiers returned to the barracks at night.	

5888	공무원 GRE	삽입어구, 괄호	
parenthesis			
[puh-REN-thuh-sis]		Use parentheses to write down unimportant information.	

5889		(눈의) 홍채	
iris			
[AHY-ris]		His irises are blue.	

5890		(죄의) 사면, 대사	[1785] pardon
amnesty			[2182] immunity
[AM-nuh-stee]		The military generals were granted amnesty.	[2532] forgiveness

5891		거북이	[3527] turtle
tortoise			
[TAWR-tuhs]		A tortoise can live for a long time.	

5892		1. 밀어냄 2. 틀에서 밀어내어 형태를 잡음	extrude (돌출하다)
extrusion			[5535] protrusion
[ik-STROO-zhuhn]		The machine repeats the process of extrusion.	[415] discharge
			[5349] banishment

5893 **kink** [kingk]	1. 구부러짐, 비틀림 2. 구부러지게 하다, 비틀다 3. 성격의 특이함	kinky (특이한) [2202] twist [215] problem [4064] wrinkle
	The street is not straight. There is a kink in the street.	

5894 **chestnut** [CHES-nuht]	1. 밤(나무) 2. 밤색(의)	[1858] brown
	Squirrels eat chestnut.	

5895 GRE **treachery** [TRECH-uh-ree]	배신, 배반	treacherous (예측이 힘들고 위험한, 배반하는) [4004] betrayal [4536] infidelity
	She was hurt by his treachery.	

5896 **outback** [OUT-bak]	(특히 호주의) 오지, 미개척된 땅	[3661] wilderness
	Many animals are living in the outback.	

5897 공무원 GRE **substantiate** [suhb-STAN-shee-eyt]	1. 입증하다, 증명하다 2. 구제화하다, 실체화하다	unsubstantiated (입증되지 않은) [1200] confirm [3157] affirm
	The police had a suspect but they could not substantiate his motive.	

5898 **topology** [tuh-POL-uh-jee]	체계적 분류, 배치에 대한 학문	[3852] geology
	The scientists applied topology to study the expansion of the universe.	

5899 편입 **scorch** [skawrch]	1. 그을리다 2. (자동차가) 질주하다	[1224] burn [556] blacken [1589] bake
	The fire scorched her car.	

5900 공무원 **chisel** [CHIZ-uhl]	1. 끌, 조각칼 2. (조각칼로) 모양을 내다, 파내다 3. 사기치다	[3140] carve [2010] blade [2080] knife
	The architect used a chisel to add details to the sculpture.	

5901 **citadel** [SIT-uh-dl]	(내려다보며 도시를 지키는 용도의) 성, 요새	[4675] fortress [128] place [3482] fortification [6860] bastion
	The citadel is located on a hill.	

5902 GRE **abatement** [uh-BEYT-muhnt]	감소, 완화, 경감	abate (줄어들다) unabated (줄어들지 않은) [509] reduction
	Tax abatement will help companies.	

5903 GRE **conducive** [kuhn-DOO-siv]	~에 이바지하는, ~를 일어나게 하는	[30] useful [85] helpful [284] decisive
	The couch and bed are conducive to a comfortable atmosphere.	

5904 토익 **parameter** [puh-RAM-i-ter]	1. 한계, 한도 2. 조건	[2090] criterion [2187] framework
	They need to work within the parameters.	

5905 **retrofit** [RE-troh-fit]	없던 부품을 추가하다, 개조하다	[401] improve
	The driver retrofitted her car with more comfortable seats.	

5906 **fauna** [FAW-nuh]	(특정한 시대나 지역에 서식하는 동물인) 동물상, 동물군	[907] animal
	The fauna of the desert can withstand extremely high temperatures.	

5907		받침대, 주춧대	[4832] podium
pedestal			
[PED-uh-stl]		The statue is standing on a pedestal.	

5908	편입	1. 대리의 2. 대리인	[2386] substitute
surrogate			[1259] assignee
[SUR-uh-geyt]		She is a surrogate mother.	[3513] proxy

5909		1. (병을 치료하지 않지만 고통을 완화하는) 완화제 2. (일시적인) 대처법	[1808] reassuring
palliative			[2260] calming
[PAL-ee-ey-tiv]		There are only palliative treatments for cancer.	

5910		특대의, 굉장히 큰	[5184] gigantic
jumbo			[196] large
[JUHM-boh]		He drank a jumbo-sized coke.	[417] oversized
			[6260] colossal

5911		1. 강타하다 2. (강하게) 마음이 끌리다	[1226] strike
smite			[578] hit
[smahyt]		Smite the ball with the bat.	[4795] afflict

5912		1. 술집 2. 세단형 자동차	
saloon			
[suh-LOON]		Gambling and drugs often occur in saloons.	

5913		(야생의 소인) 들소	[5500] buffalo
bison			
[BAHY-suhn]		A bison is bigger and hairier than a cow.	

5914		1. 어린이용 변기 2. 정신 나간 3. 부가적인, 중요하지 않은	[1776] crazy
potty			[2658] toilet
[POT-ee]		There is a potty in the bathroom.	

5915		1. 신음하다 2. (무거워서 사물이) 삐걱거리다	[5385] moan
groan			[1936] sigh
[grohn]		The patient groaned with pain.	[5600] grunt

5916		백분위수(의)	
percentile			
[per-SEN-tahyl]		My grades are in the 99th percentile.	

5917	공무원 GRE	기이한, 불가사의한	canny (현명한, 검소한)
uncanny			[2265] weird
[uhn-KAN-ee]		She had an uncanny feeling that she was being watched.	[1659] strange
			[4014] astonishing

5918		1. 납부금 2. (이어지는 책이나 방송의) 한 회	[160] payment
installment			[1422] chapter
[in-STAWL-muhnt]		The first installment for your car is due next week.	[1455] episode

5919	공무원	1. 폭등하다, 급등하다	[2888] rocket
skyrocket		2. (신호를 보내기 위해 하늘에서 터지는) 로켓이나 폭죽	[4057] escalate
[SKAHY-rok-it]		The price of oil has skyrocketed.	[6012] catapult

5920	편입	애도(의 말)	[2313] consolation
condolence			[3146] compassion
[kuhn-DOH-luhns]		She wrote a letter of condolence.	[3321] sympathy

5921		정액	[2699] corn
semen			[3669] berry
[SEE-muhn]		The police collected semen from the rape victim.	

5922	공무원 편입 GRE	1. 실망(시키다), 유감(스럽게 하다) 2. 당황, 경악	[2408] alarm
dismay			[1133] worry
[dis-MEY]		The fans were in dismay because their team lost the game.	[2288] anxiety

5923		음성학, 음향학	[1492] audios
phonics			
[FON-iks]		Children need to learn phonics.	

5924		(기대하거나 예상한 것에 미치지 못하는) 부족액	[2193] absence
shortfall			[2643] flaw
[SHAWRT-fawl]		The company has a budget shortfall of $2000.	[3361] deficiency

5925		1. 스포츠 경기, 경마 경기 2. 남자 챙모자	
derby			
[DUR-bee]		Are you going to bet money on the Derby?	

5926		때, 그을음	grimy (더러운)
grime			[5249] filth
[grahym]		Your car is covered with grime.	[1914] dirt
			[2102] dust

5927	토플	성추행하다	molestation (성추행)
molest			molester (치한)
[muh-LEST]		The criminal molested a child.	[3275] harass
			[2860] rape

5928		발작, 경련	[452] fit
spasm			[738] contraction
[SPAZ-uhm]		His arm went into spasm.	

5929	공무원 편입	1. 황폐한, 황량한 2. 황량하게 하다	desolation (황량함)
desolate			[2843] lonely
[DES-uh-lit]		The desolate area does not have any buildings.	[1889] empty
			[2117] bare

5930		허리(의), 요추(의)	[5794] dorsal
lumbar			
[LUHM-ber]		This chair is designed to support your lumbar.	

5931	토플	1. (액체 등이) 배어 나오다, 발산하다	[5957] ooze
exude		2. (어떤 감정을 당당히) 표현하다, 드러내다	[287] seem
[ig-ZOOD]			[5808] emanate
		The caterpillar exuded poison.	

5932		(조개의 일종인) 가리비	scalloped (테두리가 물결 모양인)
scallop			[4588] oyster
[SKOL-uhp]		Can we have scallops for dinner?	[5840] clam

5933		1. 호수 2. (바닷물이 들어온 골짜기인) 협만	[1301] lake
loch			[3832] basin
[lok]		Many creatures are living near the loch.	

5934	GRE	모음	[2998] vocal
vowel			[3560] articulate
[VOU-uhl]		A, E, I, O, and U are vowels.	[3739] choral

5935 공무원 편입 GRE	1. 가늠하다, 파악하다 2. 재다	unfathomable (가늠할 수 없는)
fathom [FATH-uhm]	I can't fathom your anger.	[1251] appreciate [1546] comprehend
5936 **pundit** [PUHN-dit]	전문가, 학자, 박식한 사람	[908] expert
	She is a sports pundit.	
5937 **taxonomy** [tak-SON-uh-mee]	분류 체계, 분류학	[1098] sort
	According to botanical taxonomy, a tomato is a fruit.	
5938 공무원 **dispel** [dih-SPEL]	(기분이나 느낌을) 떨쳐버리다, 쫓아버리다	[4160] disperse [673] replace [7386] allay
	The happy song dispelled my sadness.	
5939 편입 GRE **transgression** [trans-GRESH-uhn]	위반, 위배	transgress (위반하다) [1835] violation [967] crime [2628] breach
	Entering someone's room without permission is a transgression of privacy.	
5940 **crucify** [KROO-suh-fahy]	1. 십자가에 매달다 2. 억누르다 3. 괴롭히다	[5104] torment [709] attack
	Jesus was crucified.	
5941 편입 **erotic** [ih-ROT-ik]	성적인, 애욕의, 에로틱한	[773] sexy
	The erotic film was popular.	
5942 편입 **burrow** [BUR-oh]	굴(을 파다)	[1320] hole
	The rabbit dug a burrow.	
5943 공무원 편입 **nimble** [NIM-buhl]	민첩한, 날렵한	[3187] agile [585] fast [5598] adept
	Her nimble mind came up with the answer.	
5944 편입 **theologian** [thee-uh-LOH-juhn]	(종교를 연구하고 공부하는) 신학자	theology (신학) [2519] divine [5321] clergy
	He is a theologian who studies Christianity.	
5945 **pomegranate** [POM-gran-it]	석류	
	A pomegranate has red seeds.	
5946 토플 **nectar** [NEK-ter]	1. (꽃의) 꿀 2. (진한) 과즙 3. (신화에 등장하는) 넥타	[2603] honey
	Bees collect nectar.	
5947 **stockpile** [STOK-pahyl]	1. 비축량, 사재기 2. 비축하다, 사재기하다	[2732] accumulation
	She has a stockpile of food in her kitchen.	
5948 **cot** [kot]	1. 아기 침대 2. 간이 침대 3. 오두막집	[5544] crib [3971] bunk
	The baby is sleeping in the cot.	

5949 공무원 편입 GRE **devoid** [dih-VOID]	~이 없는, ~이 결여된	[3502] vacant [1091] lack [2117] bare [5989] barren
	Their relationship is devoid of love.	

5950 **acorn** [EY-kawrn]	도토리	
	Squirrels eat acorns.	

5951 **fad** [fad]	1. (일시적) 유행 2. 변덕	[3161] rage [1277] fantasy [1776] craze
	Wearing oversized shirts was a fad.	

5952 **mushy** [MUHSH-ee]	걸쭉한, 무른	[3346] sentimental [1245] soft [3131] muddy [외래어] spongy
	Porridge is mushy.	

5953 **preface** [PREF-is]	(책의) 서문	[761] introduction [6596] prelude [7449] preamble
	In her preface, the author thanks her family for their support.	

5954 공무원 편입 **heresy** [HER-uh-see]	1. 이교, 이단 2. 유별난 의견	[1930] evil [5726] fallacy [6343] blasphemy
	Her radical remarks were considered to be heresy.	

5955 **amortization** [am-er-tuh-ZEY-shuhn]	1. (무형 자산의) 감가상각 2. 부동산 양도	amortize (빚을 할부 상환 하다)
	The letter 'A' in the financial term 'EBIDTA' stands for amortization.	

5956 **whack** [hwak]	때리다, 치다	[578] hit
	He whacked the wall out of anger.	

5957 공무원 **ooze** [ooz]	스며나오다, 흐르다	[5646] trickle [5715] goo
	Blood oozed out of the wound.	

5958 **godfather** [GOD-fah-ther]	대부	godmother (대모) [618] figure
	Who is the baby's godfather?	

5959 **bard** [bahrd]	(음유) 시인	[2321] poet
	The bard traveled and wrote poems.	

5960 **brawl** [brawl]	말다툼(하다), 싸움(하다)	brawler (싸우는 사람) [697] fight [962] argument [6808] altercation
	You can often see drunken brawls at the bar.	

5961 **idyll** [AHYD-l]	이상적이고 한적한 (전원) 풍경	idyllic ((풍경이) 한적하게 아름다운) [2973] pastoral [1384] peace
	The rural idyll was ruined after factories entered the region.	

5962 **abyss** [uh-BIS]	1. 심연, 구렁 2. 혼돈, 혼란 3. (두 사람이나 국가간의 큰) 차이	[3800] gulf [1223] danger [7080] chasm
	The explorer fell down a dark abyss.	

5963 **borderline** [BAWR-der-lahyn]	1. 경계 2. 거의 ~인	[1823] border [557] almost [2183] marginal
	The borderline between friendship and romantic love is confusing.	
5964 **sorcerer** [SAWR-ser-er]	마술사, 마법사	sorcery (마법) [1375] magician
	Sorcerers should not use magic to harm other people.	
5965 **gazette** [guh-ZET]	신문(에 게재하다), 잡지(에 게재하다)	[1806] journal [545] periodical
	The bankruptcy of the company was published in the gazette.	
5966 공무원 편입 GRE **sporadic** [spuh-RAD-ik]	산발적인, 드문드문한	sporadically (산발적으로) [1326] occasional [33] sometimes
	The two friends had sporadic fights.	
5967 **glean** [gleen]	1. 다양한 출처에서 (정보를) 모으다, 챙기다 2. (이삭을) 줍다	[1502] gather [193] learn [5993] cull [6353] deduce
	The information is gleaned from three newspapers.	
5968 **raccoon** [ra-KOON]	(미국) 너구리	
	Raccoons eat berries and eggs.	
5969 편입 **congenital** [kuhn-JEN-i-tl]	(병이나 결함 등이) 타고난, 선천적인	[3079] inborn [6571] ingrained
	She suffers from a congenital disorder.	
5970 공무원 편입 GRE **complacent** [kuhm-PLEY-suhnt]	(가진 것에) 안주하는, 만족한, 흡족한	complacency (자기 만족) [6901] smug [594] happy
	Don't be complacent about your achievements. Try harder.	
5971 토플 **crouch** [krouch]	(몸을) 구부리다, 쪼그리다	[6485] stoop [2140] bend [5414] cower
	She crouched behind the door to surprise her dad.	
5972 **ivy** [AHY-vee]	1. 담쟁이 덩굴 2. 미국 아이비리그 대학	[4110] vine
	Ivy covered the walls of the castle.	
5973 **groin** [groin]	사타구니	
	He felt a painful sensation in the groin.	
5974 **mitten** [MIT-n]	벙어리 장갑	mitt (=mitten) [2746] glove
	It's cold outside so you should take your mittens.	
5975 편입 **annihilate** [uh-NAHY-uh-leyt]	전멸시키다, 멸망시키다	annihilation (전멸) [1255] destroy [2692] crush [6585] decimate
	The nuclear bomb annihilated the whole country.	
5976 공무원 GRE **taboo** [tuh-BOO]	1. 금기사항, 터부 2. 금기의, 터부의	[3590] forbidden [1728] shocking [2062] banned [5106] outlawed
	Talking about death is taboo.	

5977 공무원 편입 GRE **loathe** [lohth]	증오하다, 혐오하다, 싫어하다	[1599] hate [5283] despise [6745] abhor
	I loathe racist people.	
5978 **aft** [aft]	1. (배나 항공기의) 꼬리 2. 꼬리쪽의, 후미의	
	The captain made her way aft to inspect the ship's engine.	
5979 **vale** [veyl]	(계곡이 있는 산) 골짜기	[1784] valley
	Many people go to the vales during summer.	
5980 **specter** [SPEK-ter]	1. 귀신, 유령 2. 우려나 걱정을 초래하는 대상	[2546] ghost [221] sign [1963] shadow [3047] demon
	The specter haunted the town.	
5981 **gleaming** [GLEE-ming]	(깨끗한 표면이) 빛나는, 반짝이는	gleam (희미하게 빛나다) [1397] bright
	The gleaming church windows are beautiful.	
5982 공무원 편입 GRE **remuneration** [ri-myoo-nuh-REY-shuhn]	1. 급료 2. 보수, 보상	[1991] compensation [2245] wage
	The volunteers worked without any remuneration.	
5983 **nautical** [NAW-ti-kuhl]	1. 항해의, 해사의 2. 선박의, 선원의	[1950] marine [1762] navigational [4315] maritime
	All sailors know how to read nautical charts.	
5984 편입 **stifle** [STAHY-fuhl]	1. ~를 숨막히게 하다 2. (어떤 감정을) 억누르다	stifling (숨막히는, 답답한) [3210] suppress [1177] suffer [4189] curb
	The fumes stifled the inhabitants of the building.	
5985 **guerrilla** [guh-RIL-uh]	(더 큰 집단을 상대로 투쟁하는) 게릴라(병), 유격대	[5747] mercenary [6529] commando
	The guerrillas captured the town.	
5986 **hornet** [HAWR-nit]	말벌	[5347] wasp [812] ant
	Hornets will sting intruders.	
5987 **scarlet** [SKAHR-lit]	주홍색(의), 새빨간 색(의)	
	She is wearing a scarlet skirt.	
5988 **bogus** [BOH-guhs]	가짜의, 거짓의, 엉터리의	[2552] fake [1119] imaginary [4480] false
	Her resume was found to be bogus.	
5989 편입 **barren** [BAR-uhn]	1. 불모의, 황량한 2. 불임의	[2117] bare [3021] arid [5929] desolate
	No plants are growing on the barren land.	
5990 **flurry** [FLUR-ee]	1. (눈이나 비 등이) 휘몰아치는 2. 소동, 혼란 3. 들뜬	[4564] bustle [452] fit
	She got in the car to escape the flurry of snow.	

5991 **tribulation** [trib-yuh-LEY-shuhn]	역경, 고난	[215] problem [2835] adversity [3887] grief
	The politician suffered from the tribulations of being famous.	
5992 **moron** [MAWR-on]	바보, 등신	[3666] idiot [2644] fool
	He is a moron that forgot to lock the door.	
5993 **cull** [kuhl]	1. 추려내다, 선별하다 2. (동물의 수를 줄이기 위해) 사냥하다	[641] pick [1968] extract [5967] glean
	She traveled to many countries to cull legends for her book.	
5994 **stylus** [STAHY-luhs]	1. 레코드 바늘 2. (점토 등에 글을 쓰는 도구인) 첨필	
	Without the stylus, the record player cannot play music.	
5995 **lactate** [LAK-teyt]	젖을 분비하다	[1217] nurse [1033] feed [5102] cradle
	Lactating women should eat healthy food.	
5996 편입 GRE **cunning** [KUHN-ing]	교활한, 간사한	[1536] crafty [3031] clever
	She came up with a cunning plan.	
5997 **errand** [ER-uhnd]	심부름, 잡일	[1180] commission
	I'm busy today. I have to run some errands.	
5998 **actuary** [AK-choo-er-ee]	보험 계리사	[1712] statistician [318] accountant
	An actuary calculates the risk of insurances.	
5999 **bandit** [BAN-dit]	산적, 도둑, 악당	[967] criminal [2827] gangster [3663] thief
	The bandit stole my car.	
6000 **yank** [yangk]	(갑작스럽고 세게) 잡아당기다	[912] pull [2074] drag [2285] snap [4235] jerk
	My brother yanked my hair.	

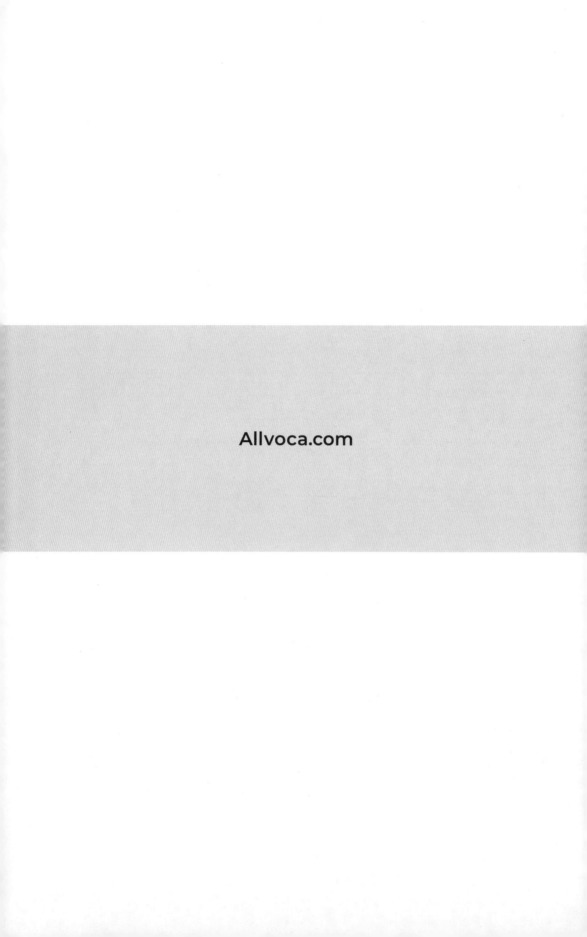
Allvoca.com

#6001~#6800

미국 상위권 대학의 학부생 수준의 어휘력이다.
밀도가 높거나 추상적인 텍스트에서도 정보 단서 간의 논리적 연결을 파악하고 적절한 추론도 해낸다. 고난도 어휘, 길고 복잡한 문장, 단락 간의 관계 이해가 관건이기에 CNN, BBC, NYT(뉴욕타임즈) 등의 해외 뉴스 매체를 학습 보조 수단으로 사용할 것을 추천한다.

LEVEL **07**

6001 공무원 GRE **attenuation** [uh-ten-yoo-EY-shuhn]	1. 저하, 해소, 완화 2. (소리나 전압 등의) 진폭을 낮춤	attenuate (약해지다)
	The attenuation of global warming is essential to achieve human happiness.	
6002 **tickle** [TIK-uhl]	1. 간지럽히다 2. 호기심을 자극하다 3. 즐겁게 하다	[966] touch [2069] delight [3634] amuse
	The man tickled his son.	
6003 **yelp** [yelp]	1. 소리 지르다, 비명을 지르다 2. 깽깽 울다	[5459] howl [6699] hoot
	The dog yelped when it saw the needle.	
6004 공무원 편입 GRE **impel** [im-PEL]	1. 추진하다 2. 재촉하다	[1935] urge [2602] compel [3288] induce
	Poverty impelled him to steal.	
6005 **liken** [LAHY-kuhn]	~에 비유하다, ~에 비교하다	[572] compare [192] relate [861] equate
	The fans likened the celebrity to a goddess.	
6006 공무원 편입 GRE **discord** [DIS-kawrd]	1. 불화, 부조화 2. 불일치 3. (서로) 반대하다	[962] argument [6937] dissonance
	Although the family was rich, there were many signs of discord.	
6007 토플 **wreak** [reek]	1. 큰 피해를 끼치다, 파괴하다 2. 원한을 갚다	[1255] destroy [4501] inflict
	The earthquake wreaked havoc in Japan.	
6008 공무원 편입 GRE **benevolent** [buh-NEV-uh-luhnt]	1. 자비로운, 친절한, 자애로운 2. 자선의	[256] caring [2507] generous [5170] benign
	She is a benevolent lady who donates to charity.	
6009 **dyslexia** [dis-LEK-see-uh]	(글자를 잘 이해하지 못하는) 난독증	dyslexic (난독증인)
	Children suffering from dyslexia often have low grades.	
6010 **whoop** [hoop]	함성(을 지르다), 환호성(을 지르다)	[3718] yell [3172] shout [6699] hoot
	After their victory, the fans whooped with joy.	
6011 **duplex** [DOO-pleks]	1. 이층 아파트 2. 두 가구 전용 건물	[1086] double
	The friends moved into the duplex flat.	
6012 **catapult** [KAT-uh-puhlt]	투석기(로 날리다)	[4544] sling [1013] push
	The children used a catapult to shoot stones at birds.	
6013 **sob** [sob]	흐느끼다, 훌쩍거리며 울다	[2068] cry
	He sobbed after being fired.	
6014 **transduce** [trans-DOOS]	(에너지나 전파를 다른 형태로) 전환하다, 변환하다	
	This bike can transduce physical energy into electricity.	

6015	GRE	1. 이제부터, 앞으로 2. 내세에서	
hereafter			
[heer-AF-ter]		You can leave early today, but hereafter you need to stay until 6 pm.	

6016	은어, (비)속어	[6101] jargon
slang		
[slang]	Many teenagers use slang.	

6017	1. 톱니 2. 베끼다	[1406] gear
cog		[6516] prong
[kog]	The cogs of the machine became blunt and rusted.	

6018	1. (특히 미국 해군의) 준장 2. (요트 클럽 등의) 회장	[5113] admiral
commodore		
[KOM-uh-dawr]	The commodore ordered the soldiers to prepare for battle.	

6019	GRE	찬미(하다), 칭찬(하다)	laudable (칭찬할만한)
laud			[2458] praise
[lawd]		The teacher lauded her as a great student.	[2728] admire
			[2940] adore

6020	편입	1. 미로, 미궁 2. 복잡한 구조	[5224] maze
labyrinth			[1926] mystery
[LAB-uh-rinth]		The explorers became lost in the labyrinth of passages.	[4158] tangle

6021	(머리나 실 따위의) 타래, 술, 다발	[5317] clump
tuft		
[tuhft]	The children pulled out tufts of grass.	

6022	귀찮은, 성가신, 폐가 되는	[2465] annoying
pesky		
[PES-kee]	The pesky mosquito kept buzzing at night.	

6023	(군대의 부대 단위 중) 소대	[2632] squad
platoon		[2662] batch
[pluh-TOON]	The platoon of soldiers was assigned to protect the queen.	[3508] detachment

6024	해바라기	
sunflower		
[SUHN-flou-er]	Sunflowers have yellow petals.	

6025	1. 밤색(의) 2. (무인도 등의) 외딴 곳에 사람을 버리다, 가두다	[3413] strand
maroon		[2243] isolate
[muh-ROON]	I have a maroon shirt.	

6026	토플 편입 GRE	1. 천재, 영재 2. 전형, 모델	prodigious ((크기나 정도가) 엄청난)
prodigy			[383] sensation
[PROD-i-jee]		He is an art prodigy.	[3360] genius

6027	(고통스러운 것의) 일시적 중지	[1528] relaxation
respite		[2018] breather
[RES-pit]	The ceasefire provided some respite from the horrors of war.	

6028	공무원	딸꾹질(하다)	
hiccup			
[HIK-uhp]		If you are hiccuping, try drinking some water.	

6029 **spar** [spahr]		1. 권투 스파링(하다) 2. (배의 돛대 등으로 사용하는) 기둥 3. (지속적으로) 다투다 The athlete was tired after sparring.	[697] fight [962] argue [4678] quarrel
6030 **palpable** [PAL-puh-buhl]	편입	1. (감정이나 분위기가) 격렬해 거의 만질 수 있을 듯한, 뚜렷한 2. 손으로 느껴지는, 분명한 Her death caused him to feel a palpable sense of loss.	palpate (만져보다) [3807] tangible [385] certain [1079] obvious
6031 **loophole** [LOOP-hohl]	토플	빠져나갈 구멍, 허술한 점 The lawyer searched for loopholes in the contract.	[1320] hole
6032 **brisk** [brisk]	토플 편입	1. 기운찬, 활발한 2. 짧은, 가벼운 She went for a brisk jog in the park.	[3873] lively [547] energetic [585] fast
6033 **subsistence** [suhb-SIS-tuhns]	공무원	1. 생존, 생활 2. (법 등이) 유효한 The minimum wage guarantees subsistence for workers.	subsist (생존하다) [2788] poverty [5502] livelihood
6034 **stutter** [STUHT-er]		말을 더듬다, 우물거리다 He stuttered when talking to the girl he liked.	
6035 **horoscope** [HAWR-uh-skohp]		(별과 행성의 위치로 사람의 운명을 예견하는) 점성술 I don't believe that horoscopes can predict our future.	[4994] zodiac [4682] astrology
6036 **blot** [blot]		1. 얼룩, 오점 2. 지우다 3. 말리다 There is a blot of paint on your white shirt.	[1896] stain [5579] blemish
6037 **plagiarism** [PLEY-juh-riz-uhm]	공무원 편입	표절 The professor said that plagiarism will not be tolerated.	plagiarize (표절하다) [2937] piracy [2419] reproduction [4026] infringement
6038 **biceps** [BAHY-seps]		이두근 The athlete has huge biceps.	[1686] branch
6039 **carcinogen** [kahr-SIN-uh-juhn]		발암성 물질 Cigarettes have more than 70 carcinogens.	carcinogenic (발암성의) [2473] toxin [2686] poison
6040 **wharf** [hwawrf]		(배가 정착해 짐을 내릴 수 있는) 부두 The sailors unloaded the packages at the wharf.	[2992] dock [5431] berth
6041 **horrendous** [haw-REN-duhs]		끔찍한, 무서운 Murder is a horrendous crime.	horrendously (끔찍하게) [2830] horrible [1728] shocking [5666] appalling
6042 **chariot** [CHAR-ee-uht]		1. (경주용의) 마차, 전차 2. (전차로) 운반하다 Chariots are pulled by horses.	[553] carriage [1049] bicycle [1775] automobile

6043	공무원 편입	1. 유토피아의, 이상적인 2. 실현될 수 없는	utopia (이상향, 유토피아)
utopian			[2667] fanciful
[yoo-TOH-pee-uhn]		In a utopian world, there would be no discrimination or poverty.	

6044		영화 촬영술	
cinematography			
[sin-uh-muh-TOG-ruh-fee]		The award-winning movie has amazing cinematography.	

6045		난동, 혼란	[2962] chaos
mayhem			[4970] anarchy
[MEY-hem]		Complete mayhem broke out after the earthquake.	[7127] commotion

6046	공무원 편입	읽을 수 있는, 명백한	illegible (읽기 어려운)
legible			legibility (읽기 쉬움)
[LEJ-uh-buhl]		Your essay is not legible.	[169] read
			[1701] distinct

6047	공무원 토플	(나무의) 가지	[915] stick
twig			[317] understand
[twig]		A bird is sitting on the twig.	[3728] limb

6048		(아래로) 급습하다, 덮치다	[2076] dive
swoop			[454] fall
[swoop]		The eagle swooped down on its prey.	[5723] plummet

6049	편입 GRE	1. 어린 새 2. 어린, 미숙한	[4392] novice
fledgling			[60] new
[FLEJ-ling]		The fledgling is learning to fly.	

6050		(요주의 인물 이름을 적어두는) 블랙리스트	[439] stop
blacklist			[5349] banish
[BLAK-list]		She is blacklisted because of her radical, dangerous political ideologies.	

6051		쉬이 소리를 내다	[4045] whistle
hiss			[3968] whisper
[his]		The audience hissed at the racist joke.	[6699] hoot

6052	공무원 편입	1. (특히 바람이) 갑작스레 방향을 바꾸다 2. 주제나 입장을 갑자기 바꾸다	[7005] swerve
veer			[2140] bend
[veer]		The car veered to the north.	[4848] deflect

6053	공무원	중재인, 심판	[504] referee
umpire			[993] judge
[UHM-pahyuhr]		He works as a tennis umpire.	[3672] arbitrator

6054	토플	1. 첨부하다, 붙이다 2. (문법) 조사	[1242] attach
affix			[4058] fasten
[uh-FIKS]		She affixed a document to the email.	[5016] append

6055		1. 꼬챙이(에 꽂다) 2. 강하게 비난하다	[4150] spit
skewer			[1766] tear
[SKYOO-er]		The meat and vegetables were held together with a shewer.	

6056		(특정한 조건을 충족해야 효력이 발효되며 제 3자에게 예탁하여 보관하는) 조건부 날인 증서	[1827] deposit
escrow			
[ES-kroh]		Her inheritance was placed in escrow until she turned 20.	

6057 공무원 편입	의지가 굳건한, 강건한, 단호한	adamantly (단호하게) [4545] stubborn
adamant [AD-uh-muhnt]	She was adamant about her decision to become a scientist.	[652] determined [2537] insistent

6058	(액체나 공기의) 소용돌이	[4494] swirl [2962] chaos
vortex [VAWR-teks]	A vortex of water destroyed the farm.	[6111] whirlwind

6059 공무원 편입 GRE	1. (장애물이나 문제를) 우회하다 2. 속이다	[4633] evade [848] avoid
circumvent [sur-kuhm-VENT]	The car circumvented the construction site.	[3567] bypass

6060	1. 가까이 붙어 운전하다 2. (자동차의) 뒷문	[6729] hatchback [453] attend
tailgate [TEYL-geyt]	The police car is tailgating the criminal's car.	[4138] escort

6061	1. (미인) 선발 대회 2. 화려한 옷을 입은 사람들의 행렬, 퍼레이드	[1134] celebration [5574] extravaganza
pageant [PAJ-uh nt]	She decided to participate in the beauty pageant.	

6062 GRE	1. 큰 도움이 되는, 요긴한 도구, 혜택 2. 요구, 부탁	[1918] blessing [991] advantage
boon [boon]	The washing machine was a boon for women.	

6063 공무원 편입	1. (직책, 권리 등을) 공식적으로 포기하다 2. (소비, 사용을) 중단하다	renunciation (포기) [1655] deny
renounce [ri-NOUNS]	The princess renounced her throne.	

6064	재주, 요령	[1372] talent [171] experience
knack [nak]	He has a knack of remembering people's names.	[4460] aptitude [6256] dexterity

6065 토플 편입	1. (머리카락 등을) 헝클다 2. (평평했던 표면에) 물결이 생기게 하다 3. 프릴 장식	[2705] upset [5326] crease
ruffle [RUHF-uhl]	She ruffled her boyfriend's hair.	

6066 토플	1. (특히 길들여진 환경을 탈출한) 야생의 2. 흉포한, 야생동물같은	[1547] wild [3470] cruel
feral [FEER-uh l]	The feral horse freely ran around the field.	[5846] ferocious

6067 공무원 편입 GRE	당혹스럽게 하다, 당황케 하다, 난처하게 하다	perplexity (당혹감) [1581] confuse
perplex [per-PLEKS]	He was perplexed by her daughter's anger.	[4014] astonish [5166] astound

6068 GRE	1. 보조의 2. 보조하는 사람	[4883] auxiliary [98] additional
ancillary [AN-suh-ler-ee]	Earphones are ancillary devices that support cellphones.	[251] secondary

6069	1. 광희, 황홀 2. 열변을 토하다	rapturous (광희의) rapt (매료된)
rapture [RAP-cher]	The fans greeted the celebrity with rapture.	[5125] ecstasy [497] contentment

6070 편입	(말할 때의) 리듬, 높낮이	[외래어] rhythm [2880] accent
cadence [KEYD-ns]	The professor spoke in a monotonous cadence.	[7154] inflection

6071 **wicket** [WIK-it]		1. 작은 문 2. 티켓 판매소	
		The workers used the wicket to enter and exit.	

6072 **glyph** [glif]		(고대 이집트 등에서 사용한) 상형 문자	
		Scholars attempted to decipher the glyphs.	

6073 **thrash** [thrash]		1. 때리다 2. (다급히) 노력하다	thrashing (때리는 행위, 매) [1187] beat [2014] defeat
		The mother thrashed her son across the shoulders.	

6074 **regal** [REE-guhl]		왕족에게 걸맞은, 위엄있는	[1539] royal
		They entered the regal building.	

6075 **outsole** [OUT-sohl]		(특히 운동화의) 구두창	insole (안창) midsole (중창)
		The outsole is made of rubber.	

6076 **mildew** [MIL-doo]		곰팡이(가 피어난)	[2342] mold [6125] blight
		There is mildew on this apple.	

6077 **silo** [SAHY-loh]		1. (곡식이나 목초) 저장고 2. 동떨어진/격리된 부서, 과정	[2053] elevator [5053] cellar
		The silo stores food for the cows during winter.	

6078 **vile** [vahyl]		1. 역겨운, 상스러운 2. 비열한	[3788] foul [2830] horrible [5010] contemptible [5666] appalling
		He has vile manners.	

6079 **teleport** [TEL-uh-pawrt]		1. 텔레포트하다, 순간 이동하다 2. (물건 등을) 염력으로 옮기다	
		I wish I could teleport to work.	

6080 **elm** [elm]		느릅나무	[1179] wood
		We sat in the shade of the elm tree.	

6081 **meek** [meek]	편입	온순한, 유화한	meekness (온화함) meekly (온순하게) [3179] humble [2065] gentle
		He is very gentle and meek.	

6082 **remorse** [ri-MAWRS]		후회, 자책, 양심의 가책	remorseful (깊이 뉘우치 는) [2972] regret [1692] sadness
		She felt remorse for the crimes she committed.	

6083 **bask** [bask]	토플	(햇볕이나 불 등을) 쬐다	
		The lizard is basking in the sun.	

6084 **profane** [pruh-FEYN]	편입	모독적인, 불경한, (신성한 것을) 더럽히는	profanity (신성 모독) [6343] blasphemous [1550] abusive [4467] secular
		Children should not use profane language.	

6085 토플 GRE **twofold** [TOO-fohld]	1. 두배의 2. 이중적인	threefold (3배의) [1086] double
	This surgery has a twofold increase in the risk of failure.	
6086 편입 **consummate** [KON-suh-meyt]	1. 온전하게 하다, 완벽하게 하다 2. 첫날밤을 치르다 3. 완벽한, 모범적인	[111] able [984] gifted [1760] accomplished
	Her book was consummated through years of research.	
6087 편입 **hiatus** [hahy-EY-tuhs]	(활동의 일시적인) 중단, 중절	[2754] interval [3165] pause [4244] lapse
	Summer vacation is a two-month hiatus from studying.	
6088 **pendulum** [PEN-juh-luh m]	1. (시계 등의) 추 2. 진자	[2186] swing [1463] transition
	The pendulum in the clock is broken. It does not swing back and forth.	
6089 **meander** [mee-AN-der]	1. 정처없이 떠돌다 2. 구불거리다 3. 들락날락하는	[3039] wander [3393] drift [3406] crawl [5289] ramble
	The girl meandered through the field.	
6090 공무원 편입 GRE **tenet** [TEN-it]	(종교나 철학의) 교리, 교의	[3022] doctrine [75] thought [1041] assumption
	Harmony with nature is one of the tenets of Buddhism.	
6091 편입 **rapport** [ra-PAWR]	(사람들 사이의 긴밀하고 친근한) 관계	[3321] sympathy [192] relationship [1964] compatibility [4725] affinity
	The teacher established a good rapport with his students.	
6092 GRE **cleat** [kleet]	1. (특히 항해 중 밧줄을 고정하기 위해 사용하는 T자형의) 고정구 2. (운동 선수의 신발 밑의) 미끄럼막이	
	The sailors attached the rope to the cleat.	
6093 공무원 편입 GRE **aberration** [ab-uh-REY-shuhn]	(정상적이거나 바른 길을) 벗어남, 일탈	aberrant (정도를 벗어난, 탈선적인) [3910] deviation [4511] peculiarity
	The protest in the region was an aberration.	
6094 편입 GRE **melancholy** [MEL-uhn-kol-ee]	멜랑꼴리한, 우울한	[5443] gloomy [1692] sadness [5034] grim
	This song is melancholy.	
6095 공무원 편입 GRE **painstakingly** [PEYNZ-tey-king-lee]	공들여서, 굉장히 열심히	painstaking (공들인) [1332] laboriously [256] carefully [2117] barely
	He painstakingly finished the project.	
6096 **keg** [keg]	(술 등의 액체를 저장하는) 작은 나무 통	[2384] barrel [6584] cask
	There is beer in the keg.	
6097 편입 GRE **ramification** [ram-uh-fi-KEY-shuh n]	(부정적인) 결과, 여파	[1686] branching [235] result [1746] consequence [1817] complication
	Skipping school will have ramifications.	
6098 **cringe** [krinj]	1. (겁이 나서) 움찔하다, 숙이다 2. 당혹해하다, 창피해하다	[5414] cower [3172] shout
	She cringed away from the ball.	

6099		
visor	1. (모자의) 챙 2. (헬멧이나 투구의) 얼굴 가리개	
[VAHY-zer]	I am wearing a black cap with a white visor.	

6100 공무원 토플 편입 GRE		audacious (용감한)
audacity	1. 용감함, 용맹함 2. 뻔뻔함, 안하무인함	[2591] boldness [929] courage
[aw-DAS-i-tee]	Her audacity is admirable.	[1110] confidence

6101 편입 GRE		[6016] slang
jargon	전문용어	[6457] idiom
[JAHR-guhn]	Doctors use medical jargon.	

6102 토플		[4938] ape
primate	1. (원숭이 등의) 영장류 2. (특정 지역의) 대주교	
[PRAHY-meyt]	Monkeys and apes are primates.	

6103		[678] degree
baccalaureate	1. 학사 학위 2. 입학 시험	
[bak-uh-LAWR-ee-it]	Students take the baccalaureate in the last year of school.	

6104 공무원 편입 GRE		stagnate (침체되다) stagnant (침체된)
stagnation	침체, 발전과 변화가 없는 상황	[82] inaction
[stag-NEY-shuhn]	Citizens are frustrated at the 5 years of economic stagnation.	[4251] sluggishness

6105 토플 편입 GRE		[2196] moderate [427] agreeable
temperate	1. 온난한, 온건한 2. 절제력 있는	[1294] weather
[TEM-per-it]	Korea has a temperate climate.	[5100] balmy

6106		acquittal (무죄 선고)
acquit	1. 석방하다, 면제하다 2. 특정하게 행동하다	[6996] absolve
[uh-KWIT]	She was acquitted on her crime.	[372] clear

6107		[1962] shine [257] light
sheen	광채, 윤기, 빛남	[3767] glaze
[sheen]	The glass window has a sheen.	[5981] gleam

6108		[3496] elaborate [542] beautiful
ornate	장식된, 화려한	[7017] baroque
[awr-NEYT]	The museum has an ornate ceiling.	

6109		[4471] prostitute
whore	매춘부	[4899] hustler
[hawr]	Whores have many sexual relationships.	

6110		[5100] balm
ointment	연고	[외래어] lotion
[OINT-muhnt]	Please rub some ointment on my scar.	

6111 공무원 편입		whirl (회전하다) [3290] hurricane
whirlwind	회오리(바람)	[2962] chaos
[HWURL-wind]	The whirlwind moved across the sea.	

6112		[1689] horse [1039] task
mare	1. 암컷인 말 2. 달의 어두운 표면	[1084] adult
[mair]	The mare gave birth.	[1438] female

6113		
inflammation [in-fluh-MEY-shuhn]	1. 선동, 자극 2. 발화 3. 염증	inflammatory (선동적인) flammable (불이 잘 붙는) [3367] ignition [1374] infection
	The man's racist remarks caused extreme inflammation amongst the group.	

6114		
fuselage [FYOO-suh-lahzh]	(비행기의) 동체, 중심부	[569] box [1120] frame
	The fuselage of the plane can accommodate 100 passengers.	

6115 토익		
broom [broom]	빗자루	[2570] sweep [5528] mop
	The children swept the room with the broom.	

6116		
atonement [uh-TOHN-muhnt]	(잘못이나 죄에 대한) 보상, 속죄	atone (보상하다) [1267] satisfaction [4605] redemption
	The parent wanted to make atonement for his child's actions.	

6117		
catfish [KAT-fish]	메기	[983] fish [1077] liar
	Catfish eat small shrimp and worms.	

6118 공무원 편입 GRE		
assailant [uh-SEY-luhnt]	공격자	assail (공격하다) unassailable (공격 불가능한) [2141] aggressor
	The identity of the assailant is still a mystery.	

6119		
hoodie [HOOD-ee]	(옷의 종류 중) 후드 티셔츠	
	She is wearing a gray hoodie.	

6120		
duet [doo-ET]	이중창, 이중주	[644] couple [3584] duo
	The couple sang a duet.	

6121 편입		
bellow [BEL-oh]	(동물이나 사람이) 소리를 지르다, 고함을 지르다	[4320] roar [3172] shout
	The lion bellowed in pain.	

6122		
fillet [FIL-it]	(동물의 갈비뼈 근처에서 발라낸) 고기	[983] fish [1755] meat
	She ordered a pork fillet.	

6123 공무원		
puberty [PYOO-ber-tee]	사춘기	[3689] adolescence
	At puberty, teenagers become moody.	

6124		
gamut [GAM-uht]	전범위, 전역	[2606] spectrum
	The singer could sing the whole gamut of notes.	

6125		
blight [blahyt]	1. (식물을 말라죽이는) 마름병 2. 망치다, 피해를 끼치다	[3766] plague [719] damage [4795] affliction
	The crops are suffering from blight.	

6126		
fruition [froo-ISH-uhn]	(어떤 과정의) 결실	[1019] realization [235] result
	Her diligence came to fruition during the exam.	

6127	초자연적인, 과학적으로 증명할 수 없는, 논리적으로 설명하기 어려운	
paranormal		
[par-uh-NAWR-muh l]	The magician has paranormal powers.	

6128	자식, 놈	[1580] fellow
bloke		[1545] male
[blohk]	He's an arrogant bloke.	

6129	막대 그래프	
histogram		
[HIS-tuh-gram]	The histogram shows changes in population.	

6130	1. (큰 덩어리에서 떨어져 나온) 조각, 가시 2. 분열되다, 쪼개지다	[3352] fragment
splinter		[409] bit
[SPLIN-ter]	There is a splinter of glass in my thumb.	[6836] sliver

6131 공무원 토플 편입 GRE	몰살, 전멸	exterminate (몰살시키다)
extermination		[5975] annihilation
		[1255] destruction
[ik-STUR-muh-ney-shuh n]	Hunting caused the extermination of buffalos.	[1626] elimination

6132	즐거운, 쾌활한	[594] happy
jolly		[2488] cheerful
[JOL-ee]	The jolly clown made the children happy.	

6133	(산)토끼	[792] rabbit
hare		[986] fly
[hair]	The hare ran away from the lion.	

6134	익살, 장난	[6875] shenanigans
antics		[2293] joke
		[6667] frivolity
[AN-tiks]	The audience is entertained by the comedian's antics.	

6135	대명사	
pronoun		
[PROH-noun]	The word 'she' is a pronoun.	

6136	투박한	[5858] clumsy
clunky		[196] large
[KLUHNG-kee]	Old machines are clunky.	

6137	1. (주차를 담당하는) 발레 서비스/요원 2. (남자의 하인인) 종자	[269] servant
valet		[453] attendant
[va-LEY]	The restaurant will valet your car for you.	

6138 공무원	홍역	
measles		
[MEE-zuh lz]	Children are suffering from a case of the measles.	

6139 GRE	1. 난해한, 이해하기 어려운 2. 비밀스러운	[1926] mysterious
arcane		[1817] complicated
		[3056] impenetrable
[ahr-KEYN]	Only scholars understood the arcane book.	[6307] esoteric

6140 공무원	(손목 발목 등을) 삐다	[2202] twist
sprain		[1043] injure
		[2286] strain
[spreyn]	I sprained my ankles.	

6141		
abomination [uh-bom-uh-NEY-shuhn]	1. 증오심을 유발하는 것, 혐오하는 것 2. 혐오, 증오	abominable (혐오스러 운) [1599] hate [53] dislike
	Child exploitation is an abomination.	

6142	토플	
carcass [KAHR-kuhs]	시체, 송장	[4693] corpse
	Birds gathered around the rotting carcass.	

6143		
plump [pluhmp]	1. 통통한, 포동포동한 2. 통통해지다 3. (쿠션이나 배게 등의 모양을) 둥글게 하다	[7063] chubby [1328] fat [2997] fleshy [3037] chunky
	Oranges are plump and sweet.	

6144		
joystick [JOI-stik]	1. (비디오 게임을 조작하는) 조이스틱 2. (비행기 등을 조정하는) 수동식 조작 장치	[915] stick
	You can use the joystick to move your character.	

6145		
barrage [buh-RAHZH]	1. (과도하게 많은) 비판, 질문 지적 2. 엄호 사격	[4939] bombardment [898] criticism [2572] blast
	The teacher received a barrage of complaints from parents.	

6146	공무원 GRE	
cosmopolitan [koz-muh-POL-i-tn]	국제적인, 전세계적인	cosmo (도시 분위기의)
	New York is a cosmopolitan city.	

6147		
convoy [KON-voi]	1. (여러 대의 선박이나 자동차의) 호위대 2. (보호 목적을 위해) 호송하다	[4138] escort [1236] traffic
	A convoy of tanks surrounded the president's car.	

6148		
heirloom [AIR-loom]	(집안에서 전해지는) 가보	[3286] antique
	The necklace I am wearing is a family heirloom.	

6149		
cliche [klee-SHEY]	(표현이나 생각 등이) 진부한, 상투적인	
	"All that glitters is not gold" is a cliche expression.	

6150	공무원 편입 GRE	
unscrupulous [uhn-SKROO-pyuh-luhs]	무법하다, 도리를 지키지 않는, 비양심적인	scrupulous (양심적인) [1404] dishonest [1536] crafty [2543] corrupt
	The unscrupulous CEO embezzled money.	

6151	GRE	
elapse [ih-LAPS]	(시간의) 경과	[448] passing [2438] expire
	Weeks elapsed after the accident.	

6152		
kilo [KEE-loh]	1. 킬로그램 2. 킬로미터	[외래어] kilogram
	Newborn babies weigh about 5 kilograms.	

6153	편입	
hoax [hohks]	장난(을 치다), 골탕(먹이다)	[1595] trick [6921] ploy
	The children made hoax calls pretending to be the police.	

6154	GRE	
herbicide [HUR-buh-sahyd]	(잡초를 제거하기 위해 사용하는) 제초제	
	The farmer sprayed his cornfield with herbicide.	

6155 **tapestry** [TAP-uh-stree]	1. (수나 무늬가 놓여진 두꺼운) 천, 벽걸이 2. 혼합, 조합	[4603] drapery [656] mixture
	This tapestry depicts the ocean.	

6156 **anguish** [ANG-gwish]	(심리적이거나 신체적인) 고통, 격통	anguished (고뇌에 찬) [3324] distress [3887] grief [4829] agony
	He cried in anguish.	

6157 편입 **gratuity** [gruh-TOO-i-tee]	(웨이터나 운전 기사에게 주는) 팁	[3831] perks [160] payment [1884] bonus
	The waiter received a large tip.	

6158 **transfusion** [trans-FYOO-zhuhn]	수혈	
	The patient needs an immediate blood transfusion.	

6159 공무원 편입 GRE **relinquish** [ri-LING-kwish]	(책임, 직무 등을) 포기하다, 양도하다	[2399] abandon [7198] abdicate
	He relinquished the company stocks to his daughter.	

6160 토플 **ghetto** [GET-oh]	(특히 사회적 소수자들이 모여사는) 빈민가	[6316] slum [500] association
	Even in New York, there are ghettos.	

6161 **squirt** [skwurt]	뿜어내다, 분출하다, (찍) 짜다	[6715] spurt [2029] wet [2230] pour
	She squirted mustard on her hotdog.	

6162 토플 **beak** [beek]	(새 등의) 부리, (거북이 등의) 주둥이	[1057] bill
	The eagle picked up the fish with its beak.	

6163 편입 **maxim** [MAK-sim]	(삶의 진리나 바람직한 처세를 논하는) 격언	[4846] proverb [6783] adage
	His maxim in life is "this too shall pass".	

6164 편입 **phobia** [FOH-bee-uh]	공포증	[1198] fear [2288] anxiety [5725] aversion
	I have a phobia of spiders.	

6165 편입 **supple** [SUHP-uhl]	1. 유연하고 민첩한 2. 사고가 유연한	[1309] flexible [2097] graceful [3187] agile [3667] elastic
	The dancer's body is supple.	

6166 **mainstay** [MEYN-stey]	중심, 핵심, (비유적 의미로의) 대들보	[2162] backbone [3920] confidant
	Trade is the mainstay of the Korean GDP.	

6167 공무원 **shiver** [SHIV-er]	(부들부들) 떨다, 전율하다	[1969] shake [6239] flutter [6740] quiver
	He shivered because of the cold.	

6168 GRE **centrifugal** [sen-TRIF-yuh-guhl]	(원의 중심에서 멀어지는 성질인) 원심력의	
	The vacuum cleaner uses centrifugal force to collect dust.	

6169	공무원 편입 GRE	1. (좋지 않은 일을) 방지하다, 막다 2. (머리나 눈을) 돌리다	[848] avoid
avert			[740] prevent
[uh-VURT]		The successful negotiation averted a protest.	[3923] deter

6170	공무원	(신문의) 사망기사	[7440] eulogy
obituary			
[oh-BICH-oo-er-ee]		He found out she passed away after reading the obituary.	

6171	공무원 토플 편입 GRE	(비용 등을) 줄이다, 단축하다	curtailment (단축)
curtail			[509] reduce
[ker-TEYL]		The dictator curtailed the freedom of the citizens.	[1756] decrease

6172		1. 전적으로 2. 진심으로	wholehearted (전적인)
wholeheartedly			[3338] sincerely
[HOHL-hahr-tid-lee]		I wholeheartedly support your decision.	[595] deeply
			[5642] candidly

6173		광견병	[2378] madness
rabies			
[REY-beez]		Rabies causes madness and trembling.	

6174		별표(를 달다)	[669] star
asterisk			[837] mark
[AS-tuh-risk]		Asterisks are used to notify the source of the information.	

6175		1. 산책 2. 산책로	[533] walk
promenade			[1743] deck
[prom-uh-NEYD]		He went on a promenade after dinner.	

6176		(은빛과 청색을 띠는 물고기인) 청어	
herring			
[HER-ing]		Bears eat herring.	

6177	공무원 토플	1. 반역 2. 배신	[4004] betrayal
treason			[967] crime
[TREE-zuhn]		The punishment for treason is life in prison.	[7210] mutiny

6178	토익 공무원 GRE	(내용을 요약하거나 단순화하여) 바꿔쓰다	[2379] rephrase
paraphrase			[1201] repeat
[PAR-uh-freyz]		You must credit the original text when you paraphrase it.	

6179		건방진, 까부는	[3614] cheeky
sassy			[547] energetic
[SAS-ee]		Many teenagers are sassy.	

6180	편입	(주장이나 사고 등이) 단호한, 강경한	emphatically (강조하여)
emphatic			[195] directly
[em-FAT-ik]		She was empathic that she did not like him.	[1122] categorical
			[2842] assertive

6181	편입 GRE	1. 불쾌한 2. (모욕스러울 정도로) 밉살스러운, 무례한	noxious (유독한)
obnoxious			[4403] repulsive
[uhb-NOK-shuhs]		Her straightforwardness is a large part of why people call her obnoxious.	[2465] annoying
			[4009] rude

6182	공무원	1. 끊임없이 힘써 일하다 2. 힘든 일, 어려운 일	[4263] exertion
toil			
[toil]		The laborers toiled away on the construction site.	

6183	토플	비몽사몽(한 상태), 최면 상태	[1073] dream
trance			[990] asleep
[trans]		The magician put him in a trance.	[5675] coma
			[6069] rapture

6184	편입	(독주 악기를 중심으로 관현악이 합주하는 형식의 음악인) 콘체르토, 협주곡	[2217] concert
concerto			[1368] arrangement
[kuhn-CHER-toh]		The flute concerto was delightful.	

6185	공무원	1. (지도자의) 탄핵 2. 비난, 고소	impeach (탄핵하다)
impeachment			[4665] indictment
[im-PEECH-muhnt]		If the sexual harassment scandals are true, the president will face impeachment.	[4101] allegation

6186	GRE	(특정 작가의 작품 등의) 전집, 총괄, 집대성	
corpus			
[KAWR-puhs]		You can borrow the Shakespearean corpus at the library.	

6187		질식시키다, 목을 조르다	[3992] choke
strangle			[682] kill
[STRANG-guhl]		The criminal strangled his victim.	[2952] inhibit
			[5310] gag

6188		(특히 범죄 사건에 대한) 조사	inquisition (조사, 심문)
inquest			[1004] investigation
[IN-kwest]		The police held an inquest regarding the murder.	[647] discussion

6189	편입	급성장하는, 빠르게 발달하는	[3945] flourishing
burgeoning			[3323] prosper
[BUR-juh-ning]		Many people are employed in the burgeoning technology industry.	

6190	편입 GRE	(원인을 ~로) 돌리다, 탓하다	[1783] attribute
ascribe			[75] think
[uh-SKRAHYB]		He ascribed his students' lack of attention to the hot weather.	[6945] impute

6191		퓨마	[외래어] puma
cougar			[4330] panther
[KOO-ger]		Cougars eat deer.	

6192	편입	(특히 건물을 허물어 발생한) 파편, 조각, 잔해	[3571] debris
rubble			
[RUHB-uhl]		Many people are trapped in the rubble of rocks.	

6193	토플	1. 열정적인, 강렬한 2. 고온에 달해 빛을 내는, 백열의	[5565] luminous
incandescent			[1397] bright
[in-kuhn-DES-uhnt]		Her performance was incandescent.	[2089] radiant

6194		애욕, 성욕	[4753] lust
libido			
[li-BEE-doh]		Depression may cause weight loss and loss of libido.	

6195	토플 편입 GRE	1. 허세를 부리는, 자부하는 2. 가식적인	pretension (허세)
pretentious			pretense (겉치레, 가식)
[pri-TEN-shuhs]		The pretentious critic acts as he knows more than he actually does.	[6815] pompous
			[316] arty

6196		(빛이나 비를 막는) 캐노피, 천막	[2191] blind
awning			[231] covering
[AW-ning]		The awning keeps the porch dry.	[외래어] tent

6197	편입	1. 떨림, 몸서리, 전율 2. (작은 규모의 지진인) 미진	[6740] quiver
tremor			[3467] earthquake
[TREM-er]		The tremor in her voice was caused by nervousness.	[6167] shiver

6198		고의성이 없는 살인	[4581] homicide
manslaughter			[967] crime
[MAN-slaw-ter]		The punishment for manslaughter is not as severe as the punishment for murder.	

6199		1. (특히 갈증을) 해소하다 2. (불을) 끄다	unquenchable (해소 불 가능한)
quench			[1267] satisfy
[kwench]		She drank lemonade to quench her thirst.	[862] drink

6200		1. 자신감, 자존감 2. 약탈된 물건, 장물	[4337] loot
swag			[6512] plunder
[swag]		The celebrity has a lot of swag.	

6201	토플	흰개미	[812] ant
termite			
[TUR-mahyt]		Termites feed on trees and wooden furniture.	

6202	편입	1. 시들다 2. (감정이) 식다 3. 쇠퇴하다	[3808] decay
wither			[6835] atrophy
[WITH-er]		The flower is withering.	

6203		연약한, 허약한	frailty (허약함)
frail			[1445] weak
[freyl]		He is a frail old man.	[2113] ill
			[3609] feeble

6204		자기애가 넘치는, 자기 도취적인	narcissism (자기애)
narcissistic			
[nahr-suh-SIS-tik]		Some beautiful people are narcissistic.	

6205		귀부인	[1662] lady
dame			
[deym]		Dame Margaret donated a lot of money to charity.	

6206		동성애를 혐오하는, 동성애 공포증의	homophobia (동성애 혐오증)
homophobic			
[hoh-muh-FOH-bik]		The younger generation is less homophobic.	

6207	공무원	(고온에서) 녹은, 용해된	[2362] melted
molten			[1055] warm
[MOHL-tn]		Molten metal is used to make many products.	

6208	GRE	1. 세 부분으로 구성된 2. 삼인조	[3927] trio
triad			
[TRAHY-ad]		The triad of exercise, healthy eating, and sleep is necessary to lose weight.	

6209	공무원 편입 GRE	기피하다, 멀리하다	[848] avoid
shun			[5283] despise
[shuhn]		The corrupt politician shunned journalists.	[6427] disdain

6210		특이한, 괴짜의	[1776] crazy
wacky			[514] funny
[WAK-ee]		The protagonist is wacky but endearing.	[4103] absurd

6211		긴급 의료원, 위생병	[1217] nurse
paramedic			
[par-uh-MED-ik]		The paramedic team treated patients at the scene of the accident.	

6212		여학생들만의 사교 동아리	[4806] fraternity
sorority			
[suh-RAWR-i-tee]		The university has many sororities and fraternities.	

6213		1. 틀에 박힌 (진부한) 생활 2. 바퀴 자국	
rut			
[ruht]		If you're in a rut, you should search for a different job.	

6214		1. (상처를 소독하는) 거즈, 스펀지 2. 상처를 소독하다	[2466] wipe
swab			[1357] wash
[SWOB]		The doctor cleaned my wound with a swab.	[5528] mop

6215	편입 GRE	1. 예상하다 2. 상상하다, 마음으로 구상하다	visage (얼굴, 용모)
envisage			[1119] imagine
[en-VIZ-ij]		It's envisaged that the project will end next year.	[1387] intend

6216	토플 GRE	1. 단축하다, 짧게 자르다 2. 단축된, 짧게 잘라진	truncation (절단)
truncate			[2263] trim
[TRUHNG-keyt]		The editor truncated the article that I wrote.	[103] lengthen
			[4590] abbreviate

6217	토익	부동산업자	real estate (부동산)
realtor			
[REE-uhl-ter]		I am looking for a good realtor.	

6218		(오징어 등의) 촉수	
tentacle			
[TEN-tuh-kuhl]		Squids have two tentacles.	

6219	편입	(사람이나 신념을) 저버리다, 떠나가다	[2399] abandon
forsake			[118] disown
[fawr-SEYK]		She would never forsake her boyfriend.	[2456] desert
			[4548] forgo

6220	공무원	양육, 가정교육	[841] raising
upbringing			
[UHP-bring-ing]		My upbringing influenced my personality.	

6221		1. (무언가를 담아두는 용도의) 그릇, 용기 2. 저장고	[503] container
receptacle			
[ri-SEP-tuh-kuhl]		There are two different receptacles for paper and plastic.	

6222	공무원 GRE	1. 재난, 사고 2. 불행, 비운	[2257] disaster
calamity			[1597] accident
[kuh-LAM-i-tee]		The huge earthquake was a calamity for the country.	[2835] adversity
			[7435] cataclysm

6223	편입	1. 무절제(적으로 행동하다) 2. 낭비	[5605] binge
spree			
[spree]		He went on a shopping spree.	

6224		1. 탁탁 소리(가 나다) 2. (매끈한 표면 위의) 자잘하게 깨진 자국	[3441] sparkle
crackle			
[KRAK-uhl]		After putting in more wood, the fire started to crackle.	

6225		육각형	
hexagon			
[HEK-suh-gon]		Bee houses resemble a collection of hexagons.	

6226		1. (지위, 권리, 소유물 등을) 박탈하다, 빼앗다	[1848] strip
divest		2. 기업이나 사업 등의 (일부를) 팔다 3. 옷을 벗다	[3326] bankrupt
[dih-VEST]		The corrupt CEO was divested of his power.	[3880] deprive

6227		1. (솟아오른) 혹 2. 어렵게 운반하다	[553] carry
hump			
[huhmp]		Camels have humps on their backs.	

6228		1. 옹기종기 모이다 2. 움츠리다	[1635] crowd
huddle			[2435] assemble
[HUHD-l]		The penguins huddled together to stay warm.	

6229	공무원 편입	현혹하다, 마음을 사로잡다	thrall (속박)
enthrall			[3366] captivate
[en-THRAWL]		The inspiring speech enthralled the audience.	[964] inspire
			[7310] beguile

6230	토플	(뱀)장어	
eel			
[eel]		Eels have slippery bodies.	

6231	공무원 편입 GRE	병렬로 놓아 대조하다	juxtaposition (병치)
juxtapose			[572] compare
[JUHK-stuh-pohz]		The skyscrapers are juxtaposed with the slums.	

6232	공무원 편입 GRE	표면적으로	ostensible (표면적인)
ostensibly			[1582] apparently
[o-STEN-suh-blee]		She borrowed my phone, ostensibly to call her mother.	[179] officially
			[956] evidently

6233		(어떤 지위나 자리로부터) 추방하다, 내쫓다	ouster (축출)
oust			[4505] expel
[oust]		The corrupt president was ousted.	[2899] dethrone
			[4976] depose

6234	GRE	아니	naysayer (반대론자)
nay			[1315] negative
[ney]		The fight will be hard, nay, almost impossible.	[67] no

6235		1. 기사의 군도, 칼 2. 칼로 베다	[2509] sword
saber			
[SEY-ber]		The knight carried a saber.	

6236	공무원 편입	1. 만족할 줄 모르는, 충족되지 않는 2. 욕심이 많은, 탐욕스러운	satiate (실컷 만족시키다)
insatiable			[4192] greedy
[in-SEY-shuh-buhl]		She has an insatiable passion for learning.	[2537] insistent

6237		수적으로 능가하다, ~보다 많다	[1983] exceed
outnumber			
[out-NUHM-ber]		Students outnumbered teachers by four to one.	

6238		1. 긴장감, 걱정 2. (신호 등의) 파동, 변화 3. 긴장하다, 걱정하다	jittery (조마조마한)
jitters			[2288] anxiety
[JIT-er z]		I get the jitters before an interview.	[1133] worry

6239 **flutter** [FLUHT-er]	토플	1. 파닥거리다 2. 끊임없이 움직이다 3. 심장이 두근거리다 Birds fluttered around the park.	[4041] flap [2186] swing [3393] drift [3841] flicker
6240 **amputation** [AM-pyoo-tey-shuh n]		(팔이나 다리의) 절단, 잘라냄 The injury was severe and required an amputation.	amputate (절단하다)
6241 **hideous** [HID-ee-uhs]	공무원 편입	끔찍한, 섬뜩한, 징그러운 That outfit is hideous.	hideously (섬뜩하게) [785] ugly [5666] appalling [6141] abominable
6242 **helix** [HEE-liks]	GRE	나선, 소용돌이 The staircase resembles a helix.	helical (나선형의) [3919] spiral [1942] screw [4158] tangle
6243 **sprocket** [SPROK-it]		사슬 톱니 바퀴 The sprocket is an essential component of bicycles.	[1406] gear
6244 **infallible** [in-FAL-uh-buh l]	공무원 편입	1. 오류가 없는, 전지적인 2. 완벽한 Teachers are not infallible.	fallible (실수 하기 쉬운) [414] perfect [2643] flawless
6245 **knead** [need]		1. (반죽이나 흙 등을) 반죽하다, 주무르다 2. 주무르다, 안마하다 Knead the dough for five minutes.	[2768] rub [외래어] massage
6246 **presumptuous** [pri-ZUHMP-choo-uhs]		주제넘은, 뻔뻔한 Sorry if I'm being presumptuous, but your fly is open.	[4589] arrogant
6247 **snuggle** [SNUHG-uh l]		1. 편히 눕다 2. ~를 끌어안다, ~에 달라붙다 She snuggled down on her couch.	[5074] cuddle [6228] huddle
6248 **goblin** [GOB-lin]		도깨비, 고블린 Goblins play tricks on people.	[6375] gnome
6249 **mane** [meyn]		1. (동물의) 갈기 2. (갈기처럼 긴) 사람의 머리 Lions have flowing, golden manes.	[891] hair
6250 **boar** [bawr]		1. 야생의 멧돼지 2. 수퇘지 Hunters shot down the boar.	[6651] swine [2872] piglet [4756] hog
6251 **handcuff** [HAND-kuhf]		수갑(을 채우다), 쇠고랑(을 채우다) The police officer handcuffed the criminal.	[6367] shackle
6252 **rye** [rahy]		호밀(로 만든) Rye bread has a darker color than ordinary bread.	[2699] corn

6253	토익 토플 편입	1. 배려심이 있는 2. 동정심이 있는	inconsiderate (배려하지 않는)
considerate			[2065] gentle
[kuhn-SID-er-it]		My neighbor is very considerate.	[7131] amiable

6254		격자무늬(의)	
plaid			
[plad]		She is wearing a plaid skirt.	

6255		행방, (대략적인) 위치, 소재	[128] place
whereabouts			
[HWAIR-uh-bouts]		Nobody knows the whereabouts of the criminal.	

6256	편입	(특히 손)재주, 능숙함	ambidextrous (양손잡이)
dexterity			[520] skill
[dek-STER-i-tee]		I was impressed by her dexterity with knitting.	[171] experience

6257	공무원 편입	1. 가난한, 빈곤한 2. 허약한	[1173] poor
impoverished			[5989] barren
[im-POV-er-isht]		The impoverished towns were quiet and empty.	[7039] destitute

6258	공무원 GRE	1. 사선의, 비스듬한 2. 완곡히	obliquely (비스듬히)
oblique			[2494] imply
[uh-BLEEK]		There is a chair oblique to the table.	

6259	토플	콧구멍	[2309] nose
nostril			[6162] beak
[NOS-truhl]		Snot is running down your nostrils.	

6260	공무원 편입	1. 거대한 2. 어마어마한, 훌륭한	[2777] enormous
colossal			[196] large
[kuh-LOS-uhl]		The company has a colossal amount of debt.	[7278] gargantuan

6261	공무원	부두, 선착장	[6040] wharf
quay			
[kee]		The boats sailed to the quay.	

6262	공무원 토플 GRE	1. 묘사하다, 상세히 설명하다 2. 경계를 표기하다	delineation (묘사)
delineate			[526] describe
[dih-LIN-ee-eyt]		The witness delineated the appearance of the criminal.	[729] define
			[2807] depict

6263		자르다	snippet (잘라낸 조각)
snip			[1866] clip
[snip]		I snipped out the picture from the magazine.	[3285] bargain

6264		침을 (질질) 흘리다	
drool			
[drool]		The smell of food made the dog drool.	

6265	공무원 토플 편입	(고기를 먹는) 육식 동물	carnivorous (육식의)
carnivore			[3377] predator
[KAHR-nuh-vawr]		Cheetahs are carnivores.	

6266		살충제	[2686] poison
insecticide			
[in-SEK-tuh-sahyd]		If there are too many mosquitos, try spraying some insecticide.	

6267 **onslaught** [ON-slawt]	1. 맹공격 2. 과도한 양의	[709] attack
		[2141] aggression
	The army launched a series of onslaughts in the capital city.	[2335] assault

| 6268 **outboard** [OUT-bawrd] | (특히 배나 자동차의) 밖의, 곁의 | |
| | He is sitting on the outboard seats of the boat. | |

6269 **brook** [brook]	시내, 실개천	[2482] tolerate
		[3590] forbid
	Children are catching fish at the brook.	

| 6270 **watermark** [WAW-ter-mahrk] | (서류나 현찰의) 진품임을 증명하기 위한 무늬, 워터마크 | |
| | If you hold money against the light, you can see the watermark. | |

6271 **reconnaissance** [ri-KON-uh-suhns]	1. 정찰 2. 정찰대	[870] exploration
		[563] war
	Reconnaissance of the enemy revealed that they were retreating.	[3478] surveillance

6272 편입 **tumultuous** [too-MUHL-choo-uhs]	1. 떠들썩한, 시끄러운 2. 혼란스러운	tumult (소란)
		[4991] turbulent
		[2261] loud
	The party was tumultuous.	[3867] fierce

6273 **splurge** [splurj]	1. 돈 낭비(를 하다) 2. 과도한 양의	[7034] squander
		[5659] disburse
	He splurged money on food.	

6274 공무원 **punitive** [PYOO-ni-tiv]	1. 형벌의, 처벌의 2. 가혹한	[2939] harsh
		[665] difficult
		[1822] disciplinary
	The UN took punitive measures against the dictator.	[2046] penal

| 6275 **lifeline** [LAHYF-lahyn] | 1. 구명 밧줄 2. 삶의 질을 개선해주는 것 | |
| | The lifeguard threw the lifeline to the drowning man. | |

| 6276 **rad** [rad] | 1. 대단한, 기막힌 2. (기하학의) 라디안 | [3791] wicked |
| | Your outfit is rad. | |

| 6277 토플 **rubric** [ROO-brik] | 1. (시험지의) 지시문 2. (지문의) 제목 | |
| | Don't forget to read the rubric. | |

| 6278 공무원 **anabolic** [uh-NAB-uh-lik] | 동화 작용의 | |
| | Some athletes use anabolic steroids to enhance their performance. | |

6279 편입 **pious** [PAHY-uhs]	신앙심이 깊은, 경건한	piety (경건, 신앙심)
		impious (신앙심이 부족한)
		[1240] religious
	My grandparents are very pious.	[6421] devout

6280 공무원 편입 **fugitive** [FYOO-ji-tiv]	1. 도망자 2. 도망치는	[83] wanted
		[4680] elusive
	Fugitives are fleeing religious persecution.	

6281 **outspoken** [OUT-spoh-kuhn]	진솔한, 거리낌 없는, 노골적인	[5642] candid [1404] honest [4649] blunt
	He is an outspoken critic of animal cruelty.	
6282 편입 **makeshift** [MEYK-shift]	임시의, 임의의	
	During the war, children studied in makeshift classrooms.	
6283 **pleat** [pleet]	주름(을 잡다)	pleated (주름을 잡은) [1182] fold [2833] cloth
	He pleated his shirt.	
6284 **bereavement** [bih-REEV-muhnt]	(죽음으로 인한 이별인) 사별	bereaved (사별을 당한) [4298] mourning [363] death [4508] sorrow
	He is suffering from the bereavement of his wife.	
6285 **bullion** [BOOL-yuhn]	1. 금덩어리, 금괴 2. 은덩어리, 은괴	[847] gold
	The ship is transporting gold bullions.	
6286 **underdog** [UHN-der-dawg]	1. 약자 2. 패배자	
	We should help the underdogs of our society.	
6287 **thump** [thuhmp]	1. 세게 때리다 2. (어떤 물건을) 거칠게 움직이다	[5956] whack [578] hit
	Her anger caused her to thump the wall.	
6288 GRE **vignette** [vin-YET]	1. (~에 대한) 간략한 설명 2. 삽화	[3085] sketch [974] scene [외래어] scenario
	She wrote a vignette of married life.	
6289 토플 편입 GRE **instigate** [IN-sti-geyt]	1. 선동하다, 추기다 2. 시작하다, 착수하다	instigator (선동자) instigation (선동 행위) [3638] provoke [7477] abet
	The media instigated citizens to vote for the old party.	
6290 **swatch** [swoch]	1. 견본, 샘플 2. 샘플을 사용하다	[1196] sample
	I would like to see a swatch of this fabric.	
6291 **decrypt** [dee-KRIPT]	(암호를) 해독하다, 해석하다	decryption (해독) [5046] decipher
	Computers can decrypt codes faster than humans.	
6292 **reindeer** [REYN-deer]	순록	
	Reindeers have large horns.	
6293 GRE **dabble** [DAB-uhl]	1. 물장난을 하다 2. 잠시 시도하다	[5120] tinker
	The children dabbled their feet in the creek.	
6294 편입 **flimsy** [FLIM-zee]	1. 조잡한, 엉성한 2. 얇은 3. 설득력이 없는	[1445] weak
	The flimsy building was destroyed in the earthquake.	

6295			
topple	1. 넘어지다 2. 쓰러지게 하다, 넘어뜨리다		[1030] overthrow [2604] collapse [6233] oust
[TOP-uhl]	The lamp post toppled down.		

6296			
doodle	낙서(하다)		[6690] scribble [670] draw
[DOOD-l]	She is doodling in her textbook.		

6297	편입		
wretched	1. 상태가 안 좋은, 비참한 2. 불행한, 불운한		[3497] miserable [3013] utterly [6912] deplorable
[RECH-id]	The condition at the refugee camp is wretched.		

6298			
thereto	1. 앞서 말한 것과 연관있는 2. 거기로, 그쪽으로		[326] connected
[thair-TOO]	The researchers studied ancient roman history and artifacts relating thereto.		

6299	공무원		
mutilation	1. 절단 2. 손상, 훼손		mutilate (인체를 훼손하다) [719] damage
[MYOOT-l-ey-shuh n]	The surgery involves mutilation of the arms.		

6300	토플		
photosynthesis	광합성		
[foh-tuh-SIN-thuh-sis]	Plants produce their food through photosynthesis.		

6301	공무원 편입 GRE		
precarious	위태로운, 불안정한		precariously (위태롭게) [531] risky [1223] dangerous [3126] delicate
[pri-KAIR-ee-uhs]	Poets make a precarious living.		

6302			
marinate	마리네이드/양념장에 (고기, 생선 등을) 담그다		[2934] steep [2367] bathe [5732] brine
[MAR-uh-neyt]	Marinate the fish in wine.		

6303			
suffocate	질식하게 하다, 호흡을 곤란케하다		suffocation (질식) [3992] choke [682] kill [4033] drown
[SUHF-uh-keyt]	The smoke suffocated the residents.		

6304			
monologue	1. 독백 2. 일방적으로 대화를 선점하다		[1813] speech [4455] discourse
[MON-uh-lawg]	The actor recited a monologue about her feelings.		

6305			
figurine	(인간 모양의) 작은 조각상		
[fig-yuh-REEN]	There is a figurine of Jesus at church.		

6306	편입		
vulgar	1. 천박한, 상스러운, 저속한 2. 널리 알려진, 모두가 아는		vulgarity (상스러움) [4802] coarse [773] sexual
[VUHL-ger]	You shouldn't make vulgar comments in public.		

6307	GRE		
esoteric	소수만 이해할 수 있는, 난해한, 비밀스러운		[3292] profound [1817] complicated [6139] arcane [7494] abstruse
[es-uh-TER-ik]	This book is too esoteric.		

6308			
numeral	숫자의, 수사		[159] number
[NOO-mer-uh l]	The numeral II represents two.		

6309	토플 편입	시대	[545] period
epoch			
[EP-uhk]		The Victorian epoch began in 1837.	

6310		1. 우연 2. 편형 기생충	[1131] luck
fluke			[1597] accident
			[1918] blessing
[flook]		Her success was not a fluke.	[4093] quirk

6311		1. 피로, 지침 2. 연소 종료	[2198] exhaustion
burnout			[2113] illness
[BURN-out]		Excessive studying results in burnout.	

6312	토플	표면에 무늬를 도드라지게 새기다	[2609] stamp
emboss			[1667] decorate
			[4509] adorn
[em-BAWS]		I embossed my name on the jacket.	

6313		다툼, 분쟁, 싸움	[1717] conflict
strife			[962] argument
			[7113] animosity
[strahyf]		There was strife within the family.	[7152] bickering

6314	공무원	저명한, 유명한	[1159] famous
illustrious			[2412] distinguished
[ih-LUHS-tree-uhs]		Michael Jordan has always been spectacular during his illustrious career.	[5148] eminent

6315		현관, 로비	[2971] lobby
foyer			
[FOI-er]		There are couches at the foyer of the hotel.	

6316	토플	빈민굴, 슬럼	
slum			
[sluhm]		Many poor people live in slums.	

6317	GRE	고안해내다, 설계하다	contrivance ((주로 억지 스러운) 고안)
contrive			[4318] devise
[kuhn-TRAHYV]		The researchers contrived a solution.	[5678] concoct

6318		1. 찌르다 2. 재수없는 사람	[4235] jerk
prick			[1766] tear
[prik]		I pricked the balloon to pop it.	

6319		빨리 걷다, 총총 걷다	[4630] jog
trot			[533] walk
			[807] hurry
[trot]		The horse trotted across the park.	[6337] amble

6320		1. (사건이) 일어나다 2. (비밀 등이) 밝혀지다	[874] occur
transpire			[370] happen
			[2035] arise
[tran-SPAHYUHR]		Anything may transpire during the elections.	[6948] befall

6321	편입	1. 봉쇄(하다) 2. 차단(하다)	[849] block
blockade			[247] closure
			[외래어] barricade
[blo-KEYD]		The government issued a blockade of American products.	

6322		1. 지글지글(거리다) 2. 매우 덥다	sizzling (매우 더운)
sizzle			[6224] crackle
			[7199] broil
[SIZ-uhl]		Sausages are sizzling on the grill.	

6323		1. (액체가) 쏟아지다, 분출하다 2. 열정적으로 말하다/쓰다	[1470] stream
gush			[2458] praise
[guhsh]		Water is gushing out of the fountain.	

6324	편입	우스꽝스러운, 바보같은, 터무니없는	[2708] ridiculous
ludicrous			[1594] comical
[LOO-di-kruhs]		His plan is ludicrous.	[1776] crazy
			[4006] bizarre

6325	공무원 편입	(무력이나 협박을 통한) 강탈, 착취	extort (강탈하다)
extortion			[6666] blackmail
[ik-STAWR-shuhn]		Extortion happens in hierarchical environments.	[2439] fraud
			[5301] coercion

6326	GRE	1. 당황하게 하다, 난처하게 하다 2. 혼동하다	[1581] confuse
confound			[887] amaze
[kon-FOUND]		His success confounded his friends.	[959] surprise
			[4014] astonish

6327	공무원 편입 GRE	간결한, 간단한, 깔끔한	succinctly (간결하게)
succinct			[1671] brief
[suhk-SINGKT]		The succinct explanation was easy for the students to understand.	[1739] quiet
			[4625] concise

6328		속눈썹	[2167] lash
eyelash			
[AHY-lash]		He has long eyelashes.	

6329		1. (그림이 그려져 있는) 퍼즐 2. 실톱	[215] problem
jigsaw			[445] break
[JIG-saw]		It took two hours to finish this jigsaw.	[1893] crack

6330	공무원 편입	1. 원한 2. 거리끼다	grudgingly (마지못해)
grudge			begrudge (시기하다)
[gruhj]		He holds a grudge against his ex-wife.	[3130] bitterness
			[7113] animosity

6331		1. 불분명하게 발음하다 2. 비난, 규탄	[5156] smear
slur			[898] criticism
[slur]		Excessive drinking causes people to slur their words.	[2120] accusation

6332	편입	(특히 종교적 이유로 인한) 은둔자	[2843] loner
hermit			
[HUR-mit]		He is a hermit who lives in the mountains.	

6333		파괴(하다), 황폐(화 하다)	[3090] devastate
ravage			[677] consume
[RAV-ij]		The army ravaged the town.	[719] damage
			[1255] destroy

6334		(경기장의 특정 구역 안인) 내야(의)	
infield			
[IN-feeld]		She is an infield player.	

6335	공무원	당혹한, 놀란	bewildering (당혹시키
bewildered			는)
[bih-WIL-derd]		My parents were bewildered by my grades.	[1581] confused

6336	공무원 편입	1. 달래다, 누그러지게 하다 2. (어떤 욕구나 기분을) 충족하다	appeasement (달램)
appease			[3926] soothe
[uh-PEEZ]		The writer made some changes to appease the critics.	[969] submit
			[4170] alleviate

6337 **amble** [AM-buhl]	1. 느릿느릿 걷다, 완보하다 2. 측대걸음 The couple ambled around the park.	ambulatory (이동하는) [3456] stroll [533] walk [3393] drift
6338 **tempest** [TEM-pist]	폭풍우, 비바람 The weather forecaster predicted a tempest this weekend.	tempestuous (비바람의) [1878] storm [1223] danger [5374] cyclone
6339 **caddie** [KAD-ee]	1. 상자, 보관함 2. 골프 캐디 There is a tea caddy in the cupboard.	
6340　공무원 **upkeep** [UHP-keep]	1. 유지, 보수, 관리 2. 유지비, 양육비 The government is responsible for the upkeep of cultural artifacts.	[600] maintenance [305] price [2748] conservation [6884] outlay
6341 **joist** [joist]	(건물 등을 받치는) 기둥, 들보 Three joists are supporting the ceiling.	[2697] beam [1120] frame [3987] stud
6342 **stipend** [STAHY-pend]	급료, 임금 My monthly stipend is $500.	[2123] salary [200] allowance [884] fee
6343 **blasphemy** [BLAS-fuh-mee]	(신성) 모독, 모욕 He was accused of blasphemy for skipping church.	blasphemous (모독적 인) [6084] profanity [5954] heresy
6344 **bonfire** [BON-fahyuhr]	(야외에서 나무 따위를 모아두고 피우는) 모닥불 The children sat down around the bonfire.	
6345 **writ** [rit]	(법원의 명령을 기록한) 영장 The judge issued a writ against the suspect.	[1079] obvious [3515] summons
6346 **moot** [moot]	1. 의제로 제안하다, 안건으로 제시하다 2. 논의할 가치가 없는 3. 모의의 The topic of climate change was mooted for the conference.	[215] problematic [665] difficult [1849] debatable
6347　공무원 **smother** [SMUHTH-er]	1. 질식시키다 2. (불을) 끄다 3. 뒤덮다 The criminal suffocated her victim.	[231] cover [3992] choke
6348 **wager** [WEY-jer]	1. 내기(를 하다) 2. 내기에 건 물건 He tried to get my number for a wager.	[2212] bet [3370] gamble
6349 **kiln** [kil]	(도자기 등을 굽는) 가마 My pottery is in the kiln.	[3387] stove [4641] furnace
6350　공무원 **hunch** [huhnch]	1. 구부리다 2. 예감 3. 밀다, 밀치다 The sad child hunched his shoulders and walked home.	[385] certainty [3528] instinct

6351	GRE	1. 복잡한, 까다로운 2. 회선상의	convolution (복잡한 것) [1088] complex
convoluted [KON-vuh-loo-tid]		I can't understand your convoluted argument.	[1817] complicated [3983] intricate

6352	공무원 편입 GRE	1. 무기력함, 활발하지 않음 2. 혼수	lethargic (무기력한) [4251] sluggishness
lethargy [LETH-er-jee]		Lethargy can be resolved with sleep and healthy eating.	[249] disinterest [3144] fatigue

6353	토플 GRE	1. 추론하다 2. 연역하다	[4210] infer [317] understand
deduce [dih-DOOS]		The investigators deduced that he was the criminal.	[2551] deduct [5967] glean

6354		1. 파괴하다, 말살하다 2. (특정한 방향으로) 움직이다, 이동하다	[682] kill
zap [zap]		Zap the enemy's weapon storage.	

6355	GRE	공리, 자명한 진리	[2290] conviction [6783] adage
axiom [AK-see-uhm]		It is an axiom that 'the whole is greater than the part'.	

6356	GRE	1. (경계 등이) 인접한, 접촉한 2. 다닥다닥 붙어있는	[3239] adjacent [347] local
contiguous [kuhn-TIG-yoo-uhs]		Korea and China are contiguous countries.	[1246] neighboring [5478] adjoining

6357	GRE	1. 역효과(를 초래하다) 2. 맞불(을 시작하다)	[2517] recoil
backfire [BAK-fahyuhr]		Criticizing his opponent backfired on him.	

6358	편입 GRE	1. (~하는) 경향 2. 버릇, 습관	[994] tendency [2103] disposition
propensity [pruh-PEN-si-tee]		She has a propensity for aggression.	[2753] bias

6359		(특정한 목적을 가진 국가나 사람들의) 연맹, 연합, 블록	[849] block [500] association
bloc [blok]		North-East Asian countries should form a trading bloc.	[3801] faction

6360		1. 창턱 2. 문지방	[3207] threshold [3199] ridge
sill [sil]		He leaned on the sill.	

6361		(말 등의 동물의) 발굽	[657] foot [533] walk
hoof [hoof]		I could hear the sound of hooves stepping against the pavement.	[4627] paw

6362	공무원 편입 GRE	비난(하다), 질책(하다)	[6859] reprimand [898] criticize
rebuke [ri-BYOOK]		My parents rebuked me for staying out late.	[6418] admonition [7141] censure

6363		1. 쓰레기 등 더러운 것, 오물 2. 퇴비	[1914] dirt [3131] mud
muck [muhk]		Please clean this muck off your table.	[5735] manure

6364		1. 주 요리, 메인 메뉴 2. 입장할 수 있는 권리, 입장권	[337] access [1078] admission
entree [AHN-trey]		I ordered steak for the entree.	

6365 **twinkle** [TWING-kuh l]	1. 빛나다 2. 빛	[3441] sparkle [1962] shine [3841] flicker [4191] blink
	Stars are twinkling in the night sky.	

6366　　　　공무원 **gall** [gawl]	1. 뻔뻔함, 염치 없음 2. 담즙	galling (짜증나는) [1833] nerve
	The customer had the gall to demand a refund.	

6367 **shackle** [SHAK-uhl]	족쇄(를 채우다), 쇠고랑(을 채우다), 속박(하다)	[720] subjection [6251] handcuff
	The police shackled the criminal.	

6368 **hulk** [huhlk]	1. 거대한, 막대한 2. 노화된 배의 선체	[1828] giant [1120] frame [4280] hull
	The hulk of a man is a basketball player	

6369 **straddle** [STRAD-l]	1. 다리를 벌리고 (걸쳐) 앉다 2. (양쪽에) 걸쳐 있다	[2587] span [1573] occupy
	The child straddled her bike.	

6370　　　　공무원 **valiant** [VAL-yuhnt]	용감한, 겁 없는	valiantly (용감하게) [929] courageous [1198] fearless [2865] brave
	She made a valiant decision to climb the mountain.	

6371　　　공무원 편입 **conglomerate** [kuh n-GLOM-er-it]	1. 대기업 2. 뭉치다, 모으다	[1053] corporation [656] mixture
	The IT conglomerate makes a lot of money.	

6372 **exponent** [ik-SPOH-nuhnt]	1. 옹호자, 추종자 2. (수학)지수	[1934] advocate [172] supporter [5047] proponent
	The professor was an exponent of equality.	

6373　　공무원 편입 GRE **timid** [TIM-id]	겁이 많은, 내향적인	timidity (겁 많음) [796] shy [6929] ambivalent [7243] bashful
	The child was too timid to make new friends.	

6374 **unison** [YOO-nuh-suh n]	1. 동시다발적 2. 조화, 화음	[2723] harmony
	The students replied in unison.	

6375 **gnome** [nohm]	난쟁이, (땅 속의 보물을 지키는) 요정	[4130] dwarf [3484] fairy
	Gnomes are often featured with pointy hats.	

6376 **restitution** [res-ti-TOO-shuhn]	1. 반환함 2. 배상, 갚음, 보상함	[160] payment [671] supply [5749] indemnity
	The restitution of cultural artifacts is important.	

6377 **baton** [buh-TON]	1. 지휘봉 2. 경찰봉	[915] stick
	The conductor controlled the orchestra with her baton.	

6378 **fang** [fang]	1. (개나 늑새 등의) 송곳니 2. 뱀의 독니	[1467] weapon
	The dog bit the prey with its fangs.	

6379	공무원 편입	암호학	cryptic (수수께끼 같은, 비밀의)
cryptography			cryptocurrency (암호화폐)
[krip-TOG-ruh-fee]		Cryptography is essential during a war.	

6380	공무원 편입	1. 압축하다, 수축하다 2. 좁아지다 3. 억제하다, 제한하다	constriction (압축)
constrict			[738] contract
			[509] reduce
[kuhn-STRIKT]		Too much fat can constrict the blood vessels.	[1959] compress

6381	공무원 편입	조짐이 되다, 나쁜 조짐을 보내다	forebode (전조가 되다)
bode			[7374] portend
[bohd]		The earthquake bodes disaster for the country.	[221] signify

6382	공무원 편입	1. 적은, 부족한 2. 인색하게 굴다	scanty (부족한)
scant			[197] little
			[1742] insufficient
[skant]		Our country has scant natural resources.	[1995] mere

6383		논문	[760] paper
treatise			[525] commentary
			[3582] thesis
[TREE-tis]		This is a comprehensive treatise on climate change.	[4455] discourse

6384	편입 GRE	1. 어둡고 탁한 2. 비밀이 많은, 투명하지 않은	[941] dark
murky			[1363] cloudy
[MUR-kee]		Fish cannot live in murky water.	

6385	공무원 편입 GRE	1. (특정 지역이나 집단에) 만연한 2. (어떤 동식물이 특정 지역에) 고유한	[485] common
endemic			
[en-DEM-ik]		Corruption is endemic in modern politics.	

6386		배출하다, 뿜어내다	[3964] vomit
spew			[4391] cascade
[spyoo]		Factories are spewing out smoke.	

6387	편입	1. 매혹하다, 사로잡다 2. 최면을 걸다	[4942] hypnotize
mesmerize			[964] inspire
			[2469] fascinate
[MEZ-muh-rahyz]		The beautiful car mesmerized her.	[6229] enthrall

6388		(음질을 높이기 위해) 다시 마스터 테이프를 만들다	[568] update
remaster			
[ree-MAS-ter]		Has this song been remastered?	

6389	공무원 편입 GRE	두 가지 뜻으로 해석될 수 있는, 애매한	unequivocal (명백히)
equivocal			equivoation (말의 애매함)
			[4259] ambiguous
[ih-KWIV-uh-kuhl]		His equivocal response confuses me.	[6929] ambivalent

6390		(어린 아이들에게 성적인 이끌림을 느끼는) 소아 성애자	pedophilia (소아성애)
pedophile			[5710] pervert
[PED-uh-fahyl]		Pedophiles need psychological counseling.	

6391	편입 GRE	상처 없는, 무탈한	scathing (신랄한)
unscathed			[1708] unharmed
			[1745] unhurt
[uhn-SKEYTHD]		Despite the accident, she is unscathed.	

6392	편입	1. 미치광이, 미친 사람 2. 기괴한, 미친	[1776] crazy
lunatic			[4871] maniacal
[LOO-nuh-tik]		The lunatic jumped in front of the car.	

6393 **gripe** [grahyp]	1. 불평하다, 투정 부리다 2. 꽉 잡다, 괴롭히다	[1782] complaint [4366] ache [5206] grievance
	"My husband doesn't wash the dishes" she griped.	
6394 **stag** [stag]	1. 남성들 전용의 2. 수사슴	[3281] deer [1902] sole [2843] lonely
	Bachelor parties are generally stag events.	
6395 편입 **accede** [ak-SEED]	1. (조약이나 요청 등에) 동의하다 2. 지위에 오르다	accession (취임) [427] agree [7207] acquiesce
	The teachers did not accede to the requests of the students.	
6396 **orthodontic** [awr-thuh-DON-tik]	치열 교정의	orthodontist (교정 전문의)
	My teeth are crooked. I need orthodontic treatment.	
6397 **rescind** [ri-SIND]	폐지하다, 무효화하다	[3960] revoke [4362] abolish [7375] abrogate
	This law was rescinded last month.	
6398 **posh** [posh]	화려한, 호화로운	[353] classy [1130] expensive [4086] chic
	She lives in a posh mansion.	
6399 편입 **smudge** [smuhj]	1. 자국, 오점, 얼룩 2. 얼룩지게 하다	[940] spot [837] mark [5579] blemish [6036] blot
	There is a smudge of paint on the table.	
6400 **armpit** [AHRM-pit]	겨드랑이	
	My armpits are sweaty.	
6401 편입 GRE **conjecture** [kuhn-JEK-cher]	짐작(하다), 추측(하다)	[1216] guess [6350] hunch
	There is a lot of conjecture about the elections.	
6402 공무원 **exhort** [ig-ZAWRT]	권고하다, 훈계하다	exhortation (권고) [1935] urge [929] encourage [1035] advise
	The teacher exhorted the students to study more.	
6403 **rewind** [ree-WAHYND]	되감다, 다시 감다	[1845] reverse
	She rewound the film to watch the movie again.	
6404 토플 **pastime** [PAS-tahym]	취미, 여가	[3904] diversion [3634] amusement
	My favorite pastime is reading.	
6405 **crutch** [kruhch]	1. 목발 2. (심리적) 지지대	[3920] confidant [4278] cane
	I've been on crutches since last week.	
6406 공무원 **drowsiness** [DROU-zee-nis]	나른함, 권태로움	drowsy (졸리는) [990] sleepiness [789] laziness [3144] fatigue
	This cold medicine may cause drowsiness.	

6407 공무원 편입 GRE	침입하다, 침범하다	encroachment (침입)
encroach		[4026] infringe
[en-KROHCH]	CCTVs are encroaching on our privacy.	[7134] impinge

6408 GRE	1. 공표하다, 발표하다 2. 퍼뜨리다	promulgation (선포)
promulgate		[2132] broadcast
[PROM-uhl-geyt]	The president promulgated the new law yesterday.	[481] notify
		[899] announce

6409 공무원 편입 GRE	경멸(하다), 멸시(하다)	[6427] disdain
scorn		[6925] derision
[skawrn]	Everyone scorned the criminal.	

6410 GRE	(의미, 권력 등을) 넘기다, 양도하다	devolution (권력 이양)
devolve		
[dih-VOLV]	A good president devolves power to the vice president.	

6411 토플 편입	열렬한, 열정적인	ardently (열렬히)
ardent		[1475] passionate
[AHR-dnt]	She is an ardent football fan.	[1268] emotional
		[4209] avid

6412	채우다, 집어넣다	
stow		
[stoh]	Please stow your toys in these boxes.	

6413 공무원 편입	1. 사이가 틀어진, 멀어진 2. 별거 중인	[2502] alienated
estranged		[2640] divorce
[ih-STREYNJD]	The fight made me feel estranged from my girlfriend.	[2843] lonely

6414 GRE	공모, 통모	collude (불법 행위를 공모하다)
collusion		[3483] conspiracy
[kuh-LOO-zhuhn]	The companies worked in collusion to increase prices.	[6915] complicity

6415 공무원	1. (글로) 적다 2. 미량, 소량	[6669] speck
jot		[168] write
[jot]	Can you jot down your phone number?	

6416	1. 이성애자 2. 이성애의	[1233] straight
heterosexual		
[het-er-uh-SEK-shoo-uhl]	Heterosexual males are attracted to females.	

6417 공무원 편입 GRE	무관심	apathetic (무관심한)
apathy		[117] indifference
[AP-uh-thee]	There is widespread apathy about politics.	[383] insensitivity
		[2460] boredom

6418 공무원 편입	1. 훈계하다, 타이르다 2. 충고하다	admonition (훈계)
admonish		[6362] rebuke
[ad-MON-ish]	The parents admonished the child for not finishing her homework.	[898] criticize
		[1035] advise

6419	1. 다항식 2. 다명의	
polynomial		
[pol-uh-NOH-mee-uhl]	$x^2 - 4x + 7$ is a polynomial.	

6420 GRE	기존 자료를 활용해 예측하다, 추정하다	[4210] infer
extrapolate		[317] understand
[ik-STRAP-uh-leyt]	The results of this experiment cannot be extrapolated to other scenarios.	[3152] hypothesize
		[6353] deduce

6421	편입	독신한, 열심인	[6279] pious
devout			[1240] religious
[dih-VOUT]		He is a devout Buddhist.	[2940] adoring
			[6411] ardent

6422		1. 속이다 2. (사기의) 피해자	[2644] fool
dupe			
[doop]		He was duped into purchasing insurance.	

6423		1. (걷잡을 수 없는) 큰 불 2. 지옥	infernal (지긋지긋한, 지옥의)
inferno			[1842] hell
[in-FUR-noh]		An hour after the fire started, the mountain was an inferno.	[655] fire

6424	공무원	(감정이나 행동 등의) 분출, 폭발	[2058] explosion
outburst			[452] fit
[OUT-burst]		Everyone was surprised by her outburst of anger.	[2828] burst
			[4109] eruption

6425	공무원 편입 GRE	1. 말살하다 2. 지우다, 흔적을 제거하다, 가리다	[1255] destroy
obliterate			[5975] annihilate
[uh-BLIT-uh-reyt]		The army obliterated the whole town.	

6426		1. 무시무시한 2. 공포스러운	[2830] horrible
gruesome			[3594] frightful
[GROO-suhm]		I couldn't sleep after watching a gruesome movie.	[5666] appalling

6427	공무원 편입 GRE	경멸(하다), 무시(하다)	[6409] scorn
disdain			[4589] arrogance
[dis-DEYN]		He sighed in disdain.	[7342] antipathy

6428	편입	1. 중얼대다, 종알대다 2. 중얼거림	[6678] mutter
murmur			[3968] whisper
[MUR-mer]		The students were murmuring during the principal's speech.	[4642] buzz
			[5031] hum

6429		야금야금 먹다, 조금 베어물다, 갉아먹다	[2061] bite
nibble			
[NIB-uhl]		He nibbled at the toast.	

6430		(어두운 분위기의) 누아르 영화	[941] dark
noir			
[nwar]		He is directing a noir.	

6431		막대 사탕	
lollipop			
[LOL-ee-pop]		The child is sucking on a lollipop.	

6432	공무원 토플 편입	해방	emancipate (해방하다)
emancipation			[2181] liberation
[ih-man-suh-PEY-shuhn]		The women's rights activist dedicated her whole life to female emancipation.	[386] independence

6433	공무원 GRE	함축 또는 내포되어있는 의미	[2752] implication
connotation			[158] meaning
[kon-uh-TEY-shuhn]		The words he chose had a negative connotation.	[1590] overtone

6434		1. (길고 튼튼한)장갑 2. 시련 3. 태형	
gauntlet			
[GAWNT-lit]		The little boy's parents bought him a toy gauntlet as his birthday gift.	

6435 **medley** [MED-lee]	1. 메들리 2. 잡동사니, 여러 가지 뒤섞인 무언가 3. 혼합 릴레이(수영)	[656] mixture
	Her wardrobe contains a medley of colorful t-shirts.	
6436 공무원 토플 GRE **domesticated** [duh-MES-ti-key-tid]	1. 가축된 2. 길들여진 3. 가정적인	domestication (길들이기) [2009] domestic
	Do you know which animals were domesticated first?	
6437 **namesake** [NEYM-seyk]	동성동명의 또는 이름이 같은 사람/곳	
	The new company is the namesake of the owner's father.	
6438 **abode** [uh-BOHD]	거주지, 거처, 주거	[145] home
	The couple moved into their temporary abode.	
6439 **hooray** [hoo-REY]	만세, 야호	
	Hooray! Today is Friday!	
6440 **wail** [weyl]	1. 울부짖다, 통곡하다, 비탄하다 2. 불평하다 3. (바람 등이)슬픈 소리를 내다	[5385] moan [2068] cry [3887] grieve [4488] fuss
	She began to wail when she realized that he no longer loved her.	
6441 **vulture** [VUHL-cher]	1. 독수리 2. 욕심쟁이	[3377] predator [4273] miser
	A couple of vultures were circling in the sky as if to look for prey.	
6442 공무원 토플 편입 **inundate** [IN-uhn-deyt]	1. 범람시키다, 침수하다 2. 몰려오다, 쇄도하다	inundation (범람) [2126] flood [396] send [3800] engulf
	The city has been inundated with floodwater.	
6443 공무원 편입 GRE **opulent** [OP-yuh-luhnt]	부유한, 풍부한, 호화로운	[1854] luxurious [1130] expensive [5574] extravagant [5731] deluxe
	He enjoys his opulent lifestyle to the fullest.	
6444 **din** [din]	소음, 소란스러움	[5557] racket [334] teach
	The din from my aunt's room irritates me so much.	
6445 **bandwagon** [BAND-wag-uhn]	1. (jump on the bandwagon의 의미로 쓰일 때) 시류 또는 유행에 편승하다 2. 행사	[4288] wagon [75] thought
	Many of the IT companies jumped on the bandwagon and started investing in AI.	
6446 **conjugate** [KON-juh-geyt]	1. 결합(하다) 2. 활용시키다, (적절히)변화하다 3. 같은 어원인	
	Some words can be conjugated for convenience.	
6447 **sonar** [SOH-nahr]	수중 음파 탐지기(초음파 방출 탐지 시스템)	
	A submarine sonar was installed to monitor any possible enemies.	
6448 **camaraderie** [kah-muh-RAH-duh-ree]	동지애, 동료의식, 우애	[288] friendship [2783] intimacy
	The team members eventually developed a sense of camaraderie.	

6449		
minion [MIN-yuhn]	1. 부하 2. 앞잡이	
	All successful leaders have intelligent minions.	

6450 공무원 토플 편입 GRE		rudiment (기본)
rudimentary [roo-duh-MEN-tuh-ree]	1. 기본의, 기초의 2. 미발달의, 원시적인	[648] basic [838] elemental
	The engineer didn't even have the most rudimentary skills.	

6451		[1230] cheap
tacky [TAK-ee]	1. 조잡한, 엉성한 2. (끈적한 물질이)덜 마른 3. 싸구려의, 저속한	[2802] faded
	She was ashamed of her tacky essay.	

6452		
abscess [AB-ses]	종기, 농양	
	The old lady had an abscess on her gum.	

6453		[1113] diner
bistro [BIS-troh]	비스트로, 작은 (선)술집 또는 식당	[1162] restaurant [2856] lounge
	He often visits a local bistro for some food and drinks.	

6454		[4373] solicitor
barrister [BAR-uh-ster]	법정 변호사	
	She failed to convince her barrister that she indeed is innocent.	

6455		[4919] potion
elixir [ih-LIK-ser]	영약, 묘약, 만병통치약	[7415] panacea
	I want an elixir that could make these worries go away.	

6456 공무원 편입 GRE		[3876] impulse
impetus [IM-pi-tuhs]	자극(제), 추진력, 박차	[323] cause [4302] catalyst
	The government's recent reforms served as growth impetus.	

6457 편입		idiomatic (관용적인)
idiom [ID-ee-uhm]	관용구, 숙어, 속담	[2379] phrase [5721] dialect [6101] jargon
	It is often hard to figure out what the idiom is trying to infer.	

6458		[1007] strength
forte [FAWRt]	1. 강점, 장점 2. (음악) 포르테	
	She spent the whole week studying math since it wasn't her forte.	

6459		[3161] rage
tantrum [TAN-truhm]	1. 울화 2. 짜증, 떼쓰기	[452] fit [6424] outburst
	After talking to his boss, he had a tantrum.	

6460		[6736] scourge
birch [burch]	1. 자작나무 2. 회초리	[4278] cane [6377] baton
	Birch water contains many healthy nutrients.	

6461 편입		[5480] turmoil
upheaval [uhp-HEE-vuhl]	격변, 대변동, 봉기	[234] effect [4119] catastrophe [7435] cataclysm
	With the fall of the dictator, the country faced an upheaval.	

6462		[5840] clam
mussel [MUHS-uhl]	홍합	
	I'd recommend white wine for the mussel pasta.	

6463		
spatula	주걱, 뒤집개	[795] spoonful
[SPACH-uh-luh]	It is easy to scrape the batter if you use a rubber spatula.	

6464		
empress	여제, 황후	[1948] queen
[EM-pris]	After her husband died, the empress succeeded to the throne.	

6465 편입		adjournment (연기)
adjourn	연기하다, 휴정하다	[4705] postpone
[uh-JURN]	The meeting has been adjourned until next month.	[439] stop [1697] delay

6466		[2129] addict
junkie	(마약)중독자, 마니아	[2131] enthusiast
[JUHNG-kee]	He is a social media junkie.	

6467		
renegade	변절자, 이탈자, 배신자	
[REN-i-geyd]	The employee became a renegade and leaked confidential information about the company.	

6468		[1854] luxurious
sumptuous	호화로운, 사치스런	[542] beautiful
[SUHMP-choo-uhs]	She was mesmerized by her friend's sumptuous birthday party.	[1130] expensive

6469		[1447] guarantee
surety	보증(금), 보증인, 담보(물건)	
[SHOOR-i-tee]	I lent him $1000 and he gave me his watch as surety.	

6470 공무원 편입 GRE		[3286] antiquated
archaic	1. 구식인, 원시적인 2. 고풍의, 고대의	[1417] old-fashioned
[ahr-KEY-ik]	He still carries around his archaic laptop from ten years ago.	[1803] ancient

6471 공무원 편입		[388] nightly
nocturnal	야행성의, 밤의, 야간의	
[nok-TUR-nl]	She became nocturnal after she quit her job.	

6472 편입		hibernate (동면하다)
hibernation	동면	[990] sleep
[HI-ber-ney-shuh n]	Many animals are capable of maintaining homeostasis during hibernation.	[1073] dream [5675] coma

6473		[1182] fold
crimp	1. (머리를)웨이브하다 2. 주름을 잡다 3. 방해하다, 훼방놓다	[949] shape
[krimp]	She crimped and curled her daughter's hair.	

6474		[5729] eczema
dermatitis	피부염	
[dur-muh-TAHY-tis]	This ointment will help soothe allergic dermatitis.	

6475 공무원 편입		[3437] clash
skirmish	작은 충돌/접전/언쟁(을 벌이다)	[563] war
[SKUR-mish]	The couple's short skirmish eventually led to the divorce.	[962] argument [6808] altercation

6476 편입		intercede (중재하다)
intercession	1. 중재, 조정 2. 기도, 간청	[2157] intervention
[in-ter-SESH-uh n]	He has been released from jail thanks to the intercession of a policeman.	[442] pressure

6477 **spoof** [spoof]	1. 패러디(하다), 흉내내다 2. 도용하다	[외래어] parody [7201] burlesque
	The movie was a spoof of high school life.	
6478 **archipelago** [ahr-kuh-PEL-uh-goh]	군도, 다도해	
	The family planned a trip to many different islands on the archipelago.	
6479 **meld** [meld]	혼합하다, 섞다	[1620] blend [656] mix [2375] merge [2582] fuse
	Her colleagues were able to meld their ideas into a viable plan.	
6480 **transpose** [trans-POHZ]	1. (순서를)바꾸어 놓다 2. 전치하다	transposition (치환) [922] transfer
	Members of the famous boy band decided to transpose their songs on the setlist.	
6481 **cubicle** [KYOO-bi-kuhl]	큐비클, 칸막이 장소/사무실	[3373] booth [833] cell
	Find me in the cubicle section of the library.	
6482 **outlier** [OUT-lahy-er]	1. 특이값 2. 국외자, 문외한 3. 영외 거주자	[3910] deviation [6093] aberration
	Being an outlier, she found it difficult to fit in at her new job.	
6483 편입 GRE **sedentary** [SED-n-ter-ee]	앉아서 일하는, 앉아 있는, 한 곳에 머물러 사는	[4823] stationary [82] inactive [142] still
	Even though he is living a sedentary life, he is not obese at all.	
6484 공무원 편입 GRE **antidote** [AN-ti-doht]	해독제, 해결책	[2239] cure [577] solution [662] corrective
	We couldn't find any antidote for that lethal venom.	
6485 **stoop** [stoop]	1. 몸/허리를 굽히다, 구부정하다 2. 현관 계단	[5971] crouch [530] commit
	He stooped to tie his shoes.	
6486 **rouge** [roozh]	1. 악당, 변질자 2. 붉은 빛의	[5511] crimson
	The US considers North Korea to be a rogue nation.	
6487 **hyper** [HAHY-per]	1. 들뜬, 흥분한 2. 극도의, 지나치게	[1028] wired [249] interested [3534] bracing [5650] exhilarating
	I cannot handle hyper kids.	
6488 **anus** [EY-nuhs]	항문	
	He couldn't sleep because his anus was so itchy.	
6489 토플 **enclave** [EN-kleyv]	소수 민족, 고립된 소수집단	[2109] territory [3548] isle [6478] archipelago
	Their town has been known as a wealthy enclave for decades.	
6490 **scum** [skuhm]	1. (더러운)거품 2. 인간쓰레기	[6742] froth [1914] dirt
	You should try to remove any scum on the surface of the boiling broth.	

6491 **tact** [takt]	편입	1. 요령, 재치, 솜씨 2. 촉감	tactful (눈치있는) [6554] finesse
		He was fired for the lack of tact in dealing with issues.	

6492 **shudder** [SHUHD-er]	1. 몸을 떨다, 몸서리치다 2. 전율	[5700] tremble [2186] swing [6167] shiver
	The little girl shuddered at the thought of ghosts.	

6493 **dismal** [DIZ-muhl]	공무원 편입 GRE	1. 음울한, 음침한 2. 질 낮은, 형편없는	[5443] gloomy [1692] sad [1780] depressing [3823] dim
		The holiday will be dismal without the love of my life.	

6494 **sesame** [SES-uh-mee]	참깨(씨)	
	My mom sprinkles sesame seeds over every dish she makes.	

6495 **fizz** [fiz]	1. (탄산)거품 2. 활기를 띠다 3. 탄산이 쉬익 빠지는 소리	[862] drink
	The soda had already lost its fizz.	

6496 **resuscitation** [ri-SUHS-i-tey-shuh n]	공무원 편입	1. 부활, 부흥 2. 소생, 의식 회복	resuscitate (되살아나게 하다) [1927] revitalization [5251] rejuvenation
		The declining industry needs resuscitation.	

6497 **ratchet** [RACH-it]	1. 단계적으로 증가시키다 2. 래칫(톱니바퀴)	[280] increase [1633] disk
	Steel prices have ratcheted up for years.	

6498 **cannibal** [KAN-uh-buh l]	1. 식인종 2. 육식동물	
	Several tourists were killed by cannibals.	

6499 **corporal** [KAWR-per-uhl]	1. 육체의 2. 상등병	
	Our school does not allow any kind of corporal punishment.	

6500 **ejaculate** [ih-JAK-yuh-leyt]	1. 사정하다 2. 갑자기 소리지르다	ejaculation (사정)
	Unlike men, women don't ejaculate.	

6501 **falter** [FAWL-ter]	공무원 편입	주춤하다, 주저하다, 더듬거리다	[3494] stumble [3227] hesitate [6992] flounder
		She hoped he would stop faltering and finally propose to her.	

6502 **barometer** [buh-ROM-i-ter]	1. 기압계 2. 지표, 표준	[1294] weather
	The barometer on the living room wall has been broken.	

6503 **hush** [huhsh]	공무원	1. 쉿(제스쳐), ~을 조용히 시키다, 쉬쉬하다 2. 침묵, 정적	[1739] quiet [142] stillness
		The teacher tried hard to hush his noisy students.	

6504 **arson** [AHR-suh n]	방화	arsonist (방화범) [655] fire [4162] torching
	The entire factory has been destroyed in an arson attack.	

6505 **sly** [slahy]	교활한, 음흉한, 익살맞은 I hate it when she puts a sly smile on her face.	[1536] crafty [3031] clever [5917] canny
6506　　GRE **intelligible** [in-TEL-i-juh-buhl]	이해할 수 있는, 알기 쉬운 His essay was far from intelligible.	unintelligible (이해하기 힘든) [3384] straightforward
6507 **privy** [PRIV-ee]	1. 비밀 따위를 공유받은　2. 옥외 변소 They are not privy to any information from the company.	[1334] secret [65] knowing
6508 **galore** [guh-LAWR]	많이, 충분히, 풍부하게 Their house is surrounded by shops and restaurants galore.	[1299] plentiful [1432] substantial
6509　공무원 편입 GRE **condone** [kuhn-DOHN]	용서하다, 용납하다, 묵과하다 She couldn't condone cheating.	[2532] forgive [1072] approve [1095] forget [2592] excuse
6510　편입 GRE **heterogeneous** [het-er-uh-JEE-nee-uhs]	1. 다양성의, 이질의　2. 불균질의 Her university has a heterogeneous student body.	heterogeneity (다양성) [1535] diverse
6511 **retroactive** [re-troh-AK-tiv]	1. (효력이)소급하는　2. 반동하는 The refund will be retroactive to July 10.	retroactively (소급하는) [4684] retrospective
6512 **plunder** [PLUHN-der]	약탈(하다), 강탈(하다) He was arrested for plundering the ATM.	[4337] loot [1736] steal
6513 **radish** [RAD-ish]	무 Radish pickle goes well with pasta.	
6514　공무원 **hind** [hahynd]	뒤의, 뒤쪽의 Frogs can jump thanks to their long hind legs.	hindsight (돌이켜 보는 것)
6515 **dandelion** [DAN-dl-ahy-uhn]	민들레 The little boy blew on a dandelion.	
6516 **prong** [prawng]	끝이 뾰족한 기구, 갈래 Forks for cheese fondue usually have 3 prongs.	[3057] spike
6517 **polio** [POH-lee-oh]	소아마비 In the modern world, polio has almost been completely eradicated.	
6518 **volley** [VOL-ee]	1. 일제 사격, 집중 공세　2. 발리킥 The soldier fired off a volley of bullets.	

6519	바퀴벌레	[812] ant
cockroach [KOK-rohch]	Do you know how to get rid of cockroaches?	

6520 편입 GRE	1. 교훈, 격언 2. 명령서, 행동 수칙, 계율	[1501] principle [516] rule
precept [PREE-sept]	She teaches her students by precept and examples.	[4847] canon [6355] axiom

6521	집착, 페티쉬	[5710] perversion [7410] proclivity
fetish [FET-ish]	He has a fetish for expensive cars.	[7423] predilection

6522 편입	융합, 합류(점)	[3741] junction [656] mixture
confluence [KON-floo-uhns]	The confluence of the scenery and the perfect weather made her wedding more special.	[2435] assemblage

6523 공무원	위반, 위배	[1835] violation [967] crime
infraction [in-FRAK-shuhn]	He was arrested for a minor infraction.	[2628] breach

6524 편입	대학살	[4387] slaughter [1223] danger
carnage [KAHR-nij]	The dreadful carnage had finally stopped with the fall of the dictator.	[4911] butchery

6525	1. 가로놓인 2. 횡단물	[1161] cross [95] uneven
transverse [trans-VURS]	The pathway has been blocked by two transverse tree limbs.	

6526	1. 확 움직이다 2. 충격을 가하다	[1728] shock [452] fit
jolt [johlt]	The truck started to jolt as we entered the rocky road.	[2332] bump [2594] punch

6527	(미국의) 주	[839] county [2244] colony
shire [shahyuhr]	Our shire has the lowest per capita income of all the shires.	

6528 공무원 편입 GRE	1. 생기 넘치는, 활기찬 2. 무성한	exuberance (생기 발랄함) [2131] enthusiastic
exuberant [ig-ZOO-ber-uhnt]	She was exuberant when her boyfriend came to see her.	[547] energetic [2031] animated

6529	1. 특공대 2. 의용군	[6676] ranger [697] fighter
commando [kuh-MAN-doh]	He wasn't ready to join the commando unit.	[1661] guard

6530	(엉덩이를)때리다, 손바닥으로 찰싹 때리다	[4125] slap [578] hit
spank [spangk]	The boy hates it when his mom spanks him on the butt.	[7048] chastise

6531	(동물의)가지진 뿔	[3045] horn
antler [ANT-ler]	The male deer sheds its antlers every year.	

6532 공무원 토플 편입	1. 극복할 수 없는 2. 이길 수 없는 3. 능가할 수 없는	surmount (극복하다, 넘다)
insurmountable [in-ser-MOUN-tuh-buhl]	The company is facing an insurmountable challenge.	[384] hopeless [448] impassable

6533	공무원 편입	1. 끊임없는 2. 계속되는	incessantly (끊임없이)
incessant			[1264] constant
[in-SES-uhnt]		The incessant noise from the construction site drove me crazy.	[260] continuous
			[3025] ceaseless

6534		1. 굉장한 2. 울려퍼지는 3. 메아리치는	[207] complete
resounding			[1015] electrifying
[ri-ZOUN-ding]		Her new novel was a resounding success.	

6535		1. 체 2. 체로 거르다, 체로 치다	
sieve			
[siv]		You should strain the pasta noodles in a sieve before adding some olive oil.	

6536		1. 콕 찌르다 2. 재촉(하다)	[442] press
prod			[1013] push
[prod]		The little boy gave the girl he likes a prod with a pencil.	[5692] nudge

6537	공무원 토플 편입	1. 비방(하다), 중상(하다) 2. 명예훼손	slanderous (명예훼손의)
slander			[1043] injury
[SLAN-der]		The journalist is well-known for slandering politicians.	[1159] defamation

6538	편입	1. (원고의)반박 2. 반대, 반증	rebut (반박하다)
rebuttal			[1655] denial
[ri-BUHT-l]		The judge patiently waited for the plaintiff's rebuttal.	[1666] reply

6539	토익	새로이, 다시, 신규로	[295] again
anew			
[uh-NOO]		After the divorce, he wanted to start his life anew.	

6540		사료, 먹이	[1033] feed
fodder			[1518] victim
[FOD-er]		What types of fodder crops are used to feed livestock?	[2699] corn
			[5236] barley

6541	공무원 편입 GRE	1. 맛 좋은 2. 마음에 드는	unpalatable (불쾌한)
palatable			[1065] tasty
[PAL-uh-tuh-buhl]		The dish was quite palatable.	[668] acceptable
			[3557] appetizing

6542		거식증	anorexic (거식증 환자)
anorexia			
[an-uh-REK-see-uh]		Anorexia is quite common in modern society.	

6543	공무원 편입	즉흥적인, 즉석에서	[1749] random
impromptu			[4078] spontaneous
[im-PROMP-too]		Not too many people came to the impromptu party she threw.	

6544		집사	[6137] valet
butler			
[BUHT-ler]		The family's butler knew how to cook very well.	

6545	공무원	1. 심술궂은, 삐뚤어진 2. 대다수는 좋아하지 않을 법한	[4545] stubborn
perverse			[306] unreasonable
[per-VURS]		He was perverse enough to torture little animals.	[3488] contradictory
			[3791] wicked

6546		1. 교묘한, 교활한 2. 기교적인	[5996] cunning
artful			[3031] clever
[AHRT-fuhl]		She used artful means to get what she wanted.	[4781] ingenious

6547 **espionage** [ES-pee-uh-nahzh]	간첩행위	[3499] spying [1588] intelligence
	As a victim of espionage, the politician has been monitored.	

6548 **plenary** [PLEE-nuh-ree]	1. 총회(의) 2. 전체적인, 충분한	
	The president raised important issues during the plenary meeting.	

6549 **toad** [tohd]	두꺼비	[811] frog
	What is the difference between a frog and a toad?	

6550 **phony** [FOH-nee]	가짜(의), 사기(의)	[2552] fake [1119] imaginary [5303] counterfeit [5988] bogus
	He bought his girlfriend a phony piece of jewelry.	

6551 **ode** [ohd]	(송)시	[외래어] ballad
	She finally finished writing an ode to her family.	

6552 **tabloid** [TAB-loid]	소형 신문 (=타블로이드)	[760] paper
	The tabloid papers called him a dumb celebrity.	

6553 **chastity** [CHAS-ti-tee]	1. 순결, 금욕 2. 정숙, 고상함	chaste (순결한) [1549] purity [2073] decency [5316] abstinence
	She considers herself a vower of chastity.	

6554 편입 **finesse** [fi-NESS]	재간, 솜씨, 기교	[520] skill [171] experience [2388] competence [6721] acumen
	The Go champion is well known for his moves with a delicate finesse.	

6555 편입 **gallant** [GAL-uhnt]	1. 용감한, 씩씩한 2. 정중한, 친절한	gallantry (용감함) [929] courageous [2865] brave [2891] courtly
	He pretended to be gallant in front of his girlfriend.	

6556 **leach** [leech]	1. 세어나오다 2. 거르다, 걸러내다	
	The extensive farming led to soil leaching.	

6557 **snore** [snawr]	코를 골다	[990] sleep [7137] wheeze
	I was snoring all night long.	

6558 토플 **bedrock** [BED-rok]	1. 기반, 기초, 기본 2. 기반암	[1219] theory
	Trust is the bedrock of a long-lasting relationship.	

6559 **allegory** [AL-uh-gawr-ee]	1. 비유 2. 우화, 풍자	allegorical (우화적인) [5607] parable
	The author used gray clouds as an allegory for the gloomy future.	

6560 공무원 **unwittingly** [uhn-WIT-ing-lee]	무의식에, 자기자신도 모르게	unwitting (모르는) [5183] inadvertently [1527] unintentionally [1597] accidentally
	He unwittingly hurt her feelings.	

6561 **collate** [kuh-LEYT]		1. 순서대로 모으다 2. 분석하다 3. 비교하다, 대조하다	collation (수집, 대조) [572] compare
		We collated data according to their priorities.	
6562 **rife** [rahyf]	공무원	만연한, 가득 찬	[2698] prevalent [485] common [2231] alive [2566] abundant
		The tourist site is rife with people from all over the world.	
6563 **hedgehog** [HEJ-hog]		고슴도치	
		I saw a hedgehog rolling itself into a ball.	
6564 **bridle** [BRAHYD-l]		1. 고삐(를 매다), 속박 2. 화내다	unbridled (구속이 없는)
		He failed to get the bridle around the horse.	
6565 **tarnish** [TAHR-nish]	공무원 토플 편입	1. 흐려지다 2. 더럽히다, 손상하다 3. 변색된 곳	[5156] smear [523] discredit [719] damage [1159] defame
		If you keep on touching that shiny faucet, you will make it tarnish.	
6566 **ebb** [eb]	편입 GRE	1. 쇠퇴하다 2. 썰물(이 되다)	[5752] wane [1756] decrease
		My passion and love for the job began to ebb.	
6567 **christ** [krahyst]		그리스도	christian (기독교 신자) christianity (기독교) [1419] lord
		She lost faith in Christ.	
6568 **apartheid** [uh-PAHRT-hahyt]		과거 남아프리카공화국 내의 인종 차별정책	[646] racism [2625] discrimination
		He was at the forefront of the anti-Apartheid movement.	
6569 **banter** [BAN-ter]	편입	1. 농담(을 주고받다) 2. 놀리다, 조롱하다	[2293] joke [1411] conversation [5009] gossip
		We spent the lunchtime exchanging banter.	
6570 **recoup** [ri-KOOP]	토플	1. 되찾다 2. 회복하다	[890] earn [1991] compensate
		The company tried hard to recoup its initial investment.	
6571 **ingrain** [in-GREYN]	GRE	1. 뿌리 깊은, 깊이 스며든 2. 염색한	[864] affect [5143] instill
		I have no studying routine ingrained in me yet.	
6572 **gist** [jist]	공무원 편입	요점, 골자	[902] essence [1764] summary [5722] tenor
		Just give me the gist of what you are trying to say.	
6573 **digress** [dih-GRES]	공무원 편입	요지/본론에서 벗어나다, 탈선하다	digression (요지에서 벗어남) [4452] stray [6089] meander
		He kept on digressing from the topic of the discussion.	
6574 **jest** [jest]	토플	농담, 장난, 웃음거리	jester (농담꾸러기) [2293] joke
		She was still hurt even though she knew he only spoke in jest.	

6575		화환, 화관	[4978] wreath
garland			[1667] decorate
[GAHR-luh nd]		She wore a beautiful garland made with lilac.	

6576	편입	1. 어떻게 될지 모르는 상태 2. 잊혀진 상태	[5292] oblivion
limbo			[385] uncertainty
[LIM-boh]		He is in limbo regarding the quitting of his job.	

6577		1. 꿀꺽 한입 2. 벌컥벌컥 마시다, 삼키다 3. 숨을 들이 마시다	[3533] swallow
gulp			[1773] mouthful
[guhlp]		She drank the vodka in one big gulp.	[2018] breathe

6578		언쟁, 논쟁, 말다툼(하다)	wrangler (논쟁자)
wrangle			[2329] dispute
[RANG-guhl]		She wrangled with her peers.	[962] argument
			[6808] altercation

6579		1. 지체, 밀림 2. 체납금	[1514] debt
arrears			[1852] liability
[uh-REERZ]		We've got 2 months' arrears to pay.	[3434] deficit

6580	편입	틈, 균열	[1893] crack
crevice			[5962] abyss
[KREV-is]		He dropped his car key in the crevice.	

6581	편입	1. (미술품 등의)감정가, 품평가 2. 전문가	[908] expert
connoisseur			[2521] buff
[kon-uh-SUR]		As a connoisseur of coffee, she doesn't like drinking instant coffee.	[4476] gourmet

6582	공무원 편입 GRE	용감한, 대담한, 두려움을 모르는	trepidation (두려움, 공포)
intrepid			[929] courageous
[in-TREP-id]		I am not intrepid enough to make big decisions.	[1198] fearless
			[2865] brave

6583	공무원	1. 작은 마을 2. 햄릿(셰익스피어 작품)	[1691] village
hamlet			
[HAM-lit]		The small hamlet has its own culture and tradition different from neighboring communities.	

6584		통(에 넣다)	[2384] barrel
cask			[6096] keg
[kask]		He drank the entire cask of wine.	

6585	토플 편입	1. 대량 학살하다 2. 크게 훼손시키다	decimation (대량 학살)
decimate			[5975] annihilate
[DES-uh-meyt]		The bomb could potentially decimate the entire population of the city.	[1255] destroy
			[6131] exterminate

6586		1. 써레 2. 써레질하다, 땅을 고르다 3. 괴롭히다	harrowing (끔찍한)
harrow			[5104] torment
[HAR-oh]		A harrow will be of great help to farmers.	[2896] spoil
			[3090] devastate

6587	GRE	1. 가짜(의) 2. 사기꾼(의) 3. ~인 척하다	[2552] fake
sham			[2315] fictitious
[sham]		He believed that the last presidential election was just a sham.	[4480] falsehood
			[5988] bogus

6588		담당자의 관리 능력	[256] care
stewardship			[573] preparation
[STOO-erd-ship]		Under her stewardship, the company overcame numerous obstacles.	[2748] conservancy

6589 　　　　토플 **introspect** [in-truh-SPEKT]	1. 자기 반성하다, 내성하다　2. 성찰하다	introspection (자기 성 찰) [4788] ponder
	He took some time to introspect into his mind.	
6590 　　공무원 편입 **shabby** [SHAB-ee]	1. 허름한, 추레한, 초라한　2. 부당한	[3808] decaying
	She was mad at him for taking her to such a shabby restaurant.	
6591 **romp** [romp]	1. 즐겁게 놀다　2. 손쉽게 이기다　3. 오락물	[96] play
	I saw many children romping around by the playground.	
6592 **popsicle** [POP-si-kuhl]	막대 아이스크림	
	Can you bring me a popsicle from the freezer?	
6593 **zoology** [zoh-OL-uh-jee]	동물학	[4546] anthropology
	She has a degree in zoology.	
6594 **typewriter** [TAHYP-rahy-ter]	타자기	[853] machine
	He kindly lent me his typewriter when mine was broken.	
6595 　공무원 토플 편입 GRE **expedient** [ik-SPEE-dee-uhnt]	1. 수단, 방편, 방책　2. (목적에)알맞은, 편리한, 적당한	expedience (편의) [1430] convenient [30] useful [991] advantageous
	The company should not resort to a temporary expedient.	
6596 **prelude** [PREL-yood]	1. 서막　2. 서곡	[761] introduction [5953] preface [6673] prologue
	The working-level meetings were a prelude to the peace agreement.	
6597 **tidbit** [TID-bit]	1. 한 입　2. 가벼운 음식　3. 토막 정보	[42] goody [120] information
	He only had a tidbit of food.	
6598 　　　　편입 **admissible** [ad-MIS-uh-buhl]	1. 인정되는, 용인될 수 있는　2. 취임할 자격이 있는	inadmissible (용인될 수 없는) [200] allowed [668] acceptable [2256] justifiable
	Such behavior is not admissible at our company.	
6599 **werewolf** [WAIR-woolf]	늑대 인간	[2799] beast [6709] behemoth
	He transformed into a werewolf at night.	
6600 **jingle** [JING-guhl]	짤랑짤랑, 딸랑딸랑 울리다	
	I noticed his presence by the jingle of his keys.	
6601 **pique** [peek]	1. 불쾌함, 성남　2. 불쾌하게 하다, 감정을 상하게 하다	[2895] irritate [270] displeasure [2465] annoyance
	He yelled at her out of pique.	
6602 **mogul** [MOH-guhl]	1. 거물, 능력자　2. 무굴인	[6967] tycoon [618] figure [758] executive [7371] magnate
	Her billionaire dad is a real estate mogul.	

6603 공무원 편입 **profusely** [pruh-FYOOS-lee]	풍부하게, 넘치도록, 실컷	profusion (풍부함) profuse (풍부한, 넘치는) [5574] extravagantly [5132] lavishly
	The student apologized profusely for the mistake he made.	

6604 공무원 **invincible** [in-VIN-suh-buhl]	천하무적의, 이길 수 없는	[1187] unbeatable [448] impassable [498] strong
	Nobody could break her invincible record.	

6605 **envoy** [EN-voi]	사절, 특사, 사신	[2900] delegate [3491] diplomat
	She was sent to the neighboring country as a special envoy.	

6606 **ditto** [DIT-oh]	위와 같음, 마찬가지로	[3337] reiterate [외래어] ok
	I ditto what she said.	

6607 **delectable** [dih-LEK-tuh-buhl]	1. 매우 맛있는 2. 매력 넘치는 3. 매우 즐거운	[1937] delicious [1065] tasty [3126] delicate [3557] appetizing
	I enjoyed the delectable meal at a small restaurant last night.	

6608 **splint** [splint]	부목	[5503] bandage [3534] brace
	She had to put a splint on her broken arm.	

6609 **fraught** [frawt]	1. ~을 내포한, ~으로 가득 차 있는 2. 걱정되는, 우려되는	[2305] tense [415] charged [685] filled [1133] worried
	Their relationship is fraught with troubles and issues.	

6610 **jagged** [JAG-id]	1. 들쭉날쭉한, 톱니 모양의 2. 다듬지 않은, 요철의	[445] broken [1719] rough
	After biting a chicken bone, his teeth became rough and jagged.	

6611 **swat** [SWOT]	1. 때리다 2. (공을)치다	[2320] knock [2594] punch
	He successfully swatted a mosquito with his hand.	

6612 **stampede** [stam-PEED]	1. 몰림, 쇄도 2. 도망가다	[2136] rush [152] run [3132] panic
	On the day of the singer's new release, the owner of the record store expected a stampede.	

6613 **heave** [heev]	1. (무거운 것을)들어올리다 2. 몸을 일으키다	[1493] lift [3442] haul [5531] fling
	He failed to heave the heavyweight.	

6614 **afield** [uh-FEELD]	1. 멀리 떨어져 2. 들에, 밭에 3. 싸움터에	[1208] distant [4452] astray
	She is working afield in a large city.	

6615 공무원 편입 **blunder** [BLUHN-der]	실수(하다)	[1513] mistake [621] fail [1092] error
	The waitress made a blunder when she wrote down the wrong orders.	

6616 **singularity** [sing-gyuh-LAR-i-tee]	특이성	singular (특이하다) [4511] peculiarity [59] otherness
	Jane has a singularity that distinguishes her from all others.	

6617 **astral** [AS-truhl]	별의	[4179] stellar [923] spirituality
	He enjoys looking at astral objects in the sky.	
6618 **peck** [pek]	1. 쪼아먹다, 쪼다 2. 가벼운 입맞춤	[2696] pile
	I saw a bird pecking at a caterpillar.	
6619　　　公務員 편입 **drench** [drench]	흠뻑 젖다, ~을 흠뻑 적시다	[2733] soak [2029] wet [6760] deluge
	I got drenched in heavy rain.	
6620 **insofar** [in-suh-FAHR]	~하는 한에 있어서는	
	The company will only hire you insofar as you work hard.	
6621 **vertigo** [VUR-ti-goh]	1. 현기증, 어지러움 2. 혼란	[4418] dizziness
	Her dizziness is caused by vertigo.	
6622　　　편입 **bane** [beyn]	골칫거리, 해, 독	[3358] curse [1039] task
	I believe that social networks are the bane of human interaction.	
6623　　　편입 **contravention** [kon-truh-VEN-shuhn]	1. 위반, 위배 2. 반대	contravene (위반하다) [2628] breach [4026] infringement
	The company's actions were in direct contravention of the domestic law.	
6624 **bib** [bib]	턱받이	
	She forgot to tie a bib around her baby's neck.	
6625　公務員 편입 GRE **predicament** [pri-DIK-uh-muhnt]	곤경, 어려움, 궁지	[5785] plight [215] problem [1735] circumstance [2063] crisis
	He found himself in a financial predicament.	
6626　　　토플 GRE **virtuoso** [vur-choo-OH-soh]	1. 거장, 명인 2. 기교를 보여주는	virtuosity (연주의 기교, 스킬) [932] master [394] musician
	Even though nobody believed in him, he eventually became a musical virtuoso.	
6627　　　편입 **secession** [si-SESH-uhn]	탈퇴, 분리 독립	secede (탈퇴하다) [892] separation
	The country wanted secession from the alliance.	
6628 **totalitarian** [toh-tal-i-TAIR-ee-uhn]	전체주의의	totalitarianism (전체주의)
	The politician is in favor of a totalitarian government.	
6629 **yawn** [YAWN]	하품(하다)	[6727] gape
	I try not to yawn in class.	
6630　　　편입 **lull** [luhl]	1. 달래다 2. 소강(상태) 3. 잠잠해지다	[1739] quiet [2018] breather [2260] calmness
	Only the mother could lull the crying baby.	

6631			
pothole	1. 깊게 파인 곳 2. 돌개구멍		[1320] hole [5398] crater
[POT-hohl]	She drove her car over a big pothole.		

6632			
prawn	대하, (큰)새우		[4186] shrimp [5840] clam
[prawn]	We had prawn curry for dinner last night.		

6633	편입		
retribution	1. 징벌 2. 응보, 보복		[5007] retaliation [1991] compensation
[re-truh-BYOO-shuhn]	He believes that evil people will eventually face retribution even after death.		[4013] revenge

6634			
viper	독사		[5269] serpent [외래어] cobra
[VAHY-per]	The viper's venom is very lethal.		

6635	토플		
saucer	(받침)접시		[1758] dish
[SAW-ser]	I poured water into a saucer so that my dog can drink some.		

6636	공무원 GRE		
redress	1. 바로잡다 2. 교정하다 3. 보상		[2428] remedy [401] improvement
[REE-dres]	The company needs to redress the balance between male and female employees.		[1947] amends [6116] atonement

6637			
crotch	가랑이		[5973] groin
[kroch]	She kicked her boyfriend in the crotch.		

6638			
droop	1. 처지다, 늘어지다 2. 풀이 죽다		droopy (처지는) [5759] wilt
[droop]	The movie was too boring that her eyelids started to droop.		[1331] hang [5103] sag

6639			
philharmonic	1. 교향악단 2. 음악 애호의		[3909] symphony
[fil-hahr-MON-ik]	She played the violin for the San Fransico Philharmonic.		

6640			
gobble	급하게 먹다, 게걸스럽게 먹다		[5375] devour [2611] tweet
[GOB-uhl]	Stop gobbling your food and just eat slowly.		[6577] gulp

6641	공무원 편입		
lukewarm	1. 미지근한, 미적지근한 2. 무관심한		[1055] warm [7385] tepid
[LOOK-wawrm]	Drinking lukewarm water is beneficial to your health.		

6642	공무원 편입 GRE		
arduous	고된, 매우 힘든		[665] difficult [2760] burdensome
[AHR-joo-uhs]	Raising children is much more arduous than working at a company.		

6643			
limelight	각광, 주목의 대상, 세상의 이목		[외래어] spotlight [2601] prominence
[LAHYM-lahyt]	AI has become the limelight of today's world.		[4557] glare

6644	공무원 편입		
fervent	열렬한, 뜨거운, 열정적인		fervently (열렬하게) [6411] ardent
[FUR-vuhnt]	Students had a fervent debate on a controversial issue.		[2131] enthusiastic [6421] devout

6645	공무원 편입	지각 있는	
sentient			
[SEN-shuhnt]		Some argue that whales are sentient beings just like humans.	

6646		불사조, 봉황새	[2963] gem
phoenix			[4196] masterpiece
[FEE-niks]		She saw a phoenix rising from its ashes in her dream.	

6647		주연 여가수, 디바	
diva			
[DEE-vuh]		This talented little girl will grow up to be a diva.	

6648		살구	[4083] peach
apricot			
[AP-ri-kot]		Apricots are my favorite fruit.	

6649		1. 마귀(귀신)쫓기, 액막이 2. 안 좋은 기억을 잊기 위한 행동	[4215] purification
exorcism			
[EK-sawr-siz-uhm]		Only those experienced priests can conduct an exorcism.	

6650	공무원 편입	1. 녹초로 만드는, 엄한 2. 봉변, 엄벌	[6642] arduous
grueling			[665] difficult
[GROO-uh-ling]		He has to manage a very grueling schedule this week.	

6651		1. 돼지 2. 나쁜 인간	[6250] boar
swine			[2084] monster
[swahyn]		He suffered from swine flu.	[4756] hog

6652	공무원 편입 GRE	분개한, 몹시 화난	indignation (분개)
indignant			[1987] angry
[in-DIG-nuhnt]		She was indignant about the way her boss treated her.	[2465] annoyed
			[3576] furious

6653	공무원 편입 GRE	1. 단호한, 확고한 2. 의지가 굳은, 결의에 찬	resolution (굳은 결심, 결
resolute			의안, 화질)
[REZ-uh-loot]		The singer's fans remained resolute in their loyalty no matter what he did.	resolutely (확고히)
			[652] determined

6654	토플 편입	1. 확고한 2. 독실한 3. 견실한	[2267] loyal
staunch			[6411] ardent
[stawnch]		I consider myself a staunch advocate of liberalism.	

6655	공무원 토플 편입 GRE	1. 참견하다, 간섭하다, 개입하다 2. 손을 대다, 건들다	[4133] hinder
meddle			[4727] impede
[MED-l]		She hates it when her mom meddles in her personal life.	

6656	편입 GRE	1. 가득 채우다 2. 스며들다	[6571] ingrain
imbue			
[im-BYOO]		The professor gave her students an encouraging comment to imbue them with confidence.	

6657		1. 난로 2. 노변 3. 가정	
hearth			
[hahrth]		We usually gather around the hearth in our living room when it gets too cold.	

6658		모루 (=달군 쇠를 올려놓고 두드릴 때 받침으로 쓰는 쇳덩이)	
anvil			
[AN-vil]		Nowadays, people don't seem to use anvil as much thanks to the invention of welding.	

6659 편입 **monotonous** [muh-NOT-n-uhs]	단조로운, 변화없는, 지루한	monotony (단조로움) [3731] dull
	She fell asleep during the monotonous lecture.	[1109] boring [6985] dreary

6660 **luscious** [LUHSH-uhs]	1. 매력적인, 매혹적인 2. 감미로운, 달콤한	[1937] delicious [773] sexy
	She put glosses over her luscious lips.	[1701] distinctive [3557] appetizing

6661 공무원 편입 GRE **altruism** [AL-troo-iz-uhm]	이타주의, 이타심, 이타적 행위	altruistic (이타적인) [1607] selflessness
	Some believe that there's no such thing as pure altruism.	[410] kindness [6008] benevolence

6662 공무원 편입 GRE **meager** [MEE-ger]	1. 빈약한, 부족한, 결핍한 2. 메마른	[5426] sparse [1742] insufficient
	He is planning on quitting his job since he only earns a meager salary.	[1995] mere [2096] inadequate

6663 **soggy** [SOG-ee]	1. 흠뻑 젖은 2. 질척한	[2029] wet [2064] moist
	My shoes became soggy after accidentally stepping in a puddle.	[3279] humid

6664 **mull** [muhl]	1. 심사숙고하다 2. 실수(하다), 실패(하다), 망치다	[4788] ponder [282] consider
	Don't make your decision before you have some time to mull it over.	[3023] deliberate [3697] contemplate

6665 편입 GRE **vindicate** [VIN-di-keyt]	1. (무죄 등을) 입증하다 2. 비난을 풀다	vindication (입증) [2256] justify
	As long as there's legitimate evidence, he will be vindicated.	[121] show [6996] absolve

6666 편입 **blackmail** [BLAK-meyl]	1. 협박(하다) 2. 갈취, 공갈	[2593] manipulation [4903] bribe
	She attempted to blackmail her boss.	

6667 공무원 편입 GRE **frivolous** [FRIV-uh-luhs]	1. 경솔한, 경박한 2. 하찮은, 시시한, 사소한	[3103] silly [1776] crazy
	I hate it when my husband spends money on frivolous purchases.	[2644] foolish [3666] idiotic

6668 **ovation** [oh-VEY-shuhn]	1. 열띤 응원, 박수 2. 갈채	[5073] applause [3724] acclaim
	After she finished her performance, the crowd gave her a standing ovation.	

6669 **speck** [spek]	작은 얼룩, 반점	[2701] particle [2478] dot
	There's a speck of dirt on your dress.	[6036] blot

6670 **peddle** [PED-l]	1. 행상하다, 이곳저곳 다니면서 팔다 2. 퍼뜨리다, 유포하다	peddler (행상인)
	The old lady peddles her products around the town.	

6671 **populous** [POP-yuh-luhs]	인구가 많은, 높은 인구 밀도의	[1635] crowded [1718] numerous
	The housing price goes up if the area becomes more populous.	

6672 **bummer** [BUHM-er]	1. 실망스러운 일 2. 기대에 어긋난 경험	[1941] disappointment
	It's a bummer that he couldn't get that job.	

6673	편입	프롤로그, 서막, 도입부	[5953] preface
prologue			[279] beginning
[PROH-lawg]		I have memorized the entire prologue to The Canterbury Tales.	[6596] prelude

6674	공무원 편입	안락사	
euthanasia			
[yoo-thuh-NEY-zhuh]		It is illegal for doctors to practice euthanasia in our country.	

6675		1. 깜빡이는 빛 2. 희미한 빛, 표시 3. 깜빡이다, 빛나다	[5981] gleam
glimmer			[257] light
[GLIM-er]		Even after failing all the exams, she still had a glimmer of hope.	[3841] flicker

6676		1. 관리원, 경비원 2. 기습 공격대원	[1661] guard
ranger			
[REYN-jer]		He was the head ranger of the park.	

6677		유령	[2546] ghost
apparition			[4480] falsehood
[ap-uh-RISH-uhn]		The little boy said he saw an apparition of a dead man last night.	

6678		1. 중얼거리다, 속닥이다 2. 불평하다 3. 중얼거림	[6896] mumble
mutter			[1782] complain
[MUHT-er]		She heard her colleague muttering complaints about their boss.	[3968] whisper
			[5915] groan

6679	편입	전국(전 세계)적으로 퍼져나간 유행병	[4538] epidemic
pandemic			[2113] illness
[pan-DEM-ik]		Washing hands thoroughly can prevent most of the pandemics from spreading quickly.	

6680	토플 GRE	1. 가정(하다), 상정(하다) 2. 요구하다	[121] show
postulate			[3152] hypothesize
[POS-chuh-leyt]		The government postulated that the economy will rebound soon.	

6681	공무원	속기	short-handed (일손이 부족한 채)
shorthand			[168] handwriting
[SHAWRT-hand]		He took notes in shorthand so that he can perform consecutive interpretation.	[1764] summary

6682	편입	1. 위엄 있는, 장엄한 2. 위풍당당한	[2405] imposing
stately			[883] slow
[STEYT-lee]		The billionaire purchased a stately mansion in a wealthy community.	[2190] ceremonial
			[2425] elegant

6683		1. 금박 입힌, 도금을 칠한 2. 부자의, 상류층의	gild (금도금을 하다)
gilded			[847] gold
[GIL-did]		The spring sun gilded their faces.	[1397] bright
			[1854] luxurious

6684	공무원 편입	1. 기괴한, 괴상한 2. 터무니없는 3. 괴물같은 인물	[6241] hideous
grotesque			[785] ugly
[groh-TESK]		She couldn't finish watching that grotesque movie.	[4006] bizarre
			[4103] absurd

6685		비듬	
dandruff			
[DAN-druh f]		I bought an expensive shampoo to treat my dandruff.	

6686		부적	[7464] talisman
amulet			[3871] ornament
[AM-yuh-lit]		She always wears her amulet given by a famous monk.	

6687			
psych [sahyk]	1. 불안하게 하다, 혼란을 가중시키다 2. 사람의 심리를 꿰뚫다		[1684] psychology [1133] worry [1402] medicine [2055] attitude
	She successfully psyched out other competitors before the match.		

6688			
fro [froh]	저쪽으로 (to and fro: 이리저리)		
	The businessman traveled to and fro between Spain and Germany.		

6689			
jackpot [JAK-pot]	거액의 상금, 잭팟		[1787] prize [991] advantage
	I wonder if I could ever hit a jackpot.		

6690			
scribble [SKRIB-uhl]	1. 낙서(하다) 2. ~을 휘갈겨 쓰다		[168] write [2247] scratch [6415] jot
	Stop scribbling on my paper.		

6691	공무원 편입 GRE		
condescending [kon-duh-SEN-ding]	1. 잘난 체하는 2. 무시하는, 비하하는		condescension (잘난 체하는 것) [3460] patronizing [4589] arrogant
	She despises his condescending attitude.		

6692	GRE		
orator [AWR-uh-ter]	연설자, 웅변가		oratory (웅변술) oration (연설) [440] speaker [2385] lecturer
	Since I'm not a skilled orator, I spend a lot of time preparing.		

6693	공무원 편입 GRE		
copious [KOH-pee-uhs]	방대한, 많은, 내용이 풍부한		[2566] abundant [196] large [608] extensive [3811] ample
	He tries to drink a copious amount of water.		

6694	GRE		
downplay [DOUN-pley]	경시하다, 얕보다		[1114] minimize [327] lessen
	The factory experienced downtime because workers downplayed the importance of inspection.		

6695			
grumpy [GRUHM-pee]	1. 성격이 나쁜 2. 심술궂은		[1692] sad
	She becomes very grumpy whenever she gets headaches.		

6696	편입 GRE		
usurp [yoo-SURP]	1. 빼앗다, 강탈하다 2. 침해하다		usurper (강탈자) [1041] assume [673] replace [4853] annex
	His younger brother usurped the king's throne.		

6697	공무원 편입 GRE		
deftly [deft-lee]	교묘히, 재빠르게, 능숙하게		deft (손기술이 좋은) [520] skillfully [111] ably
	He deftly avoided answering reporters' questions.		

6698			
budge [buhj]	1. 살짝 움직이다 2. 의견(입장)을 바꾸다		[2140] bend
	He leaned on the door but it wouldn't budge.		

6699			
hoot [hoot]	1. 비웃다, 야유하다, 콧방귀(를 뀌다) 2. 경적을 울리다 3. 부엉이가 울다		[5459] howl [1863] laughter
	People hooted at her presentation.		

6700			
osmosis [oz-MOH-sis]	삼투 현상		[1998] absorption
	Water enters plant roots by osmosis.		

6701	오목한	[3993] hollow
concave		
[kon-KEYV]	Contact lenses have a concave shape in line with the eyeball.	

6702	포주, 매춘 알선업자	[4899] hustler
pimp		
[pimp]	He saw a pimp wearing a gold chain necklace.	

6703　GRE	대중, 서민	
populace		
[POP-yuh-luhs]	The government's new policy didn't satisfy the populace.	

6704	1. 뭉치, 다발　2. 뭉치다	[2696] pile
wad		[2757] bundle
[wod]	She pulled a thick wad of hair from her husband during their fight.	[3037] chunk

6705	1. 성질이 급한 사람(여자)　2. 불을 뿜는 것	
spitfire		
[SPIT-fahyuhr]	He couldn't handle his mother being a spitfire all the time.	

6706　GRE	1. 감정이 없는　2. 금욕주의자	stoicism (금욕 스토아 철학)
stoic		[6417] apathetic
[STOH-ik]	Does that stoic man know how to smile at all?	[7215] aloof

6707　편입 GRE	예리한, 샤프한	[3031] clever
astute		[3360] genius
[uh-STOOT]	The astute student talked his teacher into changing his grade.	[5917] canny

6708	근친상간	incestuous (근친상간의)
incest		[5710] perversion
[IN-sest]	Committing incest is strictly prohibited in many countries.	

6709	1. 거대 기업(조직)　2. 큰 짐승	[1828] giant
behemoth		[2490] bulk
[bih-HEE-muhth]	This IT behemoth provides many frontier technology solutions.	[2799] beast

6710	1. 매우 고통스러운　2. 극심한, 극도의	excruciatingly (매우 고통스럽게)
excruciating		[4829] agonizing
[ik-SKROO-shee-ey-ting]	He was in excruciating pain when his leg broke.	[3013] utterly

6711	1. 코웃음(을 치다), 콧방귀(를 뀌다)　2. 코로 들이마시다, 흡입하다	[6051] hiss
snort		[1863] laughter
[snawrt]	I tend to snort whenever I laugh.	[5600] grunt

6712	1. 전력 질주하다　2. 전속력(으로 말 몰기)	[2136] rush
gallop		[986] fly
[GAL-uhp]	She was frightened by a horse galloping toward her.	[4463] dart
		[6337] amble

6713	1. 십일조　2. 세금	[297] cost
tithe		[901] contribution
[tahyth]	He was asked to give a tithe to the church.	

6714　공무원 편입 GRE	과장법	hyperbolic (쌍곡선의)
hyperbole		[1789] emphasis
[hahy-PUR-buh-lee]	Politicians always engage in hyperbole.	[3989] hype
		[4076] metaphor

6715			
spurt	1. 뿜어나오다, 분출(하다) 2. 속도를 내다, 스퍼트 내다	[6323] gush [1168] river	
[spurt]	I saw a spurt of blood coming out of the wound.	[4109] eruption [7127] commotion	

6716 토플 편입 GRE			
inert	1. 스스로 움직일 수 없는 2. 무기력한	inertia (활동없음, 관성) [948] immobile	
[in-URT]	Argon is an inert gas.	[2681] blank [5447] dormant	

6717 편입			
embargo	금수조치(를 내리다)	[2062] ban [3210] suppress	
[em-BAHR-goh]	The president is trying hard to lift the embargo.	[3449] restraint	

6718			
stalwart	1. 충실한(일꾼) 2. 튼튼한, 건장한	[3474] sturdy [386] dependable	
[STAWL-wert]	He has been a stalwart worker for many years.	[1198] fearless [2267] loyal	

6719 편입			
infuriating	1. 몹시 화가나는, 짜증나는 2. 격분하게 하는	infuriate (격분하게 하다) [2465] annoying	
[in-FYOOR-ee-ey-ting]	It's infuriating when people keep pronouncing my name wrong.	[1987] anger [4266] aggravate	

6720 공무원 토플 편입			
libel	1. 명예훼손 2. 모욕하다	[6537] slander [1159] defamation	
[LAHY-buhl]	He went to jail for libel.		

6721 GRE			
acumen	1. (예민한)감각 2. 통찰력	[4060] discernment [1021] awareness	
[uh-KYOO-muhn]	His business acumen made him very successful.	[1588] intelligence [6946] acuity	

6722			
entourage	1. 수행단, 수행원 2. 측근	[500] association	
[ahn-too-RAHZH]	The president and his entourage stay in that hotel.		

6723			
ocular	1. 눈의, 안구의 2. 눈으로 본		
[OK-yuh-ler]	Sunglasses can prevent ocular damage.		

6724			
beckon	1. 손짓하다, 손짓으로 부르다 2. 신호를 보내다	[1354] wave [1069] attract	
[BEK-uhn]	The police beckoned us to ask some questions.	[4495] entice	

6725 토익			
briefcase	서류 가방	[1052] bag	
[BREEF-keys]	He took his briefcase to work.		

6726			
uptown	1. 도심을 벗어나, 외곽으로, 변두리로 2. 상류층 지역의	[5674] affluent	
[UHP-toun]	I live in an apartment uptown.		

6727 공무원			
gaping	1. (놀라서) 입을 크게 벌린 2. 크게 벌어진, 갈라진	gape (입을 크게 벌리다) [6629] yawning	
[gey-ping]	The gaping audience stared in awe.	[196] large [2019] vast	

6728			
nemesis	1. (천)벌 2. 천적, 강적	[6622] bane [1548] enemy	
[NEM-uh-sis]	He will eventually face a nemesis.	[2835] adversary	

6729 **hatchback** [HACH-bak]	해치백, 트렁크 문이 위로 열리는 자동차(의 뒷부분) I saw a red hatchback on the road.	
6730 **pounce** [pouns]	덮치다, 덤벼들다 The lion was about to pounce.	[1276] jump
6731 **grumble** [GRUHM-buhl]	1. 투덜대다, 불평하다 2. 우르릉거리다 3. 불만, 불편 The students grumbled over their homework.	[1782] complain [4488] fuss
6732 편입 **retrograde** [RE-truh-greyd]	역행하는, 후퇴하는 Some believe that nuclear phaseout is a retrograde step.	[373] worse
6733 편입 **clamor** [KLAM-er]	1. 떠들썩함, 외침, 아우성, 소란 2. 떠들다, 시끄럽게 하다 I hear a clamor of voices inside the building.	[7132] uproar [1022] demand [4877] agitation
6734 **condiment** [KON-duh-muhnt]	양념, 조미료, 소스 Salt is the best condiment.	[5442] relish [1190] dressing [5548] gravy
6735 **leech** [leech]	1. 거머리 2. 고리 대금업자 A leech can suck the blood out of the human body.	[4069] parasite [4273] miser
6736 **scourge** [skurj]	1. 재앙, 악 2. 채찍(질 하다) Drug violence is a scourge in the US.	[3766] plague [1039] task [3358] curse [3762] pest
6737 **muddle** [MUHD-l]	1. 뒤죽박죽 만들다 2. 혼란, 혼동을 주다 He muddled up some Spanish and Italian words.	[6954] jumble [2962] chaos
6738 **antelope** [AN-tl-ohp]	영양(사슴류의 동물) I saw a small antelope jumping.	
6739 공무원 편입 GRE **ephemeral** [ih-FEM-er-uhl]	1. 덧없는 2. 수명 짧은, 단명하는 His success was ephemeral.	[1648] temporary [189] short-lived [604] variable [2554] fleeting
6740 **quiver** [KWIV-er]	떨다 His voice starts to quiver whenever talking to his boss.	[5700] tremble [2186] swing
6741 **paralympics** [PAR-uh-lim-piks]	패럴림픽(세계 장애인 올림픽) Many athletes participated in the Paralympics.	
6742 **froth** [frawth]	1. 거품(이 일게하다) 2. 들끓는 He likes to drink the froth on the top of the latte.	[2559] foam [919] stuff [6490] scum

6743	공무원 편입 GRE	1. 확증하다, 입증하다, 확실하게 하다 2. 제공하다	corroboration (확증)
corroborate			[1200] confirm
[kuh-ROB-uh-reyt]		A recent study corroborates her theory.	[121] show
			[1986] authenticate

6744		채도, 색 농도	chromatic (색채의)
chroma			[3391] saturation
[KROH-muh]		She knows how to adjust chroma very well.	[330] color

6745	공무원 편입 GRE	혐오하다, 몹시 싫어하다	abhorrent (혐오스러운)
abhor			[1599] hate
[ab-HAWR]		I abhor all forms of gender discrimination.	[5283] despise
			[7042] detest

6746		~을 아삭아삭/우적우적 먹다	[3328] chew
munch			
[muhnch]		She munched a sandwich for breakfast.	

6747		목을 베다, 참수하다	[7175] decapitate
behead			[758] execute
[bih-HED]		He was beheaded for spying.	

6748		(부정적 의미의) 엄청난, 터무니없는	[3681] outrageous
egregious			[1692] sad
[ih-GREE-juhs]			[5241] atrocious
		We must address egregious human rights violations.	[6912] deplorable

6749		반복	
reprise			
[ri-PRAHYZ]		She reprised that role in a musical version.	

6750		1. 자기 스스로 하는 2. 최소한의 자본으로 해내는 3. 가죽 손잡이	[113] reset
bootstrap			[1562] reboot
[BOOT-strap]		The company has grown through bootstrap efforts.	

6751	공무원 편입 GRE	누설하다, 폭로하다, 알리다	[1080] reveal
divulge			[1078] admit
[dih-VUHLJ]		He refused to divulge the details.	

6752	공무원	나란히, 뒤지지 않고 따라가다	
abreast			
[uh-BREST]		They walked abreast along the paths.	

6753		1. 삽화 2. 삽입물 3. ~을 끼워 넣다, 삽입하다	[1809] insert
inset			[86] include
[IN-set]			[1667] decorate
		The inset on the following page will further explain details.	[1703] import

6754	GRE	수반되는(일), 동반되는	[2060] accompanying
concomitant			
[kon-KOM-i-tuhnt]		Hair loss is a frequent concomitant of old age.	

6755	편입	1. 올바른 행동 2. 타당성, 적절성	impropriety (부적절한 행동)
propriety			[7365] decorum
[pruh-PRAHY-i-tee]		My children always behave with propriety.	[662] correctness

6756	공무원	1. 혼란스러운 2. 방향 감각을 잃은	disorientation (방향 감각 상실)
disoriented			[1581] confused
[dis-AWR-ee-en-tid]		He was feeling disoriented after an accident.	[4452] astray

6757		1. 수망아지 2. 선수	[6828] foal
colt			
[kohlt]		There is a colt inside the fence.	

6758		1. 선로를 바꾸다, 옆으로 돌리다 2. 이동하다 3. 추돌	[3567] bypass
shunt			[848] avoid
			[3923] deter
[shuhnt]		Several people died when the train was shunted.	[6698] budge

6759	공무원	(주름)장식	[1854] luxury
frill			
[fril]		She wore a beautiful frill dress.	

6760	편입	1. 폭우, 호우, 대홍수 2. 쇄도(하다) 3. 물에 잠기다	[2126] flood
deluge			[5276] avalanche
			[6145] barrage
[DEL-yooj]		Many homes were damaged in the deluge.	

6761		희열, 극도의 행복	[594] happiness
euphoria			[5650] exhilaration
			[6846] elation
[yoo-FAWR-ee-uh]		He was in a state of euphoria after winning the lottery.	

6762	공무원 편입	1. 불필요한 관심을 끌지 않는 2. 삼가는	obtrusive (튀는)
unobtrusive			[3179] humble
			[5420] inconspicuous
[uhn-uhb-TROO-siv]		He is quiet and unobtrusive at work.	

6763		1. 무대 2. (보행자용)통로	
catwalk			
[KAT-wawk]		The models walked down the catwalk.	

6764	토플 GRE	1. 중요한, 핵심적인 2. 두드러진, 현저한, 눈에 띄는	[2601] prominent
salient			[1314] relevant
			[1816] arresting
[SEY-lee-uhnt]		She only read salient points.	[5420] conspicuous

6765		1. (작은)방목장 2. 대기소	[561] track
paddock			
[PAD-uhk]		There is a horse in the paddock.	

6766		1. 발을 질질 끌며 걷다 2. 흠을 내다	[3658] scrape
scuff			[719] damage
[skuhf]		Stop scuffing your shoes.	

6767	토플	잠, 수면	[990] sleep
slumber			[5447] dormancy
			[5675] coma
[SLUHM-ber]		Let's have a slumber party!	

6768	GRE	1. 지지하다, 옹호하다 2. 신봉하다	[1431] adopt
espouse			[1934] advocate
[ih-SPOUZ]		Many men espouse gender equality.	

6769		1. 소모 2. 마찰	[563] war
attrition			[3913] erosion
[uh-TRISH-uhn]		This was a war of attrition that continued for three years.	

6770		인간과 비슷한 기계(로봇)	[907] animal
humanoid			
[HYOO-muh-noid]		We now have humanoid robots.	

6771 **sequestration** [see-kwes-TREY-shuhn]	1. 격리, 제거 2. 은퇴 3. 압류, 몰수	sequester (격리하다) [2243] isolation
	Promoting carbon sequestration is important for preventing climate change.	

6772 **trinket** [TRING-kit]	값싼(작은) 장신구	[3297] bead
	She likes to collect little trinkets.	

6773 **pubic** [PYOO-bik]	1. 치골의 2. 음부의	
	It will take some time for a fractured pubic bone to heal.	

6774 **fiend** [FEENd]	1. 악마 같은 사람, 악령 2. 열광자	fiendish (악마 같은) [3047] demon [5603] barbarian
	The little sneaky boy is such a fiend.	

6775 편입 **scoff** [skawf]	1. 비웃다, 조롱(하다) 2. 급하게 먹다	[1863] laugh [6925] deride [7120] belittle
	They scoffed at her thought.	

6776 편입 **repose** [ri-POHZ]	1. 휴식, 휴양 2. 수면	[714] rest [82] inactivity [142] stillness [2260] calm
	I need an undisturbed repose.	

6777 **hunk** [huhngk]	(큰)덩어리, 조각	[3037] chunk [3684] lump [5265] hoard
	He ate a hunk of bread for breakfast.	

6778 **blacksmith** [BLAK-smith]	대장장이	[3190] forger
	My husband works as a blacksmith.	

6779 **vice versa** [VAHY-suh vur-suh]	1. 거꾸로, 반대로 2. 반대도 마찬가지	[1411] conversely
	At our school, girls like to talk about boys and vice versa.	

6780 편입 **heyday** [HEY-dey]	전성기, 한창	[1641] prime [1868] peak
	She was very beautiful in her heyday.	

6781 공무원 **angst** [ahngkst]	1. 불안, 비관, 염세 2. 고뇌	[2288] anxiety [1133] worry [4829] agony [4835] apprehension
	Teenage angst can be very difficult for parents.	

6782 **expressway** [ik-SPRES-wey]	고속도로	[4948] freeway [124] interstate
	He took the expressway to head home.	

6783 **adage** [AD-ij]	속담, 격언	[4846] proverb [6355] axiom
	According to the well known adage, it's easier said than done.	

6784 **remand** [ri-MAND]	1. 구금, 유치 2. 송환하다	[3176] custody [3366] captivity [3443] confinement
	She is being held on remand.	

6785	편입	1. 혼란스럽게 하다 2. 신비화하다	demystify (신비성을 없애다)
mystify			[1817] complicate
[MIS-tuh-fahy]		He has failed to mystify his enemy.	[4839] baffle

6786	공무원 편입 GRE	1. 자음 2. 일치하는, 조화하는	[1337] consistent
consonant			[688] match
[KON-suh-nuhnt]		The English alphabet has 21 consonants.	

6787		버릇없는 놈, 선머슴	[4257] punk
brat			[7258] rascal
[brat]		That boy is a little brat.	

6788		1. 끼익 소리(를 내다) 2. 꽥 소리를 지르다	[2784] scream
squeal			[5459] howl
[skweel]		The truck stopped with a squeal of brakes.	[5682] peep

6789		쥐어짜다, 비틀다	[2967] squeeze
wring			[2029] wet
[ring]		Please wring the water from the wet blanket.	[6325] extort

6790		1. 변절자, 배신자 2. 탈당자	apostasy (변절)
apostate			[6467] renegade
[uh-POS-teyt]		She was viewed as an apostate when she stopped coming to the church.	

6791		1. 신들, 위인들, 영웅들 2. 신전	[2676] temple
pantheon			[867] church
[PAN-thee-on]		He deserves a spot on the pantheon of basketball legends.	[4065] chapel

6792	공무원	짓밟다, 유린하다, 무시하다	trampoline (트램폴린)
trample			[2692] crush
[TRAM-puhl]		Please don't trample on the grass.	[719] damage
			[6407] encroach

6793	공무원 편입 GRE	큰 실패, 사태	[621] failure
debacle			[445] breakdown
[dey-BAH-kuhl]		The global financial crisis is considered the greatest financial debacle.	[1187] beating

6794		속쓰림, 위산 과다 분비	[2433] indigestion
heartburn			
[HAHRT-burn]		You should see a doctor if the heartburn continues.	

6795		로그, 대수	logarithmic (로그의)
logarithm			
[LAW-guh-rith-uhm]		She didn't understand the underlying logic of logarithms.	

6796		손궤, 장식함, 작은 상자	[2173] chest
casket			
[KAS-kit]		I put my jewelry in a casket.	

6797		픽시, 작은 요정	[3484] fairy
pixie			
[PIK-see]		Both pixies and elves are imaginary creatures.	

6798		세 쌍둥이	[기타] three
triplet			
[TRIP-lit]		I am expecting triplets.	

6799 **daze** [deyz]	1. 멍해지게 하다 2. 현혹(시키다) 3. 눈부시게 하다	dazed (충격을 받아 멍한) [1958] stun [1399] tired
	She was dazed and confused by the news.	

6800 **intonation** [in-toh-NEY-shuhn]	토익 억양	intone (어조로 말하다) [4434] modulation
	Speaking with the right intonation is important.	

Allvoca.com

공무원	95~100
텝스	600
토플	120
아이엘츠	9
편입	최상위
SAT	780+
GRE	최빈출 단어

#6801~#7500

외국인으로서는 최상급 수준이자 원어민 석사 수준의 어휘력이다.
99% 이상의 영문 텍스트를 이해할 수 있다. 전문 서적 속 핵심 내용과 지문 구조를 정확히 파악할 수 있고 저자가 전달하고자하는 미세한 뉘앙스 차이까지 분별 가능하다.
레벨8을 마친 학습자에게는 최고 수준의 어휘력을 요하는 미국 이코노미스트지(The Economist)와 영국 가디언지(The Guardian)등의 학습 자료를 추천한다.

LEVEL **08**

6801 **wetsuit** [WET-soot]	잠수복	
	I bought my wetsuit just a year ago.	
6802 **defile** [dih-FAHYL]	1. 더럽히다 2. 모독하다	[719] damage
	Let no evil defile our souls.	
6803 **keepsake** [KEEP-seyk]	1. 기념품 2. 유품	[6874] memento [4760] relic
	That is one expensive keepsake.	
6804 **flexion** [FLEK-shuhn]	구부리기, 굴곡	
	A little bit of hip flexion is completely normal as it happens every time.	
6805 **wile** [wahyl]	1. 책략, 계략 2. 속이다, 사기치다	wily (교활한) [1595] trick
	She used her feminine wiles to persuade her boyfriend.	
6806 **solace** [SOL-is]	위안, 위로	[694] comfort [401] improvement [2313] consolation [5920] condolence
	She found solace in religion when her son died five years ago.	
6807 **screech** [skreech]	끼익거리는 소리(날카로운 소리)	[2784] scream [3172] shout [5459] howl
	The car stopped with a loud screech of breaks.	
6808 **altercation** [awl-ter-KEY-shuhn]	언쟁, 논쟁	[2329] dispute [962] argument [7152] bickering
	I had an altercation with my parents who were against my decision.	
6809 **carousel** [kar-uh-SEL]	1. 회전목마 2. 수하물 컨테이너 벨트	[5421] roundabout
	I had fun riding on a carousel.	
6810 **tantalize** [TAN-tl-ahyz]	애가 타게 하다, 감질나게 하다	tantalizing (감질나는) [3772] tease [964] inspire [2465] annoy
	He tantalized the dog with the smell of bacon.	
6811 **fiat** [FEE-aht]	1. 명령, 지시 2. 인가, 허가	[7424] dictum
	Leaders should be careful when issuing fiats.	
6812 **outpace** [out-PEYS]	~보다 빠르다, 앞서다	[1040] progress [1187] beat [2455] dominate
	He outpaced other runners.	
6813 　　　공무원 GRE **dichotomy** [dahy-KOT-uh-mee]	양분, 이분(법)	[1800] split [117] difference
	The dichotomy between his words and actions was very obvious.	
6814 **livery** [LIV-uh-ree]	1. (특정 회사의)상징 색 2. 제복, 정복	[2420] uniform [1190] dress [2729] costume
	The company wanted its own livery to present its identity.	

6815 **pomp** [pomp]	편입	장관, 화려함, 허식 The guests enjoyed the pomp at the celebrity's wedding.	pompous (호화로운, 거만한) [6847] fanfare
6816 **permutation** [pur-myoo-TEY-shuhn]		교환, 순열, 치환 It is impossible to count all the permutations of this set of alphabets.	[1032] switch [656] mixture
6817 **equinox** [EE-kwuh-noks]		주야 평분시, 낮과 밤이 똑같은 때 During an equinox, the lengths of daylight and nighttime hours are practically the same.	
6818 **assent** [uh-SENT]	편입	1. 찬성(하다), 동의(하다) 2. 승인 She nodded to show her assent to the decision.	[2370] consent [1072] approval [7207] acquiescence
6819 **corsair** [KAWR-sair]		해적(선) Who is the captain of this corsair?	[2937] pirate [3663] thief
6820 **troupe** [troop]		1. 극단 2. 일행 He joined a circus troupe and traveled all over Asia.	[500] association [1067] band
6821 **depravity** [dih-PRAV-i-tee]	편입	타락, 비행, 부패(행위) The author depicted the depravities of the political circle.	depraved (타락한) deprave (타락시키다) [2543] corruption [967] criminality
6822 **repatriate** [ree-PEY-tree-eyt]		1. (포로, 망명자를)본국으로 송환하다 2. 귀국자, 송환자 Many European countries are trying to repatriate refugees.	repatriation (귀국)
6823 **conundrum** [kuh-NUHN-druhm]	GRE	1. 어려운 문제, 난문제 2. 수수께끼 The company has to solve this conundrum to survive.	[5291] riddle [1039] task [1926] mystery [5599] enigma
6824 **onshore** [ON-shawr]		1. (바람이 바다에서)육지로 향하는 2. 내륙의 The wind was blowing onshore.	[690] land [2866] ashore [4658] inland
6825 **idiosyncrasy** [id-ee-uh-SING-kruh-see]	GRE	1. 특이한 습관, 습성 2. 특질 Her friends had an appreciation for her idiosyncrasy.	idiosyncratic (특이한) [266] feature [1654] mannerism [5202] eccentricity
6826 **vex** [veks]	토플 편입 GRE	1. 성가시게 하다 2. (사소한 일로)성나게 하다 It vexed him to think of others talking behind his back.	[2895] irritate [2465] annoy [4795] afflict [4877] agitate
6827 **viva** [VEE-vuh]		만세 People in the crowd shouted, "Viva democracy."	
6828 **foal** [fohl]		망아지(를 낳다) I saw a foal running on the green field.	[6757] colt [4655] offspring

| 6829 **janitor** [JAN-i-ter] | 1. 건물 관리인 2. 문지기, 수위 | [453] attendant [3176] custodian |
| | You should leave your key with the janitor. | |

| 6830 **iniquity** [ih-NIK-wi-tee] | 1. 사악 2. 부당, 부정(행위) | [3791] wickedness [1930] evil |
| | Parents are trying to protect their children from iniquity. | |

| 6831 **fidget** [FIJ-it] | 1. 안절부절 못하다 2. 가만히 못 있다 | [7129] squirm [966] touch [4539] fret |
| | Stop fidgeting over little matters. | |

| 6832 **ordain** [awr-DEYN] | 1. 임명하다, 정하다 2. 규정하다 | ordinance (법령) [1369] appoint [5750] anoint |
| | The pope will ordain ten new priests this year. | |

| 6833 공무원 편입 **derogatory** [dih-ROG-uh-tawr-ee] | 1. 경멸적인 2. 비판적인 | [7021] disparaging [1159] defamatory [3745] degrading [6409] scorn |
| | She made derogatory remarks to her friend. | |

| 6834 편입 **despicable** [DES-pi-kuh-buhl] | 1. 비열한, 야비한 2. 경멸스러운 | [6078] vile [2830] horrible [3745] degrading [5010] contemptible |
| | It is despicable to abandon your pet. | |

| 6835 공무원 **atrophy** [A-truh-fee] | 1. 쇠약(하다) 2. 위축(되다) | [3808] decay [4651] degeneration |
| | Memory can atrophy as you age. | |

| 6836 **sliver** [SLIV-er] | 조각 | [3352] fragment [409] bit [4059] flake |
| | I would like a sliver of cheese. | |

| 6837 **sickle** [SIK-uhl] | 낫 | [2010] blade [6927] bayonet |
| | He went out to buy a hammer and a sickle. | |

| 6838 **snob** [snob] | 1. 고상한/신사인 체하는 사람 2. 속물 | [7068] extrovert |
| | I hate it when she is acting like a snob. | |

| 6839 **mojo** [MOH-joh] | 1. 마력, 매력 2. 마약 | [2312] charm [1893] crack [5456] narcotic |
| | She is trying to regain her lost mojo. | |

| 6840 공무원 **barter** [BAHR-ter] | 1. 물물교환하다 2. 거래하다 | [667] trade [7241] haggle |
| | The Pilgrims bartered with Native Americans. | |

| 6841 토플 **tectonic** [tek-TON-ik] | (지질)구조의 | [854] structural [1825] architectural [3625] anatomical |
| | Constantly moving tectonic plates causes earthquakes. | |

| 6842 공무원 토플 **outcry** [OUT-krahy] | 강한 항의/반응 | [2298] protest [1228] reaction [6733] clamor [7127] commotion |
| | The government's decision provoked a public outcry. | |

6843	토플	머스킷총(구식 소총)	musketeer (머스킷총 병사)
musket			[2564] rifle
[MUHS-kit]		I used a musket for hunting.	

6844	공무원 편입	다정한, 따뜻한, 진심의	cordially (다정하게)
cordial			[288] friendly
			[3570] affectionate
[KAWR-juhl]		The Queen was very cordial to her people.	[7184] amicable

6845	공무원 토플 편입 GRE	1. 불러일으키다 2. 발생시키다	[603] generate
engender			[864] affect
			[5094] arouse
[en-JEN-der]		The president's tragic past engendered public empathy.	

6846		1. 신이 난 2. 의기양양한	elation (의기양양함)
elated			[594] happy
			[249] interested
[ih-LEY-tid]		She was greatly elated by the good news.	[2069] delighted

6847		1. 트럼펫과 드럼의 짧은 곡 (팡파르) 2. 광고, 선전	[3945] flourish
fanfare			[6815] pomp
[FAN-fair]		The ceremony started with great fanfare.	

6848		세뇌하다	[3022] indoctrinate
brainwash			[334] teach
			[354] educate
[BREYN-wosh]		The North Korean regime is trying to brainwash its people.	

6849	토플 GRE	1. 피하다, 멀리하다 2. 삼가다	[848] avoid
eschew			[2399] abandon
[es-CHOO]		We must eschew violence and conflict.	

6850		여러가지 도구/용품	[1406] gear
paraphernalia			[853] machinery
			[919] stuff
[par-uh-fer-NEYL-yuh]		Don't forget to bring all your fishing paraphernalia.	

6851	GRE	1. 중심지 2. 장소, 위치	
locus			
[LOH-kuhs]		New York City is the locus of economic activity.	

6852		보초, 감시인	[5564] sentinel
sentry			
[SEN-tree]		The sentry let the guests enter.	

6853	공무원 편입	1. 에워싸다, 포위하다 2. 공격하다	[1346] surround
besiege			[2294] invade
			[7146] beset
[bih-SEEJ]		The boyband was besieged by many people.	

6854	공무원	1. 따돌림 받는 사람 2. 버림받은 사람, 배척자	[966] untouchable
outcast			[6280] fugitive
[OUT-kast]		She was an outcast in high school.	

6855	공무원	1. 용기 2. 인내, 불굴의 정신	[929] courage
fortitude			[2591] boldness
			[2865] bravery
[FAWR-ti-tood]		He endured his pain with fortitude.	

6856		진정한, 진실의	[296] actually
veritable			
[VER-i-tuh-buhl]		This beach is considered a veritable paradise for those who love surfing.	

6857 **demote** [dih-MOHT]	1. 강등시키다 2. 지위를 낮추다	demotion (강등) [2332] bump [2703] dismiss
	He had a hard time after being demoted.	
6858 **rendezvous** [RAHN-duh-voo]	만남(의 장소), 회합	
	This place is a rendezvous for authors.	
6859 공무원 편입 **reprimand** [REP-ruh-mand]	질책하다, 꾸짖다	[6362] rebuke [898] criticize [6418] admonition [7141] censure
	His teacher reprimanded him for all the lies he told.	
6860 **bastion** [BAS-chuhn]	1. 수호자 2. 요새	[5901] citadel [2149] precaution
	My professor is my last bastion of justice.	
6861 편입 **standoff** [STAND-awf]	1. 교착 상태 2. 떨어져 있는 3. 서먹서먹한, 냉담한	[962] argument [6902] deadlock
	It is important to end the political standoff.	
6862 **sidekick** [SAHYD-kik]	1. 동료, 한패 2. 들러리	[3510] buddy [288] friend
	I have been his sidekick since college.	
6863 **throbbing** [THROB-ing]	욱신거리는, 두근거리는	throb (욱신거리다) [4366] aching [2941] pulse [6239] flutter
	My heart is throbbing with pain.	
6864 **lair** [lair]	1. 은신처 2. (소)굴, 집	[4639] den
	This place served as a thief's lair.	
6865 GRE **symbiosis** [sim-bee-OH-sis]	공생, 공존	symbiotic (공생의) [192] relationship [335] body [549] existence
	Fungi live in symbiosis with trees.	
6866 **botch** [boch]	1. 망치다 2. 엉성한 일, 망친 일	
	I am about to botch my final exam.	
6867 **crux** [kruhks]	핵심 부분, 요점	[1248] core [266] feature
	The crux of the matter is to prevent it from recurring.	
6868 **boulevard** [BOOL-uh-vahrd]	1. 도로, 대로 2. 넓은 길	[2289] avenue [3504] artery
	The complex narrow streets were replaced with a boulevard.	
6869 **glisten** [GLIS-uhn]	반짝이다, 빛나다	[4211] glitter [1962] shine [3841] flicker [5981] gleam
	Her eyes began to glisten with tears.	
6870 **pertinent** [PUR-tn-uhnt]	적절한, 적합한	[1314] relevant [140] applicable [6598] admissible
	Key details pertinent to the story were omitted.	

6871 **ravine** [ruh-VEEN]	1. 좁은 골짜기 2. 협곡, 계곡 We crossed the ravine safely.	[4262] canyon [5962] abyss
6872　　　　편입 **decoy** [DEE-koi]	1. 유인물, 미끼 2. 유인하다 The police acted as a decoy to catch the thief.	[3966] lure [2593] manipulation
6873　공무원 편입 **lenient** [LEE-nee-uhnt]	1. 관대한, 느슨한 2. 온화한 The current law is too lenient.	leniency (관대함) [1245] soft [3146] compassionate [5170] benign
6874 **memento** [muh-MEN-toh]	1. 기념품 2. 추억거리 We gave her a cup as a memento.	[5140] souvenir [4760] relic [6803] keepsake
6875 **shenanigans** [shuh-NAN-i-guhnz]	1. 허튼 소리 2. 사기, 속임수 I cannot stand his shenanigans anymore.	[6134] antics
6876 **lob** [lob]	1. 높게 던지다 2. 높게 차다 He lobbed the ball high over her head.	[1603] pitch [1030] throw [2432] flip [5297] hurl
6877 **strum** [struhm]	(기타를)치다, 퉁기다 He strummed the guitar for his wife.	[5351] pluck
6878　　　　GRE **dovetail** [DUHV-teyl]	딱/꼭 들어맞다 Her holiday plans dovetail with his.	[3224] coincide [3398] conform
6879　토플 편입 **incinerate** [in-SIN-uh-reyt]	소각하다, 태워서 재로 만들다 It is cost-effective to incinerate waste.	incineration (소각) [1224] burn [677] consume [5507] cremate
6880 **monsoon** [mon-SOON]	1. 우기, 장맛비, 호우 2. 계절풍 It is difficult to travel during the monsoon season.	[5114] drizzle [6760] deluge
6881 **handkerchief** [HANG-ker-chif]	손수건 He gave her a handkerchief as a present.	[외래어] scarf
6882 **munitions** [myoo-NISH-uhns]	1. 군수품 2. 탄약 3. 생필품 She worked in a munitions factory for several years.	[1467] weaponry
6883　공무원 편입 **insidious** [in-SID-ee-uhs]	1. (발견되지 않은 암처럼) 위험이 서서히 퍼지는 2. 음흉한 The effects are insidious and persistent.	[5996] cunning [1223] dangerous [2569] subtle
6884　　　공무원 **outlay** [OUT-ley]	경비, 지출 This work requires a lot of financial outlay.	[1130] expenditure [305] price [5659] disbursement

6885	공무원 편입	낙엽(성)의, 탈락성의	[1648] temporary
deciduous			[1671] brief
[dih-SIJ-oo-uhs]		Deciduous trees lose their leaves every autumn.	[6739] ephemeral

6886		1. 유명 디자이너 제품 2. 고급 여성복	
couture			
[koo-TOOR]		The princess wore a couture dress.	

6887		법률 전문가, 변호사	jurisprudence (법학)
jurist			[1727] counselor
[JOOR-ist]		He is an honest jurist respected by many people.	[6454] barrister

6888	토플 GRE	1. 참정권 2. 투표권, 선거권	suffragette (여성 참정권 운동가)
suffrage			
[SUHF-rij]		Universal suffrage was introduced in 1918 in Britain.	

6889		본국으로 이송하다	extradition (본국 이송)
extradite			[4558] deport
[EK-struh-dahyt]		The government refused to extradite criminals.	[2399] abandon
			[4835] apprehend

6890		1. (장식)술 2. (옥수수)수염	[6021] tuft
tassel			[3199] ridge
[TAS-uhl]		I made tassels for the cushions.	

6891		(개가 꼬리를) 빠르게 흔들다	[3837] wit
wag			
[wag]		Dogs wag their tails when they are happy.	

6892		격투, 난투	[4061] scramble
scrimmage			[697] fight
[SKRIM-ij]		Seven football players are on the line of scrimmage.	[6475] skirmish
			[7325] scuffle

6893		해적(질하다)	[2937] pirate
buccaneer			
[buhk-uh-NEER]		He played his role as a notorious buccaneer of the Carribeans.	

6894	공무원	낭패, 대실패	[621] failure
fiasco			[445] breakdown
[fee-AS-koh]		Their plan for revenge ended in a fiasco.	[6615] blunder

6895		1. 은제품 2. 식탁용 은식기류	[2016] silver
silverware			[6990] cutlery
[SIL-ver-wair]		He cleaned the silverware with a dry cloth.	

6896		1. 중얼/웅얼거리다 2. 중얼거리는 말	[6678] mutter
mumble			[6428] murmur
[MUHM-buhl]		Don't mumble, I can't hear you.	[6731] grumble
			[7124] babble

6897		1. 코담배 2. 코로 들이마시다, 냄새를 맡다	[5088] sniff
snuff			[2068] cry
[snuhf]		Not many people take snuff these days.	[5134] extinguish

6898	공무원 편입	1. 지독한 2. 무시무시한, 무서운	[6241] hideous
horrid			[2830] horrible
[HAWR-id]		He is so horrid to his little sister.	[4011] disgusting
			[5241] atrocious

6899		잠자리	
dragonfly			
[DRAG-uhn-flahy]		A dragonfly landed on me.	

6900	편입	1. 구혼자 2. 다른 기업 인수를 원하는 기업	[2728] admirer
suitor			
[SOO-ter]		She has a suitor who loves her very much.	

6901	편입	의기양양한, 우쭐대는	[7071] conceited
smug			[3754] egotistical
			[4589] arrogant
[smuhg]		He was so smug about winning that game.	[5970] complacent

6902	공무원 편입	교착 상태, 막다른/막힌 상태	[2063] crisis
deadlock			[4483] dilemma
[DED-lok]		Negotiations ended in deadlock.	

6903		강풍, 큰 바람, 돌풍	[1878] storm
gale			[1863] laughter
			[3290] hurricane
[geyl]		A gale will be blowing from the north later this week.	[5374] cyclone

6904	공무원 편입	후원자, 기증자	[105] backer
benefactor			[901] contributor
[BEN-uh-fak-ter]		A generous benefactor donated a lot of money.	

6905	공무원 편입 GRE	속이기 쉬운	[2644] foolish
gullible			[5081] naive
[GUHL-uh-buhl]		My girlfriend is very gullible.	

6906		자체적으로 붕괴하다	[621] fail
implode			
[im-PLOHD]		Some economists warn that the global economy could implode.	

6907		과시하다, 허세부리다	[704] advertise
flaunt			[2650] boast
			[7262] brandish
[flawnt]		She likes to flaunt her wealth.	

6908	공무원	1. 가장 무도회 2. 겉치레 3. 가장(하다)	
masquerade			
[mas-kuh-REYD]		Many celebrities attended the masquerade party.	

6909	편입 GRE	1. 격렬한 2. 열정적인, 열렬한	vehemently (격렬하게)
vehement			[1987] angry
		Despite vehement opposition from my parents, I didn't go to	[2769] abstract
[VEE-uh-muhnt]		university.	[6411] ardent

6910		막다	
occlude			
[uh-KLOOD]		Her arteries are occluded.	

6911		멋있는, 그럴싸한	[938] modern
groovy			[2547] fabulous
[GROO-vee]		She is wearing a groovy dress.	

6912	공무원 편입 GRE	매우 슬퍼하다, 한탄하다, 개탄하다	deplorable (슬픈, 개탄스러운)
deplore			[2972] regret
[dih-PLAWR]		The United Nations deplores violations of human rights.	[4274] bemoan

6913	괭이(로 파다)	[5033] shovel
hoe [hoh]	Use this hoe to dig up potatoes.	

6914	어리석은	[1776] crazy
daft [daft]	The daft plan will fail.	

6915 공무원 편입	공범자	complicit (공모한) complicity (공모, 연루) [500] associate
accomplice [uh-KOM-plis]	Who was the accomplice in the burglary?	

6916	1. (일시적으로 확 풍기는) 냄새, 한번 뭄 2. 흔적	[1836] smell [2018] breath [2226] trace [3604] aroma
whiff [hwif]	She caught a whiff of alcohol.	

6917	1. (주먹을) 꽉 쥐다 2. (이를) 악 물다	[2200] grip [3656] clamp [5775] clasp
clench [klench]	She clenched her fists and punched the wall.	

6918	매춘굴, 사창가	
brothel [BROTH-uhl]	Prostitutes work in brothels.	

6919 편입	1. 넘치다, 많이 있다 2. (비가) 많이 내리다, 쏟아지다	[4897] swarm [1675] rain [4564] bustle [5336] brim
teem [teem]	The forest is teeming with animals.	

6920	(책이나 계약서의) 부록	[1647] postscript [4422] appendix
addendum [uh-DEN-duhm]	The addendum of the book contained minor corrections made by the author.	

6921 편입	계략, 술책	[1595] trick [562] device [4046] maneuver [6153] hoax
ploy [ploi]	The company's donations were just a marketing ploy.	

6922	죽	
porridge [PAWR-ij]	You should eat porridge if you are sick.	

6923	도마뱀붙이	[5378] lizard
gecko [GEK-oh]	Geckos mostly live in warm countries.	

6924	1. 불만스러운 2. 시무룩한, 언짢은	[594] unhappy [1987] angry [2465] annoyed [2895] irritated
disgruntled [dis-GRUHN-tld]	The students are disgruntled with the teacher.	

6925 공무원 편입 GRE	조롱하다, 깔보다	derision (조롱) [2708] ridicule [898] criticize [6427] disdain
deride [dih-RAHYD]	Critics derided the movie as immature.	

6926	물결 모양의, 주름 잡힌	[7047] crumpled
corrugated [KAWR-uh-gey-tid]	Corrugated cardboard boxes are sturdier.	

6927	(총에 고정된 검이 있는) 총검	[2080] knife
bayonet		
[BEY-uh-nit]	The solider is holding a bayonet.	

6928　　편입	1. 움찔하다, 움츠리다　2. ~을 회피하다	[7263] wince
flinch		
[flinch]	He flinched at the loud noise.	

6929　공무원 편입 GRE	충돌되는 감정을 가진, 애증의	ambivalence (충돌된 감정을 가진 상태)
ambivalent		[385] uncertain
[am-BIV-uh-luhnt]	I feel ambivalent about breaking up with my boyfriend.	[1476] doubtful

6930	1. 족제비　2. (끈질기게 무언가를) 찾다	[1600] hunt
ferret		
[FER-it]	Ferrets eat mice.	

6931　　편입	애원하다, 간절히 부탁하다	[3511] plead
implore		
[im-PLAWR]	He implored his teacher to give him a better grade.	

6932	석궁	[2059] bomb
crossbow		[3253] ammunition
[KRAWS-boh]	Crossbows were used for hunting.	

6933	1. 통제하기 힘든　2. 질서가 없는	[1547] wild
unruly		[290] disorderly
[uhn-ROO-lee]	Unruly crowds flooded into the street.	[402] unlimited
		[5376] drunken

6934	1. (곤충이나 새가) 짹짹 울다　2. 즐겁게 얘기하다	[2611] tweet
chirp		
[churp]	The hungry birds are chirping.	

6935	예를 들다, 실증하다	
instantiate		
[in-STAN-shee-eyt]	The couple instantiates a successful long-distance relationship.	

6936　　편입	(야간) 통행 금지령, 집에 돌아와야 하는 시간, 통금	
curfew		
[KUR-fyoo]	My curfew is 11 pm.	

6937	(소리나 색 등이) 조화롭지 않은, 불협화의	dissonance (불협화음)
dissonant		[6006] discordant
[DIS-uh-nuhnt]	The dissonant music is unpleasant to listen to.	[117] differing

6938	볼록한	[5287] bulging
convex		
[kon-VEKS]	My glasses have convex lenses.	

6939	1. (누에 등의) 고치　2. (고치처럼) 둘러싸다	
cocoon		
[kuh-KOON]	Silk thread is made from cocoons.	

6940　　편입 GRE	여분의, 과다의	[658] unnecessary
superfluous		[1130] expendable
[soo-PUR-floo-uhs]	The article is too long because it has superfluous details.	[1738] excessive

6941	토플	흩뜨리다, 사이사이에 배치하다	[3539] infuse
intersperse			
[in-ter-SPURS]		Informative articles are interspersed throughout the magazine.	

6942		변덕스러운	[123] changeable
mercurial			
[mer-KYOOR-ee-uhl]		Support for the team captain was mercurial.	

6943	공무원 편입 GRE	1. 꾸짖다, 비난하다 2. 비난	[898] criticize [2097] disgrace
reproach			
[ri-PROHCH]		My teacher reproached me.	

6944		1. 윙윙하는 움직임 (움직이다) 2. 윙윙 소리 3. 명인, 전문가	[42] best [3360] genius [6026] prodigy
whiz			
[hwiz]		The bee whizzed past.	

6945	공무원 편입 GRE	(죄나 책임 등을) 돌리다, 전가하다	imputation (책임 전가) [415] charge [6190] ascribe
impute			
[im-PYOOT]		The crimes were imputed to the servants.	

6946	편입	(사고나 감각의) 예민함, 격렬함	[1588] intelligence [3187] agility [6721] acumen
acuity			
[uh-KYOO-i-tee]		I admire people with intellectual acuity.	

6947		1. 망자를 위한 예배 2. 위령곡	
requiem			
[REK-wee-uhm]		The church held a requiem mass for the victims of the earthquake.	

6948		일어나다, 벌어지다	[874] occur [370] happen [511] materialize [4553] ensue
befall			
[bih-FAWL]		A tragedy befell him.	

6949		흩뿌리다, 퍼지다	[3299] scatter [1573] occupy [3182] sprinkle
strew			
[stroo]		Toys were strewn all over the floor.	

6950		고지(대), 산지	[690] highland
upland			
[UHP-luhnd]		The school is built on an upland plain.	

6951	공무원 편입 GRE	긴밀하게, 밀접하게, 뗄래야 뗄 수 없는	extricate (탈출, 구출) [326] connected [2798] inevitably
inextricably			
[in-EK-stri-kuh-buh lee]		Success and hard work are inextricably linked.	

6952	편입	연장하다, 길게 끌다	[3680] prolong
protract			
[proh-TRAKT]		The teacher protracted the class.	

6953	공무원 편입 GRE	상응하는, 비례하는	[2241] proportionate [572] comparable [988] suitable [1964] compatible
commensurate			
[kuh-MEN-ser-it]		Your grade will be commensurate with hard work.	

6954		뒤죽박죽(되도록 만들다), 혼란(스럽게 하다)	[6737] muddle [656] mixture [4031] assortment
jumble			
[JUHM-buhl]		My clothes are in a jumble.	

6955			
domicile	1. 집, 거주지 2. 거주하는 나라		
[dom]	I am renovating my domicile.		

6956	GRE	같은 중심의, 동심의	
concentric			
[kuhn-SEN-trik]	The concentric circles have different sizes.		

6957		강탈, 도둑질	[2966] robbery
heist			
[hahyst]	The diamond heist was reported on the news.		

6958		풍자극, 익살극	[3085] sketch
skit			[5383] satire
[skit]	This is a skit regarding the corruption of the elite.		[외래어] parody

6959	공무원 편입 GRE	사소한 일, 하찮은 일	trifling (사소한)
trifle			[919] stuff
[TRAHY-fuhl]	Don't worry about such trifles.		

6960		삐걱/삑삑거리다	[5824] squeak
creak			[4646] reshuffle
			[5915] groan
[kreek]	The chair creaked when she sat on it.		[6807] screech

6961		썰매(를 타다)	
sled			
[sled]	This sled is pulled by horses.		

6962		(미사일의) 탄두	
warhead			
[WAWR-hed]	Nuclear warheads have severe explosive power.		

6963	편입	사죄하는, 뉘우치는	penitentiary (교도소)
penitent			[1682] sorry
[PEN-i-tuhnt]	The victim forgave the penitent criminal.		[2637] apologetic

6964	공무원	구름으로 덮인, 흐린	[941] dark
overcast			[6493] dismal
[OH-ver-kast]	The weather is cold and the sky is overcast.		[6985] dreary

6965		화, 분노	[3161] rage
ire			[270] displeasure
[ahyuhr]	The company provoked the ire of stockholders.		[2465] annoyance

6966		변증법, (진리를 추구하는) 토의	dialectical (변증적인)
dialectic			[235] result
[dahy-uh-LEK-tik]	The elections contributed a great deal to the dialectic surrounding politics.		

6967	편입	(어떤 업계의) 대물, 거장	[6602] mogul
tycoon			[1056] capitalist
[tahy-KOON]	He is a fashion tycoon.		[2085] boss

6968		(특히 방에 욕실이) 딸려오는	
ensuite			
[ahn SWEET]	There are four ensuite bathrooms.		

6969	공무원	인파	[1635] crowd
throng			[2070] bunch
[thrawng]		A huge throng gathered in front of the news station.	[3736] congregation

6970	공무원 편입	쇠약해지다, 힘 없이 지내다	languid (힘 없는)
languish			[1445] weaken
[LANG-gwish]		The criminal languishes in prison.	[4034] deteriorate

6971		트림(하다)	
burp			
[burp]		Babies cannot burp on their own.	

6972		출처	[1729] origin
provenance			
[PROV-uh-nuhns]		The painting is of Korean provenance.	

6973		1. (술을 마시지 않아) 정신이 멀쩡한, 취하지 않은 2. 근엄	[4868] sober
sobriety			
[suh-BRAHY-i-tee]		The driver passed the sobriety test.	

6974		1.약골, 겁이 많은 사람 2. (겁이 나서) 무언가를 하지 않음	[5414] coward
wimp			
[wimp]		I'm a wimp when it comes to swimming.	

6975	토플 편입	가짜의, 거짓의	pseudonym (필명)
pseudo			[2552] fake
[SOO-doh]		Pseudo journalists spread fake news.	

6976	토플	(황소 중 특히) 수소	[2942] bull
ox			
[oks]		The ox is pulling a cart.	

6977		1.소리지르다 2. 비명을 지르다 3. 비명	[2784] scream
shriek			[3172] shout
[shreek]		After getting a present, she shrieked with excitement.	[5459] howl
			[6807] screech

6978		종마	[1689] horse
stallion			[204] manly
[STAL-yuhn]		Stallions are raised for breeding.	[7305] macho

6979		파마(하다)	[1751] permanent
perm			
[purm]		I had a perm to make my hair curly.	

6980	공무원 편입 GRE	초기의, 발생하려고 하는, 시작 단계의	[7281] incipient
nascent			[60] new
[NAS-uhnt]		The nascent artificial intelligence industry is developing rapidly.	

6981		(방금 언급한 것) 위에, 대해	[80] afterwards
thereon			[1322] eventually
[thair-ON]		Read the newspaper and articles posted thereon.	

6982	공무원 편입	1. 기이한, 독특한 2. 이국적인, 낯선	[1659] strange
outlandish			[5202] eccentric
[out-LAN-dish]		His outlandish outfit got everyone's attention.	[5574] extravagant

6983	편입	1. 나무늘보 2. 게으름뱅이	
sloth			
[slawth]		Sloths move very slowly.	

6984		1. 격퇴하다, 무찌르다 2. ~을 역겹게 하다	repulsive (역겨운) [4403] repel
repulse			
[ri-PUHLS]		The police repulsed the protesters.	

6985	편입	음울한, 쓸쓸한	[5443] gloomy [1109] boring [5795] bleak
dreary			
[DREER-ee]		The walk to school was dreary.	

6986		여성혐오	misogynist (여성혐오자) [773] sexism
misogyny			
[mi-SOJ-uh-nee]		Misogyny is a serious problem that needs to be resolved.	

6987	공무원	소멸한, 존재하지 않는	[1186] dead [30] useless [549] nonexistent [4927] obsolete
defunct			
[dih-FUHNGKT]		Telephones are almost defunct.	

6988		1. 가시(등의 따끔한 물건) 2. 콕 찌르다	prickly (가시가 많은) [5786] tingle [1177] suffer
prickle			
[PRIK-uhl]		Eat the fish after removing the prickles.	

6989	토플	계보, 혈통	genealogist (계보 학자) [5546] lineage [1524] genetics [3455] ancestry
genealogy			
[jee-nee-OL-uh-jee]		If you trace your genealogy, you can find your ancestors.	

6990	공무원	(포크와 나이프 등) 식기	[6895] silverware [5526] tableware
cutlery			
[KUHT-luh-ree]		Please use the cutlery to eat food.	

6991	토플	(다량의) 분출, 유출	[2126] flood [2226] trace [6760] deluge
outpouring			
[OUT-pawr-ing]		There was a massive outpouring of oil from the ship.	

6992	공무원	1. 버둥거리다, 허우적거리다 2. 가자미	[3494] stumble [4365] flop
flounder			
[FLOUN-der]		He cannot swim so he is floundering in the pool.	

6993		(냄새나 맛이) 강렬한, 자극적인	[1781] sharp [1565] acid [5779] stale [7420] acrid
pungent			
[PUHN-juhnt]		The pungent smell of rotting milk spread from the trashcan.	

6994		1. 창 던지기 2. 창을 던지다	[4486] spear
javelin			
[JAV-lin]		She is champion in the javelin.	

6995		깨달음의 순간, 통찰	[1080] revelation [1650] insight [1670] flash
epiphany			
[ih-PIF-uh-nee]		After a moment of epiphany, he could understand the book.	

6996	편입 GRE	면제하다, 방면하다, 사면하다	absolution (사면) [7237] exonerate [372] clear [2700] exempt
absolve			
[ab-ZOLV]		Being forgiven absolved the criminals of their guilt.	

6997	GRE	1. 핵심 그룹 2. 그룹의 중요한 인물	[350] organization
cadre			[2380] personnel
[KAD-ree]		The small cadre of journalists researched the political corruption.	

6998		퐁당(떨어짐), 첨벙(빠짐)	[454] fall
plop			[6239] flutter
[plop]		The ball plopped into the pool.	

6999	GRE	극악한, 악랄한	[3817] villainous
nefarious			[1930] evil
[ni-FAIR-ee-uhs]		The police arrested the nefarious criminals.	[2830] horrible

7000	공무원 편입 GRE	격분케하다, (감정을) 악화하다	exasperation (격노)
exasperate			[2895] irritate
[ig-ZAS-puh-reyt]		The child exasperated her parents.	[2465] annoy
			[4877] agitate

7001		1. 쿵쿵 걷다 2. 짓밟다 3. 부랑자	[7366] vagabond
tramp			
[tramp]		When my mother is angry, she tramps around the kitchen.	

7002	편입	단조로운, 생기 없는	[3731] dull
drab			[1109] boring
[drab]		Her outfit is drab and brown.	[5795] bleak
			[5929] desolate

7003	GRE	1. 분리하다, 분리해서 생각하다 2. 거리를 두다	[572] compare
dissociate			[2502] alienate
[dih-SOH-shee-eyt]		This statement should not be dissociated from the context.	[3508] detach

7004		딱지(가 형성되다)	[4578] blister
scab			[5398] crater
[skab]		A scab formed over my wound.	

7005		1. (급격히) 방향을 틀다 2. 빗나가다	[6052] veer
swerve			[4848] deflect
[swurv]		The truck swerved around the car.	[7153] lurch

7006		할당하다, 나누다, 분배하다	apportionment (할당)
apportion			[4933] allot
[uh-PAWR-shuhn]		The roles will be apportioned based on experience.	[271] share
			[1066] administer

7007	토익 공무원 편입	시간을 잘 지키는, 시간을 엄수하는	[1890] prompt
punctual			[386] dependable
[PUHNGK-choo-uhl]		Don't be late. Be punctual.	[3554] expeditious

7008		1. (학교, 회사 내의) 매점 2. 군인들이 사용하는 물통	[5569] cafeteria
canteen			
[kan-TEEN]		The students went to the canteen to have lunch.	

7009		정신 착란, 무아지경, 망상	delirious (정신 착란의)
delirium			[5288] frenzy
[dih-LEER-ee-uhm]		The patient is in delirium because of the fever.	[788] fever
			[1581] confusion

7010	공무원 편입	1. (범죄나 잘못된 행실을) 뒤덮다, 숨기다 2. 백색도료	[617] whiten
whitewash			[6921] ploy
[HWAHYT-wosh]		The president tried to whitewash her crime.	

7011	1. 방지하다 2. 선취하다	preemption (방지)
preempt		preemptive (방지의)
[pree-EMPT]	The police preempted a protest through negotiations.	[740] prevent

7012	1. 기억상실증 환자, 건망증 환자 2. 건망증의	amnesia (기억 상실증)
amnesic		[2191] blind
[am-NEE-zhik]	Amnesics often retain memories from their childhood.	[4185] deaf

7013	구혼, 구애	[5728] wooing
courtship		[626] courting
[KAWRT-ship]	His courtship of her succeeded after 7 months.	[895] engagement

7014	지배권, 헤게모니	
hegemony		
[hi-JEM-uh-nee]	The United States united the world under its hegemony.	

7015	1. 보조개(가 움푹 들어가다) 2. 홈, 파인 구멍	[4856] dent
dimple		[5019] imprint
[DIM-puhl]	He has blue hair and dimples.	

7016 공무원 편입	1. 몹시 추운, 차가운 2. (성격이나 태도가) 쌀쌀한, 냉담한	[1163] cold
frigid		[288] unfriendly
		[1579] freezing
[FRIJ-id]	He jumped into the frigid water.	[2763] chilly

7017	1. 기괴한, 이상한 2. 바로크 양식의	[6108] ornate
baroque		[1817] complicated
[buh-ROHK]	His signature is baroque, yet sophisticated.	

7018	~가 빠진 자리, ~를 대신하는 자리	[673] replace
stead		
[sted]	When the principal was absent, the vice principal was appointed in her stead.	

7019 편입	열정, 열의	[1475] passion
fervor		[2131] enthusiasm
		[4770] earnestness
[FUR-ver]	She talked about her favorite movie with fervor.	

7020 토플	땀이 나다, 땀이 흐르다	perspiration (땀)
perspire		[2391] sweat
[per-SPAHYUHR]	Exercising caused students to perspire.	[4609] secrete

7021 공무원 편입 GRE	비난하다, 얕보다	disparaging (험담하는)
disparage		[7120] belittle
		[6409] scorn
[dih-SPAR-ij]	The president's new legislation was disparaged as pointless.	[7089] decry

7022 GRE	1. 특정 집단의 대화법 2. 은어	[5721] dialect
vernacular		[3278] indigenous
		[6306] vulgar
[ver-NAK-yuh-ler]	The actor spoke in the vernacular.	

7023	가리개(로 가리다)	[2191] blind
blindfold		[외래어] curtain
[BLAHYND-fohld]	If it is too bright, use a blindfold to go to sleep.	

7024	(특히 일본식) 종이접기	
origami		
[awr-i-GAH-mee]	He is an expert in origami.	

7025 **distraught** [dih-STRAWT]	마음이 상한, 몹시 속상한	[2705] upset [1581] confused [2288] anxious [4877] agitated
	My parents were distraught because of my illness.	
7026 GRE **extant** [EK-stuh nt]	현존하는, 존재하는	[549] existent [1212] surviving
	The original cultural artifact is no longer extant.	
7027 **exhale** [eks-HEYL]	(공기나 숨을) 발산하다, 내쉬다	exhalation (내쉬기) [2018] breathe [2259] emit
	He exhaled deeply to become calmer.	
7028 공무원 GRE **prerogative** [pri-ROG-uh-tiv]	특권, 특전	[2489] privilege
	Having a smartphone is no longer the prerogative of the rich.	
7029 **bootleg** [BOOT-leg]	1. 불법의, 밀수된 2. 밀매하다, 밀수하다	[7183] contraband [732] illegal [5630] illicit
	Bootleg alcohol was popular in the United States.	
7030 **czar** [zahr]	1. (옛 러시아의) 군주 2. 특정 분야의 정책을 담당하는 사람	[516] ruler
	Czars have a lot of wealth and power.	
7031 편입 **quell** [kwel]	(사태를) 진압하다, 가라앉히다	[673] replace [3501] conquer [5975] annihilate
	The police quelled the protesters.	
7032 공무원 GRE **expound** [ik-SPOUND]	1. (주장 등을) 제시하다 2. 설명하다, 해석하다	[630] explain [2184] clarify [6262] delineate
	The politician expounded a persuasive argument.	
7033 **umbilical** [uhm-BIL-i-kuh l]	1. 배꼽의 2. 밀접한, 긴밀한	
	The doctor cut the umbilical cord of the baby.	
7034 공무원 토플 편입 **squander** [SKWON-der]	1. 낭비하다 2. (기회 등을) 놓치다	[1370] waste [1130] expend [1568] blow
	He squandered his wage buying a new car.	
7035 **grasshopper** [GRAS-hop-er]	메뚜기	[3853] cricket
	There are a lot of grasshoppers in the field.	
7036 공무원 편입 GRE **haphazard** [hap-HAZ-erd]	어질러진, 무계획의	[1749] random [854] unstructured [1319] aimless [4123] arbitrary
	My closet contains a haphazard collection of clothes.	
7037 공무원 편입 **semblance** [SEM-bluhns]	1. 유사함, (외관이) 비슷함, 유사성 2. 외관	[614] measure
	Tigers bear some semblance to cheetahs.	
7038 **moat** [moht]	1. (성을 둘러싸는) 호 2. 호로 둘러싸다	[4047] ditch [4050] trench
	There is a moat protecting the castle.	

7039	공무원 편입 GRE	궁핍한, 빈곤한, 결핍한	[1173] poor
destitute			[2198] exhausted
[DES-ti-toot]		The charity assists destitute women.	[3326] bankrupt

7040	공무원 편입	잘 속는, 잘 믿는	incredulous (의심많은)
credulous			credence (신빙성, 신뢰)
[KREJ-uh-luhs]		The credulous audience believed the magician's tricks.	[5081] naive

7041	공무원	근절하다, (문제 등을) 뿌리째 뽑다	[4887] eradicate
uproot			[3962] demolish
[uhp-ROOT]		The gardener uprooted a tree.	[5975] annihilate

7042	공무원 편입	증오하다, (매우) 싫어하다	detestable (증오할만한)
detest			[1599] hate
[dih-TEST]		Many people detest politicians.	[5283] despise
			[6745] abhor

7043		(짓궂은) 웃음, 능글맞은 웃음	[7196] sneer
smirk			[1931] smile
[smurk]		She smirked after her opponent failed.	[4850] grin

7044		포물선	parabolic (포물선의)
parabola			[2702] bow
[puh-RAB-uh-luh]		The ball reached the top of the parabola and dropped.	[2767] arch
			[3559] arc

7045		휴전, 중지	[1384] peace
truce			[427] agreement
[troos]		The protesters proposed a three-day truce.	[479] accord

7046		후세, 후세대	[4655] offspring
posterity			
[po-STER-i-tee]		History is recorded so that the posterity can learn from it.	

7047		구기다, 찌부러뜨리다	[4064] wrinkle
crumple			[4431] buckle
[KRUHM-puhl]		She crumpled a piece of paper.	[5326] crease

7048		혼내다, 꾸짖다	chastisement (꾸짖음)
chastise			[898] criticize
[chas-TAHYZ]		The employer chastised the employee for being late.	[7223] berate

7049	공무원 GRE	1. 조화로운, 어울리는 2. (도형 등의 모양이) 동일한	congruence (일치)
congruent			congruous (일치하는)
[KONG-groo-uhnt]		This employee is not congruent with our company.	[582] similar

7050	GRE	적의, 적대심	inimical (해로운, 적대적인)
enmity			[3603] hostility
[EN-mi-tee]		Colonialism caused enmity between Japan and Korea.	[7355] acrimony

7051	토플	1. 영향력, 파급력 2. (주먹으로) 때리다	[2594] punch
clout			[131] leadership
[klout]		She has a lot of clout in the field of journalism.	[1203] influence
			[3143] prestige

7052	공무원 편입 GRE	1. 항복하다 2. 포기하다	capitulation (항복)
capitulate			[3682] surrender
[kuh-PICH-uh-leyt]		The protesters capitulated to the government.	[427] agree
			[2702] bow

7053			
squint [skwint]	힐끗 보다, 눈을 찡그리고 보다	[4310] peek [5682] peep
	The children squinted because of the bright light.	

7054	편입 GRE		
verbose [ver-BOHS]	1. 간결하지 않은, 장황한 2. 말이 많은	
	This book is too verbose.	

7055	공무원 토플 편입 GRE		
judicious [joo-DISH-uhs]	현명한, 분별력이 있는	judiciously (현명하게) [4610] prudent [256] careful [3360] genius
	The judicious use of the death penalty is important.	

7056			
caress [kuh-RES]	1. 애무하다, 어루만지다 2. 애무	[2340] stroke [외래어] kiss
	The mother caressed her baby.	

7057			
juncture [JUHNGK-cher]	1. (특정한) 시점 2. 연결, 이음매, 접합	[3741] junction
	At this juncture, we cannot predict the success of the project.	

7058	편입		
primordial [prahy-MAWR-dee-uhl]	1. 원시부터 존재하는, 태고의 2. 근본적인	[7293] primeval [341] prehistoric [1641] primal
	Cockroaches are primordial insects.	

7059			
ginseng [JIN-seng]	인삼	
	Ginseng is used as medicine in many Asian countries.	

7060	편입		
pretext [PREE-tekst]	구실, 변명	[2592] excuse [306] reason [외래어] alibi
	The pretext of sending soldiers to Iraq was combatting terrorism.	

7061			
quotient [KWOH-shuhnt]	1. 나눗셈의 몫 2. (특정한 자질이나 성격의) 양, 정도	[930] factor
	Dividing 24 by 4 results in the quotient of 6.	

7062	GRE		
attune [uh-TOON]	1. 익숙하다, ~에 적응된 2. 조율하다	[1680] tune [1618] accommodate [4534] accustom
	Children these days are not attuned to thinking creatively.	

7063			
chubby [CHUHB-ee]	토실토실한, 통통한	[6143] plump [1328] fat [3037] chunky
	Children have chubby cheeks.	

7064	공무원 편입		
recuperate [ri-KOO-puh-reyt]	1. 회복하다, 건강해지다 2. 되찾다	recuperation (회복) [231] recovery
	She is recuperating from a car accident.	

7065	공무원 토플 편입 GRE		
repudiate [ri-PYOO-dee-eyt]	거절하다, 사절하다, 거부하다	repudiation (거절) [2030] reject [2329] dispute [2399] abandon
	She repudiated the plans of the opposition party.	

7066			
twirl [twurl]	1. 빙글빙글 돌다 2. 돌리다	[1960] spin [3522] pivot
	The ballerina twirled three times.	

7067 **brash** [brash]	1. 경솔하고 뻔뻔한 2. (맛이나 냄새 등이) 강력한	[2591] bold [3614] cheeky [4589] arrogant
	I dislike her brash personality.	

7068　공무원 편입 **extrovert** [EK-struh-vurt]	1. 외향적인 사람 2. 외향성	extroverted (외향적인) [1150] outgoing
	She is an extrovert who has a lot of friends.	

7069 **honeycomb** [HUHN-ee-kohm]	(꿀)벌집	[5499] puncture
	Bees store honey in honeycombs.	

7070　편입 **surmise** [ser-MAHYZ]	추측하다, 예측하다	[1216] guess
	He surmised that he passed the exam.	

7071　공무원 편입 **conceit** [kuhn-SEET]	1. 자만함, 자부심 2. (예술적 효과인) 형상화	conceited (자만심이 강한) [2436] pride [4589] arrogance
	Success filled her with conceit.	

7072　공무원 편입 **dissuade** [dih-SWEYD]	단념시키다, 포기시키다	[3923] deter [929] encourage [3662] discourage
	Her friends dissuaded her from sky diving.	

7073 **diminutive** [dih-MIN-yuh-tiv]	1. 작은, 아담한 2. 별명	[1869] tiny [219] small [4114] miniature
	A diminutive child dressed in blue is walking this way.	

7074　GRE **hitherto** [HITH-er-too]	지금까지, 그때까지	[406] already [513] past [916] formerly
	The weather had hitherto been sunny.	

7075 **derange** [dih-REYNJ]	1. 미치게 하다 2. 혼란스럽게 하다	deranged (미친) derangement (교란) [2665] disturb
	The busy schedule deranged her.	

7076 **bequest** [bih-KWEST]	유산	[2471] legacy [2907] inheritance [4264] endowment
	She left a large bequest for her children.	

7077　공무원 토플 편입 GRE **clandestine** [klan-DES-tin]	(특히 불법이기에) 은밀히하는, 남몰래하는	[1334] secret [2439] fraudulent [5524] covert
	The CEOs held clandestine meetings with their employees.	

7078 **peacock** [PEE-kok]	1. 공작 2. 화려하게 행동하다	
	Peacocks have colorful feathers.	

7079　공무원 편입 GRE **extraneous** [ik-STREY-nee-uhs]	1. (현재 주제와) 무관한, 관련이 없는 2. 외부에서 시작된	[1442] foreign [98] additional [511] immaterial [1314] irrelevant
	He gave an extraneous response to my question.	

7080　편입 **chasm** [KAZ-uhm]	(신체적이거나 정신적인) 폭, 틈, 간격	[5962] abyss [117] difference [5398] crater [5562] cleavage
	There is a chasm between men and women.	

7081 snarl [snahrl]	1. 으르렁거리다/ 으르렁거림 2. 뒤엉킴/ 엉클어지게 하다	[4158] tangle
	The wolf snarled at the lion.	
7082 swish [swish]	1. 휘두르다 2. 쓱 소리를 내며 빠르게 지나가다	[3432] splash
	The wizard swished his magic wand and cast a spell.	
7083 편입 swagger [SWAG-er]	거들먹거리며 걷다, 뽐내다	[5028] strut [533] walk [7309] bluster
	The model swaggered across the runway.	
7084 inoculate [ih-NOK-yuh-leyt]	예방접종하다	inoculation (예방접종) [외래어] vaccinate [2205] inject
	Children should be inoculated against diseases.	
7085 공무원 편입 GRE tacit [TAS-it]	암묵의, 침묵의	taciturn (과묵한) [440] unspoken [2494] implied [4673] implicit
	Silence does not imply a tacit agreement.	
7086 outlast [out-LAST]	보다 오래 지속되다	[1212] survive
	Nature will outlast humans.	
7087 scapegoat [SKEYP-goht]	1.희생양 2. 죄를 뒤집어 씌우다	[1518] victim [845] target
	The student was made a scapegoat for the teacher's failure.	
7088 impunity [im-PYOO-ni-tee]	면죄, 벌을 받지 않음	[2182] immunity
	Diplomats enjoy immunity during their work.	
7089 공무원 편입 decry [dih-KRAHY]	비난하다, 질책하다	[7021] disparage [3417] condemn [7120] belittle
	The NGO decried child exploitation.	
7090 slouch [slouch]	수그리다, 구부정하게 있다	[5260] slump [533] walk [5971] crouch [6638] droop
	She slouched on the couch.	
7091 편입 GRE xenophobia [zen-uh-FOH-bee-uh]	외국의 사람이나 물건에 대한 혐오	xenophobic (외국혐오의) [646] racism [2753] bias [7113] animosity
	Xenophobia is on the rise in America.	
7092 편입 GRE onerous [ON-er-uhs]	부담이 되는, 어려운	[2760] burdensome [665] difficult [6642] arduous
	He found his career in teaching onerous.	
7093 midget [MIJ-it]	1. 매우 작은 2. 난쟁이	[4130] dwarf [219] small [7073] diminutive
	This is a midget car.	
7094 GRE heuristic [hyoo-RIS-tik]	1. (학생이) 스스로 발견하는, 체험적인 2. 체험적 교수법	[7447] didactic
	I think a heuristic approach to learning is better for students.	

7095 **navel** [NEY-vuh l]	1. 핵심적인 장소, 중심 2. 배꼽	
	Silicon Valley is the navel of the technology industry.	

7096 **scrumptious** [SKRUHMP-shuh s]	1. 매우 맛있는 2. 잘생긴	[1937] delicious [1065] tasty
	This strawberry ice cream is scrumptious.	

7097　　　　편입 **insinuate** [in-SIN-yoo-eyt]	암시하다, 빗대어 말하다, 둘러서 말하다	insinuation (암시) [591] suggest [2494] imply
	Are you insinuating that this is my fault?	

7098 **taut** [tawt]	1. 팽팽한 2. (목소리 등이) 긴장된	[2305] tense [1474] tight
	The seatbelt will stay taut.	

7099 **cologne** [kuh-LOHN]	향수	[4294] perfume
	I would like a bottle of cologne.	

7100　　　　공무원 **bygone** [BAHY-gawn]	과거의, 지나간	[916] former [513] past
	Latin is a bygone language.	

7101　　　공무원 편입 **omnipotent** [om-NIP-uh-tuhnt]	전능한, 능통한, 무한한 능력의	omnipotence (전능) [5229] almighty [201] powerful
	God is omnipotent.	

7102　　공무원 편입 GRE **supplant** [suh-PLANT]	(능가하여) 대체하다	[673] replace [1030] overthrow [1649] succeed
	Scientific theories are constantly being supplanted.	

7103 **trailblaze** [TREYL-bleyz]	개척하다	trailblazer (개척자)
	The electric car will trailblaze the market for environmentally friendly products.	

7104 **gizmo** [GIZ-moh]	(특정한 기능이 있는) 장치, 장비	[3950] gadget [2766] appliance
	This is a communication gizmo.	

7105 **myopic** [mahy-OP-ik]	1. (멀리 있는 것을 잘 보지 못하는) 근시의 2. 미래에 대한 준비성이 떨어지는	myopia (근시) [3452] shallow
	I have a myopic vision.	

7106　　공무원 편입 **claustrophobia** [klaw-struh-FOH-bee-uh]	폐쇄 공포증	claustrophobic (폐쇄 공 포증의)
	I can't close my bedroom door because I suffer from claustrophobia.	

7107 **echelon** [ESH-uh-lon]	(군대나 회사 등의 특정한) 직위, 계층	[1274] rank
	The government increased taxes for the highest echelon of society.	

7108　　공무원 편입 GRE **innocuous** [ih-NOK-yoo-uh s]	1. 독성이 없는 2. 해를 끼치지 않는 3. 악의가 없는	[1708] harmless [391] safe [5518] bland [7418] banal
	This spider is innocuous.	

7109 **regurgitate** [ri-GUR-ji-teyt]	1. (음식물을) 되새김질하다 2. 역류하다 3. (정보를 이해하지 않고) 되뇌다	regurgitation (역류) [3964] vomit [1201] repeat
	Cows regurgitate food.	

7110 **infatuated** [in-FACH-oo-ey-tid]	미쳐 있는, 얼빠진	infatuation (금방 빠진 사랑) [2427] devoted
	He is infatuated with the celebrity.	

7111　　　　편입 GRE **flamboyant** [flam-BOI-uhnt]	1. 화려한 2. 대담한	[1670] flashy [1677] grand [2178] brilliant [7392] bombastic
	The celebrity had a flamboyant lifestyle.	

7112 **geyser** [GAHY-zer]	1. (간헐적으로 물을 분출하는 온천인) 분천 2. 분출하다	[3756] fountain
	Geysers contain hot water.	

7113　　　　토플 **animosity** [an-uh-MOS-i-tee]	증오심, 악의	[3603] hostility [1599] hatred [7355] acrimony
	I feel animosity towards companies that pollute the environment.	

7114 **leeway** [LEE-wey]	(시간이나 공간의) 여유	[2153] scope
	The students have a few weeks' leeways to finish the project.	

7115 **mackerel** [MAK-er-uhl]	고등어	[983] fish
	The fisherman caught a mackerel.	

7116　　　공무원 편입 **forbear** [fawr-BAIR]	참다, 자제하다, 억제하다	forbearance (자제) [4708] refrain [1697] delay
	After getting a good grade, he could not forbear a smile.	

7117 **whatnot** [HWUHT-not]	(앞에 언급된 것들과 유사한) 등등	[251] secondly
	My grandfather grows potatoes, carrots, peas, and whatnot.	

7118 **billiards** [BIL-yerdz]	당구	
	You can play billiards with fifteen balls.	

7119 **cuckoo** [KOO-koo]	1. 뻐꾸기 2. 뻐꾹 울다 3. 미치광이	[2693] insane
	The cuckoo laid an egg.	

7120 **belittle** [bih-LIT-l]	무시하다, 얕보다	[7021] disparage [898] criticize [7089] decry
	My employer constantly belittles me.	

7121　　　공무원 편입 **impregnate** [im-PREG-neyt]	1. 임신시키다 2. (감정, 사상 등을) 스며들게 하다, 주입하다	impregnable (확고한) [5056] permeate [2512] fertilize [6619] drench
	My neighbor's dog impregnated my dog.	

7122　　　　　GRE **replete** [ri-PLEET]	~로 가득한, ~이 넘치는	[2566] abundant [228] full [685] filled
	Modern movies are replete with violence.	

7123	편입	터무니없는, 지나친, 엄청난	[3681] outrageous [1130] expensive
exorbitant [ig-ZAWR-bi-tuhnt]		I cannot afford the exorbitant price of rent.	[2777] enormous [7411] inordinate

7124		1. 조잘거리다, 종알거리다 2. 허튼소리	[2045] chatter [6896] mumble
babble [BAB-uhl]		The fans babbled about the celebrity.	

7125		(용액을) 붓다, 따르다	decanter (양주를 따르는 유리병)
decant [dih-KANT]		You should decant the wine before dinner.	[2230] pour [396] send

7126	편입	악취	[5121] stink [1599] hatred
stench [stench]		The stench of rotting fish spread in the kitchen.	[1836] smell

7127	편입	소동, 법석	[2665] disturbance [2465] annoyance
commotion [kuh-MOH-shuhn]		The large commotion kept her from falling asleep.	[4877] agitation

7128	공무원 편입 GRE	1. 영리한, 판단력이 좋은 2. 차가운	[3031] clever [3360] genius
shrewd [shrood]		You cannot fool shrewd people.	[6707] astute

7129		꿈틀거리다, 몸부림치다	[4873] blush [6992] flounder
squirm [skwurm]		The worm is squirming on the pavement.	

7130	편입	용기	[929] courage [2591] boldness
valor [VAL-er]		Soldiers have a lot of valor.	[2865] bravery

7131	편입 GRE	붙임성 있는, 친근한	[288] friendly [7184] amicable
amiable [EY-mee-uh-buhl]		All of my friends are amiable.	[7413] affable

7132	편입	1. 격노, 격분 2. 소란	[7127] commotion [1782] complaint
uproar [UHP-rawr]		The government corruption caused a public uproar.	[5960] brawl [7152] bickering

7133		사기꾼, 사칭하는 사람	[2439] fraud
imposter [im-POS-ter]		The imposter pretended to be a police officer.	

7134	GRE	1. 부정적인 영향을 미치다, 악영향을 미치다 2. 침해하다	impingement (영향, 침 범)
impinge [im-PINJ]		The divorce impinged on the lives of the children.	[6407] encroach [4026] infringe

7135		막간, 틈새 시간	[2754] interval [3165] pause
interlude [IN-ter-lood]		He is enjoying a breaktime interlude.	[5961] idyll

7136	공무원 편입	1. ~으로 영향받지 않는 2. (액체나 공기가) 통과하지 않는	[3056] impenetrable [448] impassable
impervious [im-PUR-vee-uhs]		She is impervious to my criticism.	[2182] immune [2681] blank

7137 **wheeze** [hweez]	1. 헐떡거리다, 씩씩거리며 말하다 2. 가쁜 숨	[5372] gasp [2018] breathe [3620] cough
	His asthma often causes him to wheeze.	
7138　　　편입 GRE **culpable** [KUHL-puh-buhl]	과실이 있는, 책잡힐 만한, 비난할 만한	culpability (과실이 있음) [2118] guilty [651] responsible
	The student is culpable of stealing exam keys.	
7139 **dainty** [DEYN-tee]	1. 앙증맞은 2. 우아한, 품위 있는 3. 진미	[3126] delicate [2366] cute [2425] elegant [3259] slim
	Her baby tickled her face with his dainty fingers.	
7140 **salamander** [SAL-uh-man-der]	도롱뇽	[5758] amphibian
	He saw a salamander with yellow spots on its skin.	
7141　　　공무원 편입 **censure** [SEN-sher]	1. 비난(하다), 질책(하다), 견책(하다) 2. 불신임	[6859] reprimand [898] criticism [3417] condemnation [6362] rebuke
	The employee was given a censure for not working hard enough.	
7142 **adrift** [uh-DRIFT]	1. 표류하는 2. 방황하는, 떠도는 3. (점수가)뒤져있는	[3393] drifting [2143] afloat
	A fisherman found a small boat adrift in the ocean.	
7143　　　토플 **ablate** [a-BLEYT]	제거하다, 제거되다	ablation (제거)
	The tumor has been ablated with a laser.	
7144 **teeter** [TEE-ter]	넘어질 듯 움직이다, 불안정하게 서다	[3494] stumble [5774] dangle [6501] falter
	After drinking too much, he started to teeter on his feet.	
7145　　　공무원 편입 GRE **inept** [in-EPT]	1. 서투른, 미숙한 2. 부적절한, 부주의한	[2388] incompetent [3424] awkward
	She still is an inept driver, not knowing how to park properly.	
7146　　　공무원 **beset** [bih-SET]	1. 괴롭히다, 공격하다 2. 포위하다, 둘러싸다	[3766] plague
	He was beset by the knee injury.	
7147 **freckle** [FREK-uhl]	주근깨, 기미	[4324] mole [5579] blemish
	Her cute face is covered with brown freckles.	
7148 **etymology** [et-uh-MOL-uh-jee]	어원(학)	[1729] origin
	Do you know the etymology of this term?	
7149　　　편입 GRE **tenable** [TEN-uh-buhl]	1. 방어할 수 있는, 지킬 수 있는 2. ~동안 유지될 수 있는	untenable (방어할 수 없는) [672] defensible [962] arguable
	The scientist's theory was not tenable.	
7150　　　편입 **vanquish** [VANG-kwish]	1. 격파하다, 완파하다 2. ~을 정복하다	vanquished (완파당한자) [2014] defeat [2692] crush [3501] conquer
	Our military force successfully vanquished terrorist groups.	

7151	GRE	대리의, 간접적인, 대신의	vicariously (대리로)
vicarious			
[vahy-KAIR-ee-uhs]		He experienced vicarious pain as his friend fell down the stairs.	

7152		말다툼하다, 언쟁하다, 옥신각신하다	bickering (말다툼)
bicker			[427] disagree
[BIK-er]		My friends always bicker with one another over minor issues.	[4678] quarrel

7153	편입	1. 휘청, 비틀거림 2. 요동, 떨림	[3494] stumble
lurch			[5432] twitch
[lurch]		The huge truck stopped with a lurch.	

7154		굴곡시키다, 변화시키다, 영향을 끼치다	inflection (굴곡)
inflect			
[in-FLEKT]		History inflects the present in many different ways.	

7155		1. 연결된, 연쇄된, 이어진 2. 결부시키다	concatenation (연결)
concatenate			
[kon-KAT-n-eyt]		A recipe is composed of several steps that are concatenated.	

7156	GRE	뜻밖의 발견/행운	serendipitous (우연히 발생한)
serendipity			[733] chance
[ser-uhn-DIP-i-tee]		We met each other simply by serendipity at the airport.	[1597] accident

7157	편입	악의 있는, 심술궂은	[3963] malicious
malevolent			[1930] evil
[muh-LEV-uh-luhnt]		She got chills when she noticed a malevolent look on his face.	[4986] malignant

7158	공무원 편입 GRE	다루기 쉬운, 온순한	intractable (다루기 어려운)
tractable			[1469] compliant
[TRAK-tuh-buhl]		Unlike her stubborn brother, she has a tractable personality.	[165] easy

7159		1. 엎드린, 몸을 가누지 못하는 2. 쓰러지다	prostration (배 대고 엎드리기)
prostrate			[1398] flat
[PROS-treyt]		She couldn't move her body after sleeping in a prostrate position all night.	

7160		(운전)기사	
chauffeur			
[SHOH-fer]		My father's chauffeur drove me to school yesterday.	

7161		썰매	[6961] sled
sleigh			
[sley]		The little boy enjoys a sleigh ride across the snow.	

7162	공무원 GRE	1. 노예 상태 2. 복역, 징역	[1707] bondage
servitude			[2121] enslavement
[SUR-vi-tood]		He has been living a life of servitude because of the huge debt he has to pay off.	

7163		1. 난잡한, 문란한 2. 마구잡이의, 되는 대로의	promiscuity (난잡함)
promiscuous			[1891] loose
[pruh-MIS-kyoo-uhs]		She used to date a promiscuous man.	[1980] immoral

7164		1. 손으로 더듬어서 찾다 2. 몸을 더듬다	[5587] fumble
grope			[6992] flounder
[grohp]		The baby groped around in the dark in search of his mother.	

7165			
thoroughbred	1. 순종, 순혈종 2. 출신이 좋은 사람		
[THUR-oh-bred]	Thoroughbred dogs tend to have many genetic disorders.		

7166			
drawdown	1. 축소(량), 삭감 2. 사용(액)		
[DRAW-doun]	The president called for the drawdown of troops located in the neighboring country.		

7167 편입			subjugation (정복, 억압)
subjugate	1. 예속시키다, 복종시키다 2. 정복하다, 퇴치하다		[2121] enslave
[SUHB-juh-geyt]	The dictator successfully subjugated the people.		[2294] invade [3501] conquer

7168 공무원			belatedly (뒤늦게)
belated	1. 뒤늦은, 연착된 2. 밀린		[199] late
[bih-LEY-tid]	She threw a belated birthday party.		[1697] delayed

7169			[6933] unruly
wayward	1. 다루기 힘든 2. 고집이 센 3. 변덕스러운, 흔들리는		[854] unstructured
[WEY-werd]	The mother was fed up with her son's wayward behavior.		[5391] delinquent [7268] capricious

7170			[1570] row
oar	노		
[awr]	This boat is missing oars.		

7171			[6555] gallantry
chivalry	1. 기사도(정신) 2. 예의 바름		[2891] courtesy
[SHIV-uh l-ree]	In a gesture of chivalry, the boy held the door open for other girls.		

7172 토플 편입			transmutation (변화)
transmute	바꾸다, 변화(변질)시키다		[1453] transform
[trans-MYOOT]	It takes a lot of effort to transmute negative thoughts into positive ones.		[123] change [3606] mutate

7173 공무원 편입 GRE			[6294] flimsy
tenuous	1. 미약한, 희박한, 미미한 2. 빈약한, 허약한		[604] variable
[TEN-yoo-uhs]	The investigation team only found a tenuous connection between the two crimes.		[3126] delicate [5685] dubious

7174			[1398] flat
outstretched	힘껏 뻗은, 펼친		
[out-STRECH d]	Ted caught all the balls with his outstretched hands.		

7175			decapitation (목을 자르기)
decapitate	1. 참수하다, 목을 자르다 2. 해고하다		[682] kill
[dih-KAP-i-teyt]	The king decapitated the head of his enemy.		

7176			levitation (공중부양)
levitate	공중부양하다		[2143] float
[LEV-i-teyt]	She levitated and flew away in her dream.		[1493] lift

7177 공무원 편입			perjury (위증)
perjure	위증하다		
[PUR-jer]	He was too afraid to perjure in front of the judge.		

7178 편입 GRE			obfuscation (혼란시키는 일)
obfuscate	혼란스럽게 하다, 어리둥절하게 하다, 애매하게 만들다		[3751] obscure
[OB-fuh-skeyt]	Try not to obfuscate your thesis statement and supporting ideas.		[1817] complicate

7179	토플	1. 서두르다, 급히 가다 2. 잰 걸음, 종종걸음	[2136] rush
scurry			[152] run
[SKUR-ee]		The frightened mouse tried to scurry under the porch.	[4463] dart
			[4564] bustle

7180	공무원 토플 편입	1. 겁에 질리게 하다 2. 석화하다, 돌이 되다 3. 꼼짝 못하게 하다	petrified (겁에 질린)
petrify			[1699] terrify
[PE-truh-fahy]		Zombies petrify her so much.	[3594] frighten

7181	편입	1. 정점, 절정 2. 천정	[1868] peak
zenith			
[ZEE-nith]		He is at the zenith of his career.	

7182		(서류 등에서)이하에, 하기에, 아래에	
hereinafter			
[heer-in-AF-ter]		The company is hereinafter referred to as A.	

7183		밀수품, 금지품	[732] illegal
contraband			[5630] illicit
[KON-truh-band]		A passenger was caught carrying contraband out of the country.	[6512] plunder
			[7029] bootleg

7184	공무원 편입	1. 우호적인, 원만한 2. 평화적인	amicably (우호적으로)
amicable			[288] friendly
[AM-i-kuh-buhl]		Even though he wasn't amicable, he still had many friends.	[1284] civil
			[7131] amiable

7185	편입	1. 휘말리게 하다, ~을 끌어들이다 2. 혼동하다	[4158] tangle
embroil			[3167] enmesh
[em-BROIL]		He was embroiled in a fight with his colleagues.	[5011] ensnare

7186	공무원 편입	구어(체)의, 회화체의	colloquially (구어체로)
colloquial			[1747] informal
[kuh-LOH-kwee-uhl]		You shouldn't be writing your essay in colloquial language.	[1411] conversational
			[7022] vernacular

7187		1. 듬뿍(바르다) 2. 대량, 다수 3. 낭비하다	[1373] spread
slather			[231] cover
[SLATH-er]		He always slathers a thick layer of suncream.	

7188	편입	1. 풍자적인, 비꼬는 2. 뒤틀린, 일그러진, 찌푸린	wryly (비꼬는듯하게)
wry			[3248] ironic
[rahy]		She hated him so much that she could only put on a wry smile.	[514] funny

7189		잘못된, 미흡한, 적절하지 않은	[906] wrong
amiss			[665] difficult
[uh-MIS]		It was amiss of her to skip the lecture this morning.	[879] improper
			[7303] awry

7190	공무원	1. 상처를 입히다, 거칠게 다루다 2. 혹평하다 3. 큰 나무망치	[2104] batter
maul			[709] attack
[mawl]		A lion mauled the man to death with its huge claws.	

7191	공무원 편입	화합, 일치, 조화	concordance
concord			(=concord)
[KON-kawrd]		The two countries finally reached concord.	[2723] harmony
			[288] friendship

7192		엄니/송곳니, 상아	[5057] ivory
tusk			
[tuhsk]		Sadly, many elephants are still killed for their tusks.	

7193 **paragon** [PAR-uh-gon]	모범, 본보기, 귀감	[262] ideal [5868] epitome
	The politician is viewed as a paragon of integrity.	

7194 **insurrection** [in-suh-REK-shuhn]	반란, 폭동	[2690] rebellion [5036] coup [5811] insurgency
	Unfortunately, the insurrection against the dictator was not successful.	

7195 **convoke** [kuhn-VOHK]	(의회, 회의를)소집하다	convocation (소집) [1578] convene
	The secretary-general will be convoking another meeting soon.	

7196 **sneer** [sneer]	1. 경멸, 비웃음 2. 비웃다, 냉소하다	[6409] scorn [6925] deride [7120] belittle
	She was hurt when he looked at her with a sneer.	

7197 편입 GRE **conciliate** [kuhn-SIL-ee-eyt]	달래다, 회유시키다, 설득하다	conciliation (달램) conciliatory (달래는) [3552] reconcile
	He tried to conciliate his girlfriend by buying her a diamond ring.	

7198 편입 **abdicate** [AB-di-keyt]	1. 퇴위하다, 물러나다 2. 포기하다	abdication (사직) [2399] abandon [1655] deny [4548] forgo
	The CEO decided to abdicate his title after he found out that he had a lethal disease.	

7199 **broil** [broil]	1. 굽다 2. 싸움(하다), 말다툼(하다)	[1589] bake [2362] melt [2685] roast
	My mother put the seasoned chicken in the oven to broil.	

7200 **conjunct** [kuhn-JUHNGKT]	1. 결합된, 공동의, 긴밀한 2. 접속형의, 접속사	[1488] joint [420] collective [2217] concerted
	The army conducted conjunct operations with its allied force.	

7201 **burlesque** [ber-LESK]	1. 풍자적 희극 2. 희화화하다, 익살스럽게 흉내내다	
	The burlesque musical had an intention to mock politicians.	

7202 편입 GRE **amenable** [uh-MEE-nuh-buhl]	1. ~을 잘 받아들이는 2. 순종하는, 말을 잘 듣는	[1469] compliant [20] willing [427] agreeable [756] responsive
	Young students are more amenable to changes than the old.	

7203 **upstart** [UHP-stahrt]	벼락 출세자, 갑자기 잘된 사람, 건방진 사람	
	Her parents didn't allow her to marry an upstart man.	

7204 **compatriot** [kuhm-PEY-tree-uht]	동포, 동국인	[154] national
	The family ran into a compatriot at a local restaurant in Province.	

7205 GRE **devious** [DEE-vee-uhs]	1. 속이는, 기만적인 2. 우회하는, 둘러가는	[1536] crafty [1282] calculating [3031] clever [3383] deceitful
	He approached her with devious intentions.	

7206 편입 GRE **antecedent** [an-tuh-SEED-nt]	1. 선례, 전례, 선조 2. 선행하는, 이전의	[3894] predecessor [5953] preface
	Wired phones are the antecedent of cellphones.	

7207	공무원 편입 GRE	1. 동의하다, 따르다 2. 묵인하다	acquiescence (조용한 동의)
acquiesce			[427] agree
[ak-wee-ES]		The employees had to acquiesce in the CEO's decision.	[6395] accede

7208		1. 건물, 전당 2. 조직, 체계	[854] structure
edifice			[1116] modality
		People from all over the world come to visit the magnificent edifice	[2171] skyscraper
[ED-uh-fis]		in our town.	[3195] monument

7209	공무원 편입 GRE	전지의, 모든 것을 알고 있는	omniscience (전지)
omniscient			[65] knowing
[om-NISH-uhnt]		If they were omniscient, they wouldn't have made that decision.	

7210		반란, 폭동, 저항	[1804] revolt
mutiny			[7194] insurrection
[MYOOT-n-ee]		The dictator could not stop the mutiny.	

7211	공무원 편입 GRE	1. (피부가)굳어진, 못박힌 2. 무감각한, 냉담한	[619] heartless
callous			[256] careless
			[2681] blank
[KAL-uhs]		My mom's callous hands made me burst into tears.	[6417] apathetic

7212		1. 허리둘레, 둘레의 치수 2. (말의)뱃대끈	[5638] circumference
girth			[103] length
[gurth]		Her girth was smaller than the dress.	

7213	공무원 편입 GRE	길조의, 행운의	[991] advantageous
auspicious			[3908] feasible
[aw-SPISH-uhs]		The coupled picked an auspicious date for the wedding.	

7214		무궁화	
hibiscus			
[hahy-BIS-kuhs]		It is well known that hibiscus teas have health benefits.	

7215	공무원 편입 GRE	1. 냉담한, 초연한, 무관심한 2. 떨어져서	[1163] cold
aloof			[249] disinterested
			[1208] distant
[uh-LOOF]		The aloof student didn't talk to anyone.	[3508] detached

7216		손도끼	
hatchet			
[HACH-it]		He doesn't know how to use a hatchet properly.	

7217	공무원	풍문, 소문, 전해들은 이야기	[2852] rumor
hearsay			[120] information
			[5009] gossip
[HEER-sey]		She is famous for spreading hearsay.	

7218		1. 불확실한, 애매한 2. 의심스러운 3. 이상한	[512] unlikely
iffy			
[IF-ee]		He was iffy about his answer to his boss's question.	

7219	공무원 편입	1. 냉혹한, 가차없는, 무정한 2. 멈출 수 없는, 피할 수 없는	inexorably (가차없이)
inexorable			[4249] relentless
			[1801] inescapable
[in-EK-ser-uh-buhl]		She couldn't accept the inexorable truth that he left her.	[2798] inevitable

7220	GRE	~의 경계를 정하다/구분짓다	demarcation (구분)
demarcate			
		My father decided to demarcate our land so that nobody could	
[dih-MAHR-keyt]		intrude.	

7221	편입 GRE	1. 대충 하는, 피상적인, 겉핥기의 2. 형식적인	
cursory		Even a cursory glance at her grade report will tell her that she has failed this semester.	
[KUR-suh-ree]			

7222	(문구 등을)새기다, 장식하다	[1667] decorate
emblazon		[5090] embellish
[em-BLEY-zuhn]	The employees were allowed to wear t-shirts only if they agree to emblazon the company logo.	

7223	질책하다, 꾸짖다	[829] scold
berate		
[bih-REYT]	He berated himself for being a bad student.	

7224	1. 출구, 배출구 2. 떠남, 탈출	[2032] exit
egress		[2236] departure
[EE-gres]	Our house has an egress in the front and another one in the rear.	

7225	차익거래, 중개거래	[3672] arbitration
arbitrage		
[AHR-bi-trahzh]	The investor is actively looking for any arbitrage opportunities.	

7226	1. (나무의)마디, 혹 2. 비틀다	gnarled (비틀린)
gnarl		[3344] knot
[nahrl]	Their wooden table had knots and gnarls of real wood.	[1942] screw
		[4158] tangle

7227	공무원 편입 GRE	1. 평온한, 차분한, 잔잔한 2. 온건한	[2260] calm
placid			[3077] easygoing
[PLAS-id]		After taking a deep breath, she became placid.	

7228	무겁게 터벅터벅 걷다	[7001] tramp
trudge		[533] walk
[truhj]	She trudged on foot for several hours after getting fired.	[4726] lumber

7229	결혼(생활), 혼인	matrimonial (결혼의)
matrimony		[1018] marriage
[MA-truh-moh-nee]	The couple is happily living in a state of matrimony for two years.	

7230	편입	비방하다, 비난하다, 헐뜯다	[4986] malign
vilify			[709] attack
[VIL-uh-fahy]		People easily vilify celebrities on the internet.	[6118] assail
			[7223] berate

7231	1. 몹시 까다로운 2. 주의를 요하는	[4488] fussy
finicky		[387] choosy
[FIN-i-kee]	She is finicky and will only eat a certain type of food.	[7343] fastidious

7232	편입	1. 내뿜다, 방출하다, 유출하다 2. 토로하다	effusion (액체 유출)
effuse			effusive (감정이 넘쳐 표
[ih-FYOOZ]		He smelled gas effusing out of the broken gas pipe.	현하는)
			[5931] exude

7233	(스페인이나 라틴 아메리카 국가의)축제	[1204] holiday
fiesta		[3578] feast
[fee-ES-tuh]	The citizens were happy to celebrate the fiesta.	

7234	가게에서 슬쩍 훔치다	shoplifting (절도)
shoplift		[1736] steal
[SHOP-lift]	He was caught shoplifting.	

7235			
gratuitous [gruh-TOO-i-tuhs]	1. 불필요한 2. 무료의	[256] careless [4078] spontaneous	
	There was too much gratuitous nudity in the movie.		

7236	편입 GRE		
mortify [MAWR-tuh-fahy]	1. 수치심을 주다, 굴욕을 느끼게 하다 2. 억제하다	mortification (굴욕) [4701] humiliate [2465] annoy	
	She was mortified by her son yelling directly at her at the mall.		

7237	공무원 편입		
exonerate [ig-ZON-uh-reyt]	1. 혐의를 벗다, 무죄임을 밝혀주다 2. 면제하다 3. 해방하다	[372] clear [6996] absolve	
	The newly found DNA evidence will exonerate him of the charges.		

7238			
leer [leer]	추파(를 던지다), 곁눈질(하다)	leery (의심하는) [7196] sneer	
	She was scared by a man leering at her on the street.		

7239	편입 GRE		
minuscule [MIN-uh-skyool]	1. 극소의, 아주 작은 2. 소문자	[1869] tiny [219] small [221] insignificant [3790] microscopic	
	He decided to quit his job because of the minuscule salary.		

7240			
feisty [FAHY-stee]	거침없는, 적극적인, 당돌한	[923] spirited [547] energetic [929] courageous [2535] bubbly	
	The shy boy admired his feisty girlfriend.		

7241			
haggle [HAG-uhl]	1. 흥정(하다), 값을 깎다 2. 입씨름(하다)	[3285] bargain [6840] barter	
	She always haggles to get a good bargain.		

7242	GRE		
veracity [vuh-RAS-i-tee]	진실성, 정확성	[1285] truth [1127] accuracy [1404] honesty [1986] authenticity	
	The public doubted the politician's veracity.		

7243			
abash [uh-BASH]	당황하게 하다, 부끄럽게 하다, 무안하게 하다	unabashed (부끄러워하 지 않는) bashful (부끄러운) [3088] embarrass	
	She could no longer tolerate her boyfriend's tendency to abash her.		

7244			
welt [welt]	채찍 자국, 부은 자국	[3133] whip [4284] bruise [7357] contusion	
	She put some ointment over her son's welt on the foot.		

7245	공무원 편입		
embezzle [em-BEZ-uhl]	횡령하다	embezzlement (횡령) [979] misappropriate [1736] steal	
	The CEO decided to embezzle his company's money.		

7246	공무원 편입		
dilapidate [dih-LAP-i-deyt]	1. (건물 등을)헐다, 파손하다 2. 탕진하다, 낭비하다	dilapidated (무너져가는) [3808] decay	
	Their dilapidated house needs renovation immediately.		

7247			
oddball [OD-bawl]	괴짜, 별종	[5202] eccentric	
	She is considered an oddball among her colleagues.		

7248			
cohabit [koh-HAB-it]	동거하다	cohabitation (동거)	
	They decided not to cohabit before getting married.		

7249	편입	괴롭히다, 귀찮게 하다, 성가시게 하다	[3275] harass
pester			[2465] annoy
[PES-ter]		Her friend enjoys pestering her with a bunch of questions.	[5344] badger
			[5597] nag

7250		필기체	[495] functioning
cursive			[1264] constant
[KUR-siv]		He doesn't know how to write in cursive.	

7251	공무원 편입 GRE	달래다, 진정시키다	implacable (확고한)
placate			[6336] appease
[PLEY-keyt]		The mother tried to placate her son but to no avail.	[7289] assuage

7252	공무원 편입 GRE	1. 무정형의 2. 애매모호한, 특징 없는	[949] shapeless
amorphous			[3812] vague
[uh-MAWR-fuhs]		To her, love is amorphous.	

7253		후회하다, 유감으로 여기다, 뉘우치다	[2972] regret
rue			
[roo]		She will soon rue the fact that she has dumped him.	

7254	공무원	1. 과민한, 민감한 2. 다루기 어려운	[383] sensitive
touchy			[3126] delicate
[TUHCH-ee]		He gets touchy if anyone mentions his height.	

7255	편입	활기가 넘치는, 야단법석의, 소란스러운	[1547] wild
boisterous			[547] energetic
[BOI-ster-uhs]		The parents let their children be boisterous at home.	[2261] loud

7256		1. 덤불, 풀숲 2. 얽힘, 뒤얽힌 것	
thicket			
[THIK-it]		Some children were playing hide and seek behind a thicket of bushes.	

7257		1. 늦은, 지각한 2. 더딘, 느린	tardiness (지각)
tardy			[789] lazy
[TAHR-dee]		He got fired for being tardy to work too many times.	[1697] delayed
			[7168] belated

7258	편입	악당, 악동, 불량배	[4089] rogue
rascal			[1077] liar
[RAS-kuhl]		The rascal is known for causing trouble everywhere.	[5237] bum

7259	편입 GRE	순진한, 꾸밈없는, 천진난만한	disingenuous (솔직하지 않은)
ingenuous			[5081] naive
[in-JEN-yoo-uhs]		Her ingenuous daughter still believes in Santa Claus.	[171] inexperienced

7260	공무원 편입 GRE	1. 공격적인, 호전적인 2. 교전국(의)	[2141] aggressive
belligerent			[1987] angry
[buh-LIJ-er-uhnt]		The belligerent driver almost got in a fight with a truck driver.	[5020] antagonistic

7261	공무원 편입	1. 터무니없는, 비상식의 2. 파격적인	[4103] absurd
preposterous			[1776] crazy
[pri-POS-ter-uhs]		It is preposterous to believe you can seduce him.	

7262	토플	휘두르다	[1354] wave
brandish			[1670] flash
[BRAN-dish]		A thief brandished a knife right in front of her.	

7263 **wince** [wins]	주춤하다, 움츠리다	[6928] flinch [4873] blush
	She winces every time she sees a spider.	
7264 공무원 편입 **subliminal** [suhb-LIM-uh-nl]	잠재의식의, 의식하의	[1888] subconscious [372] unclear [2319] intellectual [7402] cerebral
	Propagandas are an effective tool for implanting subliminal messages.	
7265 **disarray** [dis-uh-REY]	혼란, 난잡, 무질서	[2962] chaos [4970] anarchy
	The disorganized lady's house is in disarray.	
7266 공무원 **defuse** [dee-FYOOZ]	1. 완화/진정시키다 2. (폭탄의)신관을 제거하다	[1001] disarm [82] deactivate [3926] soothe [4170] alleviate
	As a means to defuse the tension, he walked away from the negotiating table.	
7267 **snot** [snot]	1. 콧물 2. 버릇없는 사람, 망나니	snotty (콧물을 흘리는)
	She looked funny with her snot hanging from the nose.	
7268 공무원 토플 편입 GRE **caprice** [kuh-PREES]	변덕, 예측 불허의 변화, 충동	capricious (변덕스러운) [5618] whim
	It is almost always wrong to act on caprice.	
7269 편입 **swindle** [SWIN-dl]	사취(하다), 사기(치다), 협잡	swindler (사기꾼) [2774] cheat [3383] deceit
	The sneaky man tried to swindle his colleagues out of their money.	
7270 편입 **eavesdrop** [EEVZ-drop]	엿듣다	[3499] spy [379] overhear
	The little children wanted to eavesdrop on their parents.	
7271 **hobble** [HOB-uhl]	1. 발을 절다, 절뚝거리다 2. 다리를 묶다 3. 방해하다	[5465] limp [3494] stumble [3827] halt [6501] falter
	After hurting her ankle, she hobbled over to her car.	
7272 **stiletto** [sti-LET-oh]	1. 뾰족 구두 2. 가는 단검, 단도	[2010] blade [6927] bayonet
	She bought a pair of red stiletto heels.	
7273 **upend** [uhp-END]	뒤집다, 거꾸로 하다	[3779] overturn [278] turn
	The baby upended his mom's bag.	
7274 **holler** [HOL-er]	외치다, 큰소리로 부르다	[3718] yell [2488] cheer [3172] shout
	I hate it when people holler at me.	
7275 공무원 **putative** [PYOO-tuh-tiv]	추정상의	[1312] supposed [1582] apparently [2795] presumed
	The scientist conducted research to test if his putative theory is correct.	
7276 **ostrich** [AW-strich]	1. 타조 2. 현실도피자	
	Did you know that ostriches cannot fly?	

7277 **hideout** [HAHYD-out]	은신처 He ran into the criminal's hideout by accident.		[2448] refuge
7278 **gargantuan** [gahr-GAN-choo-uhn]	엄청난, 원대한 My dad makes a gargantuan amount of money.		[939] huge [196] large [2777] enormous [6260] colossal
7279 공무원 GRE **blithe** [blahyth]	1. 태평스러운 2. 쾌활한, 유쾌한, 명랑한 She loves drinking so much so that she is blithe to its threats to health.		blithely (즐겁게) [594] happy [3452] shallow
7280 **bookworm** [BOOK-wurm]	독서광 He is a bookworm who reads about 10 books a month.		[4901] nerd
7281 편입 GRE **incipient** [in-SIP-ee-uhnt]	막 시작된, 초기의, 발단의 She still felt so sick even though her pneumonia was incipient.		[1105] initial [60] new [4395] embryonic [6980] nascent
7282 **cicada** [si-KEY-duh]	매미 She gets annoyed by the sound of cicada.		
7283 공무원 토플 편입 GRE **gregarious** [gri-GAIR-ee-uhs]	1. 사교적인 2. 무리의, 군생하는 There are many gregarious students in my class.		[288] friendly [405] sociable [7413] affable
7284 편입 **ostracize** [OS-truh-sahyz]	1. 배척하다, 외면하다 2. 추방하다 She has been ostracized by her colleagues.		[1206] exclude [848] avoid [6050] blacklist
7285 **oxymoron** [ok-si-MAWR-on]	모순 어법 He is an expert at coming up with brilliant oxymorons.		
7286 **trident** [TRAHYD-nt]	삼지창 It isn't easy to catch fish with a trident.		[6208] triad [2010] blade [6927] bayonet
7287 **cacophony** [kuh-KOF-uh-nee]	불협화음 She couldn't stand the cacophony coming from the classroom.		[1673] noise
7288 공무원 편입 **pacify** [PAS-uh-fahy]	1. 가라앉히다, 달래다 2. 평화를 수립하다 A bottle of milk wasn't enough to pacify the crying baby.		[2260] calm [7386] allay [7422] ameliorate
7289 편입 **assuage** [uh-SWEYJ]	누그러지게하다, 진정시키다 Lemon honey tea will help assuage her sore throat.		[3926] soothe [1721] relieve [4170] alleviate [7386] allay
7290 **proctor** [PROK-ter]	1. 시험 감독관 2. 대리인 3. 감독하다 If you have any questions about the instruction, go talk to the proctor.		[1089] monitor

7291	GRE	말투, 어조, 전문 용어	[1813] speech
			[6101] jargon
parlance			
[PAHR-luhns]		She is oblivious to the parlance youngsters use.	

7292	편입	진퇴양난, 곤경	[6625] predicament
			[665] difficulty
quandary			[4483] dilemma
[KWON-duh-ree]		He found himself in a quandary about whether or not he should quit the job.	

7293		태고의, 원시의	[7058] primordial
			[341] prehistoric
primeval			[1641] primal
[prahy-MEE-vuhl]		The little boy thought he found some primeval dinosaur bones in the backyard.	

7294		(풍경, 얼굴 등)촬영에 알맞은, 사진이 잘 받는	[1069] attractive
photogenic			
[foh-tuh-JEN-ik]		She has a photogenic face.	

7295	편입	꾸짖다, 비난하다	reprehensible (비난받아 마땅한)
reprehend			[6943] reproach
[rep-ri-HEND]		The teacher reprehended her student for not doing his homework.	

7296		재택(원격)근무, 텔레커뮤팅	
telecommuting			
[TEL-i-kuh-myoo-ting]		More and more people favor telecommuting.	

7297	GRE	폄하하다, ~을 더럽히다, 평판을 떨어뜨리다	[7021] disparage
			[898] criticize
denigrate			[1159] defame
[DEN-i-greyt]		He denigrated his colleague by spreading false rumors.	

7298		소란스러운, 난폭한	[6933] unruly
			[290] disorderly
rowdy			[2261] loud
[ROU-dee]		She didn't know how to deal with her children getting rowdy before going to bed.	

7299		적당한, 알맞은	[988] suitable
befitting			
[bih-FIT-ing]		His behavior is not befitting that of a future president.	

7300	공무원 토플	태풍	[3290] hurricane
typhoon			
[tahy-FOON]		The school was closed because of the typhoon.	

7301		지각(력)의	
perceptual			
[per-SEP-choo-uhl]		He is suffering from perceptual difficulties.	

7302		달팽이관의	[1241] circling
			[2517] coiled
cochlear			
[KOK-lee-uhr]		She needs cochlear implants.	

7303	편입	빗나간, 잘못되어, 엉망이 된	[4894] crooked
			[4452] astray
awry			[4525] untidy
[uh-RAHY]		The company had to come up with another plan after its initial one went awry.	

7304		신성(함), 존엄성, 성스러움	[1393] godliness
			[237] importance
sanctity			[1380] faith
[SANGK-ti-tee]		She appreciates the sanctity of all human life.	[2519] divinity

7305 **macho** [MAH-choh]		사내다운, 남자다운 He is too macho to admit that he has been hurt.	[1545] male [2141] aggressive [4166] cocky
7306 **coagulate** [koh-AG-yuh-leyt]	편입	응고하다, 굳어지다 Milk will coagulate in this hot weather.	[4617] clot
7307 **retort** [ri-TAWRT]	편입	대꾸(하다), 반격(하다), 역습 She decided not to retort to her husband's argument.	[1666] reply
7308 **brevity** [BREV-i-tee]	공무원 편입	간결함, 짧음 I was able to finish that novel in no time thanks to its brevity.	[1739] quiet
7309 **bluster** [BLUHS-ter]	공무원 편입	거세게 몰아치다, 엄포를 놓다 The angry boss blustered about all of the troubles the employee had caused.	[2650] boast
7310 **beguile** [bih-GAHYL]	편입 GRE	1. 현혹시키다 2. 기만하다, 속이다 3. 사취하다 He is very well known for his ability to beguile many women.	[2312] charm [3383] deceive [4495] entice
7311 **stymie** [STAHY-mee]		1. 방해하다 2. 스타미(골프에서의 방해구) The jealous girl tried her best to stymie her friend from getting into a prestigious school.	[3783] obstruct [6473] crimp
7312 **larceny** [LAHR-suh-nee]	편입	절도(행위), 도둑질 Committing larceny cannot be justified in normal circumstances.	[2985] theft [4498] burglary
7313 **vixen** [VIK-suhn]		암여우, 여우같은 여자 Vixens normally weigh less than male foxes.	
7314 **extrinsic** [ik-STRIN-sik]	토플 편입	외부의, 외래적인, 외적인 What are the extrinsic factors that led to the global economic crisis?	[7079] extraneous
7315 **euphemism** [YOO-fuh-miz-uhm]	편입	완곡어법, 완곡한 표현 The politician is good at using appropriate euphemisms to talk about sensitive issues.	
7316 **procreate** [PROH-kree-eyt]	토플	아이/새끼를 낳다 Many animals intuitively feel the need to procreate.	procreation (생식, 출산) [2419] reproduce
7317 **stingy** [STIN-jee]	공무원	1. 인색한, 부족한 2. 쏘는, 독기 있는 My mom is very stingy with her money.	[4192] greedy [5325] thrifty [5592] frugal
7318 **herbivore** [HUR-buh-vawr]	토플	초식 동물 Herbivores, in general, cannot digest meat.	[3866] vegetarian [3404] vegan

7319			[5122] whine
whimper	훌쩍훌쩍 울다, 낑낑거리다		[4702] weep
[HWIM-per]	Her baby kept on whimpering.		[5385] moan

7320			[4013] revenge
vendetta	(피의)복수, 앙갚음		[962] argument
[ven-DET-uh]	The team waged a vendetta against the opponent.		[6330] grudge
			[7152] bickering

7321			clairvoyance (예지력)
clairvoyant	예지력이 있는, 통찰력이 있는, 투시의		[3973] psychic
[klair-VOI-uhnt]	The desperate lady relied on the psychic's clairvoyant abilities too much.		

7322			[549] existing
afoot	1. 진행중에 2. 걸어서, 도보로		
[uh-FOOT]	He has plans afoot to leave his job.		

7323			aggrieved (괴롭혀진)
aggrieve	괴롭히다, 압박하다		[3887] grieve
[uh-GREEV]	The thought of her failed marriage would aggrieve her forever.		[3815] oppress

7324			
epithet	1. 별명, 통칭 2. 욕설		
[EP-uh-thet]	The celebrity earned the epithet of "an angel in a human form."		

7325			[697] fight
scuffle	실랑이(를 벌이다), 난투		[5960] brawl
[SKUHF-uhl]	The residents often scuffle over property boundaries.		[7127] commotion

7326	공무원 편입	1. 고집 센, 완고한 2. 난감한	[4545] stubborn
obstinate			[5572] dogmatic
[OB-stuh-nit]	The obstinate little girl never admitted her fault.		[6057] adamant

7327	편입	목 쉰	[2939] harsh
hoarse			[4234] gravelly
[hawrs]	The professor's voice sounded hoarse.		[6006] discordant

7328	편입	날카로운 소리(의), 높은 소리로	[3818] piercing
shrill			[2261] loud
[shril]	The scared woman's voice was shrill.		[4185] deafening
			[6006] discordant

7329	토플 GRE	~에 버금가는, 동등한	[2013] equivalent
tantamount			[688] match
[TAN-tuh-mount]	To leave a dog alone is tantamount to maltreatment.		[2820] identical
			[6953] commensurate

7330	공무원	불쾌한, 아주 싫은	[4403] repulsive
repugnant			[2830] horrible
[ri-PUHG-nuhnt]	The smell from the trash can is completely repugnant.		[6141] abominable
			[6745] abhorrent

7331	공무원 편입	유순한, 온순한	[2988] obedient
docile			[2065] gentle
[DOS-uhl]	The angry chihuahua is far from docile.		[2260] calm
			[3077] easygoing

7332	GRE	1. 조숙한 2. 숙성한	[1588] intelligent
precocious			[1397] bright
[pri-KOH-shuhs]	Her precocious little daughter wants to wear heels to school.		[3360] genius
			[4166] cocky

7333 GRE	복수심이 있는, 앙심을 품은	[3883] spiteful
vindictive [vin-DIK-tiv]	My friend is a vindictive young lady who slashed the tires of her ex's car.	[3470] cruel [3963] malicious

7334 공무원 편입 GRE	정직, 솔직함	[195] directness
candor [KAN-der]	The candidate's candor attracted many followers.	[886] fairness [1404] honesty

7335 편입	1. 극악무도한, 악명 높은 2. 명백한	[2591] bold
flagrant [FLEY-gruhnt]	The criminal's flagrant violation of the law put him behind the bars.	[4623] unashamed [5241] atrocious

7336	엄청난, 거대한, 굉장한	[6026] prodigious
stupendous [stoo-PEN-duhs]	The celebrity was greeted by a stupendous crowd at the airport.	[196] large

7337 편입	악당, 깡패	[4089] rogue
scoundrel [SKOUN-druhl]	The scoundrel stole her laptop.	[1077] liar [4894] crook [7258] rascal

7338 편입 GRE	무례한, 건방진, 버릇없는	insolence (거만함)
insolent [IN-suh-luhnt]	He was fired for speaking to his boss in an insolent tone.	[4009] rude

7339 공무원 편입	거만한, 오만한	[4589] arrogant
haughty [HAW-tee]	That haughty girl didn't have any friends.	[288] unfriendly [5010] contemptuous [5386] cavalier

7340 편입	생기, 활기, 활발, 쾌활	vivacious (활발한)
vivacity [vi-VAS-i-tee]	After he left her, she lost her vivacity.	[547] energy [594] happiness [2131] enthusiasm

7341 공무원 편입 GRE	마음이 잘 맞는, 같은 성질의, 성미에 맞게	congeniality (친화력)
congenial [kuhn-JEEN-yuhl]	His congenial nature made him a successful businessman.	[288] friendly [427] agreeable [7413] affable

7342 공무원 토플 편입 GRE	반감, 악감정	[1599] hatred
antipathy [an-TIP-uh-thee]	She couldn't hide her antipathy towards her boss.	[7113] animosity

7343 공무원 편입 GRE	1. 까다로운, 깐깐한 2. 꼼꼼한	[4488] fussy
fastidious [fa-STID-ee-uhs]	Nobody wanted to invite him to the party because he was too fastidious.	[256] careful [387] choosy [2625] discriminating

7344	(문이)조금 열린	[186] open
ajar [uh-JAHR]	She never leaves her bedroom door ajar.	

7345 토플 편입	고압적인, 거만한, 오만한	[1109] overbearing
imperious [im-PEER-ee-uhs]	He was so glad that his teacher wasn't imperious at all.	[1110] confident [4589] arrogant

7346	탐욕, 욕심	[4192] greed
avarice [AV-er-is]	She was sick of her husband's avarice for money.	

7347	편입	1. 수척한, 여윈 2. 삭막한, 황량한	[749] skinny
gaunt			[1572] angular
[gawnt]		He became gaunt and weak after losing her appetite.	[1768] thin
			[6542] anorexic

7348	공무원 편입	1. 큰 행복, 경사 2. 적절함, 들어맞음 3. 적절한 표현/비유	[594] happiness
felicity			
[fi-LIS-i-tee]		She smiled with felicity when he responded to her text.	

7349	공무원 편입 GRE	1. (기질, 행동 등이)성급한, 충동적인	[3986] rash
impetuous		2. (바람, 흐름, 속도 등이)격렬한, 맹렬한	[3452] shallow
[im-PECH-oo-uhs]		He quit his job out of an impetuous decision.	[3876] impulsive
			[6411] ardent

7350	공무원 편입 GRE	1. 게걸스레 먹는, 대식하는 2. 열렬한, 대단히 열심인	voracity (폭식, 탐욕)
voracious			[4192] greedy
[vaw-REY-shuhs]		The swimmer is a voracious eater.	[2131] enthusiastic
			[4209] avid

7351		맞춤(형), 주문제작한	[2756] tailored
bespoke			[2494] imply
[bih-SPOHK]		His fancy sports car has been made bespoke.	

7352		과찬, 아첨	[4293] flattery
adulation			[478] commendation
[aj-uh-LEY-shuhn]		The professor wasn't comfortable with the adulation from his students.	[2458] praise
			[5073] applause

7353	편입	구제 불능인, 고쳐지지 않는	[308] hardened
incorrigible			[1930] evil
[in-KAWR-i-juh-buhl]		She didn't know what to do with her incorrigible son who constantly gets into trouble.	

7354	공무원 편입	인색(함), 절약	[5592] frugality
parsimony			
[PAHR-suh-moh-nee]		Her dad's parsimony was so extreme that he didn't even buy a car.	

7355	공무원 편입 GRE	악감정, 신랄함	acrimonious (신랄한)
acrimony			[3130] bitterness
[AK-ruh-moh-nee]		They put an end to their marriage without acrimony.	[7113] animosity

7356	GRE	원한, 악의, 적의	[3130] bitterness
rancor			[7355] acrimony
[RANG-ker]		She feels rancor towards her ex-boyfriend.	

7357		타박상, 좌상, 멍	[4284] bruise
contusion			[2740] swelling
[kuhn-TOO-zhuhn]		A tennis ball hit him in the leg, leaving a severe contusion.	

7358	토플 편입	호전적인	[7260] belligerent
bellicose			[962] argumentative
[BEL-i-kohs]		Nobody could tolerate his bellicose nature.	[2087] combative
			[5020] antagonistic

7359	편입	1. 노출이 심한, 꼭 끼는 2. 적은, 빈약한, 불충분한	[6382] scanty
skimpy			[1742] insufficient
[SKIM-pee]		She didn't look that good in her skimpy dress.	[2096] inadequate
			[6662] meager

7360		크게 놀란, 기절초풍하는	[887] amazed
flabbergasted			[959] surprised
[FLAB-er-gas-tid]		He was flabbergasted by his daughter's phone bill.	[4014] astonish

7361	토플	불법 자금 갈취	
racketeering			
[rak-i-TEER-ing]		The lawyer has been accused of racketeering.	

7362	GRE	1. (위험을) 제거하다 2. (대책을 써서) 미연에 방지하다	[740] prevent
obviate			[82] counteract
[OB-vee-eyt]		A peaceful nuclear treaty with the North would obviate the need for a military build-up.	[673] replace [3274] forestall

7363	GRE	톱니 모양의	[1805] toothed
serrated			
[SER-ey-tid]		A serrated knife was used as the murder weapon.	

7364	편입 GRE	태연한, 무심한	[2260] calm
nonchalant			[6417] apathetic
[non-shuh-LAHNT]		A student should never be nonchalant about failing a test.	[7215] aloof

7365	편입 GRE	단정, 예의바름	[6755] propriety
decorum			[662] correctness
[dih-KAWR-uhm]		A true gentleman should act with decorum.	[1284] civility [2891] courtesy

7366	GRE	1. 방랑자, (정처없는) 나그네 2. 방랑하는	[7001] tramp
vagabond			
[VAG-uh-bond]		After years of being a vagabond, he finally settled in.	

7367	토플	1. 격납고 2. 헛간, 오두막	[2481] shed
hangar			[2311] garage
[HANG-er]		Airplanes are kept in hangars.	

7368	GRE	1. 어리석은, 얼빠진 2. 거짓의, 공허한 3. 허공	[3103] silly
inane			[306] unreasonable
[ih-NEYN]		All these inane comments are wearing me out.	

7369	편입 GRE	1. 불가지론의 2. 불가지론자 (인간은 신을 인지할 수 없다고 믿음)	[3696] skeptic
agnostic			[4467] secular
[ag-NOS-tik]		An agnostic believes that the very knowledge of whether God exists is questionable.	

7370	GRE	1. 진통제 2. 무통의	[863] painkiller
analgesic			
[an-l-JEE-zik]		Analgesics are merely a temporary solution to pain.	

7371	편입 GRE	부호, 거물	[914] king
magnate			[618] figure
[MAG-neyt]		Andrew Carnegie was one of the richest steel magnates in the world.	[1056] capitalist [5484] aristocrat

7372	GRE	소량, 조금	[3003] dash
modicum			[614] measure
[MOD-i-kuhm]		Anyone with a modicum of common sense would understand the situation.	[2616] ounce

7373	편입	몹시 건조한, 목이 마른	[900] dry
parched			[3021] arid
[pahrch d]		Apply some lip balm on those parched lips.	[5899] scorched [5989] barren

7374	GRE	~의 불길한 전조가 되다, 예시하다	[1396] warn
portend			
[pawr-TEND]		Black cats are believed to portend bad luck.	

7375	편입 GRE	(법률을) 폐지하다	[4279] repeal
abrogate			[4362] abolish
[AB-ruh-geyt]		Congress abrogated the new immigration law.	

7376	공무원 편입	낙담한, 낙심한 (사람)	[1780] depressed
despondent			[1692] sad
[dih-SPON-duhnt]		Despondent about the amount of work, the student gave up finishing homework.	[3662] discouraged

7377	공무원 토플 GRE	1. 흔들거리다 2. (마음이) 동요하다	[1354] waver
vacillate			[3888] fluctuate
[VAS-uh-leyt]		Do not vacillate so much over your options.	

7378		1. 취임한 자, 가입된 자 2. 징집병	
inductee			
[in-duhk-TEE]		Following his illustrious career, Lebron James is sure to be a Hall of Fame inductee.	

7379	GRE	1. 고위 인사 2. 존엄한	[2722] celebrity
dignitary			[618] figure
[DIG-ni-ter-ee]		Government dignitaries were indicted for bribery.	[5565] luminary

7380	GRE	학자, 석학	[1485] scholar
savant			
[sa-VAHNT]		Gwen is a self-proclaimed savant with card games.	

7381	토플	농작, 경작 가능한	
arable			
[AR-uh-buhl]		He discovered a continent rich in arable land.	

7382	GRE	1. 강한 감정의, 본능적인 2. 내장의	[2935] intuitive
visceral			[5266] innate
[VIS-er-uhl]		He displayed a visceral response towards the bad news.	[6571] ingrained

7383	공무원 편입	입이 무거운, 과묵한	[1225] reserved
reticent			[2494] imply
[RET-uh-suhnt]		He is extremely reticent about his personal life.	[3227] hesitant
			[7243] bashful

7384	공무원	낙천적인, 쾌활한	[1110] confident
sanguine			[2488] cheerful
[SANG-gwin]		Head coach Mourinho is sanguine about tomorrow's game against Chelsea.	[5194] buoyant

7385	편입 GRE	미지근한, 열의가 없는	[6641] lukewarm
tepid			[3731] dull
[TEP-id]		Her performance brought a tepid response from the audience.	

7386	편입 GRE	완화하다, 경감하다	[7289] assuage
allay			[3926] soothe
[uh-LEY]		Herbal tea helps allay pain in the throat.	[4170] alleviate

7387	편입	1. 역량, 우수성 2. 총 구멍의 직경	[111] ability
caliber			[450] standard
[KAL-uh-ber]		High caliber athletes are very rare.	[2388] competence

7388	토플 GRE	속이다	[3488] contradict
belie			[1315] negate
[bih-LAHY]		His appearances belie his skills.	

7389	공무원	뒤죽박죽(으로 만들다)	[6954] jumble
hodgepodge			[656] mixture
[HOJ-poj]		His argument was a hodgepodge of logical fallacies and assumptions.	

7390	GRE	조달(공급)업자	[671] supplier
purveyor			[453] attendant
[per-VEY-er]		His company is known to be the best purveyor of fine wine.	[1066] administrator

7391	GRE	선견지명이 있는	[2347] prophetic
prescient			[1452] predict
[PRESH-uhnt]		His projections of the collapse of Lehman Brothers proved prescient.	

7392	공무원	허풍스러운	[2579] inflated
bombastic			[1677] grand
[bom-BAS-tik]		His speech was so bombastic.	

7393	GRE	오만, 자만	[2436] pride
hubris			[2650] boast
[HYOO-bris]		Hitler's political hubris was the cause of defeat for Nazi Germany.	[6100] audacity

7394	GRE	1. (하기 힘든 이야기를) 꺼내다 2. 쇠꼬챙이	[761] introduce
broach			[876] mention
[brohch]		I am anxious about broaching the subject of marriage to my parents.	

7395	공무원	1. 둔한, 둔감한 2. 둔각(90도 이상)	[3731] dull
obtuse			
[uhb-TOOS]		I am not trying to be obtuse, but I just don't understand.	

7396	공무원 토플 편입	잘못된 이름, 오칭	
misnomer			
[mis-NOH-mer]		It is a misnomer to call the inexperienced boy a professional.	

7397	GRE	큰 책, 학술서	
tome			
[tohm]		It was challenging for her to carry around the weighty tome all day.	

7398	편입 GRE	1. ~의 결핍, 부족함 2. 기근	[1091] lack
dearth			[2096] inadequate
[durth]		Japanese companies are suffering from a dearth of young workers.	[2193] absence
			[3361] deficiency

7399	GRE	경향, 기호, inclination	[7423] predilection
penchant			[53] liking
[PEN-chuhnt]		Males tend to have a penchant for sports.	[3570] affection
			[4725] affinity

7400	GRE	해로운, 유해한	[1708] harmful
deleterious			[1223] dangerous
[del-i-TEER-ee-uhs]		Marijuana may have deleterious effects on the nervous system.	

7401	GRE	1. 농사 2. 절약	[1050] farming
husbandry			[573] preparation
[HUHZ-buhn-dree]		My farm was accused of poor husbandry by the Environmental Protection Agency.	

7402	토플 GRE	1. 대뇌의 2. 지적인	[2319] intellectual
cerebral			[871] analytical
[suh-REE-bruhl]		My handicapped friend is suffering from cerebral palsy.	[1588] intelligent
			[1817] complicated

7403	GRE	신문 기사에 필자명이 적힌 부분	
byline			
[BAHY-lahyn]		My name wasn't listed on the byline of this article.	

7404	GRE	다양하거나 잡다한	[1535] diverse [762] various
sundry			[1717] conflicting
[SUHN-dree]		National parks are open to all and sundry.	[4031] assorted

7405	GRE	1. 큰 소용돌이 2. (사회적) 대혼란	[6058] vortex [2962] chaos
maelstrom			[4991] turbulence
[MEYL-struhm]		Nowadays, many adolescents are caught up in a maelstrom of early-age alcohol and nicotine consumption.	

7406	GRE	후각(기관)의	
olfactory			
[ol-FAK-tuh-ree]		Olfactory nerves are crucial to sensing smell.	

7407	GRE	난폭한, 사나운, 제멋대로의	[7298] rowdy [547] energetic
rambunctious			[1673] noisy
[ram-BUHNGK-shuhs]		Parents are obliged to take care of their rambunctious child in public spaces.	[7255] boisterous

7408	GRE	1. 피부가 찢긴 상처 2. 괴롭힘, 고뇌	lacerate (찢다) [4340] lesion
laceration			
[las-uh-REY-shuhn]		Peter got multiple lacerations to the face from falling down the stairs.	

7409	토플 편입 GRE	1. 두드려 펼 수 있는, 가단성의 2. 영향받기 쉬운, 융통성 있는	[4470] pliable [1309] flexible
malleable			[1415] adaptable
[MAL-ee-uh-buhl]		The self-identity of adolescents is highly malleable.	

7410	공무원 GRE	성향, 기질	[2140] bent [1979] habit
proclivity			[7399] penchant
[proh-KLIV-i-tee]		Sexual proclivities cannot be an excuse for crime.	[7423] predilection

7411	편입 GRE	과도한, 지나친	[1738] excessive [196] large
inordinate			[4418] dizzying
[in-AWR-dn-it]		She had to spend an inordinate amount of time to finish all of her work.	

7412	GRE	평정, 침착, 냉정	[775] composure [2260] calmness
equanimity			
[ee-kwuh-NIM-i-tee]		She handled the complex situation with equanimity.	

7413	공무원 토플 편입 GRE	상냥하고 친절한	[288] friendly [696] approachable
affable			[7131] amiable
[AF-uh-buhl]		She was popular in school thanks to her affable personality.	

7414	토플	1. 획기적인, 비약적인 2. (물리학) 양자	[614] measure [160] payment
quantum			
[KWON-tuhm]		She wasn't able to offer a quantum of evidence to the judges.	

7415	편입 GRE	만병통치약	[577] solution [6455] elixir
panacea			
[pan-uh-SEE-uh]		Technological advancement is not a panacea for all of humanity's problems.	

7416	편입 GRE	~인 체하다, 가장하다	feigned (거짓의) [3162] pretend
feign			
[feyn]		Ted feigned illness to skip class today.	

7417	공무원	깔깔거리는 웃음	[1863] laugh
guffaw [guh-FAW]		The audience exploded into a huge guffaw of laughter.	

7418	편입 GRE	진부한, 흔해 빠진	banality (따분함) [7463] trite [1109] boring [2699] corny
banal [buh-NAL]		The banal proposal was disapproved by the executive board.	

7419	GRE	1. 파괴하다 2. (기억에서) 지우다	[3962] demolish
raze [reyz]		The bombers razed the city to the ground.	

7420	편입 GRE	1. (냄새나 맛이) 맵고 쓴 2. 신랄한, 혹독한	[3130] bitter [4019] stinging [5779] stale [6993] pungent
acrid [AK-rid]		The burning building was covered in acrid smoke.	

7421	편입 GRE	경솔한 행위, 경거망동	[6667] frivolity [외래어] humor
levity [LEV-i-tee]		The busy operation leaves no room for levity.	

7422	GRE	개선하다, 향상시키다	amelioration (개선) [257] lighten [1631] heal [4170] alleviate
ameliorate [uh-MEEL-yuh-reyt]		The caretaker worked hard to ameliorate the lives of her patients.	

7423	편입 GRE	애호, 편애, 두둔	[3341] inclination [53] liking [2304] leaning [3856] fondness
predilection [pred-l-EK-shuhn]		The child's predilection for sweets resulted in serious cavity.	

7424	GRE	1. (공식적인) 선언, 의견 2. 격언, 속담	dicta (dictum의 복수) [4479] decree [6783] adage
dictum [DIK-tuhm]		The Chinese government made an official dictum on the deployment of THAAD on the Korean peninsula.	

7425	GRE	절벽, 벼랑, 위기	precipitous (가파른, 급작스런) [3566] cliff [1223] danger
precipice [PRES-uh-pis]		The company was standing on the precipice of bankruptcy.	

7426	GRE	그만두다, 단념하다	[439] stop [3025] cease [5316] abstain
desist [dih-ZIST]		The court ordered Brian to desist from stalking his girlfriend.	

7427	GRE	1. 방종한, 음탕한 2. 바람둥이	[1891] loose [1223] dangerous [3681] outrageous
wanton [WON-tn]		The criminal was charged with hate crimes in wanton beating of innocent civilians.	

7428	GRE	아는 체하는 사람, 사기꾼	[2439] fraud [1077] liar
charlatan [SHAHR-luh-tn]		The doctor seems to be a charlatan.	

7429	GRE	(특히 비난하는) 장황한 연설	[4952] rant [898] criticism
tirade [TAHY-reyd]		The employee launched into a furious tirade about how he had been underpaid.	

7430	편입 GRE	1. 간결한, 간단명료한 2. 퉁명스러운	[4625] concise
terse [turs]		The employee was reprimanded for her terse response to the supervisor.	

7431	공무원 편입 GRE	박식한	[1485] scholarly
erudite			[354] educated
[ER-yoo-dahyt]		The erudite student graduated valedictorian.	[772] knowledgeable
			[3138] literate

7432	편입 GRE	1. 낭비하는, 방탕한 2. 방탕한 사람, 탕아	[5132] lavish
prodigal			[1370] wasteful
[PROD-i-guhl]		The executive has allegedly been prodigal with company funds.	

7433	공무원 GRE	1. 밑줄 (긋다) 2. 강조하다	[837] mark
underscore			[1382] highlight
[UHN-der-skawr]		The findings underscore the importance of a healthy diet.	[2880] accentuate

7434	편입 GRE	1. (지난 일을) 아쉬워하는, 그리워하는, 탐내는 2. 생각에 잠긴	[6094] melancholy
wistful			[1073] dreamy
[WIST-fuhl]		The general showed a wistful smile upon hearing the success of the operation.	[1692] sad
			[3697] contemplative

7435	GRE	1. (대)변동 2. 대홍수	[2257] disaster
cataclysm			[234] effect
[KAT-uh-kliz-uh m]		The Great Depression was a cataclysm for all of America.	[4119] catastrophe
			[6222] calamity

7436	GRE	(당연하거나 필연적인) 결과	[1304] conclusion
corollary			[493] link
[KAWR-uh-ler-ee]		The Greek financial crisis was a corollary of populist welfare policies.	[4056] analogy
			[7459] upshot

7437	편입 GRE	해이한, 태만한	laxity (태만함)
lax			[1309] flexible
[laks]		The investigators were lax in looking into the evidence.	[117] indifferent
			[256] careless

7438	GRE	법적 허가 없이 사람을 (주로 교수형으로) 사형시키다, 린치를 가하다	lynching (폭력적 제재)
lynch			[682] kill
[linch]		The KKK used lynchings to terrorize the African-American community.	

7439	GRE	청각의	[4866] audible
aural			
[AWR-uh l]		The lyrics of the song gave her aural sensations.	

7440	편입 GRE	1. 추도 연설 2. 찬사	[2458] praise
eulogy			[2142] citation
[YOO-luh-jee]		The minister sincerely pronounced a eulogy to the deceased.	

7441	공무원	익명의(으로)	[2368] anonymous
incognito			[1334] secret
[in-kog-NEE-toh]		The movie star traveled incognito to protect her privacy.	

7442	편입 GRE	(형 집행, 공장 폐쇄 등의 계획을) 취소/보류/유예(하다)	[1785] pardon
reprieve			[740] prevent
[ri-PREEV]		The murderer is looking to get a reprieve from prison.	[5902] abatement
			[6996] absolution

7443	GRE	1. 유기된, 버려진 2. 직무태만자	[2399] abandoned
derelict			[1889] empty
[DER-uh-likt]		The neighborhood was derelict for many years before redevelopment kicked off.	

7444	GRE	1. 부식성의 2. 날카롭고 비꼬는	[3130] bitter
caustic			[4813] abrasive
[KAW-stik]		The new drama series was subject to caustic remarks from critics.	

7445	GRE	계략, 책략	[1595] trick
ruse			[6921] ploy
[ROOz]		The Normandy Invasion was an elaborate ruse to fool Hitler.	

7446	GRE	특별한 특징이 없는, 막연한	[2503] ordinary
nondescript			[964] uninspiring
[non-di-SKRIPT]		The office is located in a nondescript building just around the corner.	[1944] unremarkable

7447	GRE	1. 교훈적인 2. (못마땅함) 남을 가르치려 하는	[881] instructive
didactic			[1234] opinionated
[dahy-DAK-tik]		The old lady I met in the subway was very didactic.	

7448	GRE	은둔한, 쓸쓸하고 적막한	recluse (은둔자)
reclusive			[5262] solitary
[REK-loo-siv]		The old man led a reclusive life in the woods.	[2243] isolated

7449	GRE	서론	[5953] preface
preamble			[630] explanation
[PREE-am-buhl]		The preamble seems unnecessarily lengthy.	

7450	편입 GRE	1. (도덕적) 문제, 폐해 2. 만성 질병	[960] disease
malady			[1074] cancer
			[2113] illness
[MAL-uh-dee]		The president was to blame for this nationwide malady.	[4366] ache

7451	GRE	잡색의, 다채로운	[7456] motley
variegated			[1717] conflicting
[VAIR-ee-i-gey-tid]		The presidential candidate boasted a variegated career.	

7452	GRE	찬란한, 눈부시게 빛나는	[5199] splendid
resplendent			[146] lovely
			[2178] brilliant
[ri-SPLEN-duhnt]		The princess appeared at the party in a resplendent dress.	[4174] blazing

7453	공무원 편입 GRE	요약하다	[1201] repeat
recapitulate			[1592] recap
[ree-kuh-PICH-uh-leyt]		The professor recapitulated his lecture.	

7454	GRE	1. ~을 상실한 2. 상실감에 빠진	bereaved (사별당한)
bereft			[6284] bereaved
[bih-REFT]		The protestors were bereft of all hope after a new dictatorship came into power.	[2843] lonely

7455	편입 GRE	칭찬하다, 격찬하다	[2133] glorify
extol			[2458] praise
			[3724] acclaim
[ik-STOHL]		The rebels extolled the virtues of freedom.	[5073] applaud

7456	GRE	1. 잡다하게 섞인 2. 잡동사니 3. 얼룩덜룩한 옷	[1535] diverse
motley			[4458] disparate
[MOT-lee]		The subway was a motley crew of the young and old.	

7457	편입 GRE	1. 격분한, 화난 2. (멍같이) 검푸른	[3576] furious
livid			
[LIV-id]		The teacher turned livid over the student's disobedience.	

7458	GRE	평등주의(자)의	[861] equal
egalitarian			[1596] democratic
			[5071] equitable
[ih-gal-i-TAIR-ee-uhn]		The United Nations is known to pursue egalitarian values.	

7459		결말, 결론	[235] result
upshot			[6572] gist
[UHP-shot]		The upshot was that I failed the test due to procrastination.	

7460	GRE	마법, 주문	[1797] spell
incantation			[3998] enchantment
[in-kan-TEY-shuhn]		The wicked witch chanted an incantation.	[4859] hymn

7461	GRE	결핍, 모자람	[1091] lack
paucity			[409] bit
[PAW-si-tee]		There is a paucity of generosity in this nation.	[1742] insufficiency
			[7398] dearth

7462	GRE	(사회문화적) 환경	[718] situation
milieu			[1346] surroundings
[mil-YOO]		There is not much hope for the Republicans in this political milieu.	[3914] ambience

7463	편입 GRE	진부한	[5779] stale
trite			[1109] boring
[trahyt]		This may sound trite, but safety always comes first.	[2699] corny
			[7418] banal

7464	GRE	부적	[6686] amulet
talisman			
[TAL-is-muhn]		This medal is a talisman for good luck.	

7465	GRE	쓰레기	[3571] debris
detritus			[4865] rubbish
[dih-TRAHY-tuhs]		Those corrupt politicians are the detritus of Japanese Imperialism.	[6192] rubble

7466	GRE	1.(태양의 열로) 그을린, 바싹 마른 2. 열렬한	[655] fiery
torrid			[1268] emotional
[TAWR-id]		Tim had a torrid love affair with Sarah.	[3021] arid
			[4174] blazing

7467	GRE	1. 광내다, 닦다 2. (실력을) 갈고닦다 polish	[1962] shine
burnish			[401] improve
[BUR-nish]		Tom burnished his Excel skills over the summer.	

7468	GRE	사후의	[363] death
posthumous			
[POS-chuh-muhs]		Vincent van Gogh gained worldwide fame posthumously.	

7469		1. 말뚝 울타리(를 치다) 2. (강가나 해안의) 벼랑	[2584] fence
palisade			
[pal-uh-SEYD]		We need to set up a palisade to defend the premises.	

7470	GRE	심술 부리는, 짜증을 잘 내는	[2895] irritable
petulant			[1987] angry
[PECH-uh-luhnt]		What a petulant man my professor is!	[3591] cranky

7471	편입 GRE	끔찍한, 소름돋게 싫은	[4403] repulsive
odious			[2830] horrible
[OH-dee-uhs]		What an odious man he is!	[6141] abominable
			[6745] abhorrent

7472	GRE	표현할 수 없을 정도로 엄청난	[542] beautiful
ineffable			[1994] heavenly
[in-EF-uh-buhl]		Winning the lottery gave him an ineffable feeling of joy.	

7473	공무원 편입	근면하는, 꾸준한, 부지런한	assiduity (근면함)
assiduous			[3701] diligent
[uh-SIJ-oo-uhs]		The government was assiduous in the fight against Covid-19.	[256] careful

7474	공무원	은밀한, 몰래하는	[1334] secret
surreptitious			[5524] covert
[sur-uh p-TISH-uh s]		The girl was caught making surreptitious glances at her crush.	[7077] clandestine

7475	GRE	거짓의, 가짜의	[4480] false
spurious			[1582] apparently
[SPYOOR-ee-uhs]		Most of the claims made by the criminal are spurious.	[5988] bogus

7476	토플 편입 GRE	치명적인, 해로운	[1708] harmful
pernicious			[719] damaging
[per-NISH-uhs]		The pernicious nature of negativity was the topic of the psychology lecture.	[1223] dangerous

7477	편입 GRE	부추기다, 선동하다	[636] assist
abet			[85] help
[uh-BET]		Matt aided and abetted her into committing financial fraud.	[5780] incite
			[6509] condone

7478	GRE	1. 편협한, 배타적인 2. 섬과 관련된	[1894] provincial
insular			[2243] isolated
[IN-suh-ler]		People tend to become more insular as they age.	[5262] solitary

7479	GRE	1. 소름끼치는, 너무 자극적인 2. 색이 화려한, colorful	[1728] shocking
lurid			[4242] exaggerated
[LOOR-id]		The lurid details of his wrongdoings were released by the media.	

7480	공무원	1. 진실된, 진짜의 2. 선량한	[87] real
bona-fide			
[BOH-nuh fahyd]		Pete was confident that the firm based overseas was not a bona fide company.	

7481		우연의, 행운의	[1597] accidental
fortuitous			[992] fortunate
[fawr-TOO-i-tuhs]		In retrospect, the encounter with Susan was a fortuitous opportunity for my career.	

7482	편입 GRE	(법, 규칙, 전통 등을) 업신여기거나 어기다	[3862] defy
flout			[445] break
[flout]		Many millennials choose to flout national holiday traditions.	[654] disregard

7483	GRE	겉만 멀쩡하고 그럴듯하지만 실상은 그렇지 못한	[1582] apparently
specious			[3383] deceptive
[SPEE-shuhs]		The boy made specious excuses to his girlfriend.	[5538] erroneous

7484	공무원 토플 GRE	경멸적인	
pejorative			
[pi-JAWR-uh-tiv]		Please refrain from using pejorative terms directed at specific ethnicities.	

7485	편입 GRE	대충하는, 형식적인, 열의 없이 겉치레로 하는	[7221] cursory
perfunctory			[256] careless
[per-FUHNGK-tuh-ree]		The interviewer asked a few perfunctory questions before ending the interview short.	

7486	편입 GRE	텅 빈, 알맹이가 없는	vacuity (멍청함)
vacuous			[3502] vacant
[VAK-yoo-uh s]		Professor Kim could tell from the student's vacuous question that he had not been paying attention.	[3452] shallow

7487	편입 GRE	관대한	magnanimity (관대함)
magnanimous [mag-NAN-uh-muhs]		The politician was magnanimous in defeat, congratulating his rival on the big win.	[2507] generous [1840] charitable [2532] forgiving
7488	GRE	공격적인, 논쟁하는	polemic (논쟁)
polemical [puh-LEM-i-kul]		Most debate shows are overly polemical.	[2538] controversial [7260] belligerent
7489	편입 GRE	1. 무기력, 휴면 2. 동면 (=겨울잠)	[6352] lethargy [2460] boredom
torpor [TAWR-per]		Many students fall into a state of torpor during summer vacation.	
7490	GRE	1. 맹비난하다 2. 피부가 벗겨지게 하다	
excoriate [ik-SKAWR-ee-eyt]		The media bombarded the movie with excoriating reviews.	
7491	GRE	1. 의지박약한, 무책임한 2. 쓸모 없는	[234] ineffective
feckless [FEK-lis]		No feckless student would have been able to reach the end of this book.	
7492	GRE	간결한, 재치 있는, 말이 짧지만 강렬한	[1671] brief [1739] quiet
laconic [luh-KON-ik]		Tyler was not talkative but still enjoyable to be around since he was laconic.	
7493	GRE	인습 타파주의자	[2690] rebel
iconoclast [ahy-KON-uh-klast]		Steve Jobs was an iconoclast in the field of design.	
7494	편입 GRE	이해하기 난해한, 심오한	[3751] obscure [4259] ambiguity [6067] perplexing [6307] esoteric
abstruse [ab-STROOS]		My brother loves reading abstruse scientific papers.	
7495	GRE	고집스러운, 굽히지 않는, 완고한	intransigience (완고함) [4545] stubborn
intransigent [in-TRAN-si-juhnt]		The president was intransigent on his policy against foreign aid.	[1309] inflexible [6057] adamant
7496	GRE	가치를 떨어뜨리다, 해치다, (평판 등을) 오염시키다	[373] worsen [1315] negate
vitiate [VISH-ee-eyt]		The celebrity's reputation was vitiated by the deluge of allegations.	[5975] annihilate
7497	편입 GRE	호전적인, 싸우기 좋아하는	[2087] combative [962] argumentative
pugnacious [puhg-NEY-shuhs]		The pugnacious president fired his staff member.	[7358] bellicose
7498	공무원 토플	쉽게 사라져 덧없는	[604] variable
evanescent [ev-uh-NES-uhnt]		The monk emphasized that our time on earth is evanescent.	
7499	편입 GRE	아부하는	
obsequious [uhb-SEE-kwee-uhs]		Mr. Kim was known to be obsequious to the wealthy.	
7500	GRE	수다스러운, 말이 많은	loquacity (수다스러움) [392] talkative
loquacious [loh-KWEY-shuhs]		I can understand why taxi drivers are loquacious.	[2045] chatty

외래어 및 기타 표현

| 외래어 및 기타 표현

무료 MP3 파일 제공 | Allvoca.com

외래어	
Accordion	아코디언
Adrenalin	아드레날린
Album	앨범
Algorithm	알고리즘
Alibi	알리바이
Almond	아몬드
Alphabet	알파벳
Alps	알프스
Aluminum	알루미늄
Amateur	아마추어
Amen	아멘
Ammonia	암모니아
Antenna	안테나
Asparagus	아스파라거스
Asphalt	아스팔트
Aspirin	아스프린
Audition	오디션
Avocado	아보카도
Bacon	베이컨
Bacteria	박테리아
Badminton	배드민턴
Bagel	베이글
Balcony	발코니
Ballad	발라드
Ballet	발레
Banana	바나나
Banner	배너
Barbecue	바비큐
Barbell	바벨
Barricade	바리케이드
Bartender	바텐더
Basil	바질
Bazaar	바자회
Beaver	비버
Beige	베이지
Bench	벤치
Bikini	비키니
Biorhythm	바이오리듬
Biscuit	비스킷

Blog	블로그
Blouse	블라우스
Blu-Ray	블루레이
Bonnet	자동차 본넷
Bouquet	부케
Bourgeois	부르주아
Brassiere	브래지어
Broccoli	브로콜리
Brownie	브라우니
Brunch	브런치
Bulldog	불도그
Bulldozer	불도저
Burger	햄버거
Burrito	브리또
Bus	버스
Cafe	카페
Caffeine	카페인
Cake	케이크
Calcium	칼슘
Calorie	칼로리
Camcorder	캠코더
Cameo	까메오
Camera	카메라
Campus	캠퍼스
Canoe	카누
Caramel	카라멜
Cardigan	가디건
Carol	캐럴
Carpet	카펫
Cashmere	캐시미어
Casino	카지노
Catholic	가톨릭
Cauliflower	콜리플라워
Celery	셀러리
Cello	첼로
Cellphone	핸드폰
Centimeter	센티미터
Cereal	시리얼
Chameleon	카멜레온
Champagne	샴페인

Chandelier	샹들리에
Checkout	체크아웃
Cheetah	치타
Chef	셰프
Cherry	체리
Chess	체스
Chilli	칠리
Chimpanzee	침팬지
Chiropractic	카이로프랙틱
Chocolate	초콜릿
Cholesterol	콜레스테롤
Christmas	크리스마스
Cigar	시가
Circus	서커스
Clarinet	클라리넷
Clover	클로버
Cobalt	코발트색 (푸른)
Cobra	코브라
Cocaine	코카인
Cocktail	칵테일
Cocoa	코코아
Coconut	코코넛
Codec	코덱
Coffee	커피
Coke	콜라
Cola	콜라
Colon	콜론 (:)
Colosseum	콜로세움
Condom	콘돔
Cookie	쿠키
Copywriter	카피라이터
Cork	코르크
Corset	코르셋
Coupe	쿠페
Coupon	쿠폰
Cowboy	카우보이
Coyote	코요테
Cranberry	크랜베리
Crayon	크레용
Cream	크림

Crowdfunding	크라우드펀딩	Freestyle	프리스타일	Internet	인터넷
Curry	카레	Gallon	갤런	Ipod	아이팟
Cursor	커서	Gamma	감마	Italics	이탤릭체
Curtain	커튼	Gel	젤	Jab	잽
Custard	커스터드	Genie	지니	Jacket	자켓
Cuticle	큐티클	Genome	게놈	Jaguar	재규어
Cyber	사이버	Genre	장르	Jazz	재즈
Cymbal	심벌즈	Golf	골프	Jeep	지프
Database	데이터베이스	Gondola	곤돌라	Jelly	젤리
Debut	데뷔	Gorilla	고릴라	Kale	케일
Denim	데님	Gradation	그라데이션	Kangaroo	캥거루
Dessert	디저트	Graffiti	그래피티	Karate	가라테
Diamond	다이아몬드	Gram	그람	Kayak	카약
Diesel	디젤	Graph	그래프	Ketchup	케첩
Disco	디스코	Greenhouse	그린하우스	Keyboard	키보드
Dna	DNA	Guitar	기타	Khaki	카키색
Dollar	달러	Gypsy	집시	Kilogram	킬로그램
Domino	도미노	Halloween	할로윈	Kilometer	킬로미터
Donut	도넛	Ham	햄	Kiss	키스
Dopamine	도파민	Hammock	해먹 침대	Kiwi	키위
Download	다운로드	Hamster	햄스터	Koala	코알라
Drone	드론	Hardware	하드웨어	Koran	코란
Drum	드럼	Harp	하프	Lavender	라벤더
Dynamite	다이나마이트	Hectare	헥타르	Lasagna	라자냐
Email	이메일	Helicopter	헬리콥터	Laser	레이저
Emerald	에메랄드	Helmet	헬멧	Latex	라텍스
Emulsion	에멀션	Heroin	헤로인	Latin	라틴
Encore	앙코르	Herpes	헤르페스	Latte	라떼
Engine	엔진	Hippie	히피	League	리그
Epoxy	에폭시	Hipster	힙스터	Lemon	레몬
Escalator	에스컬레이터	Hobbit	호빗	Lemonade	레몬에이드
Espresso	에스프레소	Hockey	하키	Lens	렌즈
Estrogen	에스트로겐	Homo Sapiens	호모사피엔스	Lesbian	레즈비언
Etiquette	에티켓	Hormone	호르몬	Lifeguard	라이프가드
Eureka	유레카	Hose	호스	Lifestyle	라이프스타일
Euro	유로	Hotel	호텔	Lime	라임
Fax	팩스	Humor	유머	Limousine	리무진
Feminism	페미니즘	Hyphen	하이픈	Linen	리넨
Fender	펜더	Igloo	이글루	Lingerie	란제리
Flute	플룻	Inch	인치	Lipstick	립스틱
Font	폰트	Ink	잉크	Liter	리터
Franc	프랑	Inning	이닝	Lithium	리튬
Franchise	프랜차이즈	Insulin	인슐린	Lobster	랍스터

Logo	로고	Neanderthal	네안데르탈인	Pickle	피클
Lotion	로션	Network	네트워크	Picnic	피크닉
Macaroni	마카로니	Neuron	뉴런	Pie	파이
Mafia	마피아	News	뉴스	Pineapple	파인애플
Mahogany	마호가니	Newsletter	뉴스레터	Pink	핑크
Makeup	메이크업	Nicotine	니코틴	Pint	파인트
Malaria	말라리라	Nightclub	나이트클럽	Pizza	피자
Mango	망고	Ninja	닌자	Placebo	플라시보
Manicure	매니큐어	Notebook	노트북	Playoff	플레이오프
Marathon	마라톤	Nylon	나일론	Podcast	포드캐스트
Marshmallow	마시멜로	Oasis	오아시스	Polo	폴로
Martini	마티니	Octave	옥타브	Polyester	폴리에스터
Mascara	마스카라	Ok	오케이	Popcorn	팝콘
Mascot	마스콧	Olive	올리브	Pretzel	프레젤
Massage	마사지	Omega	오메가	Pudding	푸딩
Mayonnaise	마요네즈	Omelette	오믈렛	Puma	퓨마
Mediterranean	지중해(의)	Online	온라인	Pump	펌프
Megaphone	메가폰	Opera	오페라	Putt	퍼트
Melody	멜로디	Opioid	오피오이드	Pyramid	피라미드
Melon	멜론	Orange	오렌지	Quinoa	퀴노아
Memo	메모	Orchestra	오케스트라	Quiz	퀴즈
Mentor	멘토	Orgasm	오르가즘	Rabbi	라비
Menu	메뉴	Oven	오븐	Radio	라디오
Message	메시지	Page	페이지	Ramadan	라마단
Methane	메탄	Pajamas	파자마	Rap	랩
Microphone	마이크	Palette	팔레트	Raspberry	래스베리
Milligram	밀리그램	Pamphlet	팜플렛	Rehearsal	리허설
Millimeter	밀리미터	Panda	팬더	Repertoire	레퍼토리
Mini	미니	Panty	팬티	Rhythm	리듬
Missile	미사일	Paprika	파프리카	Ribbon	리본
Mocha	모카	Parody	패러디	Robin	로빈
Modem	모뎀	Pasta	파스타	Robot	로봇
Montage	몽타주	Pecan	피칸	Rodeo	로데오
Mosaic	모자이크	Pedal	페달	Roommate	룸메이트
Mosque	모스크	Pedicure	페디큐어	Ruby	루비
Motel	모텔	Pelican	펠리칸	Rugby	럭비
Moto	모토	Pen	펜더	Rupee	루피
Mozzarella	모짜렐라	Penguin	펜귄	Sadism	사디즘
Muffin	머핀	Penthouse	펜트하우스	Safari	사파리
Mustang	머스탱	Percent	퍼센트	Salad	샐러드
Mustard	머스터드	Percentage	퍼센트	Samurai	사무라이
Nano	나노	Pharaoh	파라오	Sandal	샌들
Napkin	냅킨	Piano	피아노	Sandwich	샌드위치

Satan	사탄	Storytelling	스토리텔링	Url	유알엘
Sauna	사우나	Strawberry	스트로베리	Vaccine	백신
Sausage	소시지	Studio	스튜디오	Valentine	발렌타인
Saxophone	색소폰	Suede	스웨이드	Vampire	뱀파이어
Scarf	스카프	Suite	스위트룸	Vanilla	바닐라
Scenario	시나리오	Sunscreen	썬스크린	Velvet	벨벳
Scooter	스쿠터	Supermarket	슈퍼마켓	Veranda	베란다
Scrum	스크럼	Superstar	슈퍼스타	Video	비디오
Scuba	스쿠버	Sushi	초밥	Violin	바이올린
Sedan	세단	Sweater	스웨터	Virus	바이러스
Semicolon	세미콜론	Sweatshirt	스웨트 셔츠	Visa	비자
Seminar	세미나	Syrup	시럽	Vitamin	비타민
Shale	셰일	Taco	타코	Vodka	보드카
Shampoo	샴푸	Taliban	탈레반	Waffle	와플
Shirt	셔츠	Tampon	탐폰	Waltz	왈츠
Sigma	시그마	Tango	탱고	Watt	와트
Silicon	실리콘	Tar	타르	Website	웹사이트
Siren	사이렌	Tarot	타로카드	Wheelchair	휠체어
Sitcom	시트콤	Tart	타르트	Whiskey	위스키
Ski	스키	Tattoo	문신	Wine	와인
Skirt	스커트	Taxi	택시	Wink	윙크
Skunk	스컹크	Telepathy	텔레파시	Workshop	워크숍
Slipper	슬리퍼	Tennis	테니스	X-Ray	엑스레이
Slogan	슬로건	Tent	텐트	Yacht	요트
Smartphone	스마트폰	Tequila	데킬라	Yen	엔화
Smog	스모그	Terrace	테라스	Yoga	요가
Smoothie	스무디	Terrier	테리어	Yogurt	요거트
Sneakers	스피커즈	Tomato	토마토	Yuan	위안
Snorkeling	스노클링	Tractor	트랙터	Zombie	좀비
Soda	소다	Trademark	트레이드마크		
Sofa	소파	Tram	트램		
Software	소프트웨어	Trauma	트라우마		
Sonata	소나타	Truck	트럭		
Soprano	소프라노	Truffle	트러플		
Spa	스파	Tsunami	쓰나미		
Spaghetti	스파게티	Tulip	튤립		
Spam	스팸	Tunnel	터널		
Sponge	스폰지	Tumbler	텀블러		
Sport	스포츠	Tuxedo	턱시도		
Spotlight	스포트라이트	Tv	텔레비전		
Spreadsheet	스프레드시트	Ukulele	우쿨렐레		
Steak	스테이크	Unicorn	유니콘		
Steroids	스테로이드	Upload	업로드		

기타	
Monday	월요일
Tuesday	화요일
Wednesday	수요일
Thursday	목요일
Friday	금요일
Saturday	토요일
Sunday	일요일
January	1월
February	2월
March	3월
April	4월
May	5월
June	6월
July	7월
August	8월
September	9월
October	10월
November	11월
December	12월
P.M.	오후
A.M.	오전
Zero	0
One	1
Two	2
Three	3
Four	4
Five	5
Six	6
Seven	7
Eight	8
Nine	9
Ten	10
Eleven	11
Twelve	12
Thirteen	13
Fourteen	14
Fifteen	15
Sixteen	16
Seventeen	17
Eighteen	18
Nineteen	19
Twenty	20

Thirty	30
Forty	40
Fifty	50
Sixty	60
Seventy	70
Eighty	80
Ninety	90
Hundred	100
United States	미국
European Union	유럽 연합
China	중국
Japan	일본
United Kingdom	영국
Germany	독일
France	프랑스
India	인도
Italy	이탈리아
Brazil	브라질
Canada	캐나다
Russia	러시아
Korea	한국
Spain	스페인
Australia	호주
Mexico	멕시코
Indonesia	인도네시아
Saudia Arabia	사우디아라비아
Netherlands	네덜란드
Turkey	터키
Switzerland	스위스
Taiwan	타이완
Poland	폴란드
Sweden	스웨덴
Belgium	벨기에
Argentina	아르헨티나
Thailand	태국
Iran	이란
Norway	노르웨이
Nigeria	나이지리아
Ireland	아일랜드
Israel	이스라엘
Hong Kong	홍콩
Singapore	싱가포르
Malaysia	말레이시아

Denmark	덴마크
Columbia	컬럼비아
Philippines	필리핀
Pakistan	파키스탄
Chile	칠리
Bangladesh	방글라데시
Finland	핀란드
Egypt	이집트
Vietnam	베트남
Portugal	포르투갈
Iraq	이라크
Peru	페루
Greece	그리스
New Zealand	뉴질랜드
Scotland	스코틀랜드
Nepal	네팔
Europe	유럽
Asia	아시아
Africa	아프리카
Atlantic	대서양
Pacific	태평양

INDEX

| INDEX

alumni	5361	amphibian	5758	annexation	4853	anxiety	2288
alumnus	5361	amphibious	5758	annihilate	5975	anxious	2288
always	225	ample	3811	annihilation	5975	any	48
am	2	amplifier	2915	anniversary	2480	anything	48
amalgam	5809	amplify	2915	annotate	4517	anyway	3110
amalgamation	5809	amplitude	5688	annotation	4517	apart	1710
amass	5509	amputate	6240	announce	899	apartheid	6568
amateur	외래어	amputation	6240	announcement	899	apartment	1759
amaze	887	amulet	6686	annoy	2465	apathetic	6417
amazing	887	amusement	3634	annoying	2465	apathy	6417
ambassador	3319	anabolic	6278	annual	1031	ape	4938
amber	4156	anaemia	4990	annuity	4740	aperture	4005
ambidextrous	6256	anal	5422	annum	5784	apex	4870
ambient	3914	analgesic	7370	anoint	5750	apical	4870
ambiguity	4259	analog	5367	anomalous	4640	apiece	599
ambiguous	4259	analogous	4056	anomaly	4640	apocalypse	4833
ambition	2711	analogy	4056	anonymous	2368	apocalyptic	4833
ambitious	2711	analysis	871	anorexia	6542	apologize	2637
ambivalence	6929	analyst	871	anorexic	6542	apology	2637
ambivalent	6929	analytical	871	another	190	apostasy	6790
amble	6337	analytics	871	answer	540	apostate	6790
ambulance	4127	analyze	871	ant	812	apostle	3409
ambulatory	6337	anarchism	4970	antagonism	5020	appalled	5666
ambush	5766	anarchy	4970	antagonist	5020	appalling	5666
ameliorate	7422	anatomy	3625	antagonistic	5020	apparatus	5017
amelioration	7422	ancestor	3455	antagonize	5020	apparel	4021
amen	외래어	ancestry	3455	antarctic	3965	apparent	1582
amenable	7202	anchor	2679	antecedent	7206	apparently	1582
amend	1947	ancient	1803	antelope	6738	apparition	6677
amendment	1947	ancillary	6068	antenna	외래어	appeal	1365
amenities	3009	and	4	anterior	4858	appear	367
america	567	anecdotal	4723	anthem	4752	appearance	367
amiable	7131	anecdote	4723	anthology	5764	appease	6336
amicable	7184	anemia	4990	anthropological	4546	appeasement	6336
amicably	7184	anesthesia	2165	anthropologist	4546	append	5016
amid	4003	anew	6539	anthropology	4546	appendage	5016
amidst	5270	angel	2221	anti	4784	appendix	4422
amiss	7189	anger	1987	antibiotic	3134	appetite	3557
ammonia	외래어	angle	1572	anticipate	2207	applaud	5073
ammunition	3253	angry	1987	antics	6134	applause	5073
amnesia	7012	angst	6781	antidote	6484	apple	1238
amnesic	7012	anguish	6156	antipathy	7342	appliance	2766
amnesty	5890	anguished	6156	antiquated	3286	applicable	140
among	631	animal	907	antique	3286	applicant	140
amongst	631	animated	2031	antiseptic	5256	application	140
amorphous	7252	animation	2031	antler	6531	apply	140
amortization	5955	animosity	7113	antonym	4382	appoint	1369
amortize	5955	ankle	3284	anus	6488	appointment	1369
amount	455	annex	4853	anvil	6658	apportion	7006

audit	2020	await	625	baggy	2500	barely	2117
audition	외래어	awake	2819	bail	4037	bargain	3285
auditorium	5207	awaken	2819	bailout	4037	barge	5839
augment	4129	awakening	2819	bait	3861	bark	3729
augmentation	4129	award	681	bake	1589	barley	5236
August	기타	aware	1021	bakery	1589	barn	3793
aunt	809	awareness	1021	balance	897	barometer	6502
auqa	3607	away	358	balcony	외래어	baroque	7017
aura	4768	awe	1407	bald	4593	barracks	5887
aural	7439	awesome	1407	bale	5306	barrage	6145
auspicious	7213	awful	3052	ball	1054	barrel	2384
austere	5590	awhile	3899	ballad	외래어	barren	5989
austerity	5590	awkward	3424	ballast	5672	barricade	외래어
Australia	기타	awning	6196	ballet	외래어	barrier	2350
authentic	1986	awry	7303	ballistic	5219	barring	4308
author	1024	ax	4361	balloon	794	barrister	6454
authoritative	771	axe	4361	ballot	3742	bartender	외래어
authority	771	axiom	6355	ballroom	1054	barter	6840
authorize	771	axis	2893	balm	5100	base	250
autism	3301	axle	3906	bamboo	4438	baseball	2322
auto	1775	azure	4462	ban	2062	basement	3178
autobiography	2850			banal	7418	bash	4412
autograph	5211	**B**		banality	7418	bashful	7243
automated	1973			banana	외래어	basic	648
automatic	1158	babble	7124	band	1067	basil	외래어
automotive	3459	baby	970	bandage	5503	basin	3832
autonomous	3653	babysit	2984	bandit	5999	basis	1229
autonomy	3653	baccalaureate	6103	bandwagon	6445	bask	6083
autopsy	5680	bachelor	2416	bane	6622	basket	2813
autumn	3376	back	105	bang	2991	basketball	2268
auxiliary	4883	backbone	2162	Bangladesh	기타	bass	2333
avail	209	backfire	6357	bangs	2991	bastard	5239
available	209	background	1258	banish	5349	bastion	6860
avalanche	5276	backlash	2167	banishment	5349	bat	2104
avarice	7346	backlog	5689	bank	628	batch	2662
avatar	4759	backpack	1482	banking	628	bath	2367
avenge	5118	backwards	105	bankruptcy	3326	bathe	2367
avenger	5118	backyard	2981	banner	외래어	bathroom	1481
avenue	2289	bacon	외래어	banquet	5155	baton	6377
average	727	bacteria	외래어	banter	6569	battalion	4666
averse	5725	bad	373	bar	851	batter	2104
aversion	5725	badge	3421	barb	5625	battery	1170
avert	6169	badger	5344	barbarian	5603	battle	1214
aviation	3234	badminton	외래어	barbecue	외래어	battlefield	1214
avid	4209	baffle	4839	barbed	5625	battleship	1214
avidly	4209	baffling	4839	barbell	외래어	bay	1564
avocado	외래어	bag	1052	barber	5817	bayonet	6927
avoid	848	bagel	외래어	bard	5959	bazaar	외래어
avoidance	848	baggage	1052	bare	2117	be	2

bulge	5287	butcher	4911	callous	7211	capsule	3120
bulk	2490	butchery	4911	calm	2260	captain	2048
bull	2942	butler	6544	calorie	외래어	caption	3848
bulldog	외래어	butter	1774	calve	3997	captivating	3366
bulldozer	외래어	butterfly	799	camaraderie	6448	captive	3366
bullet	2677	button	944	camcorder	외래어	captivity	3366
bulletin	4379	buy	274	camel	5048	capture	1344
bullion	6285	buyout	3304	cameo	외래어	car	346
bully	3097	buzz	4642	camera	외래어	caramel	외래어
bum	5237	by	28	camouflage	5449	caravan	4442
bummer	6672	bye	817	camp	1275	carbohydrate	2670
bump	2332	bygone	7100	campaign	1006	carbon	1834
bumpy	2332	bylaw	4921	campus	외래어	carcass	6142
bun	4541	byline	7403	can	24	carcinogen	6039
bunch	2070	bypass	3567	Canada	기타	carcinogenic	6039
bundle	2757	bystander	3305	canal	3229	card	418
bunker	3971			cancel	1713	cardboard	3969
bunny	4368	**C**		cancer	1074	cardiac	3878
buoy	5194			candid	5642	cardigan	외래어
buoyancy	5194	cab	3716	candidate	1353	cardinal	3678
buoyant	5194	cabbage	4715	candidly	5642	cardiovascular	3878
burden	2760	cabin	2642	candle	3125	care	256
bureau	2811	cabinet	2372	candor	7334	career	706
bureaucracy	4397	cable	1436	candy	2694	careful	256
bureaucrat	4397	cache	3431	cane	4278	careless	256
bureaucratic	4397	cacophony	7287	canine	4906	caress	7056
burgeoning	6189	cactus	5416	canister	5508	cargo	3422
burger	외래어	caddie	6339	cannabis	3255	carnage	6524
burglar	4498	cadence	6070	cannibal	6498	carnival	4348
burglarize	4498	cadet	4969	cannon	4233	carnivore	6265
burglary	4498	cadre	6997	canny	5917	carnivorous	6265
burlesque	7201	cafe	외래어	canoe	외래어	carol	외래어
burn	1224	cafeteria	5569	canon	4847	carousel	6809
burnish	7467	caffeine	외래어	canopy	4378	carpenter	5039
burnout	6311	cage	783	canteen	7008	carpentry	5039
burp	6971	cake	외래어	canvas	3092	carpet	외래어
burrito	외래어	calamity	6222	canyon	4262	carpool	외래어
burrow	5942	calcium	외래어	cap	1592	carriage	553
burst	2828	calculate	1282	capability	1195	carrier	553
bury	2393	calculated	1282	capable	1195	carrot	804
bus	외래어	calculation	1282	capacity	1457	carry	553
bush	3546	calculator	1282	cape	5423	cart	2717
business	1657	calculus	5451	capital	1056	cartel	5596
businessman	1657	calendar	1972	capitalism	1056	cartilage	5388
bust	3329	calf	3997	capitalize	1056	carton	5684
bustle	4564	caliber	7387	capitulate	7052	cartoon	3553
bustling	4564	calibrate	3721	capitulation	7052	cartridge	3154
busy	135	calibration	3721	caprice	7268	carve	3140
but	29	call	129	capricious	7268	cascade	4391

his	21	honeymoon	4875	however	222	hyperbole	6714
hispanic	4575	Hong Kong	기타	howl	5459	hyperbolic	6714
hiss	6051	honk	3068	hub	2476	hypertension	5069
histogram	6129	honor	1151	hubris	7393	hyphen	외래어
historical	341	honorable	1151	huddle	6228	hypnosis	4942
history	341	hood	3250	hue	4062	hypnotize	4942
hit	578	hoodie	6119	hug	3564	hypocrite	5771
hitch	4934	hoof	6361	huge	939	hypocritical	5771
hitherto	7074	hook	2003	hulk	6368	hypothesis	3152
hive	4347	hoop	4490	hull	4280	hypothetical	3152
hoard	5265	hooray	6439	hum	5031	hysteria	5402
hoarder	5265	hoot	6699	human	463		
hoarse	7327	hop	2631	humane	4513		
hoax	6153	hope	384	humanely	4513		
hobbit	외래어	hopefully	384	humanitarian	463	**I**	
hobble	7271	horde	5133	humanity	463		
hobby	2969	horizon	3080	humanoid	6770	I	9
hockey	외래어	horizon	2812	humble	3179	ice	1249
hodgepodge	7389	horizontal	2812	humid	3279	iceberg	5581
hoe	6913	hormone	외래어	humidifier	3279	icon	1554
hog	4756	horn	3045	humidity	3279	iconoclast	7493
hoist	5695	hornet	5986	humiliate	4701	icy	1249
hold	265	horoscope	6035	humiliation	4701	idea	262
hole	1320	horrendous	6041	humility	5217	ideal	1901
holiday	1204	horrendously	6041	humor	외래어	ideal	262
holistic	4199	horrible	2830	hump	6227	identical	2820
holler	7274	horrid	6898	hunch	6350	identification	539
hollow	3993	horrific	4836	hundred	기타	identify	539
holster	5377	horrifically	4836	hunger	2470	identity	539
holy	1737	horror	2585	hungry	2470	ideology	3642
homage	5087	horse	1689	hunk	6777	idiom	6457
home	145	horseback	1689	hunt	1600	idiomatic	6457
homecoming	145	hose	외래어	hurdle	4265	idiosyncrasy	6825
homeless	145	hospital	1016	hurl	5297	idiosyncratic	6825
homestead	5539	hospitality	3365	hurricane	3290	idiot	3666
hometown	2441	host	855	hurry	807	idle	3403
homework	1145	hostage	5231	hurt	1745	idol	4325
homicide	4581	hostel	4659	husband	1347	idolize	4325
homo sapiens	외래어	hostile	3603	husbandry	7401	idyll	5961
homogeneity	5843	hostility	3603	hush	6503	idyllic	5961
homogeneous	5843	hot	926	hustle	4899	if	31
homophobia	6206	hotel	외래어	hustler	4899	iffy	7218
homophobic	6206	hotline	5555	hut	4622	igloo	외래어
homosexual	4040	hound	5107	hybrid	2555	ignite	3367
hone	4449	hour	310	hydrate	2905	ignition	3367
honest	1404	house	267	hygiene	4007	ignorance	3291
honestly	1404	household	267	hymn	4859	ignorant	3291
honey	2603	hover	3875	hype	3989	ignore	1793
honeycomb	7069	how	62	hyper	6487	ill	2113
						illegal	732
						illegible	6046

illicit	5630	imperative	4261	impulse	3876	income	1063
illiteracy	3138	imperfect	414	impulsive	3876	incoming	81
illogical	1859	imperial	3349	impunity	7088	incompetent	2388
illuminate	3254	imperious	7345	imputation	6945	incomplete	207
illusion	3462	impermeable	5056	impute	6945	inconclusive	1304
illusory	3462	impersonate	3925	in	7	inconsiderate	6253
illustrate	1696	impersonation	3925	inaccurate	1127	inconsistency	1337
illustration	1696	impervious	7136	inadequate	2096	inconspicuous	5420
illustrious	6314	impetuous	7349	inadmissible	6598	incorporate	1750
image	397	impetus	6456	inadvertent	5183	incorrigible	7353
imagination	1119	impinge	7134	inadvertently	5183	increase	280
imagine	1119	impingement	7134	inane	7368	increasingly	280
imbalance	897	impious	6279	inappropriate	979	incredible	1209
imbedded	5458	implacable	7251	inaudible	4866	incredulous	7040
imbue	6656	implant	3385	inaugural	4535	increment	3615
imitate	4095	implausible	4652	inauguration	4535	incremental	3615
imitation	4095	implement	1038	inborn	3079	incubate	4814
imitator	4095	implicate	2752	inbound	1881	incubation	4814
immaculate	5515	implication	2752	incandescent	6193	incubator	4814
immaculately	5515	implicit	4673	incantation	7460	incumbent	5030
immature	2155	implicitly	4673	incapable	1195	incur	3155
immediate	918	implied	2494	incapacitate	1457	incurable	2239
immediately	918	implode	6906	incarcerate	5072	incursion	3155
immense	3448	implore	6931	incarceration	5072	indebted	1514
immerse	3523	imply	2494	incarnation	4353	indeed	1583
immersion	3523	impolite	3824	incense	5754	indefinite	933
immigrant	2423	import	1703	incentive	2712	indelible	1740
immigration	2423	importance	237	inception	4579	indemnify	5749
imminent	4940	important	237	incessant	6533	indemnity	5749
immobilize	948	impose	2405	incessantly	6533	indent	5182
immoral	1980	imposing	2405	incest	6708	indentation	5182
immortal	2721	impossible	246	incestuous	6708	independent	386
immune	2182	imposter	7133	inch	외래어	in-depth	3469
immunity	2182	impotence	623	incident	1567	indeterminate	652
immunization	2182	impoverished	6257	incidentally	1567	index	1722
impact	831	impregnable	7121	incinerate	6879	India	기타
impairment	2957	impregnate	7121	incineration	6879	indicate	872
impart	5112	impress	1096	incipient	7281	indication	872
impartial	2037	impression	1096	incise	4918	indicative	872
impatient	501	impressive	1096	incision	4918	indicator	872
impeach	6185	imprint	5019	incisive	4918	indict	4665
impeachment	6185	imprisonment	1561	incisor	4918	indictment	4665
impeccable	5419	impromptu	6543	incite	5780	indifferent	3961
impeccably	5419	improper	879	inclination	3341	indigenous	3278
impede	4727	impropriety	6755	inclined	3341	indigestion	2433
impediment	4727	improve	401	include	86	indignant	6652
impel	6004	improvement	401	inclusive	86	indignation	6652
impending	5339	improvisation	4401	incognito	7441	indignity	3897
impenetrable	3056	improvise	4401	incoherent	3572	indigo	5820

jest	6574	jungle	3613	kindergarten	4098	laceration	7408
jester	6574	junior	2093	kindle	3885	lack	1091
jet	2556	junk	3461	kindred	5393	lackluster	5859
jewel	2229	junkie	6466	kinetic	5162	laconic	7492
jewelry	2229	jurisdiction	2771	kinetics	5162	lactate	5995
jigsaw	6329	jurisprudence	6887	king	914	lad	4550
jihad	5438	jurist	6887	kingdom	914	ladder	3418
jihadist	5438	jury	2919	kink	5893	laden	5029
jingle	6600	just	57	kinky	5893	lading	5029
jitters	6238	justice	1505	kinship	5393	lady	1662
jittery	6238	justification	2256	kiosk	5214	lag	3691
job	345	justify	2256	kiss	외래어	lagoon	5304
jockey	5844	juvenile	3896	kit	1391	lair	6864
jog	4630	juxtapose	6231	kitchen	1394	lake	1301
join	642	juxtaposition	6231	kite	5058	lamb	3892
joint	1488			kitten	4317	lame	4964
joist	6341	**K**		kiwi	외래어	lament	5032
joke	2293			knack	6064	lamentable	5032
jokingly	2293	kale	외래어	knead	6245	lamentation	5032
jolly	6132	kangaroo	외래어	knee	2127	laminate	4088
jolt	6526	karate	외래어	kneel	5330	lamp	2851
jot	6415	karma	5441	knife	2080	lance	4504
journal	1806	kayak	외래어	knight	3719	land	690
journalism	2213	keen	2938	knit	3298	landlord	2901
journalist	2213	keenly	2938	knob	3708	landmark	3389
journey	1484	keep	147	knock	2320	landscape	1820
joy	378	keepsake	6803	knot	3344	landslide	1574
joyful	378	keg	6096	know	65	lane	2112
joystick	6144	kennel	5575	know-how	65	language	880
jubilant	5756	kernel	4111	knowingly	65	languid	6970
jubilation	5756	ketchup	외래어	knowledge	772	languish	6970
jubilee	5756	kettle	5083	knowledgeable	772	lantern	4681
judge	993	key	486	knuckle	5530	lap	3064
judgment	993	keyboard	외래어	koala	외래어	lapse	4244
judgmental	993	keynote	2158	koran	외래어	laptop	2445
judicial	3287	khaki	외래어	Korea	기타	larceny	7312
judicious	7055	kick	1555	kudos	5741	large	196
judiciously	7055	kid	554			larva	4855
jug	5487	kidnap	4165	**L**		lasagna	외래어
juggle	5136	kidnapper	4165			laser	외래어
juice	1909	kidnapping	4165	lab	1426	lash	2167
juicy	1909	kidney	2845	label	1339	last	143
July	기타	kill	682	labeled	1339	lasting	143
jumble	6954	kiln	6349	labor	1332	lastly	143
jumbo	5910	kilo	6152	laboratory	1426	latch	4698
jump	1276	kilogram	외래어	laborious	1332	late	199
junction	3741	kilometer	외래어	labyrinth	6020	lately	199
juncture	7057	kin	5393	lace	3331	latency	4352
June	기타	kind	410	lacerate	7408	latent	4352

port	1389	pounding	1645	predominantly	4140	presumably	2795
portable	2629	pour	2230	predominately	4140	presume	2795
portal	2793	poverty	2788	preeminence	5148	presumption	2795
portend	7374	powder	2041	preempt	7011	presumptuous	6246
portfolio	1999	power	201	preemption	7011	pretend	3162
portion	1672	powerful	201	preemptive	7011	pretender	3162
portrait	2808	powerhouse	3075	preface	5953	pretense	6195
portray	3139	practical	2282	prefer	888	pretension	6195
portrayal	3139	practice	492	preferable	888	pretentious	6195
Portugal	기타	practicum	492	preference	888	pretext	7060
pose	2194	practitioner	2678	prefix	4669	pretty	551
posh	6398	pragmatic	5250	pregnancy	1638	pretzel	외래어
position	487	pragmatism	5250	pregnant	1638	prevail	2698
positive	1020	prairie	4491	prejudice	3243	prevalent	2698
positivity	1020	praise	2458	preliminary	3619	prevent	740
possess	1610	prank	5593	prelude	6596	prevention	740
possession	1610	prankster	5593	premarital	4944	preview	116
possessor	1610	prawn	6632	premature	4108	previous	674
possibility	246	pray	1508	prematurely	4108	prey	3868
possible	246	prayer	1508	premier	2199	price	305
possibly	246	preach	2989	premiere	3473	priceless	305
post	217	preacher	2989	premise	2789	pricey	305
postal	217	preamble	7449	premium	1676	prick	6318
poster	217	precarious	6301	prenatal	4664	prickle	6988
posterior	4925	precariously	6301	preoccupation	2036	prickly	6988
posterity	7046	precaution	2149	prep	573	pride	2436
postgraduate	866	precede	2306	preparation	573	priest	2472
posthumous	7468	precept	6520	prepare	573	primacy	1641
posting	217	precinct	5541	preposterous	7261	primal	1641
postnatal	4664	precious	2910	prequel	3931	primarily	968
postpone	4705	precipice	7425	prerequisite	3221	primary	968
postponement	4705	precipitate	4357	prerogative	7028	primate	6102
postulate	6680	precipitation	4357	preschool	163	prime	1641
posture	3865	precipitous	7425	prescient	7391	primeval	7293
postwar	563	precise	1767	prescribe	1867	primitive	4367
pot	1796	precision	1767	prescription	1867	primordial	7058
potable	1796	preclude	5608	presence	313	prince	1790
potato	2398	precocious	7332	present	313	princess	1790
potent	623	precursor	5315	presentation	313	principal	2005
potential	623	predator	3377	preservation	1791	principle	1501
potentially	623	predecessor	3894	preserve	1791	principled	1501
pothole	6631	predetermined	652	preset	113	print	624
potion	4919	predicament	6625	preside	5180	printer	624
pottery	1796	predicate	5869	president	584	prior	712
potty	5914	predict	1452	presidential	584	prioritize	712
pouch	4180	predictable	1452	press	442	priority	712
poultry	4816	prediction	1452	pressure	442	prism	5413
pounce	6730	predilection	7423	prestige	3143	prison	1561
pound	1645	predominance	4140	prestigious	3143	prisoner	1561

pristine	4720	profuse	6603	prophecy	2347	prudence	4610
privacy	610	profusely	6603	prophet	2347	prudent	4610
private	610	profusion	6603	propogate	4202	prudential	4610
privilege	2489	prognosis	5430	proponent	5047	prudently	4610
privileged	2489	program	141	proportion	2241	prune	4514
privy	6507	programmer	141	proportional	2241	pruning	4514
prize	1787	programming	141	proposal	1115	pry	5615
prized	1787	progress	1040	propose	1115	psalm	4124
pro	321	progressive	1040	proposition	1115	pseudo	6975
proactive	3648	prohibit	2343	proprietary	3194	pseudonym	6975
probability	458	prohibited	2343	propriety	6755	psych	6687
probable	458	prohibition	2343	prosaic	5252	psychiatric	3396
probably	458	project	277	prose	5252	psychic	3973
probation	3643	projectile	5519	prosecute	2337	psycho	5176
probe	3372	projection	277	prosecution	2337	psychological	1684
problem	215	proliferate	4714	prosecutor	2337	psychology	1684
procedure	776	proliferation	4714	prospect	1786	psychotic	5176
proceed	776	prolific	4996	prospectus	5838	pub	3033
process	198	prologue	6673	prosper	3323	puberty	6123
proclaim	3611	prolongation	3680	prosperity	3323	pubic	6773
proclamation	3611	prolonged	3680	prosperous	3323	public	333
proclivity	7410	prom	5061	prostate	4002	publication	565
procrastinate	5825	promenade	6175	prostitute	4471	publicity	333
procrastination	5825	prominent	2601	prostitution	4471	publicize	333
procrastinator	5825	promiscuity	7163	prostrate	7159	publish	565
procreate	7316	promiscuous	7163	prostration	7159	publisher	565
procreation	7316	promise	1300	protagonist	4530	puck	4549
proctor	7290	promising	1300	protect	429	pudding	외래어
procurement	3454	promo	774	protection	429	puddle	5789
prod	6536	promote	774	protectionism	429	puff	4081
prodigal	7432	promotion	774	protein	1540	puffy	4081
prodigious	6026	promotional	774	protest	2298	pugnacious	7497
prodigy	6026	prompt	1890	protocol	2301	pull	912
produce	469	promulgate	6408	prototype	3244	pulley	5179
producer	469	promulgation	6408	protract	6952	pulp	4987
product	130	prone	3547	protrude	5535	pulse	2941
production	130	prong	6516	protrusion	5535	puma	외래어
productivity	130	pronoun	6135	proud	1636	pump	외래어
profane	6084	pronounce	3083	prove	1037	pumpkin	3276
profanity	6084	pronunciation	3083	provenance	6972	pun	5161
profession	321	proof	1883	proverb	4846	punch	2594
professional	321	prop	3247	provide	99	punctual	7007
professor	1551	propaganda	4202	province	1894	punctuate	5005
proficiency	3710	propel	3551	provision	4141	punctuation	5005
proficient	3710	propeller	3551	provocative	3638	puncture	5499
profile	1295	propensity	6358	provoke	3638	pundit	5936
profit	1087	proper	879	prowess	5707	pungent	6993
profitable	1087	properly	879	proximity	3588	punish	2344
profound	3292	property	502	proxy	3513	punishment	2344

soak	2733	someone	33	spam	외래어	spicy	2353
soap	2528	something	33	span	2587	spider	3412
soar	4036	sometimes	33	spank	6530	spike	3057
sob	6013	somewhat	1992	spar	6029	spill	3216
sober	4868	somewhere	33	spare	2504	spin	1960
sobering	4868	son	928	sparingly	2504	spinach	4487
sobriety	6973	sonar	6447	spark	2522	spindle	5203
soccer	2755	sonata	외래어	sparkle	3441	spine	2615
sociable	405	song	989	sparkling	3441	spiral	3919
social	405	sonic	4336	sparse	5426	spirit	923
socialism	405	soon	726	sparsely	5426	spiritual	923
society	405	soothe	3926	spasm	5928	spit	4150
sociology	405	soothing	3926	spatial	403	spite	3883
sock	3038	sophisticated	2627	spatula	6463	spiteful	3883
socket	3267	sophistication	2627	spawn	3379	spitfire	6705
sod	4801	sophomore	3979	speak	440	splash	3432
soda	외래어	soprano	외래어	speaker	440	splendid	5199
sodium	3536	sorcerer	5964	spear	4486	splendidly	5199
sofa	외래어	sorcery	5964	special	312	splice	5802
soft	1245	sore	3116	specialist	312	splint	6608
soften	1245	soreness	3116	specialty	312	splinter	6130
software	외래어	sorority	6212	species	1519	split	1800
soggy	6663	sorrow	4508	specific	434	splurge	6273
soil	1830	sorrowful	4508	specifically	434	spoil	2896
solace	6806	sorry	1682	specify	434	spoiled	2896
solar	1856	sort	1098	specimen	3687	spokesperson	2978
sold	375	sought	910	specious	7483	sponge	외래어
soldier	2015	soul	1643	speck	6669	sponsor	1621
sole	1902	sound	444	spectacle	1925	sponsorship	1621
solemn	5294	soup	2738	spectacular	1925	spontaneity	4078
solemnity	5294	sour	813	spectator	4311	spontaneous	4078
solemnly	5294	source	534	specter	5980	spontaneously	4078
solicit	4373	south	680	spectral	2606	spoof	6477
solicitation	4373	southern	680	spectrum	2606	spooky	5238
solicitous	4373	souvenir	5140	speculate	2822	spool	5468
solicitude	4373	sovereign	3589	speculation	2822	spoon	795
solid	1307	sovereignty	3589	speech	1813	sporadic	5966
solidarity	5038	sow	4305	speechless	1813	sporadically	5966
solidify	1307	sowing	4305	speed	728	spore	5738
solitary	5262	soy	4155	speedway	5097	sport	외래어
solitude	5262	soybean	2369	speedy	728	spot	940
solo	2397	spa	외래어	spell	1797	spotlight	외래어
soluble	4688	space	403	spend	424	spouse	2742
solution	577	spacecraft	403	spending	424	spout	5832
solve	1313	spacing	403	spent	424	sprain	6140
solvent	5356	spacious	403	sperm	2980	sprawl	4949
some	33	spade	5343	spew	6386	sprawling	4949
somebody	33	spaghetti	외래어	sphere	3317	spray	1997
somehow	33	Spain	기타	spice	2353	spread	1373

surge	3170	sweatshirt	외래어	synopsis	5460	tall	2022
surgeon	3008	sweaty	2391	syntax	3890	tally	4506
surgery	1429	Sweden	기타	synthesis	2923	tame	4563
surgical	1429	sweep	2570	synthesize	2923	tamper	5195
surmise	7070	sweepstake	2889	synthesizer	2923	tampon	외래어
surmount	6532	sweet	1287	synthetic	2923	tan	3453
surname	5333	swell	2740	syringe	5261	tandem	5244
surpass	3970	swerve	7005	syrup	외래어	tang	4895
surplus	4176	swift	3860	system	137	tangent	5800
surprise	959	swim	1715	systematic	137	tangible	3807
surprised	959	swimmer	1715	systemic	4407	tangle	4158
surreal	5080	swimming	1715	systemically	4407	tango	외래어
surrealism	5080	swindle	7269			tank	1408
surrender	3682	swindler	7269	**T**		tantalize	6810
surreptitious	7474	swine	6651			tantalizing	6810
surrogate	5908	swing	2186	tab	1956	tantamount	7329
surround	1346	swipe	4364	table	703	tantrum	6459
surrounding	1346	swirl	4494	tablespoon	3202	tap	1838
surveillance	3478	swish	7082	tablet	1988	tape	1815
survey	1293	switch	1032	tableware	5526	taper	4077
survival	1212	Switzerland	기타	tabloid	6552	tapestry	6155
survive	1212	swivel	5455	taboo	5976	tar	외래어
survivor	1212	swollen	2740	tabular	703	tardiness	7257
susceptible	3940	swoop	6048	tacit	7085	tardy	7257
sushi	외래어	sword	2509	taciturn	7085	target	845
suspect	1464	syllable	5626	tack	4794	tariff	4459
suspend	1846	syllabus	5690	tackle	2240	tarnish	6565
suspense	5736	symbiosis	6865	tacky	6451	tarot	외래어
suspenseful	5736	symbiotic	6865	taco	외래어	tart	외래어
suspension	1846	symbol	1700	tact	6491	task	1039
suspicion	1464	symbolic	1700	tactful	6491	tassel	6890
suspicious	1464	symbolize	1700	tactic	2248	taste	1065
sustain	1454	symmetric	4240	tactical	2248	tasteful	1065
sustainable	1454	symmetrical	4240	tactile	5886	tasty	1065
swab	6214	symmetry	4240	tad	4923	tattoo	외래어
swag	6200	sympathetic	3321	tag	1480	taught	334
swagger	7083	sympathize	3321	tail	2457	taunt	5871
swallow	3533	sympathy	3321	tailgate	6060	taut	7098
swamp	4496	symphony	3909	tailor	2756	tavern	5653
swampy	4496	symposium	5332	tailored	2756	tax	543
swan	5494	symptom	1400	taint	5814	taxation	543
swap	2649	sync	3825	Taiwan	기타	tax-free	543
swarm	4897	synchronize	3825	take	58	taxi	외래어
swat	6611	synchronous	3825	tale	2450	taxonomy	5937
swatch	6290	syndicate	4907	talent	1372	tea	1668
sway	4408	syndrome	2836	taliban	외래어	teach	334
swear	3135	synergy	4599	talisman	7464	teacher	334
sweat	2391	synonym	4382	talk	392	team	174
sweater	외래어	synonymous	4382	talkative	392	tear	1766

Allvoca advanced

초 판 1쇄 발행일 2020년 7월 20일
초 판 5쇄 발행일 2024년 8월 22일

지은이 송승호
펴낸이 양옥매
디자인 송예린

펴낸곳 도서출판 책과나무
출판등록 제2012-000376
주소 서울특별시 마포구 방울내로 79 이노빌딩 302호
대표전화 02.372.1537 **팩스** 02.372.1538
이메일 booknamu2007@naver.com
홈페이지 www.booknamu.com
ISBN 979-11-5776-914-8 (13740)

이 도서의 국립중앙도서관 출판예정도서목록(CIP)은
서지정보유통지원시스템 홈페이지(http://seoji.nl.go.kr)와
국가자료종합목록시스템(http://www.nl.go.kr/kolisnet)에서 이용하실 수 있습니다.
(CIP제어번호: CIP2020026283)